READING MICHAEL LONGLEY

FRAN BREARTON

Reading
Michael Longley

BLOODAXE BOOKS

ISBN: 1 85224 682 0 hardback edition
1 85224 683 9 paperback edition

First published 2006 by
Bloodaxe Books Ltd,
Highgreen,
Tarset,
Northumberland NE48 1RP.

www.bloodaxebooks.com
For further information about Bloodaxe titles
please visit our website or write to
the above address for a catalogue.

Bloodaxe Books Ltd acknowledges
the financial assistance of
Arts Council England, North East.

Cover printing by J. Thomson Colour Printers Ltd, Glasgow.

Printed in Great Britain by
Bell & Bain Limited, Glasgow, Scotland.

For Jude and Sean

ACKNOWLEDGEMENTS

All quotations from Longley's poetry, unless otherwise indicated,
— are taken from the collections – excluding interim pamphlets – in
which they first appeared: *No Continuing City* (1969), *An Exploded
View* (1973), *Man Lying on a Wall* (1976), *The Echo Gate* (1979),
Gorse Fires (1991), *The Ghost Orchid* (1995), *The Weather in Japan*
(2000) and *Snow Water* (2004). The 'New Poems' discussed in
chapter 4 were first published in section V of *Poems 1963-1983*
(1985). All this work is now being republished in his *Collected Poems*
(Jonathan Cape, 2006). I am grateful to Michael Longley, and to
his publishers, Jonathan Cape (part of the Random House Group
Ltd), for permission to quote from these collections. Grateful
acknowledgement is also made to the following for permission to
reproduce copyright material: Faber & Faber Ltd for poems by
Seamus Heaney, and the Gallery Press for poems by Derek Mahon.

Michael Longley's papers are held in the Special Collections of
the Robert W. Woodruff Library, Emory University, Atlanta,
Georgia, collection no. 744. All references to manuscript versions
of Longley's poems are drawn from this archive. References to
prose materials from this source are indicated in the notes as
'Longley papers, collection 744'. The dates given in the chapter
subheadings refer to the years in which poems for each collection
were written. The poems have been dated from the manuscripts in
the Emory University archive, or, where these are undated, from
information supplied by Michael Longley and Michael Allen. I am
grateful to Douglas Dunn, Seamus Heaney, Michael Longley and
Derek Mahon for permission to quote from unpublished materials;
and to David Cabot and Michael Longley for access to papers held
in their private collections. I am also grateful to Emory University
for a fellowship which enabled much of the archival research for
this book, and to the Arts and Humanities Research Council for a
study leave grant which facilitated its completion.

CONTENTS

Preface

'Tests kick off, and "cruel" poetry catches students offside.' So read an *Irish Times* headline on 6 June 2002. Many, it seems, had been hoping for Seamus Heaney and Emily Dickinson to come up on the English Leaving Certificate examination in the Republic of Ireland. Instead, the prescribed poetry – by Michael Longley and Elizabeth Bishop – was, one teacher claimed, ' "cruel" for a lot of students'. Of course, to second-guess the contents of examination papers is always a risky strategy. But perhaps, as regards the reception of Michael Longley's poetry, there is more to it than that, since his poetry does pose specific challenges in two areas much debated in recent years in criticism of Irish poetry: poetic form and the politics of identity.

One pattern has been to see the generation of Seamus Heaney, Michael Longley and Derek Mahon as formally conservative exponents of the "well-made poem" and, as such, perfect fodder for a particular kind of formalist criticism. The slightly younger generation of poets such as Paul Muldoon, Medbh McGuckian and Ciaran Carson, on the other hand, while they still draw on traditional forms, have been seen to destabilise, in a postmodern world, the well-made poem through experiments with, and within, form and language, thereby shattering assumptions their predecessors apparently hold intact.

This book argues, on the contrary, that Longley's forms have tended to be misunderstood in this context; that they have always worked as a medium for experimentation, and for risk-taking, in ways which have made him profoundly influential on, as well as contemporaneous with, that postmodern generation – perhaps, in some ways, a closer poetic ally of writers such as Muldoon than of the group with which he is more usually associated. Even in more recent studies of Irish poetry, which proclaim pluralism as their watchword, differences between Longley and his closest contemporaries, Heaney and Mahon, tend still to be elided. At the same time, ironically enough, there has been little consideration of what it is, precisely, that they share. There are moments when poets from Northern Ireland have been, as Heaney once described himself and Longley, very evidently 'tangled in the same imaginary branches'. Often, however, their relationships may be described more precisely in terms of what Heaney also calls (in a letter to

Longley in 1977) the 'capillary action between the taproots'. While
there may be an underlying consciousness in the work of all these
poets of what the others are doing, particularly in the late 1960s
and through the 1970s, it is, on closer examination, their differ-
ences which tend to become more apparent. It is also the case that
Longley is the often unrecognised inheritor of Yeats's extraordinary
formal and generic diversity. A writer who works in many differ-
ent modes – love poet, pastoral poet, war poet, elegist – Longley,
like Yeats, proves resistant to one-dimensional readings. The example
of his poetry, therefore, in its formal and thematic preoccupations,
destabilises more than one version of literary history to have taken
on some currency since the 1980s.

If Longley's poetry, properly considered, throws into question
assumptions about the workings of form and language – and the
literary histories extrapolated from those assumptions – the same
may be said of his Irish identity. Longley's father, Major Richard
Longley, was an English veteran of the First World War. He and
his wife, Constance Longley, also from England, moved to Belfast
in the 1920s, where their three children were born: Wendy Longley
in 1930, Michael Longley and his twin brother Peter on the eve
of the Second World War, in July 1939. Growing up in an English
household in Ireland (a more unusual situation than its opposite)
engendered a dual perspective in Longley at an early age, as des-
cribed in his autobiography, *Tuppenny Stung*, a duality that translates
more broadly into a dual – ultimately triple – literary and cultural
heritage as well.

Educated at Belfast's Royal Academical Institution, and then,
between 1958 and 1963, at Trinity College Dublin, Longley returned
to Belfast in 1964, where he has lived ever since, working first as
a schoolteacher, and then, from 1970 to 1991, for the Arts Council
of Northern Ireland. Since 1970, a second 'home' for Longley has
been the remote townland of Carrigskeewaun in Co. Mayo. Yet
while Ireland – North and West, urban and rural – has always been
home to Longley, he retains a consciousness that his 'ancestors lie
in English soil', that he comes, as he explains in a 2002 interview,
from a 'long line' of English 'farmers, farm labourers, shepherds,
blacksmiths, carpenters, woodcutters, game keepers, wood reeves'.

Longley is by no means the first Irish poet to express a complex
inheritance, though he may be more unusual in embracing and
celebrating so directly that confluence in himself of different cul-
tures. It is there in Yeats too, in the recognition in his 'A General
Introduction for my Work' that 'I owe my soul to Shakespeare, to
Spenser and to Blake...and to the English language in which I think,

speak, and write, that everything I love has come to me through English', an acknowledgement which causes him some torment: 'my hatred tortures me with love, my love with hate'. It is there in a different way in the tension between Louis MacNeice's Irish childhood and English education, and in the fraught 'Odi atque amo' relation with his home country. Or it may be seen in Seamus Heaney's sense, outlined in his early essay 'Belfast', of an English literary tradition colliding with his Irish experience to create his poetry ('I began as a poet when my roots were crossed with my reading').

The politics of identity in such cases have been discussed, it would seem, almost to the point of exhaustion, and a certain weariness as regards "identitarianism" in Irish poetry criticism is also now in evidence. But weariness is only permissible when the terms of the debate have been exhausted. If there is a repetitiveness about notions of "identity" and "place" in criticism of contemporary Irish poetry, it has tended to emerge from a reluctance to accommodate exceptions that do not prove the rule. In Longley's case, that he has not been easily incorporated into some versions of the "Irish tradition", that he remains seemingly difficult to "place", suggests that his Irish-English heritage still proves a disruptive force, and that he causes, as does Yeats with his literary Anglo-Irishness, ideological unease in certain quarters.

In recent years, Longley has become a poet of international reputation and stature, even as critics still sometimes tend to fight shy of close textual engagement with his poems, and with their broader implications for understanding an Irish poetic tradition. That said, there has also been, over the last decade, a significant increase in critical engagement with his work, and more particularly with the work published from *Gorse Fires* (1991) onwards. Longley's style does change fairly dramatically through his career, and it is possible to see his first four books as forming a coherent and identifiable period, *Gorse Fires* as introducing new directions, thus dividing his career into two halves. To do so is to over-simplify, however, and I have tried instead to draw attention to continuities between Longley's 1970s and 1990s writing. Nevertheless, in view of the fact that far more criticism exists in relation to the poetry published since 1991 than that which pre-dates it, I have devoted, proportionately, slightly more space in this study to the poetry written in the earlier period.

Longley has said of his readers that 'The main thing I want them to receive is pleasure...some sense of reverence for the physical world, and some sense of mystery beyond the physical world'. His poetry – perhaps all poetry – requires an attention and concentration which, in a culture where auditory, visual – even textual – stimuli are too often expected to work instantly, may be a mode of appreciation increasingly at risk. Longley's work, in which a surface lucidity is always played out against complicated depth, does make demands on its readers. That students and critics can feel themselves caught 'offside' by his poetry suggests that those demands may be different from what we expect, disrupting ways of reading established in relation to his contemporaries.

Part of the pleasure of reading Michael Longley is the extent to which his poems have the capacity to surprise, to alter perception, to make us see on more than one level simultaneously, to combine an immediacy and physicality with that 'sense of mystery'. In his poems, the known is often rendered strange and new, the unknown familiar; perhaps that might prove paradigmatic of the experience of reading, and re-reading, his work as a whole.

1

'In two minds': *No Continuing City*
1963-1968

'For, on my own, I have lost my way at last,
So far from home.'
MICHAEL LONGLEY, 1964

I

Longley's first collection, *No Continuing City*, was published in 1969.
It is, with the benefit of hindsight, an historically evocative date
for a first book by a Northern Irish poet, and one which might
seem auspicious. Many critical narratives of contemporary Irish
poetry take 1969 as their starting point, as marking the beginning
of a poetic revival spearheaded by Seamus Heaney, Michael Longley
and Derek Mahon. But they do so in part because 1969 is seen to
mark the beginning of the Northern Ireland Troubles, in which,
from the critical perspective of the time, the emergence of Northern
poetry was implicated. In as much as it may be critically mislead-
ing, the auspicious publication date thus proves, in another sense,
inauspicious.

At first glance, *No Continuing City* is an obvious candidate for
a Belfast Troubles book, but it has never met such critical expec-
tations, and for equally obvious reasons. Like most first collections,
it had a long gestation: it was written, for the most part, between
1963 and 1966; some of its preoccupations and formal principles
were conceived even earlier. As with Philip Larkin, much of whose
second collection *The Less Deceived* was written in Belfast in the
early 1950s, not in Hull where he would later reside long term, the
activity of writing for Longley was facilitated by the experience of
having been, literally and imaginatively, 'elsewhere' – in his case
the Republic of Ireland from 1958 to 1963.

No Continuing City, in direct and oblique ways, has its roots in
Longley's experience not of a "troubled" Belfast, but of Dublin in
the first part of the decade. In March 1960, he published some
short lyrics in the student magazine *Icarus* whilst in his second
year as an undergraduate at Trinity College Dublin. The first of

these, entitled 'Marigolds', reads as follows:

She gave him marigolds
the colour of autumn
to keep in his cold room;

and the late light of autumn
gilded all their moments.[1]

The poem, as with most of Longley's juvenilia – consisting largely of the poems which appeared in *Icarus* from 1960 to 1962 – is fairly slight, with none of the density of meaning that becomes the hallmark of his equally tiny lyrics later in his career. Rather, it has both the charm (and the failings) of many short imagist poems: pleasing but ephemeral. Just over three years later however, before his return to Belfast, his last contribution as a student to Icarus appears. The poem is 'Epithalamion'.[2] It later stands at the opening of his first collection, a position it has retained through various editions of Collected and Selected Poems ever since. 'Epithalamion' is a coming of age poem, the first mature product of a poetic "apprenticeship" served at Trinity College Dublin in the early 1960s. Although only three poems from Longley's Trinity period survive into *No Continuing City* – 'Epithalamion', 'A Questionnaire for Walter Mitty', and 'Graffiti' – the years 1960-1963 mark an important transition in which Longley, in effect, finds his poetic feet.

On one level, 'Epithalamion' is a formal experiment designed to test the limits of Longley's technical skill as it developed in the early 1960s. He deliberately invents a difficult stanza shape; the inflexible ababb rhyme scheme provides its own rigorous challenge; and, finally, the poem's complex syntactical structure is tightly linked to the overall movement of the poem. 'Epithalamion' consists of four carefully structured sentences. The opening stanza presents the here and now of night time; the second sentence celebrates across five stanzas the holding of that moment; the seventh stanza recognises the moment's transient quality; and the long fourth sentence of the poem imaginatively projects into the future, as night unravels into day.

'Epithalamion' is, however, much more than an example of technical assurance. In celebrating the night, even as it anticipates the day, Longley's first major love poem stands as archetype for the two modes for which he is perhaps now most celebrated – love poems and elegies. 'Epithalamion' is a love poem which is also an elegy for the moment of love itself. The poem may be the perfected edifice but its sense works against that formal stability to leave it with only the hope of 'lingering on': the darkness is finite even as the love seeks infinity. As the poem gathers momentum through the complex sentence that comprises most of its first half, the syntax leads steadily and inevitably towards its centre:

> And everything seems bent
> On robing in this evening you
> And me, all dark the element
>   Our light is earnest to,
> All quiet gathered round us who,
>
>   When over the embankments
> A train that's loudly reprobate
> Shoots from silence into silence,
>   With ease accommodate
> Its pandemonium, its freight.

More so than any other poem in Longley's *oeuvre*, 'Epithalamion' reveals his debt to the Metaphysical poets. In terms of its imagery, one obvious precursor to this poem is John Donne's 'The Sun Rising', with its bold claim 'Shine here to us, and thou art everywhere; / This bed thy centre is, these walls, thy sphere.' There are also echoes of Louis MacNeice's love poems, notably 'Trilogy for X (part II)', of Robert Graves's love poems, and of Richard Wilbur's 'Flumen Tenebrarum' – all writers absorbed by Longley during his undergraduate years in Dublin in the early 1960s. But as with MacNeice's (and, more noticeably, Robert Graves's) love poems, the measured tone has a darker side to it, all the more poignant for making itself heard without shouting.

Like Robert Graves, Longley is deeply romantic in feeling, but often more restrained and classical in expression – a Dionysian in Apollonian clothing. Far from sustaining, Donne-style, its present moment, oblivious of past, future and the world outside, 'Epithalamion' recognises the need to 'hazard all', to see the past unfold as the future is anticipated, to 'notice how the trees / Which took on anonymity / Are again in their huge histories / Displayed'. In a way, 'Epithalamion' is 'The Sun Rising' reversed: the centre once reached, when 'dark will be / For ever like this', is also therefore the point where the poem's centrifugal collapse begins – the 'small hours widening into day' and into the need to begin all over again:

> The two of us, in these
> Which early morning has deformed,
> Must hope that in new properties
>   We'll find a uniform
> To know each other truly by, or
>
>   At the least, that these will,
> When we rise, be seen with dawn

As remnant yet part raiment still,
    Like flags that linger on
The sky when king and queen are gone.

The maturity of this poem undoubtedly lies, in part, in its technical accomplishment. But there is more to it than this. Coming of age, as Longley notes, is something the poet must do not just once but time and time again.[3] The realisation of self is never final, never stable; rather it is continually reinvented. 'Epithalamion' is the first poem in which the distinctive aesthetic of Longley's 1960s poetry manifests itself. That aesthetic works with a deliberate lack of confidence that stands in marked contrast to his formal skill. Unlike the slight, earlier poems, 'Epithalamion' understands its own ephemerality; as a poem, it transcends the ephemeral precisely through such understanding.

Derek Mahon's arrival at Trinity in the autumn of 1960 was, as Longley himself notes, a key factor in giving a new impetus to his poetry, enabling the transition from the likes of 'Marigolds' to 'Epithalamion'. (Even the form of 'Epithalamion' emerges in part from the desire to invent 'a stanza shape even more difficult than the one which had 'arrived in the post from Mahon'.)[4] To some extent, that story is told in *Icarus* from 1960 to 1963, as the two Northern poets began to dominate its poetry pages, vying for space side by side. They also became acute critics of each other's work, an intense relationship which continued in that form, despite Mahon's residence in the US and Canada, and then in London, well into the 1970s.

Longley describes their relationship in the Trinity years as one where 'Our friendship and our abilities were often stretched as far as they could go.' Given the outstanding quality of Mahon's "juvenilia", his presence could have been, as Longley acknowledges, overwhelming; instead the relationship provided the means for that first 'coming of age' as Mahon also took him on a 'guided tour of poetry'.[5] Both Longley and Mahon see their undergraduate years as, in Mahon's phrase: 'More than a remarkable experience, a whole way of life…'. He continues: 'We published in the college magazines and even in the books pages of the *Irish Times*. We did readings in the rooms of the Philosophical Society…[Longley and I] read as far up as Lowell and Larkin, as far up as Kinsella and Montague…University life merged imperceptibly into literary life.'[6] Brendan Kennelly and Rudi Holzapfel were already published poets by the time of Longley's arrival in Dublin in 1958 and keen to promote poetic activity at Trinity; Eavan Boland was later to meet Mahon, and through Mahon, Longley, marking the beginning of an exchange of ideas –

stimulating if not always unproblematical – between Boland and Longley in the mid-1960s.[7] Longley's future wife, then Edna Broderick, also published reviews and essays in *Icarus* which questioned aesthetic principles and critical assumptions about poetry in ways which can be seen to feed into, and respond to, Longley's early poetic development.

Such exchanges and contacts made during this time validate Mahon's view that the Northern student who went to Trinity 'picked up an all-Ireland view instead of the provincial view',[8] as they also complicate any simple view of Longley's emergence as a "Belfast poet" in the late 1960s. Living in Trinity itself in the late 1950s and early 1960s, with its Anglo-Irish ethos, as Longley notes, also produced 'certain sorts of useful kinds of schizophrenia':

> ...one was living in this quite tangible recognisable atmosphere within the walls of Trinity and then one would walk out into the city of Dublin ...no matter how Anglo-Irish [Trinity] may have been in the past, no matter how Protestant, it just cannot avoid being part of Dublin. I regard that as an important part of my subliminal education – walking in and out of the Front Gate and being aware of the tensions in myself and within the University.[9]

Trinity is thus Longley's apprenticeship myth both in terms of his formal development, and in terms of his emerging sense of self. It is an apprenticeship that draws its strength from a certain amount of male rivalry, predominantly between Longley and Mahon. But the rivalry goes hand in hand with a sense of a shared enterprise.

From the late 1960s onwards, Longley has argued for the importance to him – emotionally and poetically – of what he calls a 'sodality of the imagination'.[10] In the early years of the Troubles, that 'sodality' takes on a new urgency for Longley, and a certain political resonance, to become a central theme of *An Exploded View*. In the Trinity years, 'sodality of the imagination' may not have been consciously advocated by Longley, but it was, nevertheless, writ large among the unwashed dishes and socks of the Merrion Square basement flat Longley and Mahon shared from 1962 to 1963.[11] It is worth noting that while the dedicatory poem 'For Edna' opens *No Continuing City*, and while 'Epithalamion' speaks in obvious ways to Longley's own marriage in 1964, the extraordinary tribute 'To Derek Mahon', written in 1966 (retitled 'Birthmarks: *for D.M.*'), is found towards its close. In a recent interview, Longley has affirmed that 'In my forty years of writing, nothing (apart from my marriage) has been more important than that first friendship with Mahon.'[12] As 'Birthmarks' affirms, the poems of Longley's first collection, with their unusual degree of formal accomplishment, owe much to the stimulating literary environment in which they were conceived, to the rigorous criticism offered by their first "audience", and to the friendly rivalry that existed between Longley and Mahon.

> You alone read every birthmark,
> Only for you the tale it tells –
> Idiot children in the dark
> Whom we shall never bring to light,
> Criminals in their prison cells –
> These are the poems we cannot write.
>
> Though we deny them name and birth,
> Locked out from rhyme and lexicon
> The ghosts still gather round our hearth
> Whose bed and board makes up the whole –
> Thief, murderer and clown – icon
> And lares of the poet's soul.

'Birthmarks' is, in some respects, a slightly cryptic, syntactically convoluted poem which seems initially to tell a tale only to its ideal – and ideally trained – reader. But it is more than a tribute; it might also be read, implicitly, as an *ars poetica*. Its biographical elements are clear: Mahon is his co-conspirator in the world of poetry, the only reader who sees 'every birthmark', every draft, every beginning of a poem. These include the ones that the poet 'cannot' write – the 'Criminals' imprisoned, the poems that, for whatever reason, do not break free into existence; or, (as an earlier draft reads), the poems that the poet 'dare not', or will not write – 'Idiot children in the dark'. In that sense, the tale every poem tells is the tale of its own emergence – or failure to do so. But in the second stanza, those failed elements, discarded ideas and aspirations, take on a further, and subversive significance.

As any trawl through Longley's early manuscripts makes evident, the 'ghosts' of discarded poems and random phrases tend to haunt the poet, sometimes for years, until they find a resting place: fragments discarded in the early 1960s sometimes come into their own in the early 1970s; Homeric poems attempted in the mid-1970s don't find their necessary form until the late 1980s. Yet it is the discards, the rejects, and the misfits, that become, in a sense, the guardians of the poetic enterprise: the 'Thief, murderer and clown' are the 'lares', the protective gods, of the poet's soul. Every unwritten or rejected poem, every abortive attempt to write, is part of the whole of a final version by virtue of not being there. The honing of technique and subject-matter is a continual learning process that is continually haunted and disrupted by that which it denies and represses. The poem is indicative of Longley's interest through

the 1960s in split personalities, conflicting versions of self, and the
buried or suppressed "other": the 'poems we cannot write' are also,
to some extent, the people we cannot be, a preoccupation running
throughout *No Continuing City*.

In 1964, Longley took up a post as an English teacher at his old
school, the Royal Belfast Academical Institution, and married, in
December of that year, Edna Broderick, who was by then lecturing
at Queen's University Belfast. Edna Longley had already, along
with Michael Allen, Seamus Heaney and others, attended Philip
Hobsbaum's Belfast 'Group'; Michael Longley too began to attend
from 1964 and his first pamphlet, *Ten Poems*, appeared in 1965,
one of a series of pamphlets published by the Belfast Festival at
Queen's. Several of the poems included had been brought to the
Belfast Group sessions the year before; most had already appeared
in, variously, *Icarus*, the *Irish Times*, the *Listener* and the *New
Statesman*; and most were later incorporated unchanged into *No
Continuing City*. Mahon, Heaney and Hobsbaum himself published
pamphlets in the same series, which received not inconsiderable
media attention, and which may be seen as the beginnings of what
would later – and controversially – be seen as an 'Ulster Renaissance'
of poetry.

Both Mahon and Longley recorded for the Poetry Room at
Harvard in 1964, and although Mahon spent much of his time in
the mid-1960s in the US and Canada, their critical exchanges – and
competitiveness – continued unabated. Both received Eric Gregory
Awards in June 1965 (on receipt of the news of Longley's award,
Mahon cabled back two words: 'Checkmate Derek').[13] Longley has
observed that he and Mahon had been far harder on each other,
and 'more hurtful' than the Group ever was.[14] Their correspon-
dence bears that out, containing as it does detailed, often ruthless,
criticism, but criticism always driven by a care for the other's
development and reputation. Their *modus operandi* in the mid-
1960s differed considerably from the more structured procedures
of the Belfast Group, where poems would be circulated in advance,
then discussed in a semi-formal session according to the principles
of the New Critical school.

In contrast to this approach, the following comments by Mahon
to Longley are typical, as is the combative tone of the letter:

> Why, do you suppose, have you not written anything for six months?
> Could it be that you are working an exhausted vein, in terms of form?
> If the words don't just fall into place any more in accord with your
> preconceived notion of what a really good, genuine, solid-gold, floodlit
> and revolving Poem should be like, why not loosen up a bit. You did

before, magnificently, with 'The Hebrides' and 'A Personal Statement'. But I mean really go slack – write humorous verse, pastiche ee cummings, a new Dingleberry Song, a Hobsbaumiad, riddles. Please don't think me flippant, but I hate to have you feeling sorry for yourself because you haven't been writing, and all for want of a companionable kick in the arse....

Go through the poems one by one, commenting as you go. If you think there's anything I should scrap, say so, with reasons...I would be interested, too, in your comments on the collection [*Night-Crossing*, but at this point provisionally titled *Night-Train Journey*] as a whole – that is to say, on any sort of unity the things might possess apart from being all written by me. I'm not really in a position to judge. Does it make sense as a "book" as well as a "collection"?...Also, if you don't like the title, suggest alternatives.

You will be pleased to find that 'Girls in their Seasons' has been allowed to stand after all, under the title *Night-Train Journey*...You will notice that a stanza has been excised from 'An Unborn Child'.... If you want to quarrel with me about it please do, but temperately. I don't think I could take another broadside like your last....'My Wicked Uncle' remains as I have rewritten it. I am adamant. You will come to realise that I have done right....['Night Train Journey"s] present form, which incidentally represents a reasonable compromise between the ur-version and the re-write of it that you abominated, should leave you fairly happy, I think.[15]

Unlike Derek Mahon, already – as the comments above indicate – in the early to mid-1960s an inveterate reviser (and this despite protests from both Michael Longley and Edna Longley), Michael Longley has rarely tinkered with his early poems. 'Epithalamion', for example, remains unchanged from its first publication in 1963 to its recent position as the opening poem of Longley's 1998 *Selected Poems*. Only a handful of poems from the individual collections are omitted from *Poems 1963-1983*. Such revisions as there are tend to consist of the merging of individual couplets into short stanzas.

In contrast, the opening poem of *Ten Poems*, 'Emily Dickinson', written in 1964, has undergone more drastic changes. In *Ten Poems* it appears with the following four stanzas:

Emily Dickinson, I think of you
Wakening early each morning to write,
Dressing with care for the act of poetry.
Yours is always a perfect progress through
Such cluttered rooms to eloquence, delight,
To words – your window on the mystery.

The candelabra there resemble trees
Too well: the clock beneath its dome of glass
Ticks without the weather, for no one's sake,
Untruthfully. Beyond the likes of these,
In wiser landscapes, through wider vistas,
You have your voyages, your points to make.

By christening the world you live and pray –
Within those lovely titles is contained
The large philosophy you tend towards:
Within your lexicon the birds that play
Beside your life, the wind that holds your hand,
Are recognised. Your poems are full of words.

In your house in Amherst Massachusetts,
Though like love letters you lock them away,
Your poems are ubiquitous as dust.
You sit there writing while the light permits –
While you grow older they increase each day,
Gradual as flowers, gradual as rust.[16]

By the time of *No Continuing City*, it has three stanzas (the second is omitted); in *Poems 1963-1983*, two stanzas (the first and fourth of the original version are retained). And only then, one might say, is it deemed 'fit for human society'.[17]

This may not be unusual in terms of Longley's habitual method of composition, in which the principle to make every word 'earn its place' tends towards a ruthless cutting of extraneous material.[18] It is only unusual in that it is played out in print. For Longley to publish a poem in three different versions indicates an unease, even with its final form, that suggests the poem touches on some central aesthetic nerves. (That unease is perhaps comparable to Mahon's own unease with his 'Courtyards in Delft' Maenads, who are variously absent, present, and absent again in different versions of the poem.)[19] Longley admits, too, that 'Emily Dickinson' is not a poem of which he is particularly fond, and although it stands at the front of his first published pamphlet, it is not included in his 1998 *Selected Poems*. But the transparent glitches in the process of bringing the poem to a final version have their own points of interest.

The publication history of 'Emily Dickinson' uncannily mirrors its subject: the poem is gradually pared away to become as elusive and secretive as the thing it describes, moving from over-explanatory 'cluttered rooms', or stanzas, to a more precisely evocative use of language. The 'perfect progress' is both an aspiration of style, and, more generally in Longley's first collection, its accomplishment, since his early poems demonstrate an extraordinary formal skill. This poem's own gradual progress has been both growth and, more literally, decline; regeneration (flowers) and decay (rust). As with the earlier 'Epithalamion', where the poem both celebrates the night and anticipates the day, acknowledges the moment as finite even as it seeks infinity, begins a centrifugal collapse as it reaches its centripetal climax, in 'Emily Dickinson' each accumulation is also an unravelling, the moment of achievement deconstructs itself. The poem has not been allowed to gather dust; but at the same time, it has, over time, gathered around it an *oeuvre* whose preoccupations the poem itself, by looking back to Dickinson's life-work, pre-empts.

'Emily Dickinson' is thus paradigmatic in more ways than one. It demonstrates, in miniature, the process of poetry for Longley as one in which the urge to explain that process (the act of naming, for instance, is here explained as 'Within those lovely titles is contained / The large philosophy you tend towards'), eventually gives way to the thing itself (a tactic which in this instance reaches its apotheosis, to a chorus of acclaim and bemusement, in the later poem 'The Ice-cream Man', from *Gorse Fires*: 'thyme, valerian, loosestrife / Meadowsweet, tway blade, crowfoot, ling, angelica...'). In looking back, it also looks forward, implicitly, to Longley's own ambitions and development, not least in its preoccupations with the relationship between public and private, local and universal. Emily Dickinson dresses 'with care for the act of poetry'. That phrase in itself drops some hints about the almost ritualistic preparation of Longley's first collection, *No Continuing City*: poetry is both a public "putting on" of styles, voices, an assemblage of the poet's own dramatis personae, as it is also (and in the case of Dickinson exaggeratedly so) a private act, a ritual performed behind closed doors.

No Continuing City leaves little doubt that the poet is both performer, ventriloquist and actor, and simultaneously the love letter writer of intimate sincerity. At once ubiquitous and invisible, poetry in 'Emily Dickinson' is also a matter of perspective: it looks from its enclosed rooms to the community outside, and draws its light from the outside in, even as it is unknown to that community. This is not Philip Larkin's 'high window'; rather, it recognises the issues of perspective and belonging which reverberate throughout Longley's work – the knowledge that one writes, even if one does not live, in isolation; that voices may go unheard, but that the point still lies as much in the sounding of them; and that the problematic relation to the community may range from strategic withdrawal to forced exclusion to empathetic belonging. And not least, Emily Dickinson's work is itself a reminder to Longley of what becomes for him an important dictum: that miniature is not the same as minor.

II

'Emily Dickinson' thus takes its place as one of a group of poems in Longley's first collection which are tribute poems, dedicated to, or at other times ventriloquising for, figures of inspiration: poets, artists, musicians and scientists from Dr Johnson to Bix Beiderbecke. Its concern is with poetry as creating a moment of recognition, with life finding itself anew in language; its quasi-religious sensibility both holds up Dickinson's work as aspiration, and reveals something of the sense (shared by Mahon and Heaney) of poetry as an alternate spirituality. But it also takes its place in the group of poems written in the same year – 'The Hebrides', 'A Personal Statement', 'En Route', and 'No Continuing City' – in which the lyric is a voyage of (self) discovery, a journey of aesthetic development.

The voyage is not the central conceit in 'Emily Dickinson'; but it is (in the early version explicitly, and in the later one obliquely) woven into the fabric of the poem. Hers, and by implication Longley's, is a poetic journey: there may be 'points to make'; but the poem is also about the search for points from which to make them, a search for different perspectives. The 'cluttered rooms' relate symbolically to stanzaic style; the phrase is also evocative of the Metaphysical poets in more ways than one, carrying its own metaphysical wit in playing on multiple (now archaic) meanings: the room, as a stanza, is also a stopping-place on a journey.

In that sense, poetry serves both as a moment of rest, a space cleared and held poised against the flow of time, and also as a marker of movement, of progress through time. With this subtext to 'Emily Dickinson' in mind, it is not surprising that Longley places the poem at the front of *Ten Poems*. While it may not be entirely successful in its original form, its concern is, at least in part, with issues revisited in the more accomplished and sustained achievement of other poems in the first collection, all written in 1964 and 1965: 'A Personal Statement', 'The Hebrides', 'No Continuing City', 'En Route' (later retitled 'Odyssey'), 'The Ornithological Section' and 'In Memoriam'.

Of these poems, 'The Hebrides', written in the winter of 1964, is in some ways the most complex – in terms of both its form and its content – and the most self-reflexive, the culmination of aesthetic ideas worked out through the early 1960s. Its complexity partly accounts for criticism's tendency to fight shy of the poem. Nevertheless, it is central not merely to Longley's first collection but to his *oeuvre* as a whole. As with 'Emily Dickinson', the poem carries some debts to the work of the American poet Richard Wilbur, whose formal precision, metaphysical conceits, and shifting perspectives – the sense of, as Wilbur phrases it, keeping a 'difficult balance' – haunt Longley's early poems. But 'The Hebrides' also consciously draws together seemingly irreconcilable influences to define something of the paradoxical poetic sensibility at the core of *No Continuing City*.

To understand that sensibility and its implications for reading Longley's poetry, it is worth considering some of the difficulties *No Continuing City* encounters in terms of its critical reception, difficulties which the critical neglect of 'The Hebrides' brings into focus. Longley's early poems are not "obscure", in that they do not possess the wilful opacity sometimes attributed to Paul Muldoon. Nor are they characterised by a neo-modernist experimentalism with form that purports to leave its readership without the security of an existing frame of reference. But at the same time they do not have the accessibility that has been seen to characterise Seamus Heaney's first volumes. Where Heaney's early poems have been exhaustively – and repetitively – analysed by critics, *No Continuing City* tends – with a very few exceptions – to be glossed over as possessing "formal tautness", after which criticism moves hastily onwards to a point where the Troubles offer a more seductive way of reading the poetry.

The problem caused by reading through the lens of the Troubles is not, of course, unique to Longley. Heaney and Mahon have also, in different ways, both suffered from, and, in terms of media profile, benefited from the perspective which begins its narrative post-1969. But in the case of Michael Longley, rather different interpretive issues had already surfaced in the mid-1960s. In November 1964, Longley brought a selection of poems to the Belfast Group which included 'The Hebrides', 'No Continuing City' and three short (uncollected) love poems. While the poems met with admiration from Heaney, they also met with some hostility and incomprehension, notably from the Group's dominating spirit, Philip Hobsbaum who, Longley writes, 'orchestrated an indifferent, even hostile reception for some pretty ambitious early pieces'.[20]

There are two questions to address here. The first of these is why poems of this stature were ambiguously received by the critical environment of the Belfast Group; the second, and related question, is why, in the decades that have followed, critics of Irish poetry have, comparatively speaking, failed to give *No Continuing City* the attention any first collection by a leading Irish poet deserves.

Longley's first collection, it seems, poses a broader interpretive problem that has not yet been resolved. It eludes categories; it offers a challenge to its readership that has not fully been met. In a more specific instance, one difficulty of the early poems is that they elude the "difficult" category. That is to say, even the obvious difficulty posed by some of Muldoon's work, for example, is rendered to some extent benign if one follows one of the critical trails he lays down. Heaney implicitly encourages a new critical approach to his own poetry, Muldoon implicitly encourages deconstructive freefall; but the practice of (self-consciously) trail-blazing for one's readership is common to both.

Longley, who rarely adopts the role of poet-critic, has always been, in that respect, in a very different position from those whose prose-writings have opened up, and helped to educate, their own critical audience. In addition, Longley's early poems don't erect any obvious sign-posts for the reader. But the complexity of his early poetry does not exist simply at the level of formal control – complicated rhyme schemes; subtle rhythmic patterning. Rather, its interpretation depends on a recognition of paradox in terms that carry implications for theoretical approaches to Longley's work.

On one level, that recognition can lead to nothing more than delineation of paradox in *No Continuing City*: as one reviewer writes, 'these poems are sophisticated but innocent, easy-minded but clever, loving but detached, literary but firmly related to real experience and the everyday voice'.[21] Such comments, although true enough, identify thematic and tonal consequences not aesthetic principles or causes, and risk a nothing-saying see-saw of indecisive praise. But on another level, paradox may be seen as a fundamental principle of the book. As Eavan Boland writes:

> ...in a sense the distinction and grace of *No Continuing City* will be at odds with some of the critical norms of the moment, which demand that emotional anguish be testified to by technical anarchy, and confusion be expressed by obscurity. But...[f]or the most part the technical composure is moving because it ritualises a need for its opposite, a search for liberation, an insight into risk. And it is these two tensions in Michael Longley's work, of on the one hand symmetry and on the other actual suffering, which force his best poems into shape.[22]

Boland is perceptive here, in the acknowledgement that technical accomplishment can lead to the unfair judgement that accomplishment is all that there is – a criticism which has, in fact, haunted some of Longley's earlier work. In addition, she recognises that the achievement of *No Continuing City* involves more than the ability to say two different things at once, or to achieve different tonal registers. Rather, the idea of tension, and of risk taken, is crucial to understanding the poetry. Boland implicitly attributes that tension, and consequent risk, to a distinction between the imagined and the actual. Symmetry is equated here with form, and with poetry; actual suffering with real life. By implication, suffering is permitted to intrude upon symmetry and thereby risk its composure. The 'vision of risk', Boland goes on to observe, 'cannot be separated from the form which it has forced'.

Yet the argument – and the paradox – may be taken a stage further than this. It is not merely that the formal control of these poems is deliberately put at risk; rather, one might also say that the formal control, far from being a refuge, is precisely the risk that is taken. Symmetry and suffering (pre-emptive of Heaney's later uneasy polarisation of suffering and song)[23] might, in other words, be usefully replaced with the paradoxical relationship between what Muldoon calls structure and serendipity. 'One of the great mysteries for me,' Muldoon writes, 'is that one can actually combine structure and serendipity to great effect, simultaneously knowing and not knowing what one is doing.' [24] At least one way of interpreting this is to suggest that the 'knowing' lies in the adoption of a particular poetic form, or rhyme scheme, with fixed parameters; the 'not knowing' in the inevitable consequence that what is to be said within those parameters is unpredictable – and is unpredictable precisely because the parameters are in place. Longley too suggests that form is its own form of accident and anarchy. He has more than once quoted Yeats's remark that he found his ideas 'looking for the next rhyme' as illustrative of his own practice. Similarly, he celebrates the moment when 'language itself takes over the enterprise'.[25] Writing, he suggests, is about 'moving into uncharted territories inside your own head, the form of a poem is like a map and a compass'.[26]

In one sense, then, Longley's early poems are, in their formal accomplishment, as amenable as Heaney's to the mode of criticism – Anglo-American new criticism – by which Heaney's poetry has been well-served. But the extent to which the poems delight in play cuts the interpretive ground from underneath the reader. His own recent (and comparatively rare) reflection on the process of composition – in the 1996 essay 'A Tongue at Play' – acknowledges that delight, in terms both erotic and, albeit unconsciously, deconstructionist. The phrase itself is at several removes from Heaney's 'The Government of the Tongue' which, despite its ambiguity (by the tongue? of the tongue?) still suggests control as opposed to 'play'. And "experimentalism", in terms of poetic form, as Longley recognises it, has less to do with the abandonment of traditional

structures than with their reinvention – a mode of writing potentially
far more subversive than one which pretends that the parameters
against which it defines itself simply aren't there. 'The rules,' he
writes, 'are there to be broken.'[27]

Such reinvention is the conscious starting-point of 'The Hebrides'.
The poem deliberately attempts to bring together irreconcilable
influences: George Herbert and Hart Crane. It borrows its stanzaic
shape (the metrical pattern of 10, 4, 8, 6, 10 and 4 syllable lines)
and its abacbc rhyme scheme from Herbert's 'Peace'. The technical
challenge posed by this – as earlier by the form of 'Epithalamion'
– is, in Longley's phrase, one of the ways he 'discovered how to
write'.[28] It also borrows, and destabilises, Herbert's understanding of
'repose'. Herbert attains this repose at the close of 'Peace' through
an ever-present sacramental life:

> Take of this grain, which in my garden grows,
> > And grows for you;
> > Make bread of it; and that repose
> > And peace, which ev'ry where
> With so much earnestness you do pursue
> > Is onely there.

"In my end is my beginning" is, in effect, Herbert's aesthetic as well
as religious premise. 'The Hebrides' also loses its way in order to
find it, but does not make the same kind of return 'home', wherever
that might be. Instead, Longley counters Herbert's repose with a
"schizophrenia" that draws on Hart Crane's more destabilising
'Voyages', his suicidal vertigo. The sea, Crane's most powerful
image, is both order and chaos, flux and tranquillity. If Herbert
signifies harmony, Crane signifies paradox and uncertainty.

In terms of his own cultural inheritance, Longley describes him-
self as 'schizophrenic', leading 'a double life', recreating himself
'twice daily'; drifting from one side of Belfast's Lisburn Road –
itself a 'schizophrenic' street, working-class and middle-class – to
the other.[29] He first defines himself in this way in 1969, at the point
when the Troubles force a self-consciousness about "identity": 'I
see that I have been schizophrenic on the levels of nationality, class
and culture.'[30] But it is also worth noting the extent to which his
interpretation of his Belfast childhood echoes his interpretation –
quoted earlier – of his Trinity undergraduate years and of the
'tensions in myself'. It seems fair to conclude that the notion of
the divided, or dual self is carried with the poet and projected onto
his environment as well as created by it. The "schizophrenia" seen
in 'The Hebrides' in terms of influence is only part of that more
complex double life, and a problematical – or rather paradoxical –

relationship with 'home' which is lost in order to be found, and
vice versa. The opening of the poem, with its Presbyterian granite,
lack of trees and orphaned stone, is irresistibly evocative of the bleak
north Antrim coast as much as of the Hebrides:

> The winds' enclosure, Atlantic's premises,
>   Last balconies
>   Above the waves, The Hebrides –
>   Too long did I postpone
> Presbyterian granite and the lack of trees,
>   This orphaned stone
>
> Day in, day out colliding with the sea.
>   Weather forecast,
>   Compass nor ordnance survey
>   Arranges my welcome
> For, on my own, I have lost my way at last,
>   So far from home

Some of this imagery haunts Derek Mahon's poetry to the extent
that it later becomes his trademark. There are other echoes and
overlaps between the two poets that are illustrative of their close-
ness in the writing process at this time, and of their shared influences
– notably Louis MacNeice and Robert Lowell (particularly the
Lowell of 'The Quaker Graveyard in Nantucket'). For both Longley
and Mahon, the rather bleak imagery is linked to the North's
repressive puritan traditions in the 1950s and 1960s, about which
they have both been openly condemnatory. But the opening of 'The
Hebrides' has a more particular resonance in terms of Longley's
personal mythology.

The poem is a search for origins, one that finds a perspective on
Antrim from the vantage point of elsewhere. The postponement
of the opening lines is as much the postponed confrontation with
the poet's own past as it is the belated arrival in the present moment.
In the beginning of a complicated conceit that runs through the
poem whereby the speaker merges into the land, and the land itself
becomes as fluid and shifting as the sea, the 'orphaned stone'
reverberates in terms of Longley's complex, and in another way
unstable sense of origins – as the Irish child with English parents;
as the Northern Protestant alienated from the trappings of Irish
Catholic culture, but alienated also from the Presbyterian ethos of
the Northern "state". Since Longley's first elegy for his father, 'In
Memoriam', also appears in *No Continuing City*, 'orphaned' regis-
ters on a more intimate level. Lacking map, compasses, markers of
who and where he is, defined through heredity but with the father
no longer there, the speaker embraces a solitude and an instability

in which, paradoxically, to lose one's way is also to find it.

'The Hebrides' posits choices – between stability and instability, continuity and rupture, flux and poise. It begins with uncertainty and indecisiveness, moves towards certainty and poise, but ends by desiring the very state of mind it had apparently transcended. At the close of section 2 of the poem, the speaker describes himself as 'in two minds'. He confronts two irreconcilable conditions. The first – which is the one decided upon – is 'shipwreck', jettisoning 'My each nostalgic scheme' and casting himself ashore as the sole survivor; the second, which is involuntary, is the recognition that memory disallows complete severance. If the poet is the 'amputee' who decides upon shipwreck, the ghosts of the past are perpetually absorbed into his present (Old neighbours... People my brain....I feel them / Put on their raincoats for ever / And walk out in the sea'). The recognition, in section 3, is thus that a journey forward is also a journey backwards:

> For these are my sailors, these my drowned –
> > In their heart of hearts,
> > In their city I ran aground.
> > > Along my arteries
> Sluice those homewaters petroleum hurts.
> > > Dry dock, gantries,
>
> Dykes of apparatus educate my bones
> > To track the buoys
> > Up sea lanes where love emblazons
> > > To streets where shall conclude
> My journey back from flux to poise, from poise
> > > To attitude.
>
> Here, at the edge of my experience,
> > > Another tide
> > Along the broken shore extends
> > > A lifetime's wrack and ruin –
> No flotsam I may beachcomb now can hide
> > > That water line.

The movement away from the shoreline through the remainder of the poem is a movement which allows the past to emerge like a palimpsest; the varying water levels and tide marks become ('I discern / My sea levels') the map and compass of his own history that were absent at the start of the poem. (There are echoes here of the inexorable impetus behind 'Epithalamion', with the 'trees... again in their huge histories / Displayed'.) In a way, then, the poem encompasses both of its two minds: it jettisons and accumulates. What it leaves behind it also takes with it. What it takes with it, it ultimately loses.

In doing so, the poem resists harmonious "closure". It tantalises
its reader with the possibility of resolution and reconciliation, but
its resistance to 'repose', to drawing its imagery into a satisfactory
unity is, in the end, unequivocal:

> Granting the trawlers far below their stance,
>   Their anchorage,
>   I fight all the way for balance –
>   In the mountain's shadow
> Losing foothold, covet the privilege
>   Of vertigo.

This privilege is vertigo in its figurative as well as literal sense as
indicative of a disordered, or divided, state of mind. 'The Hebrides'
is an ambitious poem, not least because it provides a marker at the
outset of what Longley is trying to do, an acknowledgement that
his aesthetic will always be one of a deliberate uncertainty, and
that definitions – of home, tradition, lineage – will always prove
resistant to single interpretations. 'The Hebrides', in other words,
operates on a principle of drawing parallel lines; the objective is
always out of reach; the lines never meet.

Again, that principle carries autobiographical resonance: Longley
writes of his relationship with his twin as one in which, as a child,
he felt 'completely fulfilled – fraternal, paternal, maternal. Being a
lover, a husband, a father has since enabled me to draw parallel
lines only.'[31] Longley's inheritance is a dual inheritance; many of
the early poems are concerned with division of self from self, myth-
ologised in familial terms as the perpetual adult search – doomed
to failure – for the mirror image, or alter ego that will make the
poet whole once again. 'The Hebrides' moves beyond what one
would expect to be its own beginnings and endings – the 'bridal
pools' and 'rivers where they meet the sea' of its fourth section –
and concludes by coveting as a fundamental principle risk, a kind
of schizophrenia, being in two minds and two places, balanced
and unbalanced. And not least, the application of Herbert's tight
stanzaic pattern to the more expansive and destabilising voyage
undertaken in 'The Hebrides' means that that pattern is sustained,
against the odds, almost to breaking point.

Once again, the risk is in the form itself: the edifice meticulously
built up over five sections needs to exist for that privilege of vertigo
to take on its proper meaning. It is, in other words, as if the poet
has built his own poetic structure for the purpose of destabilising
that achievement by falling from it from the greatest possible height.
The poem thus becomes an exercise in control that by definition
is finite, that exists on the edge of collapse, that is itself, like the

landscape around it, a 'suicidal...tilt'. It is in this sense that Longley has understood Yeats perfectly, particularly the Yeats of 'The Tower' sequence, whose architectural forms embody memory even as the process of writing – and reading – unravels those structures. The sensibility that informs Longley's reading of Dickinson's poems as 'gradual as flowers, gradual as rust', simultaneously writing and unwriting themselves, accumulating and jettisoning, is likewise woven into 'The Hebrides'.

'The Hebrides' will not allow itself to be read to an easier conclusion than this; parts of it remain elusive, slightly beyond control. It wilfully embraces contradiction. This also goes some way to explaining the problematical reception accorded the poem in the Belfast Group in 1964. The introduction of Longley to the Group served to expose the critical gap between critics Philip Hobsbaum and Michael Allen, a gap which led, ultimately, to Allen's being 'cast out from the magic circle'.[32] But Longley's as compared to Heaney's Group poems might be seen to open up that kind of critical gap in a broader sense. For Hobsbaum, Heaney was the undoubted star of the Group, whose densely textured, empirical mode of writing validated Hobsbaum's own critical principles. Those principles – learned in part from his former tutor F.R. Leavis – are enshrined in Hobsbaum's *A Theory of Communication*, written between 1959 and 1968, and published in 1970. (The book is also heavily indebted to I.A. Richards's 1925 *Principles of Literary Criticism*.)

In *A Theory of Communication*, Hobsbaum asserts that an unsuccessful poem will not allow itself to be read to coherent and shared conclusion; a truly great poem is one which transcends such disagreements because it manifests itself 'so tangibly and forcefully'. In the end, this translates into a dislike of poems which lead to two irreconcilable interpretations. Poems which do so are poems which contain 'fundamentally incompatible' ideas. Thus, Emily Dickinson, whose poetry, in Hobsbaum's view, is too ambiguous for an interpretive consensus to exist, is dismissed as 'a minor poet' with a 'vastly inflated' reputation.[33] (This explains why, for Hobsbaum, Heaney is a 'great' poet because for Hobsbaum there is only one way in which Heaney can be read.)

Hobsbaum's *Theory of Communication* is a text which pushes the approach current in the academy since I.A. Richards to its extreme; and it is, of course, a text which by 1970 had missed its moment. The critical climate altered so radically in the late 1960s that some of its principles were rendered anachronistic even before it appeared. That is not necessarily to claim that all Hobsbaum's assumptions – or indeed all formalist assumptions – have been

invalidated by the explosion of literary theory in the academies in
the 1960s and 1970s. But some of his conclusions about textual
stability and coherence are – rightly – now seen as bound up with
a conservative world-view that reverberates beyond the realm of
the text. Hobsbaum's *Theory of Communication* presumes, as did
Richards's *Principles of Literary Criticism*, a consensus among readers;
but the belief in such a consensus, and in the ways in which it
comes into being – through culture, class, education – cannot now
be seen as apolitical in their implications.

A Theory of Communication reveals the extent to which Hobs-
baum's method of reading poetry struggles to accommodate the kind
of disruptive aesthetic evident in Longley's early work. The critical
gap may be illuminated by comparing Longley's 'The Hebrides'
with Heaney's 'The Peninsula', poems which share some of their
imagery, and which were both written during the period of Heaney's
and Longley's involvement with the Group. 'The Peninsula', written
after 'The Hebrides' had been discussed in the Belfast Group, has
its origins, in part, in the friendship between the Heaneys and
Longleys which began in the mid-1960s, in their joint explorations
of Co. Down and elsewhere, and in their shared love of the natural
world. But it also shows the two poets working in different direc-
tions.

In Heaney's 'The Peninsula', from *Door into the Dark*, the poet
also undertakes a coastal journey in which one aims not to arrive
'But pass through'. The poem, however, also comes full circle,
'round the peninsula', to this conclusion:

> And drive back home, still with nothing to say
> Except that now you will uncode all landscapes
> By this: things founded clean on their own shapes,
> Water and ground in their extremity.

It is, both emotionally and in terms of its imagery, a perfect loop,
that finds its starting point 'back home' with a fresh clarity of vision,
a distinctness in its elements, that was lacking at the outset, notably
in its recovery of a perfect rhyme. The poem too is a thing 'founded
clean' on its own shape, its apparent simplicity rendering it possible
to "uncode" it as a poem of integrity, in that it leaves nothing
wanting, nothing broken or incomplete.

More recently, of course, criticism has called that seductive
simplicity into question: reading Heaney has gradually become a
more difficult, and more rewarding enterprise too. Yet it is easy to
see why this poem, for example, would appeal so directly to a
reading practice invested in precisely that sense of completion and

closure, since the poem's own self-reflexivity offers that mode of interpretation as indicative of the nature of poetry itself.

One might speculate that if the fourth section of 'The Hebrides' had chosen to hold 'shore and sky / In harmony', with all the trappings of formalist unity, its reception could have been very different in the context of the Belfast Group. But 'The Hebrides' is both formally and thematically resistant to the interpretation Hobsbaum's criticism avowedly prefers. Accommodation of difference is not the same as reconciliation of difference: the former is closer to Longley's (and to Crane's) method; the latter to Heaney's (and to Herbert's). Nevertheless, that 'The Hebrides' encountered a critical approach which struggled to accommodate it should not be read as an indictment of the poem; it points rather to the limitations of that approach.

Turning some of formalism's assumptions on their head, Jacques Derrida writes in 1968 that:

> ...in marking out differance, everything is a matter of strategy and risk. It is a question of strategy because no transcendent truth present outside the sphere of writing can theologically command the totality of this field. It is hazardous because this strategy is not simply one in the sense that we say that strategy orients the tactics according to a final aim, a *telos* or the theme of a domination, a mastery or an ultimate reappropriation of movement and field. In the end, it is a strategy without finality....The concept of play...designates the unity of chance and necessity in an endless calculus.[34]

This returns us to Muldoon's earlier delight in the paradoxical relation between structure (necessity) and serendipity (chance). To covet vertigo is in one sense to opt for an endless calculus. The impetus of 'The Hebrides' may be distinguished from that of 'The Peninsula' in this: for Heaney, as for Longley, the journey through space is also a journey through time, a memory trip; but 'The Peninsula' seeks – and purports to find – a transcendent truth, one which affirms Heaney's early description of 'poetry as divination, poetry as revelation of the self to the self'.[35]

'The Hebrides', too, might seek such revelation, but for Longley it is the journey and not the destination that matters – the poem, in other words, may be read as 'a strategy without finality', as a poem that detours, that 'suspends the accomplishment or fulfilment of "desire" or "will" '.[36] Memory in 'The Hebrides' is both an accretion *and* a gradual process of forgetting which "unwrites" the poem even as its structure is established. The poem is about poetic development; it understands that the poetic journey is unpredictable, hazardous, and that it is never concluded. Longley thus takes risks in searching for a truth which the poet also knows is not there to be found, and in undertaking a journey which cannot return him to something he does not possess: a stable sense of "self", "home" or "belonging".

The paradoxes that follow on from such profound uncertainty lie at the heart of *No Continuing City*. Longley's avowedly religious sensibility finds no sure theological resting-place; "home" itself may be better translated as "homes"; the rhyming is not to see oneself, as Heaney formulates it in a poem dedicated to Longley, 'Personal Helicon', but to see multiple dramatised versions of self. The early poems are about both the search for presence, and about the irreparable loss of presence. Even the collection's title, *No Continuing City*, taken as it is from St Paul to the Hebrews – 'For here we have no continuing city, but we seek one to come' – defers its object, suspends the accomplishment of desire, and posits the quest as a permanent condition.

III

In Homer's *Odyssey*, Penelope, to free herself from the importunate demands of the suitors, insists she will remarry only when the shroud she is weaving for Laertes is completed. The work, famously, is never done, but always in hand; she weaves by day and unravels by night. As she does so, Odysseus journeys back from the Trojan War, a quest for home which takes him ten years, and which renders him unrecognisable to those at home when his goal is reached. At the same time, Odysseus's own son, Telemachus, sets out on a parallel journey to find his father, and to find his own manhood.

The *Odyssey* has become the archetype of all such journeys – whether in terms of years, or, in the case of Joyce's *Ulysses*, of one day in Dublin. It is hardly surprising, then, that Longley's pre-occupation with the classics should centre itself, in the early poems, on texts (*The Odyssey* and *Ulysses*) so attuned to the broader aesthetic principles evident in his work. While the *Iliad* to some extent displaces the *Odyssey* in later collections, offering as it does a way of writing the Troubles, the *Odyssey*'s biographical and thematic appeal is obvious in the early poetry – in its concern with finding a home, its love-encounters and culmination in a resumption of married life, its parallel lives and doublings, its manipulations of space and time, its quest for the father, its journey (in Longley's as in Joyce's case through Dublin) into maturity.

In *No Continuing City* the poet is both the voyager, who transforms his past life of loves into a Homeric journey to a single resting-place, and, variously, those characters met en route to home. 'En Route' ('Odyssey') and 'No Continuing City' may be read as complementary poems, of the journey and the journey's end respectively; 'Circe', 'Nausicaa' and 'Persephone' of its various stopping-places.

Longley may be seen here as transmuting his own life into myth, notably in terms of his marriage in 1964, and of his return to a permanent home in Belfast (his twin, meanwhile, as a ship's engineer, began to travel the world in the 1960s). The *Odyssey* is a coming of age narrative, at its centre the relationship between father and son: Longley, more obliquely, is also a son in search of a lost father. The subtle weaving of the Greek myths into the fabric of contemporary Ireland, and into the fabric of Longley's own private life (or *vice versa*) permits the crossover from epic to lyric – or rather, brings public resonance on the epic scale into the intimacy of the lyric poem.

Retrospectively, one might also now read Longley's Homeric preoccupations in the early volumes as a way of understanding his own development as a poet, particularly bearing in mind that Longley's "voice" has never been easily tabulated, and that his early work is characterised by self-effacement. Odysseus may be the subject of some of these poems, learning as he goes, and the multiple voices may give the sense of divers hands working in the collection; but behind the lines is the master-craftsman who invisibly weaves the multiple threads of the myths together over time.

Both 'Odyssey' and 'No Continuing City' play on the same conceit: that of a journey through time and space as a series of sexual encounters, a slightly tongue-in-cheek Odyssean voyage through the bed and breakfast opportunities of life. The poems, as has been noted, also take their 'compass-bearings' from Hart Crane's 'Voyages', particularly in their body/voyage conceit ('Permit me voyage, love, into your hands', Crane writes).[37] In 'Odyssey', the 'Sirens and shepherdesses', like the ghosts of the past in 'The Hebrides', a poem whose 'sailors' also give it Odyssean resonance, are emotional detours that turn out not to be detours at all: they are, instead, a losing one's way which is, paradoxically, the only way home. Every stopping-place feels like an ending, but proves to be the starting-point for another journey:

> You have kept me going, despite delays –
> On these devious shores where we coincide
> I have never once outstayed my welcome
> Though you all seem last resorts, my brides –
> You faces favourite landmarks always,
> Your bodies comprising the long way home.

Odysseus's ten-year wanderings at sea are preordained, and they are interspersed with sojourns on islands (literal and metaphorical) of seductive women – Circe, Calypso, Nausicaa – as well as encounters with the monstrous females who would literally devour him: Scylla and Charybdis. The potential for masculine self-indulgence in this kind of womb and tomb narrative is one reason for the lightness of touch in these poems. And 'No Continuing City', the parallel poem to 'Odyssey', subordinates the mythic to the autobiographical, wryly undercutting such subliminal fears and fantasies. Written in December 1964, some months after 'Odyssey' was completed, and only days before Longley's marriage took place, the message of 'No Continuing City' is more explicit: 'to recognise / This new dimension'; 'to set my house in order'. But like 'Odyssey' it plays out a narrative of self-discovery.

The tales of the *Odyssey* are the pattern of the poet's own past which he can now see, objectively, as past: his former girls 'constellate such uneventful skies, / Their stars arranged each night / In the old stories / Which I successfully have diagnosed.' Both poems are also haunted by the theme central to sexual encounters in the *Odyssey*, that of memory and forgetfulness; the 'landmarks' of one poem are the billboards 'Pasted over' of the other. In 'No Continuing City', the close of 'Odyssey', and the male fear of the devouring woman, are parodied with the 'closing broadcast' to his 'last girl':

> I tell her she is welcome,
> Advising her to make this last,
> To be sure of finding room in me
> (I embody bed and breakfast) –
> To eat and drink me out of house and home.

While 'diagnosis' might seem an unusually clinical term with which to approach past loves, it sit appositely enough in a collection so preoccupied with split personalities, and with what goes on inside people's heads. 'Journey Out of Essex' opens with John Clare 'lying with my head / Over the edge of the world, / Unpicking my whereabouts'; for 'Dr Johnson Dying', 'There was no place to go but his own head'; in 'To Bix Beiderbecke', voices 'filled like an empty room your skull'; Rip Van Winkle is exhorted to 'Unlock the Sleepy Hollow of your head'; Persephone sees 'through a skylight in my brain'; in 'Circe', 'The cries of the shipwrecked enter my head'.

The list need not end here. By no stretch of the imagination does *No Continuing City* bring together a tribe of the most well-adjusted figures: its fascination with disturbed behaviour gives a surreal tone to some of these poems; others are perhaps too cryptic for comfort. But this unsettling, darker side is an essential part of the dual vision that the poet seeks overall.

Thus, Longley's 'Circe' also parallels 'Odyssey' and 'No Continuing City', but as a negative "other". Its tale is familiar, although the gender roles are here reversed, as is its language, which subtly links all three poems. Circe's past history is measured by the 'husband after husband' who 'puts in at my island'; as in 'Odyssey', each sexual encounter is both 'for ever' and one of many. But this is not a healing putting of one's house in order, reintegrating different aspects of self, as in 'No Continuing City'. The 'torn sky' and the 'sea's cracked mirror' foreshadow the fracturing of self which renders Circe's victims 'forgetful'. And the poem's end with its 'last rooms' is also a sinister alternative to 'No Continuing City''s benign invitation to the 'last girl':

> I have made of my arms and my thighs last rooms
> For the irretrievable and capsized –
> I extend the sea, its idioms.

Given Longley's study of Classics at Trinity, and his later well-known translations from Homer and Ovid, it has proved rather too easy for critics to categorise these early poems which deal with Greek myths as academic exercises. But the tone of these poems suggests that their debt is as much to Joyce as it is to Homer, and Joyce's *Ulysses* is a text with which Longley was obsessed during his Trinity years. The voice in 'No Continuing City', with its slightly ponderous humour, its preoccupation with snoozing and dining, carries echoes of Leopold Bloom ('always a favourite with the ladies').[38] 'Nausicaa', Longley later acknowledges, 'is really Gertie McDowell'.[39] The shifts of tone throughout *No Continuing City* enable Longley to play out the roles of benevolent father-figure and tormented artist – Bloom and Dedalus. The tonal as well as thematic echoes of *Ulysses* – and an apparent concern with its more surreal and fractured episodes (notably 'Circe') – render these mythic poems subtly autobiographical in a different way, suggesting that Longley's Dublin years were as unsettling as they were fruitful.

Bloom and Dedalus do, of course, finally meet, as do Odysseus and Telemachus. To find that moment in Longley's early poetry – where parallel lives meet each other – one has to go to a poem not often considered in relation to his early Homeric poems, but nevertheless obliquely part of this group – 'In Memoriam'. From the outset, it has received more critical attention than any other poem in this first collection. It is, as Peter McDonald describes it 'enormously powerful'.[40] In an elegy for his father, the poet explores his own origin in, metaphorically, the landscape of the First World War; at the same time, the poem speaks to a wider sense of that war landscape as an origin for much of what has followed in the 20th century. It demonstrates those features that will become the hallmark of Longley's elegies: in its bringing of the private into the public utterance; in its ethical concern with history, with the poet's responsibility towards past and therefore, by implication, future; in its unobtrusive shifts in and out of an intimate, familiar and colloquial linguistic register; and in its subversion of some of the conventions of elegy.

Inspired by the memories of the war his father shared with him before his death from cancer in 1960, the poet writes both 'in memory' and, by invoking 'heartbreaks' into his own hands, from memory. (The images from those anecdotes haunt Longley's work for decades: the 'turnip field' of helmets is excised from an early draft of 'In Memoriam' in 1964 to find its final resting place in 'Behind a Cloud' in 1993.) Longley's poetry is characterised by its manipulation of perspective: the poems work structurally and syntactically to give snapshots, to zoom in on detail, or to let the camera pan slowly across space and time.[41] Here, to 'see in close-up' is to claim an inherited memory, an authentic telling brought into focus across the years. That 'memory' relates both to his familial and literary inheritance, since the poem also sees Wilfred Owen's *oeuvre* in an intertextual close-up:

> Now I see in close-up, in my mind's eye,
> The cracked and splintered dead for pity's sake
> Each dismal evening predecease the sun,
> You, looking death and nightmare in the face...

As the poet travels back in time to meet his father, his own origin becomes, potentially, his own extinction – two things that for Longley habitually go hand in hand. This poem too is a narrative of birth and death, arrival and departure:

> That instant I, your most unlikely son,
> In No Man's Land was surely left for dead,
> Blotted out from your far horizon.
> As your voice now is locked inside my head,
> I yet was held secure, waiting my turn.

This is the Odysseus/Telemachus quest for each other translated from space into time, a voyage into the past and the future. His father's journey after the Great War is one which affirms his sexual prowess after injury: 'in need of proof / You hunted down experimental lovers, / Persuading chorus girls and countesses'. In one of several parallels between Longley's transmutation of his own life and his father's life into myth, the 'experimental lovers' are his father's own version of the bodies which comprise 'the long way home'.

The links are suggested in other ways too. Richard Longley is 19 when he goes to fight in the First World War; the poet is in his 19th year when his father's 'old wounds woke / As cancer'. Beginnings are also endings. Although father and son meet, they are on parallel journeys. Longley is the Odysseus figure in many of these poems; he is also, at different times, Telemachus and Laertes. The temporal displacements of 'In Memoriam' make him both father and son; and his role at the end is protective not dependent:

> I summon girls who packed at last and went
> Underground with you. Their souls again on hire,
> Now those lost wives as recreated brides
> Take shape before me, materialise.
> On the verge of light and happy legend
> They lift their skirts like blinds across your eyes.

This final stanza is an extraordinary gesture of imaginative compensation. Yet as an elegy, the poem is unusual in that its object of consolation is not those left behind to grieve, but the subject of the elegy himself. The poet turns his father's 'last confidence' – the story of his post-war love-life – into his own last confident resurrection of the 'lost wives' as consolation at the end of the poem.

A further transference has also taken place. If memory evokes only the horrors of war, the real gift or consolation is forgetfulness, is to be able not to see. The poet's 'Now I see in close-up' allows his father not to see at the close of the poem; on one level, it renders him innocent again and reverses the normal father-son relationship. The final line is, of course, evocative of Owen's 'slow...drawing down of blinds'; but its bawdy element draws on centuries of myths and traditions: skirt-lifting as dispersing evil influences, as multiplying crop yields, as banishing pests and devils. 'Underground' suggests the mythical underworld, with Persephone as death-goddess; but the triple goddess whose vulva is worshipped in myth is creative and preservative as well as destructive. The end of the journey for the poet's father is thus death and sex, a leaving and a homecoming. As in 'The Hebrides' – or as with Penelope's shroud – the poems generate their effect through the ways in which they harness contradictory impulses, seek an uneasy equilibrium which is a progression not a resolution.

IV

Throughout *No Continuing City*, Richard Wilbur's sense of the poet's task as keeping a 'difficult balance' ('Love Calls Us to the Things of This World') is to the fore. It proves particularly relevant in view of Longley's own sense of himself as poised - or perhaps at this stage more uncomfortably suspended – between different cultural inheritances, and as lacking the instantly recognisable "voice" or tradition of some of his contemporaries.

As already discussed, that division works in terms of his English-Irish inheritance, and is then mirrored in his perception of the streets on which he grew up, not only in terms of class. More recently, Longley has also suggested an urban/rural split as another variation on the theme:

> From an early age, I drifted between Englishness and Irishness, between town and country, between the Lisburn Road with its shops and cinemas and the River Lagan with its beech woods and meadows where I fell in love with wild birds and wild flowers. I am still drifting. Perhaps a certain indeterminacy keeps me impressionable.[42]

On the one hand the notion of a split self emerges in *No Continuing City* as a disturbing preoccupation with schizophrenia, or with a fracturing of identity; on the other, Longley delights in – and finds a lyric release in – a dual inheritance. To be pulled in contrary directions, as Yeats knew, can create a rich poetic tapestry. That kind of 'drifting', of suspension 'between' one thing or another may, as Longley himself argues, have made it more difficult for him to sound his own note in the early 1960s; but it has also proved a liberating aesthetic principle, one which underpins his poetic career and which serves to create, over time, a wholly distinctive voice.

No Continuing City may be read, therefore, as both the statement of a problem and its solution. A book very consciously about its own forms, the collection as a whole potentially takes the poet in two different directions. On the one hand, Longley's preoccupations lead him into the enclosed, tightened, almost repressive short poems that, however successful they may be in and of themselves, ultimately prove to be a closed circuit, trapped inside their own forms like a voice trapped inside its own head – of which more anon. On the other, the circling of subject, the location betwixt and between, in such poems as 'The Freemartin', and 'Leaving Inishmore' proves revelatory rather than restrictive.

It is in showing both sides of the coin that *No Continuing City* finds its solution – at least on the surface. Longley has always been

an advocate of advancing on several different fronts at the same
time, of resisting categorisation as a particular type of poet. The
notion that different elements should be intermingled in the self
and the poems is central to the vision outlined in 'A Personal
Statement' (1964),[43] a poem which lays down some of the aesthetic
ground rules and aspirations for the future. A highly stylised poem
(like 'The Hebrides', it borrows one of Herbert's stanzaic patterns
– in this instance from 'Denial'), and with a 17th-century meta-
physical sensibility about it, it is, in one way, an exercise in control:

> My person is
> A chamber where the elements postpone
> In lively synthesis,
> In peace on loan,
>
> Old wars of flood and earthquake, storm
> And holocaust,
> Their attributes most temperately reformed
> Of heatwave and of frost.
> They take my form,
>
> Learn from my arteries their pace –
> They leave alarms
> And excursions for my heart and lungs to face.
> I hold them in my arms
> And keep in place.

Fire, air, water and earth – the four 'elements' for the Metaphysicals
– can also be flood, earthquake, storm and holocaust; but they are
held in check in the body by the exhortation to the 'Mind' to 'Keep
my balance'. The poem, dedicated to Heaney, also marks out
Longley's difference from Heaney, whose 'Personal Helicon', dedi-
cated to Longley, is all earth and water with a physical immediacy.

In some ways an obvious companion piece to 'The Hebrides',
'A Personal Statement' recognises the 'alarms / And excursions'
beneath an outwardly controlled surface: once again, the more
stylised the form, the more impossible it seems that it will sustain
itself. But as with 'The Hebrides', having achieved a form of
stability, the poet mistrusts it. If the poem is read as affirming the
need for balance between Body and Mind ('Essential Two'), in which
Mind keeps Body in check, its final stanza shifts the emphasis:

> Lest I with fears and hopes capsize,
> By your own lights
> Sail, Body, cargoless towards surprise.
> And come, Mind, raise your sights –
> Believe my eyes.

It is as if the freight of the preceding stanzas is to be jettisoned, leaving the Body to invest in sensory surprise, and the Mind to trust the senses' evidence. Its apparent move away from the cerebral to the physical renders it a more complicated aesthetic position than it might otherwise have appeared (as the close of Heaney's 'Personal Helicon' shifts from physical to metaphysical – 'to set the darkness echoing'). The close of the poem suggests a anxiety about too much thought, about that which is predetermined by the mind; consequently, it both reaches a conclusion, and sets sail on another quest.

Yet while *No Continuing City* plays with ideas of parallel and contrary journeys, its fight for both 'balance' and 'vertigo' simultaneously has certain implications on a formal level; which, as 'A Personal Statement' anticipates, could in the long run 'capsize' the poet. 'Remembrance Day', in its final version, was completed in December 1966 (it has its origins in juvenilia from *Icarus*) and was, Longley noted on the typescript 'the first [poem] for seven months'. In 1967, only one poem was added to *No Continuing City*, 'Man Friday'; and in 1968, three final poems: the dedicatory poem, 'To Edna', 'Klondike' (one of the less successful poems in the volume) and 'Journey Out of Essex'. A slowing down may be inevitable at the point where a volume reaches completion, but has not yet been published. For Longley, however, this period marked the beginning of a more problematical writer's block, which was not to find its release until 1971.

Longley has always seen the problem as a formal one; both in 1968, and again in the 1980s when a second period of writer's block occurred – this time to last, on and off, for more than five years. Nevertheless, that formal problem is also, by default, bound up with his theme, with the unique problems posed by the Northern Irish context, and with personal circumstances.

In 1968, Longley collected nine of the last short poems to be included in *No Continuing City* into a limited edition pamphlet, *Secret Marriages*. In draft stage, it is apparent that several of these poems – notably 'Persephone', Narcissus', 'Nausicaa', and 'Rip Van Winkle' – were working out, from different angles, a preoccupation with the divided mind, with the paradox of the 'murdered killer' (the phrase appears in an early draft of 'Persephone'), with split personalities. They exist, in draft, almost as fragments of each other; to some extent, even in their final form, their originating principles are obscured unless they are read side by side. In all cases, there has been a struggle to find a formula for what Longley describes, in the introduction to *Secret Marriages*, as 'an attempt to define schizophrenia'. 'Persephone' and 'Narcissus' are indeed, he writes, 'all that remains' of that attempt (although he notes 'something schizoid' about both 'Rip Van Winkle' and 'those poems which…have one foot in the grave, conjuring up the dead as presences' too).

Offering a possible interpretation of his poems is a rare undertaking for Longley, and one which perhaps intimates his own sense that it might be as difficult for the reader to find somewhere to go with these poems as it was later to prove for the poet. 'Persephone' is as beautifully folded a poem as its central image of the bat's wing 'like a winter leaf'; where 'footsteps borrow silence from the snow', the poem also treads softly, inevitably succumbing to the desire to reach as far towards silence, and by extension into the whiteness of the page, as possible. But its effectiveness in this regard is also, as Longley defines it, part of the problem, as it retreats into itself. These poems are, he writes:

> …the logical conclusion of a long preoccupation with form, with stanzaic patterns and rhyme – pushing a shape as far as it will go, exploring its capacities to control and its tendencies to disintegrate. Six of these poems are in rhyming couplets [the exceptions are 'Remembrance Day', 'The Freemartin', and 'In a Convent Cemetery'] which are usually something of a caretaker form, I think – a temporary address between more permanent lodgings.

Perhaps this seems to be an ideal formal development for a poet whose aesthetic thrives on temporary addresses, on a deliberate lack of stability and certainty. Yet Longley's sense that the formal tautness of these short poems has driven him into a corner works against that more liberating uncertainty. As he goes on to observe, far from being a 'caretaker form', the couplets have instead become:

> …tiny units, reduced stanzas, circuits which are almost closed, relying more on their own interrelationships than would the usual cursive and open-ended kind. These poems have an air of 'end of the road' rather than 'en route' about them. The next stage in logical progression would be a blank page and dead silence: they enjoy already the brevity of epitaphs.[44]

The irony is, of course, that to be able to see the problem clearly in this way – to become self-conscious about the poetic process – also compounds that problem. The poet is thus caught in a paradox of his own making: the poems in *Secret Marriages* achieve their desired effect; but some do so by ringing their own death-knell.

Nevertheless, if the *Secret Marriages* poems mark the end of one (stylistic and thematic) journey in *No Continuing City*, the collection itself is still one of beginnings and endings. The paradox may thus be seen in two ways: first, it leads, inevitably, to a period of writer's block; second, it wipes the slate clean, allows for the future self to find new forms. *No Continuing City* finds its own balance and integrity as a collection; but it is worth noting that the book, in style and form, is also in some ways a one-off, almost as if its arrival on the scene is the cue for the poet's departure from its formal *mores*. Longley later abandons the complex stanzaic shapes and rhymes of *No Continuing City*, and for several reasons. Partly, like all first volumes, it is self-consciously about its own apprenticeship: the formal complexity can thus sometimes seem artificial in that it serves a purpose beyond the poem. This volume shows what can be done, proves that all the technical shots are to hand if need be. But with an increase in confidence and maturity, they don't all have to be played all the time.

Longley never loses his fascination with the split personality, with the life lived in two places at once (or one place twice); but it is a fascination which eventually finds more room for itself than the tight forms of *Secret Marriages* allow. *No Continuing City* marks the culmination of several years of growth as a poet but its real achievement is to function both as a formal apotheosis – a technical firework display Longley was not to repeat, at least not as transparently as this – and, rather differently, as laying the foundations for a future aesthetic development.

Those foundations are seen in the 'voyage' poems already discussed, with their tendency to destabilise themselves, as well as in some of the poems which brood, implicitly and explicitly, on the contradictory nature of place, self, and poetry: 'Leaving Inishmore', 'In a Convent Cemetery', and 'The Freemartin', all written in 1966. They do so by recognising the subversion of fixed forms, ideas and traditions, and the embracing of contradiction, of being here and nowhere, as, paradoxically, their own source of strength and security.

'Leaving Inishmore' is really the first poem which suggests the importance the West of Ireland – another 'elsewhere' – will have for Longley, particularly when it is remembered and re-imagined from the perspective of the North. Typically, however, its sense of place is also elusive. Drawing on a trip to the Aran Islands by Longley, his wife and Mahon in the mid-1960s, the poem revisits the moment of departure:

> Rain and sunlight and the boat between them
> Shifted whole hillsides through the afternoon –
> Quiet variations on an urgent theme
> Reminding me now that we left too soon
> The island awash in wave and anthem.

Its fluid and shifting landscape and its implicit placing of the self on the (stable and unstable) 'boat between' rain and sunlight, share something with Derek Mahon's sensibility in *Night-Crossing*. For both poets, and in stark contrast to Heaney's characteristic digging deeper into the one place, identity is permanently transitional, split between here and elsewhere. The poem then plays its own 'Quiet variations on an urgent theme' in the following stanzas ('on the move between shore and shore'; 'Summer and solstice as the seasons turn / Anchor our boat in a perfect standstill') to create a feeling of movement and stasis through a circling of its subject.

It transforms, imaginatively, the past into the present moment to arrive at its 'point of no return' when that moment has already gone. In that sense it is, more properly, a 'caretaker' poem, one that holds its moment, even knowing that can't be done, without becoming trapped or cornered by its own form. (Longley is obviously comfortable, in *No Continuing City*, with the five- or six-line stanza: it dominates the volume.) Its ababa rhyme scheme adds to its variation on a theme effect, as if each stanza is a self-contained invocation of a perfected moment; but in both the first and final stanzas, the slight shift into half rather than full rhyme, and its playing of a complex syntax against stanza at the close of the poem render it more ambiguous and open-ended than the tighter couplet poems of *Secret Marriages*:

> I shall name this the point of no return
>
> Lest that excursion out of light and heat
> Take on a January idiom –
> Our ocean icebound when the year is hurt,
> Wintertime past cure – the curriculum
> Vitae of sailors and the sick at heart.

As with several of Longley's poems, the ending is resistant to paraphrase, and slightly obscure. Yet it is also profoundly evocative, linking as it does the sailor, or voyager, with the 'sick at heart' – and by implication the homesick – and both with the shaping of lives through suffering. The close of the poem, even as it protects its idyllic summer memories as a 'point of no return', recognises the threat posed by winter's heartbreak: the 'light like a downpour', the lyrical fluidity and freedom suggested by the poem, may all too easily become fixed and 'icebound'.

The imagery of snow and sunlight, the thaw and the freeze, fixity and fluidity, is at the heart of Longley's later poetry; it is also imagery that is perceived to take on a particular socio-political resonance in the context of the Troubles, particularly given Mahon's oft-quoted view of the Northern Irish situation a war which 'remains to be won...between the fluidity of a possible life (poetry is a great lubricant) and the rigor mortis of archaic postures, political and cultural'.[45] Nevertheless it is worth noting that the broader concerns which underpin the imagery and interpretation – indicative also of Longley's inheritance from MacNeice – begin here, in the mid-1960s, even if in embryonic form.

If 'Leaving Inishmore' destabilises the poet's sense of belonging in terms of a particular place and time (north or west, anchored or moving, past, present or future), poems such as 'In a Convent Cemetery' and 'The Freemartin' more obliquely unsettle any easy conception of Longley's religious and cultural affiliations. As with all the Northern poets of his generation, Longley's background has been subject to a degree of biographical scrutiny by critics, which the questions of "identity" more broadly raised by the Troubles may perhaps have encouraged. It has also been subject to more misunderstanding than most.

Raised in what he describes as an 'easy-going Anglican agnosticism',[46] at several removes from the Protestantism of the North of Ireland, his Irish upbringing also led, inevitably, to some distance from the wider family circle in England. As he notes in *Tuppenny Stung*, 'there was no hinterland of aunts, uncles and cousins to which...I could escape and still feel at home'.[47] The sense of belonging and not belonging permeates his work. An Irish writer with English parents engenders suspicion from certain quarters, as if his national credentials require more than usual testing. (In MacNeice's case, his English schooling caused a similar critical response.) Longley's distance from Ulster Presbyterianism and from the Ascendancy tradition makes him exceptionally hard for some critics to "place".

His wife's equally complex "inheritance" also becomes a part of Longley's poetic landscape. Michael Longley outlines this inheritance in an interview in 1981:

> ...Professor Broderick [Edna Longley's father]...in a sense had been forced to choose between his loyalty to the Church and his loyalty to this great University [Trinity College Dublin] which happened to be Protestant but which happened to offer him, a Cork Catholic, recognition as a Mathematician. He more or less lapsed so that my wife, although she was baptised as a Catholic, was confirmed in the Anglican Church. Her mother is a Presbyterian [of Scottish descent] so my late father-in-law and mother-in-law met here and came to some compromise that somewhere between Presbyterianism and Catholicism you have Anglicanism....[W]hen he died, all sorts of cousins, second cousins, aunts, uncles, nephews, some of them priests and nuns, all came to the funeral and regretted the fact that he had felt obliged to cut himself off from

the familial hinterland...[I]t meant that my wife had to live in the
rather circumscribed Dublin Protestant...milieu which she found
restricting....This circle would have been much larger if the Catholic
side of her family had been left open to her.[48]

Conscious of both the restrictions and the potential subversion of
monolithic versions of "Irish" identity inherent in his own – and
his wife's – backgrounds, Longley has always promoted the virtues
of what he describes as a 'confluence of cultures, a cat's cradle of
cultural interrelationships'.[49] It is a description which works in terms
of self and in terms of Northern Ireland's position as 'cultural cor-
ridor', validating the peculiar artistic virtues of the region through
the individual.

Such an inheritance might seem a complicated constraint, and, as
is evident in Longley's comments above, it can cause its problems;
but once it has been recognised, it is also, in another sense, liberating.
The Protestant tradition's repressive political ethos in the North prior
to 1969 is as much called into question by the 'cat's cradle' Longley
delights in weaving and unravelling as the Republic's Catholic and
nationalist homogeneity in the late 1950s and early 1960s.

'In a Convent Cemetery' opens up the circle for the poet and
his lover to encounter a part of their history that had seemingly
been lost, 'gone for ages'.[50]

Although they've been gone for ages
On their morning walk just beyond
The icons and the cabbages,
Convening out of sight and sound
To turn slowly their missal pages,

They find us here of all places,
And I abandon to the weather
And these unlikely mistresses
Where they bed down together,
Your maidenhair, your night-dresses

The poem transforms the lovers' metaphorical union into a simul-
taneous embrace of that neglected heritage; the poem's sexual aban-
donment is also a giving over of self into a unfamiliar context and,
by implication, future. Its 'unlikely mistresses' in the second stanza
obliquely link sexual discovery with an understanding of one's past,
since the phrase links the religious sisters with the mythical women
encountered on the poet's own journey towards the 'last girl'.

The eroticism of the poem – never openly stated but relating as
much to the tentative exploration of Catholicism as to the lovers –
is held in check, as it were, by its formal measures; by the sentence
that curls back on itself to reach its objects at the point where they

are discarded, or abandoned. The rhythmic slowing down in the last line of the poem, and its rhyming, suggest closure even as the poem itself, in effect, casts off into the unknown. Like 'Epithalamion' it suggests a need to find new ways of seeing the self and of re-imagining human relations.

'In a Convent Cemetery' is also one obvious forerunner of Longley's later celebrated single-sentence poems, in whose syntax is embedded multiple layers of meaning. (The only other examples in *No Continuing City* are 'The Freemartin' and 'Klondike'.) Its fluidity of style contrasts markedly with the tight, condensed and tonally unsettling sentences of the *Secret Marriages* couplet poems, as in the close of 'Nausicaa': 'All evidence of dry land he relearns. / The ocean gathers where your shoulder turns.' Many of the poems in *No Continuing City* are self-consciously concerned to delineate aesthetic principles; to mark out future territory, or, if need be, to close it off; to try out different techniques. 'In a Convent Cemetery' is not one of them, but in its lack of self-consciousness, it is never-theless revealing.

In the various stylistic and thematic permutations of *No Contin-uing City*, there are some discoveries that serve the poet well there-after. Although Longley is a poet whose voice and style have quite obviously developed though his poetic career, 'In a Convent Ceme-tery' would not look out of place if it turned up 25 years later in *The Ghost Orchid*. Its rhyme scheme perhaps marks it out as belonging to an earlier period; but its syntactical fluidity and experimentation, its tone (with that one touch of the familiar in 'gone for ages'), its botanical merging into sexual fascinations, its imagery (the weather, the night-dress), even its ten line-length, are all now easily recog-nisable hallmarks of a Longley poem.

One of the consequences of Longley's complicated familial and poetic origins, his dual inheritance both in the context of literary traditions in Northern Ireland and in the context of his English parents and Irish upbringing, has been an influential projection of a mixed inheritance as paradigmatic of the poetic self. In that sense, Longley's 'The Freemartin' is, implicitly, a formula for under-standing poetry, another, this time parabolic, angle on the imagi-native processes explored by 'Birthmarks', but with a rather quirky autobiographical underpinning in terms of Longley's own identity:

The Freemartin

Comes into her own
(Her barren increments,
Her false dawn)

As excess baggage,
A currency defaced –
Quaint coinage

To farmhands, farmers
Crossing the yard
With lamps in the small hours

For such incorrigibles,
Difficult births
In byres and stables.

The original note to the poems reads: 'A freemartin is a heifer whose hormones have been overwhelmed in the womb by those of her male twin. She is born sterile and sexually malformed.'

Longley pre-empts here his own later autobiographical pre-occupations with the 'twin brother / Who threatened me at first like an abortionist', and to whom, elsewhere, he reads 'like a mother',[51] thus positing himself as a hybrid figure – male and female, self and other. 'The Freemartin' is the most immediate precursor to Paul Muldoon's 'Mules' which appeared some eight years later, a poem which also explores origins as irreconcilable opposites, and which seeks 'the best of both worlds'. The mulish cross-breed is, for obvious reasons, a seductive paradigm for the poetic self in a context where seemingly irreconcilable opposites have, politically, found little common ground.

But the picture in Longley's 'Freemartin' is not wholly positive. The 'barren increments' and the 'false dawn' are reminiscent of those failed, still-born poems which haunt 'Birthmarks'. It is easy to read 'excess baggage', 'currency defaced' and 'Quaint coinage' as analogous to derogatory perceptions of the value of poetry – something frivolous, devalued, anachronistic, and surplus to requirements. Nevertheless – and this returns us to the notion of "difficulty" in Longley's poetry – there is a sense that the struggle is part of the point: however unwelcome it may be, the freemartin is also, in the end, 'incorrigible[s]', a presence that has to be dealt with even if it disrupts expectations.

The disruptive and 'Difficult birth[s]' of the final stanza is also a far cry from Heaney's early view of 'poems as elements of continuity' (although both retain the sense that the poetic process must be in some way mysterious to the poet). Heaney's metaphors for the origin of a poem are habitually natural as well, but for Heaney the poem emerges, as it were, perfected and finished, like an old port that is now ready for drinking. Of 'Digging' he writes that 'I wrote it down years ago; yet perhaps I should say that I dug it

up, because I have come to realise that it was laid down in me
years before that even.'[52] The deceptive simplicity of Heaney's
early writing is, of course, the real measure of its sophistication,
in its attempt to heal fractures and, as Heaney puts it, to bring
'the subculture to cultural power'.[53] Conversely, yet perhaps with
similar ends in view, the "difficult" in Longley serves as a measure
of his poetry's own lyric integrity, in its willingness to turn (the
illusion of) simplicity on its head, to fracture unacceptable "cer-
tainties", to resist, implicitly, the stability seemingly offered by
certain interpretive models.

Such ambitions are neither entirely conscious nor fully formed
in the 1960s; nevertheless, to recognise the aesthetic principles and
preoccupations developed by Longley through the 1960s is also in
part to understand what enables his survival as a poet in Belfast
through the 1970s. *No Continuing City*'s central themes – the split
self, fractured identity; lives lived at one remove from each other;
the attempt to journey across time and space to reunite those who
have been lost – may be read as indicative, at a subliminal level, of
a society that is itself divided. It is not an overtly political collection,
but the mythic paradigms it proposes are, in their darker aspects,
pre-emptive of a society's collapse – Ithaca in chaos – as they are
also, in their gestures of imaginative compensation, potentially
redemptive models for that society's future.

It is easy to see some of the aesthetic hallmarks of a Longley
poem – the precision in language and care for words; the poem's
sense of its own vulnerability and inadequacy; and yet the belief
in the possibility of imaginative compensation – as the products of
a "troubled" Northern Ireland. To some extent, the Troubles did
render the question 'what is the use or function of poetry' more
acute, as they also brought into critical consciousness a greater
awareness of the potentially hazardous political pitfalls inherent in
language itself. Yet it is worth noting that Longley's aesthetic is not
formulated in response to such pressures; rather, his development
in the early 1960s provides him instead with a vital stay against
such pressures from 1969 onwards.

2

Stereophonic Nightmares:
An Exploded View
1969-1972

> Blood on the kerbstones, and my mind
> Dividing like a pavement
> Cracked by the weeds, by the green grass
> That covers our necropolis,
> The pity, terror...
>
> MICHAEL LONGLEY, 1972

I

On 12 August 1969, Michael Longley gave a lecture at the Yeats Summer School in Sligo in which he spoke of 'Yeats's Effect on Young Contemporary Poets'. He observed that: 'As a reviewer of new verse for the *Irish Times* I am often depressed by the decline of the subordinate clause. A deftly worked adverbial clause of concession or consequence is hard to come by nowadays.'[1] Also on 12 August 1969, the Apprentice Boys' march in Derry triggered the siege of the Bogside, which led, in its turn, to further rioting in Belfast, to the intervention of the British Army, and to the beginning of the end of the Stormont government. Passions – and rhetoric – were running high. In the days following 12 August the death toll from the Troubles was higher than it had been in such a short space of time since the 1920s. August 1969 is thus seen as marking the beginning of a new phase of Irish 'Troubles', which through the 1970s were to claim hundreds of lives, displace thousands of people, and transform Northern Ireland into a place of some international notoriety.

Looking back on August 1969 in his August 2003 opening address to the Yeats Summer School, Longley wryly noted that he'd been well and truly stitched up by the *Irish Times* following his Yeats lecture. On the Saturday following the battle of the Bogside, impassioned political comments were quoted in the paper's 'This week they said...' column. Also included among these comments on the crisis was the following sentence: '"I am often depressed by the decline of the subordinate clause" – Mr Michael Longley,

the poet.'[2] Hindsight can look at this with a knowing amusement
– the Sligo summer school happily fiddling while Rome began to
burn, and Longley on lead violin. It sounded, Longley notes,
'comically inadequate. Had I been found wanting?' But the night-
mare was, as Longley himself has rightly pointed out, a 'night-
mare happening on my home-ground'.[3] For all the commentary on
the situation from elsewhere, it is worth remembering something
Longley himself is usually loth to stress: that, unlike his closest
contemporaries Heaney and Mahon, and unlike some of those
writers and critics particularly vocal in the media on the subject of
'poetry and the Troubles', Longley lived in Northern Ireland
through the 1970s and 1980s. The proximity to the nightmare has
its effect on the way in which his aesthetic develops in these years;
it also gives him a particular insight and sensitivity into the question
of whether or not the poet-in-the-Troubles may be found 'wanting'.

Much critical attention since 1969 has been devoted to answering
that question, or variants thereof, in relation to Northern Irish poetry.
It seems to be a question that is there in Heaney's 'A Northern
Hoard' too ('What do I say if they wheel out their dead?') and
that is obliquely answered by Mahon's apparent self-castigation in
'Afterlives':

> Perhaps if I'd stayed behind
> And lived it bomb by bomb
> I might have grown up at last
> And learnt what is meant by home.

Mahon and Heaney here respectively seem to say that the poet
has responsibilities (this is part of 'growing up'); more than this,
he or she has a particular responsibility to say the right thing, to
find an 'adequate response' – whatever that might be. But this is
to over-simplify the poetry.

Heaney offers no easy answer to the question he poses. Mahon's
position in the lines quoted above is also extraordinarily complex:
a question that is not a question; a response to pressure that could
be seen to make concessions to or point up the absurdity of such
pressures; a speculation that sounds like, but is not, an answer;
and the rhyming of 'bomb' with 'home' to undercut – indeed,
explode – any straightforward attempts to "place" the poet. There
is another ambiguity here too, about what constitutes growing up.
Is to learn 'what is meant by home' to see things the way everyone
else does, and if so, what has been learned at all? It seems, in other
words, to be not so much a case of knowing the answer, but of
knowing what might be worth asking, and of which questions might

themselves be found 'wanting'. Does the poet have particular responsibilities in the face of a social and political crisis? If so, who has the right to determine what those responsibilities might be, or the form they might take? If not, for whom does the poet write, and to what end? If, as Edna Longley has argued in *Poetry in the Wars*, poets in Northern Ireland have sometimes been, as a result of the Troubles, the victims of 'improper expectations',[4] are there "proper" expectations that can reasonably be held?

From the outset, Michael Longley draws a distinction between the poet as political spokesman or political tool, and the poet as poet. Thus, to the question 'Had I been found wanting?', of course the answer is yes – for those wanting a political judgement, a public statement about the crisis; but Longley also knows the answer to be 'no'. And the answer is no on (at least) two counts: first, as a poet, the desire to see language retain and expand its vigour, inventiveness and complexity can be nothing other than a responsible position to hold; second, if the imagination has anything to bring to situations of political stalemate – and, by implication, to the hard-line positions often delineated with rhetorical force, but also with rhetorical simplicity – it is surely a willingness to see beyond such black and white categorisation on a linguistic, but also a social level. So, as Longley pointed out explicitly a year later, at the 1970 Yeats Summer School, 'political and grammatical anxieties intersect at that point where the tensions of Ulster…might be considerably alleviated by a few deftly chosen subordinate adverbial clauses of concession'. If politics matters, language and style inevitably matter too. The 'concentrated, complex lyric' is, he goes on to argue, 'a mode capable of encompassing and solving extreme experience'.[5]

Style, in other words, is at the heart of Northern Irish poetry's response to crisis. Finding an adequate response is one way of putting it; but finding an adequate form might be another. (Or, to borrow Ezra Pound's formulation, 'I believe in technique as the test of a man's sincerity'.)[6] It is Mahon's superb formal accomplishment which sends interpretations haywire in 'Afterlives', a poem whose ending exposes the reader's desire for simple interpretations as it simultaneously shows why such interpretations don't work. At a critical point in Irish history, Yeats argued not for a literature that stirred the boiling pot, nor even for one which reflected it, but for an adequate literary criticism. Perhaps a proper concern is not with what is said, but how. That the poets had – and have – something to say is not in dispute; that they wish to be heard is self-evident. Yet if any form of responsibility exists, perhaps it is not simply to do

either of these things, but to confound expectations, to reinvent
them, expand them, and re-imagine them in ways which point up
the limitations of the contexts – aesthetic and political – from which
they emerge.

The period in which Longley wrote the poems for his second
collection, *An Exploded View* – 1969-1972 – was one in which
Northern Irish poets were placed under unusual pressure to com-
ment openly and self-consciously on aesthetic principles, to for-
malise in critical language positions held and developed more or
less instinctively and intuitively. That pressure manifests itself in
various ways: in reviews, in interviews, and – less directly – in the
debates which took place in anthologies, academic journals, and the
press which while not calling directly on the Northern poets for a
response, frequently engendered a (corrective) one because of the
willingness of the contributors to those debates to make assumptions
and judgements on the poets' behalf.

In August 1970, a year after Longley's first Yeats Summer School
lecture, Eavan Boland published a series of three articles in the
Irish Times entitled 'The Northern writers' crisis of conscience'. In
the concluding article, Boland asks: 'how…will writers in Northern
Ireland articulate the crisis in progress outside and within them,
the retrospect on communities it must force, the needs it imposes
to reorder increasingly chaotic impressions?' How will writers
cope, she continues, with 'such intractable, yet urgent material'?[7]
The underlying assumptions here were – and are – questionable.
Boland implicitly assumes that Northern writers are a distinct group
(a distinct group, moreover, in which everyone suffers a crisis of
conscience); that they have responsibilities towards the Troubles
which are not necessarily shared by their southern counterparts;
that individual anxieties and conflicts manifest the anxieties of the
state; that writers are identifiable with, or speak from, a particular
religious community; and that poetry will, in MacNeice's phrase,
'make sense of the world…put shape on it' 1930s generation style.[8]

Boland's articles are, of course, only one of many early indications
that contemporary poetry in Northern Ireland, rapidly becoming
of interest to the media, was not likely to be read outside the con-
text of the Troubles, thus positing a symbiotic relationship between
poetry and violence. The tensions at work here and in much of
the literary journalism and literary criticism of the 1970s in so far
as it concerns Northern Ireland are complex to say the least, and
those tensions have to be understood as the context in which poets
engaged – in critical prose – with debates about 'Ulster Poetry' or
'Poetry and the Troubles'. It is hardly surprising, for instance, to

find Heaney through the 1970s and 1980s worrying at length in his criticism about the role and responsibility of the poet. There were – and are – plenty of reviewers, interviewers and critics keen to predict, pre-empt, or predetermine Heaney's next move. Some were tapping their fingers impatiently on the table after *Wintering Out*, waiting for him to blow off poetic steam on an epic scale: the 'Irish situation', Stephen Spender wrote (hopefully or provocatively – it isn't clear), 'must be boiling in him'.[9] Engagement or disengagement: culpability, it seems, can work either way.

As Douglas Dunn observed in a letter to Longley, Derek Mahon's depression at the Northern Irish situation was acute in 1972; Mahon seemed also, Dunn suggested, 'terribly hurt' by Simmons's castigation of him for having abandoned the North.[10] Mahon's 'Afterlives' is dedicated to James Simmons; and it goes to prove the point that dedications in Irish poetry can be a prickly subject – and a double-edged sword. This one is both compliment and challenge; a concession to this kind of criticism, and a refutation of it. 'Afterlives' is, after all, a poem far more sophisticated in its form and politics than anything Simmons would ever write about the North, and a poem whose "responsibility" is found in its complexity.

Longley has been drawn into these debates at different times in different, not always compatible roles: as poet; as Literature Officer and, later, Combined Arts Director in the Arts Council of Northern Ireland from September 1970; as a resident of Belfast. To add to the complications, the debates were configured differently in the various contexts in which they emerged– in the North's own artistic community; in a broader network of writers; in the press; in the academy. Critical perspectives have also varied considerably in Britain, the Republic of Ireland and the US. Those various aesthetic and political contexts (or agendas) have interpreted Northern poetry in notably divergent ways; and they are a product of their time as well as place.

Eavan Boland's speculations in 1970 are not only a Dublin view of the North, but also a view of literature and the Troubles almost before the ink from the earliest 'Troubles' headlines had had time to dry. Critical views have become more circumspect in expression over the last two decades, and given the controversies surrounding 'Northern poetry', it is hardly surprising that some critics have more recently, if perhaps also naively, preferred to see the slightly younger generation of Paul Muldoon, Ciaran Carson and Medbh McGuckian as in some way liberated from these critical contexts. (It is, however, worth noting the extent to which many of the same issues still underpin seemingly more advanced theoretical positions.)

Yet the often stark presentation of the issues in the early 1970s has its advantages too, not least because it serves to point up the (stylistic) caution and complexity with which such ideas are questioned, refuted, developed or endorsed by poets in the North.

Given the shifting critical sands which have surrounded him for the last 35 years, Longley's position on the related subjects of Northern Irish Poetry and Poetry and the Troubles – in so far as he has formulated it in critical prose – has been one of remarkable consistency. (One reason is that his criticism takes its bearings from his poetry; it does not predetermine the nature of that poetry.) In the early 1970s, the position is clarified across several key texts. They include his important article 'Strife and the Ulster Poet', from 1969; his introduction to the Arts Council publication *Causeway: the Arts in Ulster* (1971); his contribution by letter to a debate in the *Irish Times* in June 1974 which began with an article by Boland, 'The Weasel's Tooth', and which also triggered responses from Francis Stuart and Liam Murphy; and his forceful objections to Padraic Fiacc's 1974 anthology *The Wearing of the Black*.

'Strife and the Ulster Poet' was written in response to a request by the editors of *Hibernia* to suggest how 'the passions now loose in the North are likely to influence, and be reflected in, the work of Northern writers'. The request itself works on certain assumptions Longley is reluctant fully to accept; nor is he willing to make too many predictions: 'I'm not a prophet'; 'diagnosis of one's own work is dangerous, of one's own colleagues presumptuous'. Yet like Mahon he recognises the emergence close together of the poetry and the troubles as more than coincidental: 'the recent political explosion was preceded by a flowering of the arts. This is a fact. Are the two related? Possibly.'

Like Mahon, he also goes on to suggest, implicitly, a common source, a common energy that challenged the status quo in both positive (artistic) and negative (violent) ways. But the link established here is far more elusive than the one *Hibernia*'s request posits: the work does not simply 'reflect' current passions, nor is it 'influenced' by them in obvious ways; by, for instance, being about the conflict, or having an 'Irish' subject-matter. Rather, the work is part of those passions and is – as it has always been – enmeshed in its context in ways that may not be transparent. Longley's understanding of self and of poetry as outlined in his critical prose is, as in the early 1960s poetry, a way of articulating broader cultural themes:

> ...as Ulstermen, we [Heaney, Mahon and Longley] share a complex and confusing culture: they help me to define myself and a culture which is for me, I think, more confusing than it is for them. They

both have recourse to solid hinterlands – Heaney the much publicised farm in County Derry, Mahon his working-class background and the shipyards. My parents came to Belfast from London in the Twenties. As a child I walked out of an English household on to Irish streets....

I see that I have been schizophrenic on the levels of nationality, class and culture....If my writing is seldom Irish in its subject-matter, whatever virtues it may have were certainly born out of the unease of my Ulster background....The unease has been heightened, to put it mildly, by recent events. My precarious (and, no doubt, luxurious) cultural balance has been upset. Prior to October 1968, my attitude to the Ulster political scene had been ambivalent, well-laced with saving ironies. I see now that as a criticism of an unjust regime...ironies have proved pusillanimous...I accept, as I must, the criticism of the slogan 'Malone Road fiddles while the Falls Road burns', the implication that the still and heartless centre of the hurricane is the civic inactivity of liberals like myself. Nevertheless I have to insist that poetry is an act which in the broadest sense can be judged political, a normal human activity; that my own poetry, if it is any good, will be of value in Ulster more than anywhere else, despite my lack of Irish subject-matter, despite my having been caught out by events. Anything I may write in the future is bound to be influenced by the recent turmoil. Whether the influence will be obvious or even recognisable, I couldn't say. I can't claim now, as I might have done a few years ago, that I myself have any longer a life which is my own entirely. However, as a poet I insist that the imagination has a life of *its* own, a life that has to be saved; if it isn't, everything else will be lost.[11]

This is the rhetoric not of either-or, of black and white categories, but of a complex and uneasy dual perspective, one that has not the luxury of 'balance', if this implies resolution or a consciousness of stability, but which continually sees and tries to see more than one perspective: 'I see now that...; At the same time I...; I accept, as I must...; Nevertheless, I have to insist...; I can't claim now, as I might have done...; However as a poet I insist...'. To interpret the piece in this way is to experience some *déjà vu* in relation to Longley's 1960s poetry; it is also to suggest that Longley's aesthetic "schizophrenia" is a vital stay against the pressures of expectations. This is not a sinister form of 'double-think' but it does argue the possibility of being in two minds: of speaking variously as poet and as citizen without necessarily falling into contradiction; and of seeing, as Yeats did, the need to respond both as poet and as public figure. (Longley became, in effect, an official spokesman for the arts in the North after 1970.) He acknowledges that the artist is responsible to his imagination; and that the artist is responsible to more than his imagination.

The twist in the tail, of course, is that if the imagination thrives on dual perspectives, poetic integrity is, in such a formula, held intact. 'The Hebrides', from *No Continuing City*, is once again instructive here: Hobsbaum's promotion of a formalist empiricism in the Belfast Group provided a sure foundation for Heaney's development; Longley's aesthetic comes from a rather different psychological stable. 'The Hebrides' is about achieving the contradictorily impossible; about balancing an inner and outer life, stability and vertigo, shipwreck and salvage, past and future; it is about a life which both is and is not his own, his brain 'people[d]' by ghosts. Part of what Longley is implicitly suggesting in 1969 is that the Troubles seem to demand the impossible of poetry; but that poetry was always about attempting the impossible anyway.

In that sense, Longley's own poetry was less 'caught out' by the political scene in 1969 than he might himself have felt. The extent to which events in Ireland in the early 1970s unsettled writers is one question; the extent to which those events affected the nature of their writing is quite another. In 1974, Boland followed up her 1970 speculations about 'the Northern writer's crisis of conscience' with her own crisis of conscience, musing on 'the problem of the writer in Ireland now'.[12] Her article, 'The Weasel's Tooth', appeared at a particularly fraught time, following bombings in Dublin on 17 May 1974 (attributed to, although not claimed by, the UVF or UDA, and with rumours of security force collusion) in which 22 people were killed and over 100 injured. Her title, from Yeats's 'Nineteen Hundred and Nineteen', presumes a certain loss of innocence: 'We, who seven years ago / Talked of honour and of truth, / Shriek with pleasure if we show / The weasel's twist, the weasel's tooth'.

The article itself suggests that in another time of crisis, the poet has a duty to look at his or her self 'self-accusingly'. Yeats's cultural self-awareness in 'Nineteen Hundred and Nineteen' might suggest he is a precursor in this; but for Boland, Yeats looks more like the devil tempting Christ in the wilderness. She argues that myths in Ireland are fantasies which have led to 'the hallucination of cultural unity'. That hallucination is projected first into rhetoric, and then into 'the infinitely tragic sphere of action, of flying limbs, lost lives, broken hearts'. Since writers are responsible for sharing and spreading such 'fantasies', they are, she suggests, also partly responsible for where those fantasies have led (to violence). The 'delusion of national cultural coherence' is the 'damaging' fantasy inherited from Yeats; and it has to be 'thrown out intellectually' if the true voice of individuality is to be achieved instead. The individual voice will then be free not to collude in such collective imaginative harm, and will thus be free – one day – from collective guilt.

Boland's piece reworks Yeats's 'Did that play of mine send out /
Certain men the English shot?' from 'The Man and the Echo',
although, ironically enough, she seems to have Yeats in the dock for
not leaving this question as part of his legacy. Boland's arguments
are not entirely consistent at this stage, and she seems unsure of
her own conclusions. But what is apparent is her compulsion to
define her role(s) – as poet in Ireland in a time of crisis; as a woman
poet in Ireland (which position may automatically be seen as critical).
In a sense, there is a certain envy in Boland for the Northern writer
who has, it seems, already come to a parting of ways and taken the
road less travelled by, who has already faced the test and found the
right answer: 'I must salute Northern poets, my contemporaries,
who need no naming, who with discipline, and against pressure to
be superficially coherent, have guarded their own individuality well.'

But perhaps this attributes the right answer to the wrong question.
What is (or was), after all, 'the problem of the writer in Ireland
now'? In the North, it has not tended to be seen as one in which
the writer is faced with cultural unity and coherence. One senses
Boland's concerns are, as might be expected, with a particular kind
of male poetic inheritance, and with a male-dominated cultural
hegemony in the Republic of Ireland. Read in these terms, her
rejection of her own collusion in that State is understandable. In
Michael Longley's contribution to the debate, and from the per-
spective of the North, he interprets questions of individuality and
responsibility rather differently. His letter to the *Irish Times* is an
outline of artistic responsibility which still speaks in pertinent
ways to contemporary writers as well as to Longley's aesthetic:

> The artist's first duty, as Miss Boland and Mr Stuart imply, is to his
> imagination. But he has other obligations surely – and not just as a citizen.
> He would be inhuman if he didn't respond to tragic events in his own
> community, and an irresponsible artist if he didn't seek to endorse that
> response imaginatively. This will probably involve a deflection or zigzag
> in his proper quest for imaginative autonomy – an attempt under pres-
> sure to absorb what in happier circumstances his imagination might
> reject as impurities. But, then, who's interested in pure art anyway?
>
> The mind, as well as the heart, is a 'foul rag-and-bone shop', with
> the imagination an ordering agent which should survive its engagement
> with the "impure", just as the body is strengthened by inoculation. That
> engagement will include attempts to understand political views which
> appear repulsive. If we are going to hate one another, let us do so in an
> informed way. With the score-board reading as it does at the moment,
> the logical outcome of most calls for a certain kind of commitment
> would be IRA art, UVF art, UWC art and so on, ad nauseam...
>
> What exactly is the controversy? I duck for cover now when I am
> asked about 'the artist and the troubles'. The artists I respect are dealing

with the Irish crisis in their own way and in their own time, and, I
imagine, they would like to be left alone to get on with the job. For
my own part, I linger in Belfast because it is home, a place where I
can follow the example of the dog that returns to its vomit, or – a
nobler image, perhaps – the hare that eats its excrement; food for
thought, sustenance for our Irish imaginations.[13]

The opening sentences of this letter were re-used by Longley,
alongside phrases from 'Strife and the Ulster Poet', in his contri-
bution to the *Poetry Book Society Bulletin* in 1979 (when *The Echo
Gate* was the Poetry Book Society Choice); he has returned to them
in interviews, and quoted the arguments again in his autobiographical
pieces. That strategy is Heaney's too, although Heaney as literary
critic has tended rather to reformulate the same ideas in relation
to different writers. It suggests that an "apology for poetry" might
be forced into articulation by the pressures of a particular moment
in time, but that if the principles are worth anything for the poet,
they transcend that time and place, and those pressures. In this
letter, as in 'Strife and the Ulster Poet', Longley outlines dual
responsibilities, infinite detours in the writer's poetic journey.

The letter may also be read, implicitly, as an argument about
form. The formalist aesthetic of Longley and his contemporaries is
not a retreat from chaos and disruption inside the ordered bounds
of the well-made poem. Rather, the whole point of that formal
technique is to bring it into collision – and collusion – with a dis-
ruptive element: order meets impurity; the rewards are mutual.
That encounter of like with unlike, the mingling of different ele-
ments, becomes a paradigm of political responsibility ('attempts to
understand political views which appear repulsive'). The distinction
drawn here is between a form of political commitment in poetry
that too easily becomes a one-dimensional, even propagandist taking
of sides, and a commitment to poetry which, by default, is a polit-
ical activity. (It is this distinction that Edna Longley was also later
– and controversially – to stress when she argued that 'poetry and
politics, like church and state, should be separated'.)[14]

To transform the dog's vomit into sustenance for Irish imagina-
tions is slightly mischievous, a deliberate debunking of the rather
'grandiose terms' – Boland's own phrase – in which the debate about
the Yeatsian inheritance began. (The poet's posture, as Mahon puts
it in 'Rage for Order' is perhaps always 'grandiloquent and depre-
cating, like this'.) But it is also one which draws on that Yeatsian
inheritance to do so: Yeats, more than anyone, understood the
relationship between foul and fair, understood that 'Love has pitched
his mansion in / The place of excrement' ('Crazy Jane talks with

the Bishop'). And, not least, the image is a more poignant reminder that home is home; that to theorise about how or why one lives there – or writes there – is a far cry from actually doing so.

In other words, this is not to say that poetry and the Troubles have nothing to do with each other, or that the poet is without responsibility towards the crisis; but it is to say that the nature of the relationship, the ground that has to be travelled between poetry and politics, text and context, poet and community, is not easily measured, nor is it ground which can be prescriptively mapped by media – or even scholarly – debate. Imaginative engagement with seemingly urgent subject-matter is, for Longley, also a question of a proper perspective; the terms of a relationship – between people, or between the poet and his subject – are always about degrees of distance and dependency.

Longley's negativity towards Fiacc's controversial *Wearing of the Black* anthology, and to Fiacc's accompanying article 'Violence and the Ulster Poet', arises from the extent to which he sees these as instances where the terms of a relationship are exploited. (Longley was not alone in his criticisms: the anthology, published in 1974, has become for many an example of how *not* to anthologise the North.) Describing the anthology as 'Fiacc's Encyclopaedia of Tormented Ulster Poets', Longley objects to the presumption and 'self-regarding nonsense' which sees the Northern poets as suffering 'tragic anguish' in the face of the Troubles; he indicts Fiacc for 'voyeurism and opportunistic parasitism', and concludes that 'He buzzes around the Ulster tragedy like a dazed bluebottle around an open wound'.[15]

In the article 'Violence and the Ulster Poet', Fiacc asks the question 'Can poetry and violence mix at all?'.[16] One senses that the sheer carelessness of such observations is, for Longley, and in a context where precision in language matters so profoundly, unforgivable. Fiacc's urge to collect as many poems about violence in Northern Ireland as possible suggests that the relationship between poetry and the Troubles can all too easily become an abusive one, with publishing mileage to be gained from suffering. In Fiacc's reading, Ulster poetry tracks a movement from 'the fear that gripped the province' after World War II, through the 'sudden panic' and 'smouldering fears' (in Derry) which 'exploded into hatred and killing', and which reaches its climax 'in the terror and horror of Belfast' where 'the poetry is pervaded by the endless bombings, the sectarian bullets, the torture, murders, beatings and maiming'. After which remains only 'bitterness', 'intimidation, frustrations, the mass exodus of so many from the province, and the depression of those left behind'.[17] The anthology also implicitly presents the poets as some kind of artistic rapid response unit, and in this it runs counter to Longley's own views – and experience – as expressed in *Causeway: the Arts in Ulster* some years earlier.

Warning against false, perhaps voyeuristic expectations, Longley writes:

> Too many critics seem to expect a harvest of paintings, poems, plays and novels to drop from the twisted branches of civil discord. They fail to realise that the artist needs time in which to allow the raw material of experience to settle to an imaginative depth where he can transform it and possibly even suggest solutions to current and very urgent problems by reframing them according to the dictates of his particular discipline. He is not some sort of super-journalist commenting with unfaltering spontaneity on events immediately after they have happened. Rather, as Wilfred Owen stated over 50 years ago, it is the artist's duty to warn, to be tuned in before anyone else to the implications of a situation.[18]

Owen suggested that 'All a poet can do today is warn' in his draft preface of 1918; but what he meant by that remains ambiguous. On the one hand, perhaps he may be seen to warn against the evils of war, or against the dangers of propaganda; on the other, the preface may itself be read as a warning about what to expect – or rather not to expect – from the poet: 'these elegies are...in no sense consolatory'.[19]

Longley too is under no illusions as to what poetry might achieve in any quantifiable way: 'Warnings generally go unheeded. Art seldom changes things.' But he is implicitly endorsing Mahon's now well-known formulation from 1970, that 'a good poem is a paradigm of good politics'.[20] To be 'tuned in', to be imaginatively close to a situation, is also about establishing a proper distance from it: to 'transform' requires a particular imaginative vision, but it also takes time. 'If we are going to hate one another, let us do so in an informed way,' Longley writes. To understand that phrase properly is to recognise, as Owen explained in another war, that to get to know one's enemy over time is to find that he is no enemy at all; rather he is an alter ego, a version of oneself. Owen's 'Strange Meeting' thus imaginatively travels, and thereby collapses, the distance between self and other with 'I am the enemy you killed, my friend'.

In May 1975, Robert Graves, First World War veteran and a poet whose work was particularly influential for Longley and Mahon, visited Ireland for the first (and last) time since the 1920s. Longley wrote a short prose piece as a tribute to Graves in honour of his visit which is illuminating as a reading of the older poet, but also reflects Longley's own aesthetic principles as established through the 1960s and early 1970s:

Graves has had the courage to live up to, (and to write up to) his own uncompromising vision. His insights have been uncomfortable and unsettling as often as they have been delicate and beautiful. He has gone his own way, ignoring literary fashions and trends. He survived the No Man's Land of the Great War to occupy more bravely than any other contemporary poet the No Man's Land between one human being and another – this has remained his central concern, the country of his imagination.[21]

Graves, as someone who always led, in Longley's phrase, a 'double life' as poet and (sometimes money-making) prose writer, has an obvious appeal to a poet who is already leading a double life as poet and Arts Council official. But his reading of Graves here maps on to his understanding of the poet's role in more ways than one. For Longley to read Graves's imaginative territory as a no man's land collapses love poet into war poet; the personal becomes paradigmatic of the political. That no man's land could only be traversed (crossed by subtle and circuitous routes, always at an oblique angle) suggests something of the care and sensitivity required to occupy what David Jones once described as 'a space between'.[22]

That space may be the ground between poetry and politics, or poet and community, as much as it is the ground 'between one human being and another' or between different versions of self. The poet's role, as it is implied in Longley's brief readings of Graves and Owen here, and as it relates to himself, seems, but is not, paradoxical: to create and hold onto the space between; to collapse the distance between by crossing divides. Or, to resist 'calls for a certain kind of commitment', and at the same time to be committed to 'attempts to understand'.

II

In July 1972, Longley wrote to Paul Muldoon, then an under-graduate at Queen's working on his first collection, about *An Exploded View*, evidently following up a continuing discussion about book titles and about Muldoon's response to the poems:

Dear Paul,
    Keep plugging at the two aways
    A good name for a pop group is not necessarily a bad name for a book of poems. The point about a title is that it should reveal its relevance after a complete reading of a collection and, in particular, the poem which suggested it. I've just posted off Mark II, christened An Exploded View, a phrase from a poem called Skara Brae. Heaney tells me there is a pop group called the Skara Brae. There you are. An

E.V. will appear parasitic on the troubles until the relevant poem is read – sez he hopefully.

My swan-song isn't competing with Leda, naughty boy: and the business of 'leagues' is complex, mercifully fluid and not really to be broached.

Look after yourself, yours Michael.[23]

The collections published by Longley, Heaney, and Mahon in the early 1970s (Heaney's *Wintering Out* and Mahon's *Lives* were published in 1972, *An Exploded View* in 1973) all show a consciousness of the 'Poetry and the Troubles' context, if not, perhaps, in accordance with 'expectations'. *An Exploded View* in particular, because of its title, might seem to cater to expectations in more obvious ways. As Douglas Dunn noted, '…"exploded" does have Ulster associations which might put an emphasis on the book you might not want'.[24] Longley's own consciousness of this is all too evident in his letter to Muldoon. Since the book marks, to some extent, a change in style for Longley after the formal experiments of *No Continuing City*, it is easy to draw the inference that the onset of the Troubles completely transformed his world view, aesthetic, and style. The tempting conclusion is that the Troubles have radically altered the poet's perception of his home ground, shattered his illusions of stability.

An Exploded View, however, both plays on reader expectations and thwarts them. The phrase, when it appears in 'Skara Brae', is used as an architectural term: an 'exploded view' is to see everything at once, as if opening the front of a doll's house to look inside. Or, in design terms, an 'exploded' drawing of a piece of machinery shows how it works, sketching its components to see how the whole is made up from the inside out.

Longley visited the prehistoric site of Skara Brae on Orkney in 1966; the poem emerged a few years later, in 1971.[25]

A window into the ground,
The bumpy lawn in section,
An exploded view
Through middens, through lives,

The thatch of grass roots,
The gravelly roof compounding
Periwinkles, small bones,
A calendar of meals,

The thread between sepulchre
And home a broken necklace,
Knuckles, dice scattering
At the warren's core,

> Pebbles the tide washes
> That conceded for so long
> Living room, the hard beds,
> The table made of stone.

The 'exploded view' is the ability to see both surface and depth – and with an eye for detail. In that sense, it does not so much signify something in ruins, or a vision shattered, as something seen – and therefore understood – more completely than ever before.

The poem has about it an air of revelation, of the window in the ground opening up, Alice-style, a new world; it discovers what constitutes that world bit by bit, and moment by moment. 'Skara Brae' digs downwards for its archaeological discoveries to see time in reverse: the 'thread between sepulchre and home', the 'broken necklace', works both literally as regards the landscape (there are architectural similarities between the village and grave-yard at Skara Brae, and decorative beads were found when the site was excavated), and metaphorically in that the poem traces such a thread through to the gradual erosion by the tide of living space, finds links in a temporal as well as spatial chain. To see through the passages that connect the houses – 'Through middens' – is also thus to see 'through lives'.

'Skara Brae' hardly seems implicated in a Northern Irish context – or at least, not in any predictable way. (Needless to say, it isn't suitable for something like *The Wearing of the Black*.) But Longley's archaeological poems, and his explorations of the natural world, are by no means remote from that context, as has already been seen in 'The Hebrides'. It may be more than coincidental that he, Mahon and Heaney are drawn to such archaeological and anthropological explorations at around the same time. Heaney's bog poems – inspired in part by P.V.Glob's 1969 *The Bog People*, which both Longley and Heaney read in 1969-70 – are avowedly (and controversially) a response to the early years of the Troubles, a way of understanding place through time, the contemporary through the archetypal. Longley's 'Skara Brae' may well be seen as an influence on Heaney's *North*.

Similarly, Mahon's apocalyptic imagination in the early 1970s leads him to envision a future which understands its own inevitable erosion: in 'An Image from Beckett', 'Our hair and excrement / Litter the rich earth, / Changing, second by second, / To civilisations'. Mahon is also drawn to anthropological and archaeological themes in 'What Will Remain' (retitled and rewritten as 'The Golden Bough') and 'The Archaeologist' (retitled 'A Stone Age Figure Far Below'). The preoccupation is to do with finding new perspectives on who, what and where they are, to see beyond the limitations of one particular time and place, partly as a way of understanding that time and place.

'Skara Brae' may also be interpreted in such terms. On one level, it is a poem about a home under threat, whose disappearance is imminent. It is also, in a way, an elegy for home, for a lost community. There is something of an Old Testament austerity in the 'hard beds' and stone table of the final lines which speaks across the millennia to the Scottish and Irish contexts from which the poem emerges. Its poignancy comes from its detail ('small bones, / A calendar of meals'), in which the poem pre-empts Longley's later elegies for his father, for victims of the Troubles, and of the world wars. The detail gives the poem an intimacy that translates into an immediacy – as if this were only yesterday, and the people only just gone. (One might see a faint echo behind it of Philip Larkin's 'Home is so Sad'.) As an elegy that reverberates in the present as well as the past, the poem is itself suspended as a (single sentence) 'thread between sepulchre / And home'.

Understood architecturally, the 'exploded view' of 'Skara Brae' is connected to the ways in which perception – and the relations between different elements – are worked out through Longley's 1970s poetry, culminating in *The Echo Gate* (1979), a collection in which the finding of different angles of vision is a central concern. But the phrase is also, if more obliquely, pertinent to an understanding of form, and to the way in which *An Exploded View* as a whole is structured. Peter McDonald suggests that 'A Personal Statement' from *No Continuing City* 'sets the terms for what was to be...Longley's point of growth' in the 1970s, taking on board 'more and more of the senses' evidence'. To do so has formal implications: for McDonald, Longley's 1970s work 'sets about removing the kinds of formality the early poems had so brilliantly put on, which might become obstacles in the way of an immediacy or naturalness of voice'.[26]

In 1972, Longley published a pamphlet of twelve poems, *Lares*, most of which were still in the mode of *Secret Marriages* – short, tight forms, couplet poems. Not all of them were included in *An Exploded View*: 'Out of the Sea', 'The North', 'Keaton', 'Ex-Champ' and 'Celeste' were dropped; 'Mountain Swim' was not collected until 1979; and 'Love Poem' underwent considerable revision between *Lares* and *An Exploded View*. Longley explains the problems with form at the time, and in relation to the writer's block he experienced in 1968-69, as follows:

> The last poem I wrote for *No Continuing City* in the summer of 1968,
> 'Journey Out of Essex', explores John Clare's psychological crisis. Despite
> the theme its relaxed movement suggested a way out of the woods. But
> I didn't take the hint and went on to produce more knotty wee poems
> which are placed towards the start of *An Exploded View*. So the thaw
> was glimpsed in the John Clare poem but didn't get underway until
> later with 'Caravan' (at the very end of 1970). I wrote 'Caravan' in a
> happy trance, the words melting down the page, the quatrains and the
> rhymes easy-going. 1971 was a good year....Problems had been solved
> at a subconscious level.[27]

Those 'knotty wee poems' – 'To the Poets', 'A Nativity' 'Lares',
and 'Miscarriage' – do run counter to the movement of *An Exploded
View* as a whole. (Unsurprisingly, Longley's 1998 *Selected Poems*
does not include any of these poems: instead, it presents a pro-
gression that for Longley now makes sense: moving seamlessly
from 'Journey Out of Essex' to 'Caravan'.) The loosening of rhythms
and the move away from the complex rhyme schemes of the first
volume "explode" Longley's forms in the early 1970s – as seen in
such poems as 'Skara Brae', 'Caravan', 'Casualty' or 'Alibis'. Where
the complex formal structures give a tension to some of the 1960s
poems pushed as far as it can go, that tension finds its more relaxed
counterpart after 1969.

In what is probably the definitive analysis of Longley's rhythmic
development in this period, Michael Allen suggests that the poet's
'rhythmic consciousness has always been responsive to the prob-
lematic nature of ever-changing experience'. That rhythmic con-
sciousness is also, as Allen shows, bound up with 'the characteris-
tic duality of Longley's poetic voice'. He points out that Longley
may be seen as structuring his work from 1970-71 onwards 'by way
of paired poems...which mime a kind of hesitant progress, two steps
forward and one step back (or *vice versa*)'. (Some of the 'twinned'
poems he identifies in *An Exploded View* are: 'Altera Cithera' and
'Three Posthumous Pieces'; 'Options' and 'Alibis'; 'The Fairground'
and 'Nightmare'; 'Caravan' and 'The Ropemakers'; 'Swans Mating'
and 'Galapagos'; 'Weather' and 'Flora'; 'Stilts' and 'Master of Cere-
monies'.) As with the earlier 'No Continuing City' and 'Circe', the
poem-pairs afford poet and reader a kind of double-take, a view from
different perspectives. Michael Allen also sees the pairs as working
in systolic and diastolic ways, expanding and contracting rhythmi-
cally as a way of 'dramatis[ing] the creative process itself', with its
pull in potentially contradictory directions, its 'regressive and asser-
tive components'.[28] *An Exploded View* is designed with such comple-
mentary poems often on facing pages; the book as a whole projects
its different dimensions as part of an architecturally envisaged whole.

Early in 1972, and before the collection as it finally appeared was complete, Longley contemplated structuring the book in three parts: Lares; Letters; Zones.[29] The idea was abandoned, since such structures don't really need to be visible, but it is noteworthy for two reasons: first, it gives some insight into the care with which an individual collection is put together; second, it explicitly places the 'Letters' sequence at the heart of the whole enterprise. An 'exploded view' is to see the individual poem *and* the collection itself as possessing their own integrity; poems may be read against each other in ways which are mutually reinforcing, and with a connective tissue linking them under the surface. In that sense, 'Skara Brae' earns its place as the (oblique) title-poem for his second collection in part because the architecture of the site may be read as paradigmatic of the way in which the book itself has been designed.

III

The newspaper reviews of *An Exploded View* suggest a desire to identify it, as far as possible, as a "Belfast" book. Most frequently quoted is 'Letter to Derek Mahon' – 'Our ears receiving then and there / The stereophonic nightmare / Of the Shankill and the Falls'; most often singled out for high praise is Longley's first poem directly concerned with sectarian killing, which is also a Belfast poem, 'Wounds'.

Whilst commending his style, reviewers also commended his engagement with the crisis. For Martin Dillon, the points in the book where 'the hatred, fears and violence in the community force a reaction from the poet' disturb 'the calm created by poems such as "Caravan" and "Swans Mating"'; they show 'that the poet has the courage to face the reality of his surroundings'.[30] Peter Porter, quoting the same poems as Dillon, notes that they are 'marked by the province's present despair and illuminated by a long vista of Irish uneasiness'.[31] The reviews are perceptive, partly because they pick up on, and promote, what was at the time likely to be the book's most obvious appeal to a wider readership for whom Northern Ireland's Troubles were an international media phenomenon (and *An Exploded View* sold out in just over a year, far more rapidly than Longley's other collections). But with the benefit of hindsight, Longley's own comments from 1969 quoted earlier are instructive: 'Anything I may write in the future is bound to be influenced by the recent turmoil. Whether the influence will be obvious or even recognisable, I couldn't say.'

Although some of the early reviews may have given a different impression, Longley has not written extensively about Belfast – or at least not directly. Over half of his poems are inspired by his "elsewheres". But what constitutes a 'Belfast' poem is not limited to the kinds of urban consciousness found in Mahon's, or, later, Ciaran Carson's *oeuvres*. (Heaney's *Wintering Out* shows one different Belfast mode, for instance.) In 1970, Longley first visited the cottage at Carrigskeewaun in Co. Mayo which was to become a second home to him over the next 35 years. Mayo offers a vital perspective on, and, one might think, relief from, Belfast. But this is not a pastoral escape from the urban 'nightmare' in which he finds himself. Longley's concern is by no means with nature only in its idealised or benign aspects, and relief here should probably be understood in the sense of heightening perceptions of Belfast, and *vice versa*, rather than escaping from it. In other words, Longley's 'elsewhere' throws Belfast into relief. It provides him with another point of the compass; it enables a form of double-take on his home ground. As with MacNeice before him, and as in 'Skara Brae', his western landscapes are also reflections on – and of – home.

Dillon's sense of opposites in *An Exploded View* – the tranquil natural world *versus* the violent and disturbed urban landscape – is thus too uncomplicated a binary to hold up for long in a more sustained analysis. The poems in *An Exploded View* inspired either directly by Longley's visits to Mayo, or more generally by the natural world – including 'The West', 'Carrigskeewaun', 'Swans Mating', 'Badger' and 'Casualty' – mark the beginning of a pastoral, or perhaps more accurately anti-pastoral strand in Longley's work that draws its influence from John Clare, Edward Thomas (and others of the English First World War poets), as well as from Kavanagh, MacNeice and Yeats. They bring to versions of Irish pastoral a new precision of observation, a naturalist's eye – the West of Ireland as place not Revival myth – and to versions of English pastoral something of the uncontrolled sensibility that also appealed to Robert Graves in 'Lost Acres' – a landscape often beautiful, but unpredictable and sometimes harsh. Longley, in other words, is unafraid to look at nature 'red in tooth and claw', in a version of pastoral that works not so much through traditional pastoral techniques – where an idealised alternative vision offers, implicitly, an indictment of a corrupt civilisation – as by showing us a disturbing "other", one which reflects back a "civilised" society to itself in sometimes uncomfortable ways. The wilderness is something internalised as well as external. The 'exploded view' of 'Skara Brae' has, for instance, a different resonance in 'Casualty' (1971), which explores, in clinical fashion, the gradual decomposition of a ram's carcass:

> Its decline was gradual,
> A sequence of explorations
> By other animals, each
> Looking for the easiest way in –
>
> A surgical removal of the eyes,
> A probing of the orifices,
> Bitings down through the skin,
> Through tracts where the grasses melt,
>
> And the bad air released
> In a ceremonious wounding
> So slow that more and more
> I wanted to get closer to it.
>
> A candid grin, the bones
> Accumulating to a diagram
> Except for the polished horns,
> The immaculate hooves.
>
> And this no final reduction
> For the ribs began to scatter,
> The wool to move outward
> As though hunger still worked there,
>
> As though something that had followed
> Fox and crow was desperate for
> A last morsel and was
> Other than the wind or rain.

The language of 'Casualty' suggests it is concerned with both natural phenomena and human society, with 'decline' in its symbolic as well as literal manifestations. (In this, it might be read as a precursor to Mahon's 'Matthew V. 29-30'.) '[E]xplorations' implies analytical curiosity as much as instinctive feeding; the scientific 'surgical' and 'probing' take us into hospital wards and operating theatres rather than open fields; 'polished' is also suggestive of human agency rather than a natural wearing smooth. The 'candid grin' of the fleshless animal is also to reappear in the 'deadly smile' of Longley's father in another poem about slaughter, 'The Linen Workers'. That the speaker is drawn almost against his will to the carcass, slowly and instinctively, that he wants to 'get closer to it', says something about a human capacity to be fascinated by gruesome events that "civilisation" might prefer not to acknowledge, as it also suggests an animal instinct at work.

The clinical incisiveness of the poem is sinister in other ways too: the forensic feel to the tone and language inevitably – given the slippage between human and animal – brings more disturbing possibilities to mind. 'Casualty' offers, literally, an exploded view – in the diagrammatic sense – of the animal, its gradual decay revealing what is not usually seen: the inside structures. The poem's form too is clinical, accumulating to its own 'diagram' of its subject. Decline runs away with itself in the sentence that encompasses the first three stanzas, coming to a halt only when we're literally up against 'it'. The fourth stanza – a close-up view of the bits that are left – is itself a grammatically incomplete, one might say skeletal sentence, in which one feels the pauses and ellipses of immediate description. But its full stop is deceptive, since there is further to fall. As the something nameless, and indefinable emerges in the final two stanzas, the enjambment begins, almost, to take on an invisible, seemingly unstoppable, 'desperate' impetus of its own, echoing the poet's earlier instinctive compulsion to 'get closer to it'. The 'something...other' of the poem's close suggests not metaphysical consolation, but, more bleakly, a fear of the unknown and an always unfulfilled need. (In this it shares, and owes a debt to, a sensibility found frequently in Mahon's early poems – the 'nameless hunger' of 'Canadian Pacific'; the 'immeasurable erosions' and 'vain / Overtures to the mindless wind and rain' of 'Day Trip to Donegal'.)

Longley's nature poems are not anthropomorphic projections; in one sense, rather than attributing to his animals the characteristics of humans, the poems work the other way around. But, as with many poets before him, the natural world offers a way of understanding the creative process. For Longley, that process is, as seen in 'The Freemartin', sometimes strained and difficult, and by no means as seamless as Heaney's nature/creativity paradigm. In 'Badger', the self-reflexivity implicit in the forms of both 'Skara Brae' and 'Casualty' is more evidently at work in Longley's subject. The badger:

> ...excavates down mine shafts
> And back into the depths of the hill.
>
> His path straight and narrow
> And not like the fox's zig-zags,
> The arc of the hare who leaves
> A silhouette on the sky line.

Douglas Dunn's description of Longley's poems as 'always at an imagined angle to reality';[32] the obliquity and the varied perspectives of his aesthetic; his syntactical detours; the doublings of the poems; the moral overtones of 'straight and narrow': all these suggest different artistic options, reflections on stylistic possibilities in himself and his contemporaries. If in this instance the badger's 'path straight and narrow' is preferred, the baiting of the third part of the poem also suggests the difficulty of that path:

> For the digger, the earth-dog
> It is a difficult delivery
> Once the tongs take hold,
>
> Vulnerable his pig's snout
> That lifted cow-pats for beetles,
> Hedgehogs for the soft meat,
>
> His limbs dragging after them
> So many stones turned over,
> The trees they tilted.

It is hard not to associate these lines, as Michael Allen has done, with the 'difficult births' of 'The Freemartin', or the 'idiot children' that never see the light in 'Birthmarks'.[33] All three instances may be read as reflections on the writing of poems, which seem here to be dragged out from under cover in a mixture of ruthlessness and compassion – a combination superbly and disturbingly implicit in the badger's 'Vulnerable...snout' that once sought out for food, but is now paralleled with, the 'soft meat' of the hedgehog's underside. This makes it at once both a scene of destruction – the badger, the 'earth-dog', "delivered" to its death by mankind – but also one of creation. Behind the 'tongs' hover forceps, and this is a birth as well as a death – one, moreover, which turns over the stones and tilts the trees. If this is an upheaval, it is also an uncovering of what is not seen on the surface, a differently angled view.[34]

Longley's nature poems, as suggested earlier, owe a debt to Edward Thomas (in the case of 'Badger', most noticeably to Thomas's 'The Combe') as well as to John Clare, with whom Longley shares – as becomes increasingly evident through his poems – a particular ecological conscience. *An Exploded View* is also, however, about Longley's relation to, and placing of himself in, an Irish tradition that runs back through MacNeice and Kavanagh to Yeats. In 'Swans Mating' and 'The West', debts – and differences – are acknowledged directly. Despite Longley's disclaimer in his letter to Muldoon quoted earlier – 'My swan-song isn't competing with Leda' – Yeats's 'Leda and the Swan' is, of course, for most readers a poem brought to mind by Longley's 'Swans Mating', the more so given the Yeatsian echoes elsewhere in the book, notably in the 'Letters' sequence. (It is also his own version of a Kavanagh-esque Canal Bank in Dublin epiphany.)

The two poems point up obvious differences between the poets – as well as shared preoccupations. In 'Swans Mating', and its companion piece, 'Galapagos', Longley defines both the kind of nature poet he is, and the kind of love poet. 'Swans Mating' is a remembered event which recreates imaginatively the climax over again:

> This was a marriage and a baptism,
> A holding of breath, nearly a drowning,
> Wings spread wide for balance where he trod,
> Her feathers full of water and her neck
> Under the water like a bar of light.

The phenomenon here is at several removes from Yeats's mythological rape in 'Leda and the Swan', even if in this second stanza it picks up some of the terror and excitement of Yeats's deliberately overblown rhetoric. Yeats's historical vision in 'Leda' – 'A shudder in the loins engenders there / The broken wall, the burning roof and tower / And Agamemnon dead' – likewise seems remote from Longley's intimate, experiential moment in time recaptured.

Yet 'Swans Mating' is also a love poem. 'Even now', it begins, 'I wish that you had been there / Sitting beside me'. That context renders the 'This' of its second stanza quoted above subtly ambiguous: why 'This' not 'It', for instance? Partly because 'This' seems to implicate the speaker in the act itself. The presence of the 'you' to whom the poem is addressed, and the frequent conceit in Longley's early writings of the lover as voyager, suggests that it too is 'sailing in rhythm' towards its own 'Wings spread wide for balance'. And it is as a love poem that it owes something to Yeats. At the close of *The Poetry of W.B. Yeats*, MacNeice quotes 'Leda and the Swan' as an instance of 'leaping vitality – the vitality of Cleopatra waiting for the asp'. The image conjoins sex and death, beginnings and endings – in Yeats's gyres 'the deaths and births of history'[35] – in a way Longley's often sacramental imagination can also encompass: 'a marriage and a baptism...nearly a drowning'. 'Swans Mating' also links, once again, balance with risk, creation with imminent loss.

In the light of Michael Allen's identification of poem-pairs in Longley, 'Swans Mating' may also be read as the assertive, rhythmically expansive love poem; 'Galapagos' as the other side, as an exploration of the hesitancy and elusiveness of an object of desire 'scattered into islands'. The 'Heraldic moment' of unity in 'Swans Mating' and its rhythmic momentum contrast with the rather bumpier rhythmical ride and syntactical 'throw-backs' and 'hold-ups' of 'Galapagos'. The "source" for 'Galapagos' is Darwin's journal – *Voyage of a Naturalist* – describing his travels around the world as a scientist on HMS *Beagle* from 1832 to 1836, and in particular the visit in 1835 to the Galapagos archipelago, which consists of ten small (volcanic) islands. 'Galapagos' too is a love poem, not quite willing to profess itself as such, where the encounter may be interpreted as a hesitant courtship.

In Longley's first collection, islands of mythological women punctuated the voyage; here, the female body becomes a series of different islands to be explored and understood on their own terms. The voyage of the naturalist is a love quest and an interior journey, one which evokes many of Longley's familiar psychological and mythological preoccupations. 'Galapagos' merges the conceit of woman as land with the 'exploded view' of different elements, a gradual understanding of the parts that make the whole, which reverberates through the collection. It is also a poem – like 'The Ropemakers', or like 'Readings' with 'Kay and Gerda in their separate attics' – preoccupied with the no man's land between one human being and another, taking steps forwards, backwards and sideways.

> Now you have scattered into islands –
> Breasts, belly, knees, the Mount of Venus,
> Each a Galapagos of the mind
> Where you, the perfect stranger, prompter
> Of throw-backs, of hold-ups in time,
>
> Embody peculiar animals –
> The giant tortoise hesitating,
> The shy lemur, the iguana's
> Slow gaze in which the *Beagle* anchors
> With its homesick scientist on board.

'Galapagos' is by no means a straightforward poem, rhythmically or structurally. Compared with the simultaneous flow and poise of 'Swans Mating', it is convoluted and unsettled, suggestive of a more uncertain, or perhaps more laboured (sexual) exploration than that seen through the seamless 'cob and his pen sailing in rhythm' to meet each other. The self-consciousness about presence – increasingly apparent in Longley's later poems with his habitually delayed entry of the 'I' voice into the scene – is implicit here too, in the embodiment of the 'you' of the poem in the 'shy lemur'. The stance taken is eco-centric rather than egocentric.

This speaker is, as a result, treading carefully, in a poem which could be seen to carry serious implications, but which inclines, tonally, towards the wryly comedic. The Darwinian paradigm implicitly suggests that the voyage of the naturalist is potentially an intrusive enterprise – in ecological, sexual or, in Darwin's case, colonial terms; Darwin's own journal, on the other hand, is often more frivolous, light-hearted and affectionate towards its subjects than one might expect. (If the speaker of the poem is not necessarily the Darwinian figure, that distinction blurs in the poem's final line; and Darwin could be seen, in some ways, as an alter ego working through the poem.)[36] The poems read as a pair in this way serve to show two sides of the same coin, contradictory impulses at work. They both, in another sense, close with a difficult, and precarious balance: in 'Swans Mating' this is present in the mating itself, where the moment cannot hold beyond the poem; in 'Galapagos' in the ambiguous and transient 'anchor' cast in 'the iguana's / Slow gaze'.

That the poet can be in two minds, as suggested earlier, is increasingly implicated in the problematic of his home ground. The divided mind, the dual rhythmic impulses Allen identifies in the early 1970s poems, also reverberate in terms of place. There are twin poems; there are twin homes. To be in two places at different times – Mayo and Belfast – is also, as Longley formulates it in 'Alibis', to be 'in two places at the one time'. In that sense, a key to understanding the relation of North and West in Longley's work can be found in the short poem 'The West', written in late August 1972.

The timing of the poem is significant. In January 1972, the events of Bloody Sunday caused the Northern Irish situation to destabilise to the extent that 1972 was – and remains – the bloodiest year of the Troubles to date, with 467 deaths and over 10,000 shootings. On 21 July 1972 – dubbed 'Bloody Friday' – after a series of bombings in Belfast, some of the victims were so badly dismembered, their remains had to be swept up and collected in plastic bags.[37] The horrors of that year had obvious implications for the cultural life of Northern Ireland. Longley's correspondence for 1972 to 1973 makes evident the increasing difficulty in persuading poets and critics to visit a place habitually depicted as a war zone;[38] Heaney's own departure to Dublin in 1972 was, understandably, deeply felt by Longley and by others in the North; and the pressures of living in Belfast at that time – even in its more protected middle-class areas – affected the quality of everyday life to a degree it is now difficult to imagine.

'The West' is a poem which reflects on the North. The choice of title carries behind it awareness of a tradition in Irish writing that reaches back to the Revival, when 'the West' signified a realm uncontaminated by outside (primarily British) influences. The emotional investment in a concept of 'the West' from the urban

perspective of Dublin partly accounted for the violent reaction to
Synge's *The Playboy of the Western World*, where, as Nicholas Grene
has pointed out, the cry heard from the audience was 'That's not
the West of Ireland'.[39]

That 'the West' still retains a romantic revivalist aura may also
be inferred from the *Irish Times* readership's vote for Yeats's 'The
Lake Isle of Innisfree' as the best Irish poem of the last millennium.
But Longley's West owes more to the western settings of Yeats's
'Nineteen Hundred and Nineteen' and 'Meditations in Time of
Civil War', as well as to the different perspectives brought to bear on
Irish poetry by Kavanagh and MacNeice in the mid-20th century.
Kavanagh's 'black hills' in 'Shancoduff' 'Eternally...look north
towards Armagh'. MacNeice's 'Neutrality' takes issue with both
Revivalist idealism and Irish neutrality in World War II. Violence
and political turmoil, the wireless's 'talk of war', also permeate the
seemingly protected space of the west of Ireland in MacNeice's
'The Closing Album'.

Like MacNeice's 'The Closing Album', Longley's 'The West' is
subtly evocative of crisis elsewhere, through its tone, and through
what is left unsaid:

> Beneath a gas-mantle that the moths bombard,
> Light that powders at a touch, dusty wings,
> I listen for news through the atmospherics,
> A crackle of sea-wrack, spinning driftwood,
> Waves like distant traffic, news from home,
>
> Or watch myself, as through a sandy lens,
> Materialising out of the heat-shimmers
> And finding my way for ever along
> The path to this cottage, its windows,
> Walls, sun and moon dials, home from home.

In this poem, the poet is metaphorically in two places, watching and
listening. If he is forever returning home along the path to the
cottage, he also constantly hears an urban echo in the background.
In 'Letter to Derek Mahon', he describes the 'persistent...under-
tow' of the west from the north; here it works the other way around.
The instinctively suicidal moths of the opening lines bring in a
wartime vocabulary – gas, bombardment – followed through in
stanza two with the evocation of desert warfare in the sandy lens,
the heat-shimmers. The sound of the sea mutates into the 'crackle'
of a radio, as if Belfast were the shell held up to the ear and the
sounds of 'news from home' eternally carried with the poet; and
where Yeats on his London roadside heard the call of Innisfree,
here it is, implicitly, the call of the North, the other urban home

heard like 'distant traffic' in the crashing of the Atlantic waves. In 1973, Longley wrote in a letter describing the isolation of the cottage in Co. Mayo that there was 'No radio, no tv, and papers only at the weekend – though I must confess we devour these for news of the North'.[40] Yet as this poem suggests, geographical isolation never means imaginative disengagement. The 'spinning driftwood' subtly implies that wreckage, the fragments of 'news from home', are constantly brought ashore to haunt memory. Longley works here with 'atmospherics', not with direct comment, to complicate his sense of place. '[N]ews from home' and 'home from home' are poised in a particular relationship – origins and destinations, beginnings and endings, here and elsewhere – with each serving as a refracting prism for the other, both contrast and conscience. In the end, the poem's only full rhyme is 'home' with 'home'.

IV

Sometime late in 1975 or early in 1976, Longley drafted a very long letter to Marie Heaney which he never sent.[41] In it, he explains what seemed to him to be the main impetus behind *An Exploded View*:

> My friendships, first with Mahon, then with Heaney, have been of central importance to me and contributed greatly to my own develop-ment as a man and poet: that's what my second book was all about. It explored the notion of an artistic community, a poetic sodality, though, as I admitted in an Irish Times interview, this was probably a fiction because, frankly, there didn't seem to me to be any takers! I realise of course that there are cultural reasons why I should need such a fiction and why my colleagues might find it an embarrassment. Given all that, their poetry matters to me and to <u>my</u> poetry since my talent is not homo-genous like theirs: I have to borrow roots! What I'm talking about, I think, is friendship lifted into the imagination...

The 'poetic sodality' that Longley invokes here is seen in embryonic form in the 1969 'Strife and the Ulster Poet': 'they [Mahon and Heaney] help me to define myself and a culture which is for me, I think, more confusing than it is for them. They both have recourse to solid hinterlands...'. *An Exploded View* is his concerted attempt to transform a 'poetic sodality' into his own hinterland. The 'Letters' sequence, and the dedicatory poem of the collection, 'For Derek, Seamus and Jimmy', are rare occasions where Longley speaks with a collective voice, where 'I' mutates into 'we', as part of what the poet means by his 'exploded view'.

In formal terms, the sequence also has a more avowedly public resonance. As Douglas Dunn observes:

> While "epistolary", and, therefore, to an extent, personal, the formal ploy of 'Letters' [octosyllabic couplets, in six or eight-line stanzas] associates it with public poetry – the same rhythm as Robert Lowell's 'Waking Early Sunday Morning', but also a Yeatsian measure ('Under Ben Bulben', for example, 'An Irish Airman Foresees His Death', or 'In Memory of Eva Gore-Booth and Con Markiewicz'), with many examples by Auden ('New Year Letter', part of 'In Memory of W.B. Yeats), MacNeice ('Letter from India') and a solid 17th-century pedigree in Ben Jonson, Marvell, and Milton. Public statements have often been disguised as private epistolary poems – Burns's and Pope's are two obvious instances.[42]

Longley's poems are concerned with the distance between private and public. Working out how to traverse that distance is central to *An Exploded View*, and to the 'Letters' sequence in particular. The risk, as Longley is aware, is that the 'public utterance' can also be an intrusion on the private – one which may also be presumptuous if it takes 'the agony of others as raw material for…art, and…art as a solace for them in their suffering'.[43] The 'public utterance' is thus mediated through privacies, rather than existing as an abstract meditation on such privacies.

The intimacy characteristic of that approach, in which the urgency of emotion may be deeply private, but also deeply political in the broadest sense of the word, is now easily recognisable as one of the most distinctive aspects of Longley's aesthetic development. The 'Letters', in the context of that development, may be read as transitional – not in themselves a final answer, but a necessary identification of the problem, and a "detour" that had to be tried. As Michael Allen notes, they proffer a 'vision of a united literary community to set against social discord and violence'; but that sense of an alliance later diminishes, he suggests, in part because it was a 'vision' and never really existed in the first place.[44]

The 'Letters' thus exist on a complex trajectory between private and public: on the one hand they posit a secure hinterland from which to speak, a sense of "belonging" in, and identification with, a literary community. But that illusory security doesn't really survive beyond this sequence; indeed, there are qualifications raised even within the sequence itself. It gives way, ultimately, to a renewed confidence in the imaginative hinterland that had been there from the beginning. In the 1960s and early 1970s Longley identifies that original hinterland as part of the problem because it was indeterminate and 'confusing'; by the mid to late 1970s the problem has become the solution: the 'certain indeterminacy', which keeps him 'impressionable'.[45]

The dedicatory poem to *An Exploded View*, 'For Derek, Seamus and Jimmy', one of the very last poems to be written for the volume, is itself a testing of the collection's ambitions and achievements, a working out of the terms in which a 'sodality of the imagination'[46] might be understood. Its ambiguities also open up that sodality to questions:

> We are trying to make ourselves heard
> Like the lover who mouths obscenities
> In his passion, like the condemned man
> Who makes a last-minute confession,
> Like the child who cries out in the dark.

The single sheet draft of the poem – incidentally a classic instance of Longley's reversals in the process of composition, since the poem's first and final lines initially appear the other way around – shows the poem emerging in first person singular, with the shift to first person plural introduced in the uneasy formulation, soon deleted, 'We are trying to make ourselves heard / And, I insist, to mean what we say'. That over-emphatic cancelled line says something about the pressures brought to bear on poetry at the time of writing – the sense that commitment of some kind is called for, even if this is commitment only to truth, integrity, or plain-speaking. It pleads for relevance; it also suggests consensus between the poets on a matter of principle. The final version above retains that slightly embattled tone, but its claims, properly examined, are strangely elusive.

Read alongside 'Letter to Derek Mahon', with its 'stereophonic nightmare', the opening line seems to place Longley's agenda firmly in a Troubles context – the poetry rendered all the more urgent by the probability that in the midst of crisis its message could fall on deaf ears. But Longley is resistant to the notion of poet as political interventionist, public speaker or preacher, even if such resistance does not preclude a belief in the transformative possibilities of art. So from his opening 'We', he shifts through the three similes that constitute the poem into increasingly isolated, solitary and private positions. Where the opening line suggests conscious endeavour, all his comparisons are with involuntary articulation at a critical or climactic point. His cancelled line ('to mean what we say') is, in a slightly different sense, thus implicit in his choice of moments where anything other than truth seems inconceivable. Yet those moments also suggest various possibilities

for what is meant by the need to 'make ourselves heard': the inti-
macy, and privacy, of the lover's obscenities, heard by no one else;
the confession that cannot change the outcome; and finally, the
child's cry which is beyond or before words (the monosyllabic
simplicity of the closing line speaks volumes) and which seeks –
rather than offers – consolation.

His sodality of the imagination, then, is not so much indicative
of a shared agenda here as it seems to reinforce the integrity of
the individual voice – heard or unheard, but at least sounded. But
that position is, given the public resonance and first person plural
of the 'Letters' sequence, an ambiguous one to hold. And it may
be one reason why opinion about the 'Letters' sequence has been
divided – not least among the poet-recipients themselves: Longley
has noted the poets' unease with their role as 'muses'; Simmons
disliked the whole enterprise (although this was not an unusual
response to much of the work by his contemporaries); Mahon, alert
to some of the complexities involved in what Longley was trying
to do, worried about whether the letter could be seen to speak *to*
him or *for* him.

The Letters sequence was written between March 1971 and April
1972.[47] As the manuscript drafts of the poems make clear, the sense
of them as linked together was present from an early stage, and
material shifted around between poems in the process of composi-
tion. 'Letters' has Yeatsian echoes, in the way it links the poems
into an "epic" sequence, in its vision of a literary community, and,
unusually for Longley, in language and tone. More particularly, it
is the Yeats of the 1920s and 1930s who appears to be providing
precedent and example here, in the Civil War poems, in 'A Prayer
for my Daughter', and in 'The Municipal Gallery Revisited' ('my
glory was I had such friends'). Yeats's sense, in some of his 1920s
poems, of the spirit of imagination under threat, and his post-1916
anxieties about the fate of the Revival find their echo in Longley's
desire to try and safeguard, against the odds, the idea of a shared
imaginative enterprise. There are 1930s models for the 'Letters'
too, most noticeably Auden and MacNeice's *Letters from Iceland*.

In the first poem of the sequence, 'To Three Irish Poets', the
birth of Longley's son brings into focus anxieties about the North,
and urges the creation of the literary community as an alternative
family: his son becomes the 'godchild' of the poets, and 'About his
ears our province reels / Pulsating like his fontanel'. Responsibility
for the child thus becomes, by implication, responsibility for the
North; making 'room' for Daniel takes on symbolic resonance in
terms of what the artistic community might achieve, and his birth

is the conceit through which both crisis and consolation are understood:

> For this, his birthday, must confound
> Baedekers of the nightmare ground –
> And room for him beneath the hedge
> With succour, school and heritage
>
> Is made tonight when I append
> Each of your names and name a friend:
> For yours, then, and the child's sake
> I who have heard the waters break
> Claim this my country, though today
> *Timor mortis conturbat me.*

Longley's epigraph to 'To Three Irish Poets' is taken from Keith Douglas's Second World War poem, 'Vergissmeinnicht': 'returning over the nightmare ground / we found the place again'. His own ground, too, has become a nightmare ground, a 'necropolis', reminiscent of Yeats's terrain in 'Nineteen Hundred and Nineteen'. Through the choice of epigraph, Longley suggests as part of his literary heritage the tradition of 20th-century war poetry, a heritage that becomes increasingly important to him through the 1970s. But the nightmare ground in this poem also has its continuities with Longley's 1960s preoccupations. For Longley, as also for Douglas, the ground is both landscape and mindscape, external and internal, private and public (as 'the waters break' is evocative of the child's birth and the country's collapse). Longley's fascination with schizophrenia in the mid-1960s, with the divided self, here becomes symbolic of a divided society, of an unstoppable force pushing its way to the surface of consciousness: 'Blood on the kerbstones, and my mind / Dividing like a pavement, / Cracked by the weeds…'.

The 'Letters' propose, implicitly, a way of reintegrating self and other, of healing fractures, through their creation of a 'poetic sodality'. To inhabit imaginatively each other's space is for Longley in 'To Three Irish Poets' a way of redefining himself, and where he comes from:

> In order to take you all in
> I've had to get beneath your skins,
> To colonise you like a land,
> To study each distinctive hand
> And, by squatter's rights, inhabit
> The letters of its alphabet…

Longley's ambiguous feelings as regards identity and place are to the fore here. On the one hand, he suggests that his fellow poets are accommodated – with all their differences – within the scope of his own imagination; on the other, this is a reaching out into their ground, the borrowing of roots he talks about in the letter to Marie Heaney. '[S]quatter's rights' serves as a compressed image of his insecurity about that lack of a 'solid hinterland'; it may also be read with a consciousness of ways in which Longley has been placed – or misplaced – in critical readings of the Irish tradition, where 'squatter's rights' are sometimes all that he has been granted.

Yet here, and elsewhere in the sequence, Longley holds together difference and sameness (since 'each distinctive hand' is colonised), individual and collective, as regards the group of poets in a slightly uneasy relation. Its uneasiness may be one reason why the idea of the poetic sodality is largely abandoned after this sequence (and not simply because 'there didn't seem...to be any takers'). While certain ideas, principles, and poetic strategies, may be shared by the Northern poets of this generation, the invisibility of those links, or at least a lack of self-consciousness about them on the part of the writers themselves, may have facilitated fruitful intertextual relationships and the emergence of strong individual talents. Longley's need – for various reasons – to make those relationships text not subtext is a need which belongs to a particular moment in time, and which, in finding its expression, doesn't have to be revisited in the same way again.

His awareness of the elusive nature of the relationship between the four poets – elusive, that is, in its resistance to easy explication of its terms [48] – is apparent in 'Letter to James Simmons':

> True to no 'kindred points', astride
> No iridescent arc besides,
> Each gives the other's lines a twist
> Over supper, dinner, breakfast
> To make a sort of Moebius Band,
> Eternal but quotidian....

Longley's note in *An Exploded View* on the Moebius Band is instructive: it is, he writes, 'an example of a non-orientable surface. It can be illustrated by taking a strip of paper several times longer than it is wide and sticking the two ends together after twisting one of them by a half turn. It is one-sided in the sense that an ant could crawl along the whole length of the strip without crossing the bounding edge and find himself at the starting point on "the other side".'

Again, the image plays with the idea of difference and sameness: although the poets are not all writing the same script, they are sharing their imaginative territory, travelling the gyres together,

crossing – and thereby eliminating – boundaries. (In earlier drafts
of the 'Letters', Longley included epigraphs taken from the poets
themselves, scripting them, in a sense, into his own poems. In
this stanza, the quotation from Wordsworth and the evocation of
Shelley also return us to an earlier group of poets in revolutionary
times.) That vision is mirrored in the twists and turns of the verse
form in 'Letter to James Simmons', with its energetic, convoluted
and unstoppable syntax, and in the enjambment that works against
the apparent boundaries introduced by the rhyming couplets. Poetry,
the final line of the stanza suggests, is both transcendent and grounded
in the real world. As such it is also the exemplar of social possi-
bility: it is 'non-orientable', unconstrained by limited and divisive
political categories. This is one-sidedness not in the sense of choosing
one side or the other, but in the sense that there are no "sides":
the artistic community is the ideal – or idealised – community.

This aspiration also underpins the closing stanza of 'Letter to
Seamus Heaney':

> So let it be the lapwing's cry
> That lodges in the throat as I
> Raise its alarum from the mud,
> Seeking for your sake to conclude
> Ulster Poet our Union Title
> And prolong this sad recital
> By leaving careful footprints round
> A wind-encircled burial mound.

The poem was written at a time when Heaney was still based in
Belfast, although he had been in California for a year; it also belongs
to a time when Northern poetry was a fledgling enterprise, at least
in terms of public perception. Over the last 30 years, poetic maps
have been redrawn to the extent that they are now seen by some
as distorted in the North's favour. But at the time, the poetic
flowering in the North reversed traditional stereotypes about the
spiritual south and the unimaginative north, and questioned
Dublin's literary centrality in important ways. Those writing in
the North at that time were conscious of those attitudes, and to
some degree self-conscious about the need to overcome them.
Heaney noted, for example, that the reviews of his 1975 collection
North indicated it had 'conquered the Dublin resistance, or
begrudgers', that 'the pressure of feeling got through to people'.[49]
Mahon argued in 1970 that 'Montague and Heaney, by reasons of
their Northernness have avoided (Dublin literati please note) the
narcissistic provincialism in which "Irish" literature is currently
sinking'.[50]

For Longley, promotion of the arts in Ulster was of course his day job; but both he and Mahon affirmed a distinctiveness in their context of production which, they suggested, should affect the ways in which Northern poetry was to be understood. Mahon has more recently rejected the idea that distinctions can be made between 'Northern' or 'Southern' poetry ('As far as I'm concerned, it's all one');[51] and such has been its profile in recent decades, the need to counter negative perceptions of the North's literary potential belongs in the past. But in 1971-72, these poets did work with the sense of a uniquely complex inheritance in Ireland which found its "voice" through the 1960s and 1970s for the first time – and against the odds.

At the close of 'To Seamus Heaney', the 'Union Title' of 'Ulster Poet' Longley grants is something of a poisoned chalice, given his earlier description in the poem (punning on Northern Ireland as the 'Six Counties') of 'the sick counties we call home'. The 'Union Title', historically, is a tainted one, and it symbolises here a responsibility inherited, a burden placed on the poets, and a problematical concept (of the 'Ulster poet') attributed to them, rather than a condition or allegiance sought. Longley and Heaney see that inheritance differently, and they see it, of course, in terms of their own individual aesthetic preoccupations (preoccupations which are also politically charged). For Longley, the North as a 'limbo' land, somewhere and nowhere, has both negative and positive connotations, and he cultivates an aesthetic which is itself in a kind of limbo, drawing on multiple perspectives. 'The Irish psyche', Longley wrote in the mid-1970s, 'is being redefined in Ulster, and the poems are born...out of a lively tension between the Irish and the English traditions'.[52]

Heaney places the emphasis, and his emergent sense of self, differently: 'I was symbolically placed between the marks of English influence and the lure of the native experience.' For Heaney, the poems are, in a sense, born out of that 'native experience' and modified by their social and cultural context: 'my roots...crossed with my reading'. His sense of poetry as 'restoration of the culture to itself' is some distance away from Longley's sense of "redefinition".[53] The phrasing in each case reveals much about their political differences, and a 'lively tension' between the two writers informs 'Letter to Seamus Heaney' itself. Yet it is also poem which broods on the themes which have been at the heart of both poets' work from the early 1970s onwards: responsibility, the burden of the past, and the role of the poet.

The 'Letter', significantly, is written while they are away from

Belfast, Longley in his home from home of Carrigskeewaun, Heaney
in the US. The poet recognises the desire:

> ...to leave the past
> Across three acres and two brooks
> On holiday in a post box
> Which dripping fuchsia bells surround,
> Its back to the prevailing wind,
> And where sanderlings from Iceland
> Court the breakers, take my stand,
>
> Disinfecting with a purer air
> That small subconscious cottage where
> The Irish poet slams his door
> On slow-worm, toad and adder:
> Beneath these racing skies it is
> A tempting stance indeed...

That stance would put history in suspended animation in a post-box,
slamming the door, metaphorically, on the problems of politics. The
insular purism that rejects any outside, contaminating influences
on poetry is symbolised by the rejection of the toad and adder,
creatures that don't belong in an "authentic" Irish landscape. (It is
also a different take on Yeats's stance towards the close of 'Meditations
in Time of Civil War – 'I turn away and shut the door...' – at
another point of crisis in history/history in crisis.) But as Longley
has observed in his critical prose, the artist 'has other obligations'
besides imaginative self-indulgence. However idyllic that 'purer air'
might seem, it is an illusion – about the self and history – which,
in its passivity, has problematical consequences for society and for
the poet: 'we may / Scorch our shins until that day / We sleepwalk
through a No Man's Land / Lipreading to an Orange band'.

   In effect, retreat into that 'small subconscious cottage', the
denial of history, is as indictable a position for the poet as
'[l]ipreading' reductive versions of history. The poet's responsibility
is thus to avoid the kind of posturing that betrays the self:

> Continually, therefore, we rehearse
> Goodbyes to all our characters
> And, since both would have it both ways,
> On the oily roll of calmer seas
> Launch coffin-ship and life-boat,
> Body with soul thus kept afloat,
> Mind open like a half-door
> To the speckled hill, the plovers' shore.

Longley revisits here, and develops, some of the concerns of the
earlier 'A Personal Statement', also dedicated to Heaney. The per-
sonal statement on the complex 'balance' between mind and body

becomes a coded statement about the responsibility of the poet
more generally. The poet casts off dramatised versions of self to
reach a definition of the poetic self held in suspension between
past and present, life and death, mind and body, art and nature.
Longley's 1974 letter to the *Irish Times* quoted earlier thus does no
more than articulate a position already inherent in his poetry: the
seductiveness of purity; the necessary engagement with impurity;
the door half open between the two. 'Letter to Seamus Heaney'
recognises a life that both is and is not his own entirely.

Thus, while the poem claims a shared burden of that 'Union
Title', it also asserts Longley's own distinctive aesthetic principles,
familiar from the 1960s, although taking on a new urgency here.
It is notable, too, that 'To Seamus Heaney' closes with a (poetic)
strategy – 'leaving careful footprints round / A wind-encircled burial
mound' – that is quintessential Michael Longley. The image of
the burial mound, which appears here for the first time, becomes,
as will be seen, central to his poetic landscape. The 'careful foot-
prints' around it are redolent of his care and precision in language,
of his reluctance to place himself in the centre of the frame, of his
ambiguous insider/outsider relation to place, and of his poetry's
capacity to mourn.

The 'Letters' are letters from home to (absent) friends. But they
are also letters to home, letters which try to define Belfast to itself;
define the poet's own particular relation to home; create home in
that they claim a country of the imagination; and attempt to trans-
form the poetic community to which they are addressed into a home
from home. Their origin, however, is simpler and more personal
than this suggests, and accounts for the fact that 'Letter to Derek
Mahon' stands in some respects apart from the rest of the sequence.

In early 1971, and as a spur to lift Longley out of a fallow period
of writing, Mahon suggested a verse correspondence, with a bottle
of whiskey as the price for failing to keep up the bargain. Mahon
began the exercise, with a 7-stanza poem – never published – in
octosyllabic rhyming couplets: 'wryly conscious too, perhaps, / of
certain precedents in kind / (Letters from Iceland comes to mind)'.
He speculates on the 'impulse' to start the dialogue, attributing it
both to friendship and to a deeper restlessness, a 'crying need / in
that dark cave which is indeed // the heart of the artistic life / un-
filled by mistress or by wife'. The poet's task, Mahon's verse letter
suggests, (and with an echo of Longley's earlier 'Birthmarks: *for
D.M.*'), is to rouse from sleep by 'naming' them, bringing them
into language, the 'dark, strange creatures' who 'keep / hibernatory
silence, scared / until we wake them with a word'. It is a poem

about the emergence of poems, a self-reflexive enterprise that broods directly on creativity, and whose purpose is to inspire creativity in the recipient. But the final stanza draws a political parallel:

> The same is true of politics.
> Way back in nineteen sixty-six
> who besides <u>Seamus</u> would have dreamed
> the past more wakeful than it seemed?
> And who, 'all ancient tricks unlearned',
> was not amazed when <u>Derry</u> burned
> if not the ideologues themselves
> with <u>Connolly</u> and <u>Fanon</u> on their shelves? [54]

The parallel between the process of poetry and the Troubles is a complex one, and an idea Mahon formulates elsewhere in interview – 'the poetry and the "troubles" had a common source, the same energy gave rise to both' [55] – if not directly in his published poetry. The link is not one of simple cause and effect: Mahon, like Longley, points out that the poetry preceded the Troubles. It is this connection, with all it implies for the role of the poet, that Longley responds to in the opening of his verse letter to Derek Mahon, written to follow directly on from Mahon's poem, and picking up on its closing questions with Longley's own question/ answer. The 'And' with which Longley's 'Letter to Derek Mahon' opens should then be read in the sense of 'moreover', or 'in addi-tion', Longley picking up the narrative strand:

> And did we come into our own
> When, minus muse and lexicon,
> We traced in August sixty-nine
> Our imaginary Peace Line
> Around the burnt-out houses of
> The Catholics we'd scarcely loved,
> Two Sisyphuses come to budge
> The stick and stones of an old grudge,
>
> Two poetic conservatives
> In the city of guns and long knives,
> Our ears receiving then and there
> The stereophonic nightmare
> Of the Shankill and the Falls,
> Our matches struck on crumbling walls
> To light us as we moved at last
> Through the back alleys of Belfast?

The question posed across these two stanzas is an ambiguous one, equivalent in its own way to Mahon's 'I might have grown up at last / And learnt what is meant by home' from 'Afterlives'. To 'come into our own' implies, variously, the attainment of a poetic

maturity; a recognition of the true nature of an inheritance that had
been deceptively "sleeping" peacefully through the 1960s; or a re-
definition of self in relation to home. It is also a buried allusion to
Mahon's own ambiguous 'Walking among my own' in 'The Spring
Vacation' (retitled 'Spring in Belfast'), a poem dedicated to Longley.

The question is not answered explicitly, although by the close of
the poem the "answer" has been suggested. The encounter with a
"troubled" Belfast initially leaves the poet exposed, strips away the
trappings of poetry – the 'muse and lexicon'. In an image which cap-
tures precisely Longley's complex position on the old question 'what
is the use or function of poetry', the 'two Sisyphuses' suggest both
the virtue and the futility (if one wants measurable or quantifiable
outcomes) of the poetic enterprise, as well as its incorrigibility, the
compulsion, like it or not, to keep trying. '[P]oetic conservatives',
which plays on the idea that art conserves, that poetry embodies
memory, also implicates both poets in a formalist tradition, with the
suggestion that the forms developed through the 1960s are facing
their ultimate test. Part of that test is to see Belfast anew, to go,
'at last', beneath the surface into its symbolic 'back alleys' and, in
doing so, to explore formerly repressed areas of consciousness.

The 'back alleys of Belfast' mutate through the rest of the poem
into the highways and byways of the past and the West. While the
encounter with a troubled Belfast is the shock of the new, it is
one which has a parallel for the poet in a visit with Mahon to the
Aran Islands in 1966. On Inishere, their footsteps echo 'down that
darkening arcade / Hung with the failures of our trade', and they
are 'tongue-tied / Companions of the island's dead', with echoes of
the 'Sisyphuses' who are 'minus muse and lexicon'. They are out-
siders at home in Belfast, and outsiders in Inishere – 'strangers in
that parish', with 'a Jesus who spoke Irish'. But they are also
insiders, in silent communion with what is beyond language.

The poem draws on the mysteries of Easter as paradigmatic of
a state of mind, a metaphysical condition:

> Black tea with bacon and cabbage
> For our sacraments and pottage,
>
> Dank blankets making up our Lent
> Till, islanders ourselves, we bent
> Our knees and cut the watery sod
> From the lazy-bed where slept a God
> We couldn't count among our friends,
> Although we'd taken in our hands
> Splinters of driftwood nailed and stuck
> On the rim of the Atlantic.

Christ's tomb (the lazy-bed), the cross (driftwood): both images, alongside the Lenten hardships, translate Good Friday into Ireland, and *vice versa*. Good Friday is, of course, a day of paradox, a day of murder and mourning that nevertheless carries within it the promise of redemption (in a manner akin to the 'coffin-ship and life-boat' of 'Letter to Seamus Heaney'). When the poets become 'islanders themselves', they do so, ambiguously, at a moment of transition and profound uncertainty, between death and resurrection. Good Friday in Inishere thus has implications for understanding Belfast's own darkness in the opening stanzas.

This poem does not promise a resurrection. On the contrary, it renders the poetic self as vulnerable as the city with its 'crumbling walls' (with an echo here of Yeats's 'my wall is loosening' from 'Meditations in Time of Civil War'). Fragmentation, and fragmenting lines of communication, are everywhere in the poem. But it leaves itself open to possibilities, and its final stanza implies one potentially redemptive mode:

> That was Good Friday years ago –
> How persistent the undertow
> Slapped by currachs ferrying stones,
> Moonlight glossing the confusions
> Of its each bilingual wave – yes,
> We would have lingered there for less....
> Six islanders for a ten bob note
> Rowed us out to the anchored boat.

Longley once described this poem as 'an attempt to define my Irishness'.[56] The poet is located, at the end, in the 'anchored boat', neither rooted nor floating free. In a critical tradition in which "Irishness" has sometimes called for very particular commitments, and at a time when the "Irishness" of a Northern protestant with English parents might have been called in question, the poem's ambiguous definition of self in relation to community has the effect of rendering "Ireland" ambiguous too. The 'undertow' that persists in this final stanza carries its own ambiguities: it is the memory of Inishere that haunts the poet in the back alleys of Belfast, constantly trying to pull him back; but the undertow that haunts the poem throughout is the memory with which it began – the 'burnt-out houses', the 'stereophonic nightmare'. The pull to-and-fro between Inishere and Belfast (places which have been more than usually subject to outside stereotyping), the complex identification with neither and both simultaneously, offers an alternative to the 'stereophonic nightmare' of one-dimensional communal loyalties: it suggests at least the possibility of both/and not either/or, a redefinition of what is or is not 'our own'.

The publication of 'Letter to Derek Mahon' caused some friction between its author and "recipient", brought latent tensions about poetry, politics and the North – or at least about the media involvement in these things – to the surface. The poem appeared in the *New Statesman* on 3 December 1971, alongside 'Letter to Seamus Heaney', and prompted a letter from Mahon to the journal dissociating himself from two of the phrases in the poem – 'the Catholics we scarcely loved' (this was the line as printed in the *New Statesman*) and 'Two poetic conservatives'.[57] He outlines his feelings more fully in a private letter sent to Longley at the same time:

> I realise that 'The Catholics whose full human reality our upbringing might well have prevented us from recognising' is not susceptible to scansion or paraphrase, but 'The Catholics we scarcely love' [*sic*] still reads to me too much like 'The Catholics we didn't much like and hadn't any time for.'...As regards the poetic tories...There's a difference between theory and practice...[and] you saying it in a poem dedicated to me, with however much irony, looks like we have an agreed platform hewn out of Yeats and Robert Graves.[58]

In retrospect, the issues here are not really to do with sectarianism or formalism, but with public *versus* private, individual *versus* community.

Part of what Longley's poem confronts is a (collective) protestant guilt, an acknowledgement of culpability – collusion through a lack of understanding. '[F]rom about 1968 to 1973,' he says later, 'I was consumed with Protestant guilt.' [59] That guilt is implied in 'scarcely', with the implication that provision for the Catholics of Northern Ireland – in terms of civil rights, jobs and housing – had been scarce too. The change of tense Longley introduced ('we'd scarcely loved') diffuses some tension, by placing that attitude firmly in the past, and before coming 'into our own' – both in terms of understanding and in terms of the poets' growing public profiles. (At the same time, it renders the implication of 'scarcity' of provision, and the guilt implied therein, far less evident.)

The question, in a sense, is how 'we' in the opening stanza of Longley's poem is to be understood. For Mahon, it means two individuals – Mahon and Longley – rather than protestant poets taking on a burden of responsibility for a community. For Longley, perhaps it means both these things. But irony as a way of dealing with an undefined guilt is there in Mahon's (published) writings too, and while his own verse letter may have been a private enterprise, its wry consciousness about its literary heritage obviously affects the terms of Longley's published, and therefore public response.

It is the Auden/MacNeice parallel that springs most obviously to mind for Mahon, and not only in terms of formal influence. While *Letters from Iceland* might begin in holiday mood, the book is also about shared beliefs, and the likely impact on the poets of imminent European war – 'Our prerogatives as men / Will be cancelled who knows when; / Still I drink your health before / The gun-butt raps upon the door.' [60] For MacNeice, one of those shared beliefs was in 'system against chaos...a positive art against a passive impressionism',[61] which is an argument about style reiterated by Mahon and Longley – 'No art without the resistance of the medium.' [62]

But in 1971 there were other issues for the Northern poets to deal with: they were often reviewed together; their work was habitually seen as implicated in the Troubles, and in some of the same ways. In some respects (as regards publicity), the Northern Irish group identification served them well; but it also served them ill by compromising critical awareness of their differences. Yeats may have bemoaned the passing of cultural coherence and the emergence of 'protesting individual voices';[63] but assertion of difference against critical assumptions about 'the Northern poets' was – and is – a measure of aesthetic achievement, which the habitually embattled and protesting Yeats in another context knew perfectly well too. As Mahon observed to Longley, 'Poetically the only ways are separate ways.' [64] The poets are 'trying to make [themselves] heard' – but against each other as well as against their context.

The 'Letters' sequence as a whole is the first and last manifestation of an insecurity that needed to be written out in order to be overcome, and which dramatises, through its imagined engagement with its subjects, debates of central importance to Longley's aesthetic development. Its centrality to *An Exploded View* should be understood in those terms, even though its strategies sometimes lead the poet into uneasy or unsustainable positions.

Mahon's anxieties about it aside, 'Letter to Derek Mahon' is the strongest poem of the sequence, partly because this poem draws its inspiration from a long-standing and intimate personal friendship rather than from a Northern poets' alliance. (From one point of view, the fact that Longley and Mahon could squabble about details in the poem, even in public, is testimony to closeness, not to distance.) It rings true because the speaker here is at ease with his subject, because his voice is not pushed out of shape. The first of the letters to be written, it is also the poem least imbued with the 'sodality of the imagination' agenda, an agenda which becomes more self-conscious – and consequently more laboured – as the composition of the sequence progresses. It doesn't compromise its own voice and its own style by getting inside Mahon's skin (which, ironically, is what gets under Mahon's skin). Its strength, in other words, lies not in its sense of a poetic alliance, but in its forging of a distinctive voice, and in the extent to which it stands on its own terms outside the context of the sequence and beyond any associations with its addressee. In this, it reinforces, even if inadvertently, Mahon's point that 'Poetically the only ways are separate ways', itself a rephrasing of MacNeice's comment on Yeats's influence: 'Go thou and do otherwise.' [65]

V

The idea of the poetic community may be one way of finding public resonance, but in *An Exploded View* the rewards yielded by that strategy are ambiguous. There are obvious difficulties with attempting to implicate other writers in one's own work in this way. Retrospectively, it is apparent that the collection looks forward and outward as much, if not more, through those poems which subtly merge public resonance into private experience – the elegies 'Kindertotenlieder', 'Wounds' and 'In Memory of Gerard Dillon' for example – as well as those which offer a self-deprecating dissection of the individual voice – 'Alibis', 'Options', or 'Ghost Town'.

Also apparent in these two strands is the versatility of Longley's voice which, while often celebrated for its elegiac seriousness is sometimes overlooked in its humour and – seemingly an old-fashioned word in poetry criticism now – wit. (These latter traits in particular make Longley an important precursor to Paul Muldoon.) In 'Alibis' and 'Options', Longley moves into the quasi-autobiographical mode that dominates the later *Man Lying on a Wall*, with a lightness of touch that differentiates such poems from the 'Letters' sequence; in 'Wounds' and 'Kindertotenlieder', towards a merging of public and private, history and autobiography, past and present, that resolves some of the problems of 'Letters', and looks forward to the elegiac mode of *The Echo Gate*.

In April 1972, James Simmons sent a postcard to Longley objecting to 'Letter to James Simmons', a copy of which Longley had just sent him; Longley responded, with 'anger and disappointment', by writing 'Alibis'.[66] 'Alibis' and the earlier 'Options', which may be read as the companion piece to 'Alibis', are oblique essays in self-criticism – of the life and the work respectively; they are also, implicitly, acts of dissociation from a 'poetic sodality'. In contrast to 'Letters' they make their point negatively: they consider and discard what might have been or used to be rather than promote a vision of what is or could be.

'Options' is an oblique reflection on some of the directions Longley's work could have taken, and a recognition of certain temptations faced by the poet. As Michael Allen notes, its gibes are 'self-aware', and its character 'humorously querulous'. 'Options' also serves as a comment on Longley's views of poetry (and criticism) more generally. The first option is:

> To have gone on and on –
> A garrulous correspondence
> Between me, the ideal reader
> And – a halo to high-light
> My head – that outer circle
> Of critical intelligences
> Deciphering – though with telling
> Lacunae – my life-story...

It is possible for a critical reputation to be developed in part through a suspect, if unspoken, liaison with that 'outer circle'; self-deception on the part of both may be intrinsic to the enterprise, and the 'candours in palimpsest' little more than an artfully constructed treasure hunt laid on for the critic.

At the opposite pole to this kind of garrulity – but equally artful in its audience cultivation perhaps – is the work of the tormented, isolated poet 'Scorched by nicotine and coffee' who, 'at a pinch... could have / Implied in reduced haiku / A world of suffering'. (The pun on 'at a pinch' should serve at the outset as an indication of the way in which, tonally, the poem should be read.) These 'options', along with the 'species of skinny stanza...In laborious versions / After the Finnish...' and 'the hushed hexameters / Of the right pastoral poet / From the Silver Age', may be read as parodic comments on some of Longley's earlier enterprises; but they are all roads now marked no entry, options which are:

> Pointing towards the asylum
> Where, for a quid of tobacco
> Or a snatch of melody,
> I might have cut off my head
> In so many words – to borrow
> A diagnosis of John Clare's –
> Siphoning through the ears
> Letters of the alphabet
> And, with the vowels and consonants,
> My life of make-believe.

'Options' picks up on the earlier 'Journey Out of Essex' in *No Continuing City*, which tells the story of John Clare's escape from the asylum, and his four-day walk home across country. Here, Clare is back in the asylum, and Longley quotes almost verbatim Clare's comments to the historian Agnes Strickland in 1860, when he explained that he could not write because 'they have cut off my head, and picked out all the letters of the alphabet – all the vowels and consonants – and brought them out through my ears; and then they want me to write poetry! I can't do it.' [67]

For all the humour of 'Options', there is a serious point at issue, since Clare's inability to write is associated with a descent into madness, a loss of language, and therefore a loss of selfhood. What constitutes the self and its individuality is, for both Clare, and for the poet of 'Options', the 'life of make-believe'. The creativity of that life has nothing to do with the 'blotting papers', 'clenched fist', and 'laborious versions' of the previous three stanzas; rather, it is one which seemingly marries imagination and truth – a 'life of make-believe' that can also, in another sense, make believe.

'Alibis' is, in a way, about a 'life of make-believe', a complex exploration of selfhood. The self, as so often in Longley's poetry, is, as Neil Corcoran notes, rendered oblique; the 'lyric first person wanders in and out of a set of variant selves'.[68] These include botanist, saxophonist, diarist, music teacher, composer, religious, football supporter – and poet. 'Alibis' is autobiography (in early drafts its first section was variously titled 'Curriculum Vitae', and 'Apologia'), but, to borrow Douglas Dunn's phrase again, it is autobiography 'at an imagined angle to reality'. The comic hero of the poem is an imaginary figure (as in Mahon's 'Lives', with which the poem has an obvious intertextual relation), but one not remote from Longley's own life.

'Alibis' is also an extended play upon the question of origins. Although the distance between the poet and his hero (who is also his alibi for a disguised self) is such that an over-literal reading risks a misreading of the tone of 'Alibis', one might gloss the poem in terms of Longley's self-awareness. The speaker's 'botanical studies' are a means of finding 'ancestors', identifying the self; but the connection is elusive – 'I used to appear to them at odd moments – / With buckets of water' – and the ironic playfulness of the poem constantly shifts the ground under the reader's feet, as if this persona too is only appearing at 'odd moments...in the distance'. There are glimpses of the familiar Longley figure: the botanical interest, the fascination with music, the ornithological ambitions. There is also a wry awareness of the fundamentally egotistical nature of the poet ('I wanted this to be a lengthy meditation / With myself as the central character – '). But 'Alibis' deflates egotism, mocking

the artist's anxious footnotes to posterity ('At present I am drafting
appendices / To lost masterpieces, some of them my own – ') as
well as the ambitions which hide vainglory under self-sacrifice –
notably here the desire to become a St Francis-like 'saviour of
damaged birds'. The desired religious and artistic retreat in and
into a medieval past, 'managing daily after matins / And before
lunch my stint of composition', like the 'Irish poet' who 'slams his
door', is impossibly remote from the present day 'idea of myself /
Clambering aboard an express train full of / Honeymoon couples
and football supporters'.

'Alibis' is a poem entirely concerned with self (and its relation
to society) and simultaneously a critique of self-indulgence. The
word 'myself' appears six times; 'I', 'me' and 'my' almost 30 times.
(One precedent for this is Yeats's insistent repetition of 'I', 'me'
and 'my' in 'Meditations in Time of Civil War'.) That makes it,
of course, a 'lengthy meditation / With myself as the central char-
acter', but 'myself' is almost impossible to pin down. The reaction
against a communal stance into a seemingly obsessive self-absorption
(my wants, my ambitions) is undercut by the deprecatory humour
of the poem, and by the transformation of self into selves. 'Alibis'
is about pleasing everybody and pleasing nobody, being different
things to different people, all things to all people, nothing to any-
one. It is about planning and improvising simultaneously.

Perhaps it is to take too much of an interpretive liberty to read
its narrative entirely in relation to its trigger – the negative response
to 'Letters' – but nonetheless, there is a sense in which the poem
allegorises the poet's recent experiments as much as it projects into
an imaginary 'final phase':

> I had folded my life like a cheque book,
> Wrapped my pyjamas around two noggins
> To keep, for a while at least, my visions warm.
> Tattered and footloose in my final phase
> I improvised on the map of the world
> And hurtled to join, among the police files,
> My obstreperous bigfisted brothers.

This identity is in stark contrast to the elusive, self-effacing and
healing opening figure with his 'medicaments' of 'badger grease
and dock leaves', although a (poetic) vision is still protected and
kept 'warm' beneath the surface here.

What 'Alibis' suggests, through the 'simple question / Of being
in two places at the one time', is a way of holding these twin –
even multiple – identities simultaneously, of developing a (self)
confidence in contrariety. But there is more to it than this, and

the temptation to read the 'simple question' as a simple answer may
be deceptive, as the poem's final section indicates:

> I could always have kept myself to myself
> And, falling asleep with the light still on,
> Reached the quiet conclusion that this
> (And this is where I came in) was no more than
> The accommodation of different weathers,
> Whirlwind tours around the scattered islands,
> Telephone calls from the guilty suburbs,
> From the back of the mind, a simple question
> Of being in two places at the one time.

The final line finds its full rhyme – indeed the only full end-line
rhyme in the poem – at the close of section I ('My one remaining
ambition is to be / The last poet in Europe to find a rhyme'), thus
locating itself, through rhyme, in two places at once. But the opening
line of this section internally rhymes 'myself' with 'myself'. The
alternatives implied by those different rhymes may be another way
in which the poem finds itself in two places at the one time.

The poem does not reach a 'conclusion', quiet or otherwise; it
recognises only the possibility of doing so in an ambiguous sen-
tence comparable in its way to the close of Mahon's 'Afterlives'. If
that possible conclusion is reducible to the mundanity of the sub-
urban adulterer's lies and telephone calls, it is not enough for the
poet: such a life might seem to be risky, but in fact it risks nothing
of the poetic self. To have 'kept myself to myself' is to circum-
scribe the self and to collapse difference into sameness – rhyming
like with like in one line. On the other hand, to posit, but not
accept, that conclusion leaves the poet with 'rhyme' and 'time' –
sameness in difference – and with the 'simple question' transformed,
through the enactment of its answer, into a more complex one. (In
that sense it finds an alternative to the sameness and difference of
the 'Moebius Band', one which does not rely on group identification.)

The poem plays off different versions of identity one against the
other, and in their simultaneity they too act as alibis for each other;
but it also plays off variant selves against keeping 'myself to myself'.
(More of those variant selves appear in 'Ghost Town', 'Three
Posthumous Pieces' and 'Altera Cithera'.) And variant readings of
'Alibis' may thus be part of the point. Establishing alibis (fake ones
particularly) is a tricky business. (It's unsurprising that Muldoon
– trickster *par excellence* whose disappearing acts are notorious –
owes a debt to this poem, both in his bold claim to tell 'new
weather' ('Wind and Tree'), and in the trick in 'Twice' of 'Two
places at once was it, or one place twice?'.) Unpicking 'Alibis' is

rather like peeling an onion; the poem is in two places at the one time, but each of those places is itself, in one way or another, in two places as well, simple and complex.

In its more complex interpretation, being in two places at once is bound up with the ways in which the poet imbricates past, present and future. 'Alibis' and 'Letters' might thus be seen as taking two different approaches to the same task: that of finding ways in which responsibilities to the self, and to the imagination, can chime with responsibilities to history. If the 'Letters' are self-consciously pre-occupied with the latter, 'Alibis' is a slightly mischievous retreat into the former. But the poem is significant because it is a blueprint for understanding how different versions of self enable the workings of an historical imagination. The final section of the poem, after all, projects into what could have been, into what could still be, *and* takes us back to the point where he 'came in'; the narrative structure of the poem as a whole complicates any single placing of poet – or speaker – in space and time. From the solitary medieval poet-monk figure to the obstreperous football supporter who is one of the crowd, 'Alibis' makes quantum leaps in time. To rhyme with time is not just to be in two places at once, but is to encompass more than one time in a single place/ poem. (Muldoon's 'Twice' understands the trickery of 'Alibis' in both these senses.)

VI

It is in the handful of elegiac poems in *An Exploded View* that the balance one senses Longley has been seeking, between private and collective concerns, between self and history, is found. The genre brings some of the problems, questions and ideas about responsibility articulated by poets in relation to Northern Ireland's Troubles into particular focus.

In Longley's early 1970s elegies and, as will be seen, in his elegiac practice more generally, some of those difficult questions find their most effective – and affecting – mode of expression. 'Wounds', 'Kindertotenlieder' and 'In Memory of Gerard Dillon' were all written between May and August of 1972. In part, that is because they respond to specific events; but it also suggests that the poet's development of concerns about public and private through 'Letters', as well as through the autobiographical and reflective 'Options' and 'Alibis', has helped to release the elegiac voice. It is here in the elegies, in other words, that positions formulated and reformulated through the earlier poems are properly tested.

'Wounds', written in May 1972, follows hard on the heels of 'Alibis'. With the possible exception of 'Ceasefire' from 1994, it may well be the best-known of Longley's poems – and for good reasons. The poem mediates public utterance through private grief, and mediates between past and present. Longley takes his father's experience in the First World War as a point from which to find perspectives on Northern Ireland's present, and its politically fraught history. The 'two pictures from my father's head' of 'the Ulster Division at the Somme / Going over the top...' and the 'London-Scottish padre / Resettling kilts...' share intimate memories of Richard Longley's experiences in the London-Scottish division, and also open up to scrutiny one of the more sensitive aspects Ireland's past.

While Ulster Unionism has never forgotten the role played by the Ulster Division in the Battle of the Somme (on 1 July 1916, the casualties for that Division numbered around 6,000, of which a third or more were fatalities), the way in which it is remembered has tended to be dictated by political necessity, and the individual experience lost to sight. 'Wounds' is one of the few, and earliest, imaginative evocations of the Unionist experience of the Great War which, in linking the experience with personal suffering, and with sectarian killing in Ireland, breaks tribal taboos 'kept...like secrets', and restores to history an intimacy of detail.

'Wounds' is an elegy for Longley's father; for sometimes mis-guided innocence in whatever form it might take; and for victims of both the Northern Irish Troubles and the First World War. His father metaphorically 'followed...for fifty years' the London-Scottish padre 'Over a landscape of dead buttocks'. By implication, that landscape has become a permanent condition; past and present are telescoped in ways which re-define perspectives on both. His death thus becomes, in the poem, a First World War death out of sequence: fifty years later he is a 'belated casualty'. On a personal level, the poem dignifies the Great War death whilst it simultaneously, and poignantly, ironises the terms by which that death would have been officially commemorated in wartime, with: 'I am dying for king and country, slowly'. All the horrors of a slow and painful death from cancer are encompassed in that one addition to a somewhat clichéd phrase. But the line also says something about the long-term psychological as well as physical damage caused – to an individual or a society – through inherited strife.

The poem travels backwards and forwards through time to con-nect the 1914-18 war with 1970s Northern Ireland. In burying the poet's father alongside recent Troubles casualties, the poem also disinters those things people might rather want to forget – about themselves, their own culture, and their own history.

> ...I bury beside him
> Three teenage soldiers, bellies full of
> Bullets and Irish beer, their flies undone.
> A packet of Woodbines I throw in,
> A lucifer, the Sacred Heart of Jesus
> Paralysed as heavy guns put out
> The night-light in a nursery for ever;
> Also a bus-conductor's uniform –
> He collapsed beside his carpet-slippers
> Without a murmur, shot through the head
> By a shivering boy who wandered in
> Before they could turn the television down
> Or tidy away the supper dishes.
> To the children, to a bewildered wife,
> I think 'Sorry Missus' was what he said.

Part of the concern of this poem is to attempt to understand actions and events that are repulsive. It forces sympathies (the 'shivering boy', the 'boy about to die / Screaming "Give 'em one for the Shankill!"') where they are difficult to share, and in doing so, it broadens what – and who – we understand by victims in society. '[I]t seems to me', Longley writes, 'important...to imagine how one can be so brainwashed or so angry or in a sense perhaps even so innocent that one can drive in a car and go into somebody's house and shoot that person stone dead.'[69]

The 'shivering boy', the 'teenage soldiers', the innocent civilian victim (whose status is poignantly reinforced by the 'uniform' he wears) – all these things are redolent of the 'innocence' that characterised the 1914 generation, and inspired the futile attacks on the Somme in 1916. The certainty of purpose in the screaming boy of the first stanza might contrast with that of the boy who 'wandered in' in the second; but the contrast serves only to throw the futility of both actions into sharper relief.

The slippage between youth and age, innocence and experience, past and present, is subtly suggested by the metaphorical expansion of the First World War 'lucifer' into the image of the Sacred Heart, and into the (obliterated) night-light in the nursery.[70] The image also crosses the line between the war zone and the domestic sphere. 'Home' is a violated space. It is also a space of which we are given, in its most disturbing form, an 'exploded view', through the poignant inclusion of domestic details – the carpet-slippers, the dirty supper dishes, the blaring television set. In the randomness of this kind of killing, 'Wounds' implies, what is "private" is exposed in the cruellest of ways, and retreat into a protected and inviolate (imaginative) space impossible.

This feeling is echoed in the short elegy 'Kindertotenlieder':

There can be no songs for dead children
Near the crazy circle of explosions,
The splintering tangent of the ricochet,

No songs for the children who have become
My unrestricted tenants, fingerprints
Everywhere, teethmarks on this and that.

Here, 'home' is also one's consciousness, a state of mind. In 'Wounds', the private space is literally invaded by a gunman; in 'Kindertotenlieder', the dead children metaphorically invade the poet's home, trespass uncontrollably in his thoughts. The poem responds, implicitly, to the deaths in the Troubles of several children in 1971 and 1972 which imprinted themselves on the society's consciousness.[71] In its title, borrowed from Ruckert's German songs for Mahler's song cycle, and in its intertextual relation to Dylan Thomas's 'A Refusal to Mourn the Death, by Fire, of a Child in London', it is also evocative of the Second World War. In the same way, in 'In Memory of Gerard Dillon', the painter becomes, after death, 'a room full of self-portraits, / A face that follows us everywhere'.

'Wounds' is, in one sense, an exploded view of his earlier elegy for his father, 'In Memoriam'. It renders 'In Memoriam' inadvertently prophetic, since his father's 'old wounds' that 'woke / As cancer' in 'In Memoriam' reverberate in 'Wounds' in the wider context of Northern Ireland and the resurfacing of the Troubles, as well as in the unresolved historical trauma induced by the First World War. The word expands beyond the literal wounds in the poem – the cancer, the bullet-holes – to encompass the psychological wounds inflicted by violence; the open wounds of history (aggravated in Northern Ireland in the early 1970s); the wounding of the innocent; and the invisible wounds left on a society.

The modern elegy itself, as Jahan Ramazani has suggested, 'resembles not so much a suture as "an open wound", in Freud's disturbing trope for melancholia'. From being an 'art of saving', elegy has become, in Elizabeth Bishop's phrase, an 'art of losing'.[72] 'Wounds' shares with 'Kindertotenlieder' the anti-elegiac mode that is central to the development of 20th-century elegy. The poem understands grief as an open wound that needs to be healed; it never presumes to be able to do so, not least because the grief is the poet's as well, in the loss of his own father. The 'bewilderment' of the bus-conductor's wife and of the poet's father, which unites the actions in both stanzas if only in their incomprehensibility, is there too in the poet's refusal to make sense of the events through conventional forms of consolation.

Elegy is a paradoxical genre, one which celebrates life and mourns its end, commemorates absence through imaginative presence. That paradoxical sensibility is at the heart of Longley's work, and its origins are best seen here in the early elegies in *An Exploded View*. The rhythmic repetitions of 'Kindertotenlieder' create the song the poem will not create; 'Wounds' inters its bodies, with the mourning rituals that are, conventionally, part of a healing process, an acceptance of loss; but in doing so it also ensures their imaginative presence.

The first part of 'Wounds' moves from the visual to the haptic, from the 'two pictures' to 'I touched his hand, his thin head I touched'; the second part brings tokens of remembrance to the graveside – 'A packet of woodbines...A Lucifer...a bus-conductor's uniform'. The repetition of 'touched', its almost touching each end of the line, struggles to render tangible in language and form that aspect of a relationship which can never be recreated after death: if sounds and visual images can remain, touch, taste, and smell are lost forever, always absent. The ritual burial of the graveside tokens of remembrance might suggest a form of closure, as with the 'Christening robes, Communion dresses' and 'blind drawn on the Lower Falls' of 'In Memory of Gerard Dillon'; but in the end, the poem leaves the dishes unwashed, the television still on, the bewilderment and grief present as an open wound.

Inevitably, and as discussed at the beginning of this chapter, the onset of violence in Northern Ireland prompted self-questioning, at times self-doubt, on the part of its "responsible" artists ('Had I been found wanting?'). Not least of the extraordinary achievement of these poems is, paradoxically, a recognition of what poetry cannot do. 'Wounds' offers no easy answers, no immediate consolations; but its real accomplishment is to expose through those absences what is found wanting in the 'Sorry Missus' of the final line.

3

'There's no such place as home':
Man Lying on a Wall
1973-1975

Should you take away the supporting structure
The result would be a miracle or
An extremely clever conjuring trick.

MICHAEL LONGLEY, 1974

I

In the 1971 poem, 'The Adulterer', from *An Exploded View*, the serial killings by John Christie, the notorious 10 Rillington Place murderer, are the original inspiration for what becomes a complex exploration of guilt, repression, betrayal and the workings of memory:[1]

> I have laid my adulteries
> Beneath the floorboards, then resettled
> The linoleum so that
> The pattern aligns exactly,
>
> Or, when I bundled into the cupboard
> Their loose limbs, their heads,
> I papered over the door
> And cut a hole for the handle.
>
> There they sleep with their names,
> My other women, their underwear
> Disarranged a little,
> Their wounds closing slowly.

The careful disposal of bodies works metaphorically here to suggest the repression of memories. The poem offers a more sinister perspective on the 'ancient histories', the past lovers who are 'Pasted over' in anticipation of the 'last girl' in the earlier 'No Continuing City'. The 'adulterer''s betrayals are 'papered over' in the recesses of the mind in order to present a seamless picture to the outside world. Physical and emotional upheavals are 'resettled'. On a literal level the 'loose limbs' and 'heads' are evocative of corpses and body parts, but 'bundled' and 'cupboard' also suggest something doll-like about the 'other women' – a sinister version of toys labelled ('with their names') and tidied away. The tone in the third stanza disturbingly verges on the paternal (maternal?) in its affectionate possessiveness, and in its undoubted tenderness. The 'underwear / Disarranged' implies sexual activity; but although disarranging is an action carefully not attributed to the speaker, the lines are, given the resettling, bundling, papering and arranging of the previous stanzas, more precisely suggestive of uninvited sexual interference (perhaps necrophilia), with 'a little' reading as a denial of responsibility, playing down the truth. The process of trying to forget is encapsulated in 'Their wounds closing slowly'. But the phrase is a complex and deceptive one. It equates forgetting with healing, but the dead can't be healed; the 'wounds' are suggestive of the open wound of the violated female body's sexual organs; and it may also be read as a concern with emotional wounding, as the abandoned past lovers of the adulterer slowly recover from the end of the affair.

Nevertheless, even if the wounds close on the surface, disease and infection are spreading underneath. The principle of 'out of sight, out of mind' may be all very well in theory; but as this poem shows, there is no such thing as out of mind:

> I have watched in the same cracked cup
> Each separate face dissolve,
> Their dispositions
> Cluster like tea leaves,
>
> Folding a silence about my hands
> Which infects the mangle,
> The hearth rug, the kitchen chair
> I've been meaning to get mended.

The faces which 'dissolve' are perhaps gruesomely redolent of the disposal of body parts, but the 'other women''s 'dispositions' haunt the speaker every time he reads his own life to become the accumulated detritus of memory. Their absence is also their presence, an infection which can't be seen, but can't be repressed, and which colours – or rather contaminates – perceptions of everyday life. Guilt and responsibility go hand in hand: those feelings, pushed to the back of the mind and papered over, make their way back through the cracks in the surface of the poem – in the 'cracked cup' where the pattern no longer 'aligns exactly' – to reappear as guilt about 'the kitchen chair / I've been meaning to get mended'.

'The Adulterer' is a poem which assumes the voice of a murderer and adulterer: it understands imaginatively what is alien and repulsive. But the speaker here is also another variant self, and the poem is disturbing because it begins to erode distinctions between what is ordinary and extraordinary, acceptable and unspeakable. The poem literally brings home things that are normally kept out of sight. It recognises that the outwardly tranquil domestic sphere may be a place of secrets, lies, and repressed horrors, and it blurs the boundaries between the voice of the killer and the voice of the ordinary suburban adulterer. By its closing stanzas, this speaker could almost be anyone, the procrastination of the final line all too familiar.

Yet more than this, 'The Adulterer' also reflects, in uncomfortable ways, on the process of writing. In a 1981 interview, Longley observed that 'the poet, like the scientist, tries to elicit from the chaos, from the great mess of being alive, patterns and shapes'.[2] Elsewhere, he objects to what he calls the 'pejorative phrase, "the well made poem"' on the grounds that: 'If it's not "well made"... then it isn't a poem. You might as well talk about a well made flower or a well made snowflake (both of which are patterned but organic). Symmetry is part of biological life.'[3] The points are not incompatible. Patterns can be discerned, but they can also be made; the two things, indeed, may be indistinguishable, since the perception of symmetry is also its creation on the part of the perceiver. If writing is always about creating patterns, those patterns are also, in a sense, always fictions.

'The Adulterer' is on one level a poem about creating – and trying to sustain – an illusion. The inside workings of its speaker's mind can also be read as the workings of text itself, which creates 'patterns and shapes', but can also, as T.S. Eliot's puts it in 'Burnt Norton', 'strain, / Crack and sometimes break, under the burden, / Under the tension, slip, slide, perish...'. Longley's poetry creates 'patterns and shapes', but this is not an organic or natural process; there is an awareness that writing can be about deception, and that it can also be a form of deception, if the 'pattern aligns exactly'. (Even the title of *Man Lying on a Wall* carries that ambiguity within it.) Certain criticisms of the so-called 'well-made poem' in Ireland – that it is conservative, determinate, unselfconscious about the problematic of language in the modern world[4] – don't tend to hold up when the claims are properly tested against the texts themselves. In Longley's case, the too-easy critical demarcations that exist between the 'well made' or 'experimental' poem, opacity and simplicity, lyric integrity and postmodern rupture, are more than usually unhelpful, since his 1970s poems are often concerned with the play between these things, knowingly caught in their forms and simultaneously pushing beyond their boundaries.

The tension between surface and depth, what we see and don't see, which is the subject of 'The Adulterer', is present in the poem at a formal level. It is also a tension between freedom and restraint. Longley describes his early poetic efforts, the juvenilia dating from his first years at Trinity, as failures because 'I was writing about ten poems a day...They were all just pouring out of me...it was letting it all hang out. But there was no discipline, no shaping, no effort.'[5] There is an honesty to 'letting it all hang out', but also a self-indulgence, an immaturity, and a certain theoretical naivety. Shaping, on the other hand, involves choices about what to reveal or conceal, and 'effort' a self-consciousness about manipulation of – and being manipulated by – language.

Viewed in this way, 'The Adulterer' is a probing and self-reflexive poem. Read as a reflection on style and form, and on its own strategies, it becomes a poem about making – and breaking – shapes and patterns, about control and loss of control. Its opening clarity of diction and the solidity of its consonants ('I have laid my adulteries / Beneath the floorboards') give the illusion of transparency: there is an openness and cleanness to the lines which is at odds with the process they describe, as if we too are being given a pattern that 'aligns exactly'. But having 'papered over the door' the poet has also 'cut a hole for the handle', allowing the possibility that he – and the reader – can one day look into the less ordered depths.

The poem gives us glimpses into more disturbing areas of consciousness even while its precision and control of language are generally maintained on the surface. The line length of 'Or, when I bundled into the cupboard' won't quite be bundled into shape with the rest of the poem. Concise, hard, exact, and monosyllabic it may be at times, but the sibilance associated with the 'other women', from 'loose limbs', 'sleep', 'names', 'disarranged', and 'wounds closing slowly', gradually infects the whole poem: 'separate face dissolve', 'dispositions', 'cluster', 'leaves', 'silence'. The words themselves will not stay still, they disarrange a surface order: what is shut away finds its way back – in the poem's diction and into the speaker's consciousness.

'The Adulterer' has obvious links with other poems in *An Exploded View* which deal with fictionalised selves, the violation of home, and the wounds of memory. But it differs from the general tenor of *An Exploded View* in that it works from the inside out: home is not invaded or violated from outside; rather, what is repressed within the self emerges to contaminate those things outside and around it. To some extent it may only be a matter of nuance – from the cracked pavement of the necropolis to the cracked cup in the kitchen, both of which reflect back to or from the self – but

the difference in emphasis is, in miniature, one way to understand
the shift that later takes place between *An Exploded View* and the
1976 *Man Lying on a Wall*. Longley describes *Man Lying on a Wall*
as 'my most personal book to date'. But it is significant that he
also insists that 'its privacies were not conceived in reaction to the
political and more public utterances of its predecessor, *An Exploded
View*: both books grew out of similar pressures.'[6]

In a sense, Longley's description of the book here is ambiguous:
he directs the reader away from certain interpretations of its 'privacies'
even as he invokes it as his most personal book. In many ways, *Man
Lying on a Wall* can be read as a collection conceived in reaction
to its more overtly political and public predecessor – or at least as
a rethinking of strategy. But Longley is also warning the reader
away from a simplistic view of the domestic sphere as the non-
political, private safe haven. As Heaney observed recently, when
questioned at a poetry reading in Belfast in March 2004 about
whether poetry had – or has – any responsibilities in relation to
the Troubles, those Troubles are not something 'out there', but
are 'in here', are also an aspect of self. In opening up some of the
cracks of 'home', in allowing the reader to see what is usually, by
most people, papered over, *Man Lying on a Wall* continues what
An Exploded View began: it questions public/private distinctions;
its insights into individual consciousness reverberate in our under-
standing of society as a whole; as in 'Casualty', it allows the reader
'to get closer', but the close-up view is profoundly disturbing.

The willingness in *Man Lying on a Wall* to take the reader into
secret places, to explore the things shifting beneath the surface, makes
it by far the most private of Longley's books; its psycho-sexual
dramas also make it the most unsettling of them. Much of the
collection is about what the poet can hardly put into words. Some
of its themes – isolation and distance, loneliness, insecurity, claus-
trophobia – can make it seem at times solipsistic and, given the more
usual compassion and humour of Longley's voice, unexpectedly
bleak. But the quasi-autobiographical mode at work in the book
serves as a conduit through which fundamental questions are asked.

Poems about home, family, love, nature, and children are per-
haps easy to misread as always benign, tranquil and affirming,
regardless of what they say. *Man Lying on a Wall* intimates surface
and depth in a way which leaves superficial or careless readings at
a loss. James Simmons rightly described the poems as 'fastidious'
and 'finely wrought'. But he struggles to see beyond the 'calm
surface' he claims is presented in all the poems, and tends to praise
the 'sharp eye, loving what it sees' as if observation were an end

in itself.[7] As a result, he finds the poet evasive; but perhaps it is the criticism that evades issues – about form, language, and fictionality, and about what Patricia Waugh has called the '*creation/description paradox*'[8] – that are at the heart of the book.

For Peter Porter, Longley 'stays away from Belfast' in this book; 'the poems are chiefly love poems'; their landscape is one of 'lakes and islands where he conjures up a poetry of departures'.[9] Douglas Dunn's comments on the book also read over underlying tensions, in as much as he makes a case for Longley's poetry more generally which *Man Lying on a Wall* disrupts:

> Longley's new collection...presents a poet among his kinsfolk and relatives; on his landscape, which is pieced together by desire and imagination as much as it is real; among his loves, children and affirmations. It is this fullness of view he has consistently worked towards. Domesticity co-exists with the world beyond his house and selves; the affectionate little details of life are seen to be as awe-inspiring as profounder designs, larger intentions.... He seeks to affirm where he can. He makes ordinary endorsements and hallows the world.[10]

This is praise, of course, and it is warranted: such affirmations, endorsements, and affectionate details are present in the book. But in the context of this collection, it is also slightly misleading.

First, affirmations are only one element of a more complex picture. As George Mackay Brown astutely notes, Longley has the 'celebrant's tongue', but also 'precision', 'tenderness and pity' alongside a 'brute directness'.[11] Second, the 'fullness of view' celebrated here suggests that the poetry's reach from the particular to the general is underpinned by phenomenological certainties; but the book's self-consciousness about textuality, about writing as fiction, continually throws such certainties into question.

As with contemporary readings of *No Continuing City*, it is Eavan Boland who is, at the time, and despite their very different aesthetic ideas, more closely attuned to the some of the ambitions and achievements of *Man Lying on a Wall*'s 'domesticity' when she writes that:

> No less than any of his previous overt statements on violence, do these poems mirror the more important violences of loss of strength and confidence, the sense of claustrophobia which a poet can have even within commitment, the fine line between obsession and love. It is far, far harder to scrutinise such violences in private situations – human relationships, the family, work – than in the more accessible realities such as public violence and loss of life. And in the sense that it is a more difficult assignment, *Man Lying on a Wall*, for all that its poems sometimes lapse from economy into obscurity, represents Michael Longley's most ambitious work...[12]

One of the 'love poems' from *Man Lying on a Wall*, 'The Goose' (1973), illustrates the way in which intimate details become the *loci* for playing out a complex emotional drama, for exploring what may be otherwise unspeakable. It is a poem for which the earlier 'The Adulterer' is in some ways a precursor, and one with which it has an obvious intertextual relation. Seemingly conventional in its opening, with its gift to the lover of 'the white goose in my arms, / A present still', it is a love poem about, in Longley's phrase, the ways 'we devour each other emotionally'.[13] 'The Goose' thus brings home some of the more sinister aspects of 'The Adulterer', and of such poems as 'Casualty':

> ...I plucked the long
> Flight-feathers, down from the breast,
> Finest fuzz from underneath the wings.
>
> I thought of you through the operation
> And covered the unmolested head,
> The pink eyes that had persisted in
> An expression of disappointment.

The poem collapses distinctions between human and animal, between the domestic task it describes and the relationship of the lovers. On one level, the narrative concerns the development of that relationship, with its disappointments, hesitations, deceptions and rewards. The 'expression of disappointment' is a silent reproach not only from a slaughtered animal, but also from the figure to whom the poem is addressed. To cover the head and eyes is a gesture of tenderness and protection; but the poet's own feelings of guilt, although their cause is unspecified, are also at work here, in a reluctance to confront the 'disappointment' for which, one senses, he must be responsible.

This poem too is about surface presentation and, underneath, the 'great mess of being alive', the things we don't usually see, or don't want to see – 'I punctured the skin, made incisions / And broached with my reluctant fingers / The chill of its intestines'. Its point is that one is dependent on, and only ever created from, awareness of the other. And when the perfected object is prepared, through discarding its more unpleasant aspects, it is then 'dismantled ...limb by limb'. The 'affirmations' of this poem run parallel to its negativities. When he finds 'Surviving there... / Nudging the bruise of the orifice...the last egg', it is 'delivered... / Like clean bone, a seamless cranium'.

Given Longley's earlier preoccupations with the birth, or delivery of poems, it is possible to see a self-reflexivity working here too;

and birth, or confinement – with its double meaning – is also a recurrent theme of *Man Lying on a Wall*. What emerges cleanly and without any cracks from this rather gruesome kind of posthumous caesarean trails some invisible baggage behind it:

> Much else followed which, for your sake,
> I bundled away, burned on the fire
> With the head, the feet, the perfect wings.

The speaker manoeuvres uneasily between what he preserves and what he destroys, what he exposes and what he hides away. What is hidden is what cannot be spoken, which is elided here in 'Much else'. Read metaphorically, this is also about areas of consciousness which are repressed, about things which are kept secret (the echoes of 'The Adulterer' bundling away his body parts are unmistakable here). But it is also done 'for your sake': responsibility, guilt and deception begin to slide into one another.

Longley offers a way in to *Man Lying on a Wall* through a series of binaries: 'The man lying on the wall might be resting between sleep and waking, dream and reality, fact and fiction, freedom and responsibility, life and death.'[14] All of these are to greater or lesser degrees deconstructed in the book; but the most ambiguous and most revealing of them at the outset is 'freedom and responsibility' since it is a false binary, an opposition constructed out of an association of responsibility with imprisonment. The association gives some indication of the poet's ambiguous attitude in *Man Lying on a Wall* towards that which he also celebrates: domesticity and family life. (It is also bound up with his feelings towards what Philip Larkin described as the 'toad *work*', as well as with the question of responsibility towards the Troubles.) Half liking it, half afraid of it, and perhaps afraid of the compromises it enjoins on the solitary poet, a darker side creeps in here and there, a fear resurfacing to take poet and reader by surprise. That darker side is what renders the ordinary, in 'The Goose', extraordinary: it is here that Longley's 'precision' meets a kind of 'brute directness'. The care taken with the poem's language and narrative is no less than the care taken with the act – the preparation of the goose – itself. But that act of preparation and creation is also one of destruction and concealment. 'Precision', in other words, is not always benign.

These contradictory attitudes also emerge in the opening poem of the collection, 'Check-up', which, like 'The Goose', is a love poem of sorts, but with a sting in the tail. Its 'check up' rests ambiguously somewhere between a clinical examination and the act of love:

> Head and ear on my chest
> To number the heartbeats,
> Fingertips or your eyes
> Taking in the wrinkles
> And folds, and your body
>
> Weighing now my long bones,
> In the palm of your hand
> My testicles, future…

There are echoes of Robert Graves's 'Counting the Beats' in the eroticism here, 'Counting the slow heart beats, / The bleeding to death of time in slow heart beats'. Indeed, *Man Lying on a Wall* is more consistently and overtly indebted to Graves than any other of Longley's collections, in its preoccupations with love and death, waking and sleeping, dream (or nightmare) and reality, and in its satirical as well as lyrical strain.

Graves is also the obvious influence behind the elegance and style of love poems such as 'Desert Warfare'. His 'Counting the Beats' brings time to a standstill even as the clock – in the heart beats – keeps on ticking. In 'Check-up', the Gravesian echo taps into an association between love and death that recurs in other poems too. Longley has suggested that 'Many of the poems in the book explore the idea that all relationships are, among other things, struggles unto death.'[15]

Love is also part of the progress towards death, as intimated by the biblical allusions (from Psalm 22) of 'Check-up' – 'I may tell all my bones: they look and stare upon me' – which seem almost to transform the speaker into the sacrificial lamb (or goose). This turns life into foreplay for death, a conceit developed more fully in 'Love Poem' in which the tantalising world of sensation is put in opposition to death, but is only a conditional tentative yearning in a single-sentence poem that inexorably unravels in a 'slow descent…towards death'. In 'Check-up', for all its eroticism, the check up is also a preparation ritual, a weighing up (and out) of what is needed

> Because if they had to
> The children would eat me –
> There's no such place as home.

With some black humour, the poem revisits the earlier invitation of 'No Continuing City' to the 'last girl' to 'eat and drink me out of house and home'; but it also revisits the fear of being devoured which is implicit in the related poem 'Circe', and is then rendered explicit in 'Nightmare' from *An Exploded View*, in which the pig

he is carrying ('I am in charge of its delivery') 'bites into my skull
...and eats my face away, / Its juices corroding my memory...'. As
Michael Allen has observed, poetry, children and death – one could
add the lover – are 'alternative agents which all consume the liv-
ing consciousness'.[16] It is as if on the one hand the poet might be
devoured by the intimacies of family life, and on the other by lan-
guage itself; to the 'binaries' he is caught between could perhaps
be added poetry and people.

These poems make incisions into the ordinary, expose depth in
surface. In doing so they question the relationship between illusion
and reality; their probing under the skin also reverberates in terms
of style and the politics of language. Plumbing those darker depths
is the impetus behind 'Riddles', 'Fury', 'Triptych' and 'Last Rites';
they are also poems whose psychological explorations come with a
degree of guilt, paranoia, and self-flagellation.

In 'Riddles', there is a desire to 'take on your stretch-marks', to
'welcome // Other stigmata', for wounds to be written on the body;
the speaker is a 'soft target' who is nailed 'to the sky'. In their
delving into hidden depths, there is a sense in which the seven short
poems which make up 'Riddles' are floundering in the riddle of
language itself, their occasional impenetrability as poems mirroring
the poet's desire to 'jumble our souls like anagrams'. This may be
one instance where, to borrow Boland's suggestion, economy lapses
too far into obscurity. But even if the riddles are not always solv-
able, their thematic concerns with 'The skeletons in our cupboard',
with the voice that might be unlocked from its cage (in 'Voice-Box')
resonate in the collection as a whole.

'Fury' also implicates birth with the problems of language, in
its 'Dithering acceptance / Of a breach birth, / A difficult name.'
It is one of a handful of poems – the others being 'Riddles', 'The
Goose', and 'Triptych' – which hint at a dark undertow to the
more celebratory mode of 'True Stories'. 'Triptych' proffers a dif-
ferent take on the iconography of the Holy Family, probes beneath
conventional imagery to give more precise detail: 'bruises', 'blue
veins', 'the elbow / She tested water with'. The poem has its ten-
derness and affirmations (in 'Baby' and 'Mother'); but it is also
riddled with anxiety and uncertainty in its opening and more evi-
dently autobiographical section, 'Father':

> I have been dressed in white
> So that I might absorb
> Your bruises, the stubble
> At your groin, the milk
> Your blue veins discolour,

And supervise his birth,
Death of the afterbirth
And my own reduction to
The ghost of a terrorist
Interrogated by you.

It is as if the birth is his own diminishment, the absorption of others an erosion of self. The poem is cryptic – perhaps too much so – and verging on solipsistic. It pre-empts the more successful 'Dead Men's Fingers' in *The Echo Gate* in which he feels 'like the ghost of a child / Visiting the mother who long ago aborted him'.

In 'Father', for all the anxiety the 'I' voice might feel, a sense of vulnerability, and the proper integration of the terrorist image with the general thrust of the poem, is missing, as is a dramatic tension.[17] But the self-absorption at work in this poem is transformed when it becomes the vehicle for playing out a tension between interiority and exteriority, as in 'Death-watch', Part I of 'Last Rites':

I keep my own death-watch:
Mine the disembodied eye
At the hole in the head,
That blinks, watches through
Judas-hatch, fontanel:

Thus, round the clock, the last
Rites again and again:
A chipped mug, a tin plate
And no one there but myself,
My own worst enemy.

This poem complicates any sense of whether it is looking from the inside out or the outside in. It is elliptical, suggestive of the interior thought processes of the blinking 'disembodied eye'. This is a consciousness trapped inside its own head, even if looking in on itself, in which the clock goes round, but time also stands still through repetition. It is reminiscent of the 'demented ...flashing round and round' in 'The Bat', as well as of Banquo with 'a hole in his head' in 'Fleance'; and its 'chipped mug' has its own intertextual pedigree.

It looks forward, also, to 'The War Poets' from *The Echo Gate*, a poem with a more obvious public resonance, but which plays out some of the same issues. The First World War echoes are more elusive here; but the scene setting, with the 'Judas hatch', the 'tin plate', and the final line's oblique evocation of Wilfred Owen, where the enemy is oneself, are suggestive. Attrition may be a state of mind, from which the only release is gained through 'a tangent in the tired skull, / A swerve, a saving miscalculation' ('The Bat').

Attrition suggests not only a trapped consciousness, but is also perhaps a way into understanding the circularity and intertextuality of these poems. To an unusual degree, they rub against one another; the temptation to read one poem as refracted through another, to build a whole from the parts, is at times, in relation to *Man Lying on a Wall*, almost irresistible. Eavan Boland suggests it is a 'weakness' of the book that 'it is not self-contained', that 'One would want to know Michael Longley's previous work' if it is to be appreciated in full.[18] From the perspective of knowing what comes after as well as before, the textual traces of earlier poems, or the foreshadowing of later ones, are more than usually evident in some of the poems of *Man Lying on a Wall*. More than that, it may be the case that meaning is sometimes dependent on the contextualisation of such traces in Longley's work as a whole. The collection is in some respects overshadowed on either side, by the public resonance of *An Exploded View*, and by the extraordinary accomplishment of *The Echo Gate*. It is possible, in other words, to read *Man Lying on a Wall* as to some extent a detour, an element in a broader intertextual web whose interest lies as much in where it has been and where it is going as in itself.

Longley's own unease with the collection may compound that feeling. None of the poems discussed so far from *Man Lying on a Wall* is included in Longley's *Selected Poems*. 'Riddles', 'Triptych' and 'The Bat' are in fact excised from his collected *Poems 1963-1983*, along with 'The King of the Island', 'Loamshire' and 'Granny' (although this last reappears as part I of 'No Man's Land' in the *New Poems* section).

Although his revisions are still comparatively few, one senses that things are not always finally settled in *Man Lying on a Wall*, that phrases, images and ideas have not yet found their final 'home': some have been tried before, and will in some cases be tried again, in *The Echo Gate* and beyond. That may contribute to Longley's own retrospective sense that the book is slightly weaker than the others, inferred from the fact that in the *Selected Poems* he affords it only half the space given to the other collections. Whatever the aesthetic judgements at work here, it is also the case that the selection gives only a very limited sense of the more disturbing elements of the original book, as if an editorial papering over has, inadvertently, taken place.

But the unease with the book may equally be read as part of the point. 'There's no such place as home' operates on a textual as well as emotional level, and in doing so brings its difficulties as well as its rewards. The irony may be that *Man Lying on a Wall*, because its thematic concerns affect its style and construction in particular ways, suffers, proportionately, more in the process of selection than the other books.

The counter-argument could easily be made that it is in fact more self-contained than its predecessors. There is a negative side to that of course, in so far as it suggests that some individual poems don't stand up on their own against Longley's best work. But *Man Lying on a Wall* weaves a dense intertextual web within itself. The weaknesses of a few of the poems notwithstanding, the collection thus reads at its best in the form in which it was originally published: its effect is diminished by breaking up the overall pattern; it makes itself felt cumulatively.

Although its poems work discretely, they also gain in particular ways from being read *in situ*. Like 'The Bat', the collection travels in circles, 'flashing round and round'; it also has its tangents, swerves, 'saving miscalculation[s]'. In the final stanza of that poem, the bat is left 'Suspended between floor and ceiling' with the possibility that it will eventually 'in our absence...drop exhausted, a full stop / At the centre of the ballroom floor'. The 'full stop' or resolution is, significantly, outside the frame of experience; for many of these poems too, their resting place is not 'home' but 'Suspended between'. That condition is, in Longley, a problem and a solution – although more frequently, as becomes evident from *Gorse Fires* onwards, the latter. *Man Lying on a Wall* is significant in his overall development, not least because it shows that the play betwixt and between can be confining as well as liberating, can be about the avoidance of rigidity, but also about the 'compasses jamming' ('Desert Warfare').

II

John Fowles refers to fiction as 'worlds as real as, but other than the world that is. Or was.' [19] When Longley describes his *Man Lying on a Wall* as 'resting between...fact and fiction', he seems to demarcate, but in fact could be seen to collapse those categories; others – dream and reality, freedom and responsibility, truth and illusion, surface and depth – collapse along with them.

His 'True Stories' in *Man Lying on a Wall* comprise the sequence of four short poems which are avowedly personal, dedicated to Longley's two eldest children; but they still carry an ambiguity within their title, a probing of what we understand by 'truth' or 'telling stories' (especially as 'true stories' for children are so often fantasy). From another angle, 'Stilts', in which 'Two grandfathers sway on stilts / Past my bedroom window' is a true story as well. The fabular mode in which poems such as 'Company' are written is relevant in this context too. Variant selves exist in variant "realities", to the point where reality is textual, or text the only reality.

The intertextual links across the book function, in a sense, as the context for the "reality" the poems create; that reality is self-consciously "staged", but it is a reality that is also a fiction existing inside the poet's head. Partly as a response to the pressure of external circumstances, the demand that poetry should communicate something of relevance to history *in extremis*, what we are given in *Man Lying on a Wall* is a reflection on the competing claims of text, self and world that destabilises the illusion of an integrity, stability or discretion each might seem to possess.

'The Lodger', the first poem of this collection to be written, gives some insight into the question of fictionality that is explored through the book, and to the development of *Man Lying on a Wall* itself:

> The lodger is writing a novel.
> We give him the run of the house
> But he occupies my mind as well –
> An attic, a lumber-room
> For his typewriter, notebooks,
> The slowly accumulating pages.

The erosion of boundaries between externalities and interior consciousness in 'Last Rites' and in the earlier 'Kindertotenlieder' is also in evidence here. Having given over domestic space to the lodger, the fictional world the lodger creates trespasses on the mind.

In a sense, the poem is about the impossibility of retreating into any "private" space and closing the door. The fictional world is 'other than' the one that is, but it displaces what 'is' to become a reality of the mind. The tension between lodger ('writing a novel') and speaker (writing a poem), between two creative acts, the first acknowledged, the second invisible, leaves the reader on slippery ground. The 'attic', 'lumber-room', and 'notebooks' could be real or metaphorical; the lodger's work space, or a state of mind. Life itself, by implication, is textual, comprising 'slowly accumulating pages', memory the 'lumber-room' in which things are stored away. The 'notebooks' and 'accumulating pages' reflect on the development of this book too, in which the poems touch upon each other with cumulative effect. But there is an implicit anxiety in the poem as well, albeit light-heartedly invoked, which provides a reverse angle on issues raised by the earlier 'Letters' sequence.

If 'Letters' scripted other figures into a particular vision, 'The Lodger' could be read as trapping the poet as a character in some-

one else's script: 'we lie here whispering, / Careful not to curtail
our lives / Or change the names he has given us'. Read straight-
forwardly, this is an acknowledgement that all fiction is drawn from
life, that they have been recreated as fictional characters, and that
in their "real" form they don't wish to disturb the flow of inspira-
tion. But as in the first stanza, the close of the poem renders the
ground between fact and fiction far more ambiguous than this,
since the implication could also be that life is lived according to the
dictates of storytelling. The final lines seem to suggest a classic
case of nature imitating art, of fiction creating, not recreating,
reality; at the same time the 'lives' are themselves, even if partly
autobiographical, fictionalised in, and by, the poem.

That sense of living out life – or rather variant, possible lives –
in someone else's story, of textual trespassing, is a motif that repeats
itself at intervals throughout *Man Lying on a Wall*. It runs along-
side a preoccupation with loss of self, or more precisely loss of
agency. In 'Belladonna', 'She and I are blood donors, prepared /
As specimens for the microscope...as anybody's future now, / Strangers,
our identities smothered'. The idea is more obliquely present in
'Desert Warfare', where the 'distances between us' are also dis-
tances between illusion and reality.

'Desert Warfare' is in part about intimacies that are also staged,
and, in a sense, about not necessarily knowing the part one is
playing in a wider drama: 'She might be a mirage, and my long /
Soliloquies part of the action.' Life as self-conscious 'action', in the
sense of acting, recurs in 'In Mayo':

> ...she and I
> Appear on the scene at the oddest times:
> We follow the footprints of animals,
>
> Then vanish into the old wives' tales
> Leaving behind us landmarks to be named
> After our episodes...

The poem itself creates scenes and episodes, conscious of is own
artifice and agency, of the poet as the director ('I clothe her now
and erase the scene').

In the way in which it peoples and vacates the landscape, sets
and erases its scenes, it owes a debt to Edward Thomas, whose
shifts in and out of his own landscape are a barometer for under-
standing his complex feelings about 'home'. (The naming of land-
marks, a familiar technique in Thomas, is also to become an
important aspect of Longley's aesthetic, particularly in the late
1980s and early 1990s.) As with Longley's lovers in 'In Mayo'

who 'Appear' and 'vanish', Thomas's lovers in 'As the Team's Head-Brass' walk in and out of the narrative, reminding us that there is always more than one story being told at any one time. In both cases, even in their absence, the lovers are implicated in the action of the poems. 'Desert Warfare' addresses 'her presence, her absence'; 'In Mayo' is also concerned with what we see and don't see; what is recorded and what is erased. It is a concern not so much with possible lives we might have led, but with variant lives led simultaneously in other, and unseen narratives, as they 'vanish into the old wives' tales'. One can be written into or out of existence, leaving traces to be deciphered and reinvented in other texts, other times.

The episodic moments of self-conscious fictionality in these poems become the central theme of the companion poems 'Man Lying on a Wall' and 'Fleance'; 'Ars Poetica' pursues the theme to its logical conclusion, in enacting variant lives, soliloquising one fiction after another. Longley describes these poems as a 'blend of paranoia, fantasy and dreams of escape'.[20] In 'Man Lying on a Wall' and 'Fleance', the 'escape' is achieved through conjuring tricks, with the poet as 'illusionist'; at the same time, there is an awareness that the idea of escape may be the greatest illusion of all. The first section of 'Man Lying on a Wall' reflects on art as illusion:

> You could draw a straight line from the heels,
> Through calves, buttocks and shoulderblades
> To the back of the head; pressure points
> That bear the enormous weight of the sky.
> Should you take away the supporting structure
> The result would be a miracle or
> An extremely clever conjuring trick.

The poem's play on truth and illusion puns on the title's 'lying'. It inverts perception ('points / That bear the enormous weight of the sky') and manoeuvres between alternate points of view: the miracle (truth as belief) *versus* trickery (truth as illusion); the 'straight line' *versus* double-dealing. Context within text – the illusion on which fiction rests, and the one which metafiction exposes – can be painted in or erased at will. In that sense, the poet is also saying something about his own formal growth. The 'conjuring trick' which takes away the visible and prominent 'supporting structures' that characterised his 1960s poems is not about an escape from form into freedom; but it is about finding freedom within form. Poetic "freedom" – for Longley as for any poet – is thus perhaps always in one sense an illusion which relies on invisible constraints.

The 'Man Lying on a Wall' is consciously staged: 'wearing the serious expression / Of popes and kings in their final slumber, /

His deportment not dissimilar to / Their stiff, reluctant exits from this world'. As with 'Fleance', the poem plays on Shakespeare's conceit of life as the 'player / That struts and frets his hour upon the stage' (or in Fleance's case his five minutes on the stage).[21] But it is a scene whose meaning is as elusive as the man lying on the wall himself: he wears the business man's uniform of 'pinstripe suit, black shoes / And a bowler hat', but he doesn't conform to expectation; the poem sets his apparent normality against the abnormality of the circumstance.

He is also reminiscent of MacNeice's alter-ego in 'The Suicide', who finds his own way of eluding the world, exiting 'By catdrop sleight-of-foot or simple vanishing act'. The sense of Longley's 'Man Lying on a Wall' as similarly trapped is suggested by the poem's final lines:

> ...on the pavement
> Below him, like a relic or something
> He is trying to forget, his briefcase
> With everybody's initials on it.

The briefcase (which takes on an intertextual afterlife in Muldoon's poetry) is almost devoured by inscriptions, and may stand as symbol for the man himself, written on and over by others. (The poem, of course, does this to him too.) Since he is 'trying to forget' it, it is also a symbol of memory, of the baggage accumulated through life which begins to write the self out of existence. ('The Suicide' is not the only one of MacNeice's last poems to prove influential in this respect, given the concerns of 'The Taxis'.)

The idea resurfaces in 'Ars Poetica', where the speaker has put himself 'in the shoes of all husbands, / Dissipated my substance', or where the judge awards first prize 'To me and to all of my characters'. In 'Man Lying on a Wall', it is as if everyone else is claiming what is his property – or prop. As a 'relic' the briefcase suggests the possibility he has escaped and left it behind as testament to a past life; but its presence also makes a different point about what might be going on under the surface. The Larkinesque ordinariness of detail – to 'return home in time for his tea' or 'arrive punctually at the office' – that intimates a structure and routine throws into sharper relief the inexplicable.

There is a clue here too as to the way many of Longley's poems in this period work, not just in terms of form but in their capacity to unsettle perception. They don't often look at the world "straight". They manipulate angles of vision to render the world as extraordinary as the man lying on the wall; or, looked at the other way around, to render the extraordinary ordinary. Differently angled perception is so habitual in this book as to becomes its own convention: it is there, for instance, in the 'rigging / Slanted across the sky' of 'Ferry'; in the island 'bumping.../ Our starboard timbers' in 'The King of the Island'; in 'Riddles''s 'answer up / Side down at the bottom of the page'; in the mallard of 'True Stories' who 'deflect[s] a danger-ous sky'; in the 'disembodied eye' of 'Last Rites'; or in the figure of Edward Thomas who 'Skirted the danger zone / To draw pan-oramas' ('Edward Thomas's War Diary').

To show things the way they are not usually seen is also the ambition of 'Fleance', which gives voice to a character virtually written out of one dramatic history. (Fleance makes only two brief appearances in *Macbeth*; after the failed attempt on his life in Act III, he disappears completely from the frame of the action for the remainder of the play.) 'Fleance' takes us beyond and beneath the "public" action being staged; in doing so it also returns to the question of what is exterior and interior, real or illusory. It is about what goes on behind the scenes; but it also stages what is "off stage", centres what would usually be in the wings. Fleance leaves a fleeting impression – or inscription – on history – 'I...cast my shadow on the backcloth / Momentarily: a handful of words, / One bullet with my initials on it – / And that got stuck in a property tree' – and then drops out of public consciousness. This is the illusionist's escape; but it is still an illusion:

> I escaped – only to lose myself.
>
> It took me a lifetime to explore
> The dusty warren beneath the stage
> With its trapdoor opening on to
> All that had happened above my head
> Like noises-off or distant weather.

That alternative reality, the world beneath the stage, slides into his own consciousness; the exploration is also a recovery of a self that has been lost. (It pre-empts the poet's own vanishing 'into the roof space' in 'The Third Light' from *New Poems*: the conceit of rooms as memory and consciousness – and also as the poetic shapes and forms which order that consciousness – is a recurrent one.)

By the end of the poem, that 'trapdoor opening' between different narratives, and between what is inside or outside one's head, is also the site of the poem, which performs a balancing act on the edge of two worlds:

> In the empty auditorium I bowed
> To one preoccupied caretaker

And, without removing my make-up,
Hurried back to the digs where Banquo
Sat up late with a hole in his head.

This locates its characters somewhere between the "made up" and
the "real". ('Ars Poetica', with its speaker 'disguised as myself',
takes this idea to its logical conclusion.) Fleance takes his bow for
a 'lifetime' lived off-stage before hurrying home. Banquo, back in
the private space of his digs, and, we might infer, without having
removed his 'make-up' – the mark of the bullet wound – either,
seems to be still haunting the play's banquet 'with a hole in his
head'. The poem begs the question whether it is possible to become
caught in fictions of one's own making; it also intimates that every
construction of self is a creative act, a performance given even if
the auditorium is empty.

Both 'Man Lying on a Wall' and 'Fleance', poems inspired by
works of art and self-consciously about the workings of art, have
autobiographical resonance in the context of the collection as a
whole. In their own way, they are 'true stories', or parables, as
well. The 'preoccupations and pressures' that inform *An Exploded
View* and *Man Lying on a Wall* include, most obviously, the
Troubles, and the questions of responsibility these bring. *Man
Lying on a Wall* internalises such pressures through its concern
with 'privacies', and with responsibility in the domestic sphere.

But there are other considerations at this time too, which may
be driving the themes and preoccupations of the book, not least of
which is Longley's fairly new – and rapidly expanding – role in
the Arts Council of Northern Ireland. He refers in a letter of 1980
to 'the schizophrenia I sometimes feel in my two roles' as Literature
Officer and as poet.[22] The tension between his public and private
personas is evident in any consideration of his activities in the
1970s and 1980s. Providing sponsorship for, and promoting the
work of his peers in his "official" role, he is also, as poet, a part
of the scene he promotes, whose engagement with those writers
works on a subtler artistic and intertextual level.

Inevitably, such distinctions were not always easy for writers in
correspondence with him to keep in mind. Perhaps purists like
Robert Graves, who argued that the poet should never compro-
mise his devotion to poetry by undertaking regular work outside
writing, had a point. But an institutional role is not necessarily
inimical to writing poetry: ideal worlds and idealised poems can
lack creative tension; splits and tensions push many of Longley's
best poems into shape. Nevertheless, holding two things in tension

may be productive; losing one's sense of self between them if they
begin to collapse in on each other is not. As already noted, being
suspended 'between' is not always a straightforwardly redemptive
or easily created poetic space; and the fear of its contracting, of
the poet's sense of being on the edge, at an angle, losing itself is
also implicit in *Man Lying on a Wall*'s ambiguous manipulation of
its binaries. In effect, there is an underlying contradiction that is
itself held in tension: to deconstruct rigid categorisations, to blur
the boundaries between seeming opposites may be read as a creative
(and liberating) act that brings fluidity and colour to lines drawn
in black and white; at the same time, the space cleared for the
self, and held against the odds, pushes between such categories
but nonetheless relies on their being in place.

It is unsurprising, then, that the space in which these poems
locate themselves is sometimes elusive. *Man Lying on a Wall* picks
up on the image from 'Letter to Seamus Heaney' of the mind 'open
like a half-door', of the ambiguous relationship between what is
seen and unseen, interior and exterior, of the whole and the part
simultaneously. The image is also indicative of the paradoxical
notion of identity as permanently transitional. Reappearing in the
'trapdoor opening' of 'Fleance', or the 'opened...window' of 'True
Stories', its more difficult implications are seen in part 5 of 'Ars
Poetica':

> Someone keeps banging the side of my head
> Who is well aware that it's his furore,
> His fists and feet I most want to describe –
> My silence to date neither invitation
> Nor complaint, but a stammering attempt
> Once and for all to get him down in words
> And allow him to push an open door.

To get things 'down in words' is to liberate them, to allow a break-
through into consciousness that eliminates the barriers between
what is sayable and unsayable as it occurs – hence the near paradox
of pushing the open door.

The phrase is also to do with agency, with whether the poet lets
speak or makes speak. Each moment in *Man Lying on a Wall* where
the poet knowingly controls the scene, as in 'I clothe her now and
erase the scene' ('In Mayo') tends to carry its opposite: 'I am clothed,
unclothed / By racing cloud shadows' ('Landscape'). But 'to get
him down in words' is also an exercise in control, a form of con-
straint/constraint in form: to put things into words is to pin them
down as shapes and definitions, as, inevitably, something less than
they are, an approximation. 'Ars Poetica' also returns us to that

earlier 'ars poetica' in *No Continuing City*, 'Birthmarks', as well as to
'The Freemartin', in its concern with the children (or poems) who
won't be completely suppressed but won't quite come into being.
The 'furore' of 'His fists and feet' is evocative of nothing so much as
the child/poem clamouring to be born; but this is also, as in 'The
Freemartin', a 'Difficult birth[s]', at once reluctance and desire.

Part of the difficulty is with confronting hidden or repressed
aspects of self. 'Ars Poetica' as a whole chases versions of self
through multiple fictional incarnations; but as in the earlier 'Alibis',
where there dawns on the poet 'this idea of myself', the implied
problem is whether these ideas, or versions, are made up by others
or by oneself – or, indeed, whether there is anything not "made
up" to be found. Does the poet 'risk [his] life in a final gesture',
'Walk the high wire' without a safety net, or 'go along with the
world and his wife'? And in any event, are these choices merely
narrative hopping, sideways moves from one story into another?

One of the most complex and significant poems of *Man Lying
on a Wall*, 'Company', may be read as an extended meditation on
themes which pervade the whole collection, and as the culmination
of ideas worked out across the preceding poems. And perhaps it
offers some resolution to such questions. A syntactical *tour de force*,
this 44-line poem comprises only one sentence; its two (equal)
parts hold two different ideas of poetry, and two possible lives, in
tension within that sentence. The tension manifests itself in subtle
parallels and differences.

In the first part, 'Love has diminished to one high room / Below
which the vigilantes patrol'; in the second, the 'far-off' rural cottage
is under scrutiny from 'households' who 'focus binoculars / On
our tiny windows'. The poet in the 'high room' creates 'fictions'
to 'placate remote customs officials, / The border guards'; under
observation in his rural isolation, he tries 'to put their district on
the map...to name the fields for them'. The 'daily bread' of the
first section (which is, ambiguously, both the essentials of survival
and 'The dissemination of manuscripts, / News from the outside
world') has its parallel in the second part's encounter with the
world outside in the 'Daily embarrassed journey' to and from the
well. The poet hesitates 'On the verge of almost total silence' at
the close of the first half; the well (of poetry) is likewise 'choked
with alder branches' in the second.

Yet these are far from being two almost identical scenarios, whose
only differences come from being staged in what could be seen as
fictionalised versions of Belfast or Mayo respectively. The first
part offers some wry revisions to earlier poems as, anticipating an

innocent second childhood, the poet finds himself instead in a
more ominous, Kafkaesque scenario. Diminishment is gradual
through the first half of the poem, suggesting both a progress
towards death, and the gradual silencing of an isolated poetic voice:
the poet has 'the only surviving copies / Of the books that sum-
marise my lifetime'. The room which 'bursts its seams' in the 1963
'Epithalamion' has 'diminished to one high room', a more embattled
image of the poet's ivory tower, or, in Larkin's formulation, his
'high windows'. The children, who have become memories and
traces, 'drawers full of soft toys', are a different version of the
memories 'bundled into the cupboard' in 'The Adulterer'.

The public persona of *An Exploded View* is also deconstructed,
the notion of 'trying to make ourselves heard' contracting to 'I
attempt to make myself heard / Above the cacophonous plumbing'.
And to see the lover as the 'solitary interpreter' who will 'lipread
such fictions as I believe / Will placate remote customs officials'
scales down the historical sensibility that underpinned the 'Lip-
reading to an Orange band' in 'Letter to Seamus Heaney'. Belief
itself, it seems, is in question, the enjambment of 'I believe / Will
placate' first permitting, then negating, any claim to integrity.
Through its parallels, the second half of 'Company' seems to
replay this scenario; but more subtly, it also reaffirms belief in
poetry, and in love, regardless of whether or not anyone is listening.
(The poem itself may seem to be 'On the verge of an almost total
silence', but, after all, the sentence does not end there.)

To create placatory fictions may be an act of survival; but naming
the fields is an act of love. The former is to respond to the pressure
to say what people (poetry vigilantes) want to hear, either ideolog-
ically or, if they are fictions which 'reassure / Anxious butchers',
in terms of consolation. The latter is, implicitly, to say that poetry
matters on its own terms; it does something for people whether
they know it and hear it or not. It is not so much about being
read by either the solitary interpreter or 'the outside world', but,
in a more delicate balance, about writing 'for them, for you'.

Perhaps, in the end, 'Company' takes a bow to what it knows
could well be an empty auditorium. It is the risk all such affirma-
tions take, and it is the reason the poem takes nothing for granted,
either about its audience, its effect, or its own survival. It explores,
rather than assumes, the nature of its own reception. The second
half of the poem is tentative, intimate, even poignant in its evoca-
tion of a rather damp, difficult and remote existence. But at the
same time, the poem's 'distances' are also about closeness ('to
overhear / A quarrel or the sounds of love-making'); a more subtle

and fluid relation with the outside world is implied by the 'thatch letting in'; and the 'rain leaning against the half-door' once again places the poet both on the edge and in between, open to more than one possibility.

Finally, instead of hesitation on the verge of silence, 'escape' is suggested by the:

> ...journey to and from
> The well we have choked with alder branches
> For the cattle's safety, their hoofprints
> A thirsty circle in the puddles,
> Watermarks under all that we say.

If the well, sometimes 'choked', as in the 'almost total silence' earlier, is the source of poetry, it is also something to which he returns again and again. In that sense, it is protected not just for the 'cattle's safety' but, given the external pressures on the poet, for its own sake. The animal prints as 'Watermarks' suggest the almost invisible imprint on a page, an underlying validation of the worth of what he is doing and writing. But the image as permanent inscription carries a more tentative possibility within it, since a watermark also measures what has been and gone. In that sense, the poem affirms a poetic vision, but it does so without complacency, and without any too easy transcendence or consolation. The poetic vision is also a permanent quest, an expression of desire, its own kind of 'thirsty circle' in the continual (circular) 'journey to and from' the well of what we 'imagine'.

III

Behind 'Company', as also to some extent behind 'Man Lying on a Wall', is discernable the influence of Larkin's 'An Arundel Tomb', particularly in its ambiguous closing affirmation (or aspiration, or negation): 'to prove / Our almost-instinct almost true: / What will survive of us is love'. The poems share a concern with truth and lies, and with the erosion of self – in Larkin's phrase 'the endless altered people... / Washing at their identity'. They are preoccupied with permanence and impermanence, fixity and fluidity, with (post-'Ozymandias') anxieties about 'what will survive' even as they make their own inscriptions on history.

Those preoccupations help to explain the 'thirsty circles' in 'Company', and the 'straight line' of 'Man Lying on a Wall'; the motif is also humorously evoked in 'Ars Poetica', where the artist-adventurer will 'Walk the high wire' and 'draw a prefect circle free-hand'. These instances are only the tip of the iceberg.

In 'The Badger', from *An Exploded View*, the poet identified with 'the fox's zig-zags, / The arc of the hare'. *Man Lying on a Wall* draws innumerable lines and circles: the circling bat; the 'V on the lake' in 'The Swim'; the lines' that 'intersect' and the 'bad line' in 'Riddles; the 'magnetic lines' of 'Love Poem'; the 'compasses jamming' in 'Desert Warfare'; circling the burial mound in 'In Mayo'; the 'circles of blue sky' in 'Weather'; the 'loop around this bollard' and 'rigging / Slanted across the sky' in 'Ferry'; the bird's wrist 'encircled…With a long number' in 'The King of the Island'; the 'catherine-wheels' of 'Fleadh'; the 'ring / Around a fledgling's leg' in 'True Stories'; the 'circle of christian names' in 'Granny'. 'Points of the Compass' encompasses both motifs in complex ways throughout: 'The four points of the compass / Or a confluence of lines, / Crossroads and roundabout'.

Both motifs relate to the poet's concern with freedom and constraint. But they are not straightforward oppositions, since both can work both ways. The circles in 'Weather', where the buckets of spring water as 'circles of blue sky' reflect 'Two lakes', like the 'wings of a butterfly' which are 'Ink blots reflecting the mind' in 'Points of the Compass', are fluid and expansive images which reflect more than themselves. They are also associated with femininity. The phallic 'standing stone' between the ink blots in 'Points of the Compass' finds its echo in the poet figure who carries – and stands between – the 'Two circles of blue sky' in 'Weather'.

The poet's willingness to render himself fluid in 'Landscape', to 'disintegrate' and disperse his identity, collapses the 'standing stone' and associates him with a circular, feminine, potentially redemptive mode, as does the close of 'Company'. But circularity is also repetition, and when the motif that repeats itself is the 'circle of christian names' that eradicates his 'jewish granny' from history in 'Granny' it is an altogether more sinister phenomenon, a destructive and inescapable cycle.

As with 'The Bat', to break a violent or claustrophobic cycle requires a creative 'tangent' or 'swerve', what Robert Graves describes as the butterfly's (and poet's) capacity for 'Flying Crooked'. Longley's preoccupation with lines and circles, with angles, tangents, repetitions, and reflections in *Man Lying on a Wall* stitches the volume together and allows him to circle around his main themes from multiple perspectives.

The collection implicitly broods on the question of 'what will survive of us'; equally importantly, its concern is with how the

things that survive will do so. It reflects, in other words, on inher-
itance, memory and form; and it is not surprising that it does so
through linear and circular motifs. It is also the case that these
motifs are self-consciously inscribed in the poems, that lines are
being drawn and shapes defined with an almost clinical precision.

Given the intertextuality of the volume, it is almost, at times, as
if poems are inscribed within each other. 'Points of the Compass',
for instance, has a ripple effect in the volume, pointing outwards
to other poems, drawing them in. Its four sections shift perspec-
tive and, by implication, posit different poetic techniques: if the
'Clapper Bridge' is 'One way to proceed: / Taking the water step /
By step', this is rarely the linear trajectory the poet follows, being
more usually 'propped / At an angle', or concerned to make 'Room
enough under the floor'. The poem also travels full circle, from the
'stone inscribed with a cross' to the 'standing stone' at its close.
Inspired in part by the remnants of the ancient monastic settle-
ment at Cong, midway between Longley's own compass points of
Belfast and Carrigskeewaun, the poem reads 'traces upon stone',
uncovers the milestone 'To understand what it says', transforms
the lakes into 'Ink blots' and the 'standing stone' into a 'record' of
'distances'. The poem interprets what remains; it also adds its own
remains and inscribes its own details onto the scene.

Yet the poems in *Man Lying on a Wall* are also underpinned by
an awareness that the impression or mark they leave may only be
a transient one. That tension, between inscription's durability and
writing's fragility, is central to the movement of 'Landscape':

> For seconds, dawn or dusk,
> The sun's at an angle
> To read inscriptions by:
> The splay of the badger
> And the otter's skidmarks
>
> Melting into water...

This not only transforms the inscription into something imperma-
nent – footprints that will eventually disappear – it makes the
moment in which they can be interpreted transient too, an elusive
matter of light, angles and timing.

'Landscape' writes the poet into the landscape, merges him with
it; but it also writes him out of existence at the same time: he is
'Erased by sea mist' and the wind 'rips thought to tatters'. The
landscape is a 'place of dispersals', where nothing remains intact.
But it also bears inscriptions, footprints reminiscent of the 'thirsty
circles' of 'Company', as if they remain under what we say even

when they can't be seen, as if the memory of absence negates absence. (Footprints are images that make their way through Longley's poetry for decades, their appeal precisely this fusion of presence/ absence, permanence/impermanence.) *Man Lying on a Wall* is full of such 'inscriptions': the initials on the briefcase and the bullet; the number tags on the birds; even, more obliquely, the flower bookmark's 'Anther staining / These pictures' in 'Flora', where the staining is also a healing and a fertilisation. The markings here – textual or otherwise – relate back to the poet's preoccupation with the body as a site to be read, fingered, and interpreted, as in 'Check-up' or 'Riddles'. They are also to do with history as inscription, with the textuality of history.

The earlier 'Kindertotenlieder' projected memory in physical terms as 'fingerprints / Everywhere, teethmarks on this and that', its inscriptions an absent presence. In *Man Lying on a Wall*, there is a dual concern with reading the body, with interpreting visible traces, and with writing it, giving it skin and bones, leaving those traces oneself. In that sense, from incision to inscription isn't as far to travel semantically as it might seem. The poet's dismantling, his probing beneath the skin, runs alongside the urge to uncover – and recover – lost areas of history and consciousness. There is, of course, a significant difference: to make incisions is seemingly a destructive act, which produces divisions by cutting things open; to write, or read, inscriptions is a preservative and potentially healing act. Thus, while 'The Goose' dismantles its subject 'limb by limb', poems such as 'Granny' or 'Edward Thomas's War Diary' reconstruct what history has missed or forgotten: 'I shall give skin and bones / To my jewish granny'. But they can also feel like two sides to the same coin, different versions of an emotional and/or historical scarification which makes its incisions in order to preserve.

The poems with a more obvious historical resonance – including 'Edward Thomas's War Diary', 'Mole', 'Granny' and 'Master of Ceremonies' – thus provide a form of reconstruction as both counter to, and complement of, the dissections and repressions elsewhere in the collection. The question they implicitly have in common with each other, and with the collection as a whole, is the one asked in 'Mole': 'Who bothers to record...?'; and it is the companion question to Larkin's 'what will survive of us'.

In 'Mole' the poem is a question in response to the question asked in Edward Thomas's diary in 1917 'Does a mole ever get hit by a shell?'; it is also the answer, not only to Thomas, but to the question it asks itself:

Who bothers to record
This body digested
By its own saliva
Inside the earth's mouth
And long intestine,

Or thanks it for digging
Its own grave, darkness
Growing like an eyelid
Over the eyes, hands
Swimming in the soil?

The anthropomorphism of the poem, and its transformation of the earth into a digestive system, implicitly revisits the fear evident elsewhere in the volume of how we 'devour each other emotionally', or, indeed, of devouring oneself. Here, that anxiety is rendered literal in the context of historical crisis.

The poem is an elegy for the dead of the First World War (including Edward Thomas himself); for those whose bodies were lost in the earth and never recovered; for those soldiers who were buried alive by shells; and more generally, for those forgotten by history, lost over time. Because the poem 'bothers to record' it negates its own premise, retrieving for posterity not just the forgotten victim, but also the diary extract that inspired the poem. Yet since it remains in the form of a question, it never quite claims to do this, leaving the 'record' as an elusive one.

'Edward Thomas's War Diary' is also inspired by the textual remains of Thomas's life in the trenches. His war diary, undiscovered for several decades, and first published in 1971, covers only a brief period, from January to April 1917. Lacking the self-conscious public overtones of many war diaries from the period, Thomas's is a private, intimate record of the detail of his everyday life and surroundings. It reads partly as if he were making notes for poems. 'Edward Thomas's War Diary' thus brings to completion the task Thomas barely had time to begin – to write the war into his poetry. In a way, Longley constructs a whole poem from what remains. It consists almost entirely of quotation adapted and rearranged into narrative shape; it is both a "found" poem, and a created one.[23]

That Edward Thomas makes his appearance in a collection which is avowedly personal also writes him into a familial narrative. (As with Robert Graves's Sergeant Lamb, one senses an extra place has been laid at table for him.) The boundaries between literary, historical or personal "inheritance" tend to collapse. Thomas's diary thus has links with the inheritance from the poet's 'jewish granny':

Who has come down to me
In the copperplate writing

Of three certificates,
A dogeared daguerrotype....

Both take us back to 'Company', where the poet broods on what will remain of his own lifetime – 'Photographs...the only surviving copies / Of the books...'.

'Granny' draws on fragments, brief inscriptions, to retrieve Jessica's 'skin and bones' for a history which is both personal and much more than personal. Her 'mislaid whereabouts' in family history is more broadly evocative of those lost, and for whom few traces remain, in the 'terrible century' of Jewish persecution that followed her death. Where history has become 'A circle of christian names', the poem writes the missing back into the script. 'Granny', rewritten to become part I of the later 'No Man's Land' may be more effective in its revised form; but it also belongs here, in as much as it reaches out from the privacies of *Man Lying on a Wall* to the major historical traumas of the 20th century, and in doing so makes it evident that "privacy", like intimacy, can be a deceptive term.

Throughout this discussion of *Man Lying on a Wall*, I have been concerned to stress the poet's deliberate self-consciousness about his art; the way in which the poetry works through, rather than in spite of, its 'privacies'; and to explore the space between writing and reality. Working out that relationship, which is also a negotiation between the imagination and history, is central to the collection. *Man Lying on a Wall* balances 'Who bothers to record' with the knowledge that such records themselves may not survive. The struggle to get things 'down in words' is always at the same time an implicit acknowledgement of what has been lost. But what this collection does affirm is the need to keep trying.

4

'The last time in reverse':
The Echo Gate and *New Poems*
1976-1983

Then cover the wound with cuckoo-sorrel
Or sphagnum moss, bring together verse
And herb, plant and prayer to stop the bleeding.
                                        MICHAEL LONGLEY, 1977

I

In the previous chapters, I have considered ways in which *An Exploded View* might be read as adopting, at times, a deliberately "public" voice, *Man Lying on a Wall* as a retreat into a more domestic, vulnerable space. In neither case, of course, is this the whole story; each collection also questions the ways in which we understand terms such as "public", "private", "domestic" and "historical". But in so far as *An Exploded View* and *Man Lying on a Wall* place the emphasis differently, it is possible to see the 1979 *The Echo Gate* as finding its own balance somewhere between the different strategies of the earlier volumes.

It is also partly for this reason that it is tempting – and in many ways justifiable – to claim *The Echo Gate* as by far the most consistently accomplished (as also the most moving) of Longley's first four books. In *The Echo Gate* the elegiac mode seen at work in *An Exploded View* becomes central to Longley's aesthetic, a mode, as suggested earlier, in which the poet may perhaps be more than usually tested in relation to "public" responsibility. The 'privacies' of this book never run the risk of solipsism or evasion; rather, *The Echo Gate*'s intimacies and introspections always expand the reader's sense of self and history.

The Echo Gate reaches a new level of poetic confidence, both formally and thematically. That confidence should not be confused with complacence; nor is this book the apotheosis of Longley's achievement. But it does suggest that his previous work may be seen in terms of a pattern of growth, and that *The Echo Gate* reaps the rewards of earlier experiments, detours and reflections on the art of poetry.

In *The Echo Gate* there are no such abstract musings on the relationship between poet and society as are seen in 'Letter to Seamus Heaney'; nor is he overtly worrying in the poems about the status of that 'half-door'. What we do see is the poet working in and at, rather than theorising about, such relationships, and mining a rich poetic seam somewhere along that symbolic "edge". Longley is still by no means assured as to whether poetry makes anything 'happen': that uncertainty, or tentativeness, is, and remains, a measure of poetic integrity. But there is none of the insecurity here that earlier pushed him either into uneasy group identification, or into a more inward, self-rebuking form of anxiety. *The Echo Gate* unerringly homes in on, and develops, the obvious strengths of his own *oeuvre* as these have emerged over the preceding ten years. Or, put another way, more cerebral explorations of how one loses one's way to find it, or speaks both for and to self and others, are less directly subject than they are subtext to an overall vision the explorations themselves have helped to make possible.

In a 1979 BBC Radio Ulster review, Anthony Thwaite, arguing that *The Echo Gate* was, at that point, 'much his [Longley's] strongest book', drew attention to its effective dramatisations, to its directness (as against what he saw as the excessive decorum of Longley's very early work), to a new kind of 'self-knowledge and asperity and wit', and to its developments in style and subject-matter. Most importantly, he notes at the outset that Longley is best understood in *The Echo Gate* not as a 'recorder', but as a 'reconstructer'. He goes on to argue that Longley is both 'reconstructing something solid' and at the same time allowing a freer flow of feeling, a rapidity of communication.[1]

Thwaite is astute here, identifying a subtle strand of Longley's work that preoccupies the poet through the 1990s as well. The argument can, however, also be taken further. As has been seen in relation to *Man Lying on a Wall*, the process of recording for Longley mutates into a process of "reconstruction"; the act of interpretation is also one of retrieval. That is to say, Longley can be understood as both 'recorder' and 'reconstructor' simultaneously. But the process of reconstructing is more ambiguous than this as well. In Longley's work, reconstruction is also deconstruction: remembering is also a form of dismembering; as history is recovered, it also needs to be forgotten – at least in its reductive forms. For Longley, as for Northern Irish society more generally, history as the remembered past is also implicated in the difficult question of how – and whether – to forget and forgive, the relationship between, as Longley terms it, 'amnesty' and 'amnesia' a complicated one.[2]

First and foremost, *The Echo Gate* picks up on and develops the reconstructive work already inherent in poems such as 'Edward Thomas's War Diary' or 'Granny'. Its title-poem puts that enterprise at the heart of the volume, and indicates something of the tension and slippage between recording and reconstructing (as also between healing and dissecting) that preoccupied the poet in *Man Lying on a Wall*:

> I stand between the pillars of the gate,
> A skull between two ears that reconstructs
> Broken voices, broken stones, history
>
> And the first words that come into my head
> Echoing back from the monastery wall
> To measure these fields at the speed of sound.

Unusually explicit for Longley in centring the 'I' voice in this way, this is still at several removes from, say, Muldoon's claim a few years earlier to 'tell new weather', partly because having begun with self-assertion, it also turns the poet into the seemingly passive receptacle who 'stand[s] between'. But to reconstruct is also to create something anew, and the passivity here is implicitly proactive: by implication, deconstruction underpins and precedes what is happening here; seamless narratives of history are fragmented before they are re-imagined.

One of the last poems in the collection to be written, in July 1978, 'The Echo Gate' can in some ways be read as a retrospective summary of what the poet has been about for the last three years. The poem encapsulates in miniature the themes, ambitions, even the poetic structures at work elsewhere in the book. In a collection haunted by fragments, echoes, and traces, the imaginative work of reconstruction claimed here gives some indication of the poet's compulsion to mend what has been broken, to recreate what has been lost. At the same time, his own art, particularly as elegist, is an 'art of losing' that tries to break the violent cycles consequent upon politicised forms of remembering: there are memory vigilantes at work in Northern Irish society too, where the past is perhaps more than usually trawled for political vindication.

'The Echo Gate' thus gives some insight into Longley's historical imagination. The poem's capacity to balance both 'history // And the first words that come into my head' locates it in past, present, and future simultaneously, its fluidities at odds with more entrenched positions. This is both an echo from a past event, but also a future projection from the moment a voice is sounded. And the present moment is a moment cleared between stanzas, a potentially redemptive space created both for the poet, and for the reconstructive act. Where the echoes 'measure these fields at the speed of sound', there is an imaginatively fluid time travel going on; but there is also a sense that poetry is about who and where we are, that it takes the measure of its own time and place.

'The Echo Gate' works with a tripartite structure – its two stanzas and the space between – that mirrors its objects: the poet between the two pillars of the gate; the 'skull between two ears'. It blends, almost imperceptibly, external circumstances and internal thought processes, as one becomes a reflection of the other. In the way the sentence echoes back on itself, the poem becomes the whole object made up of its fragments of 'Broken voices, broken stones'.

Such fragments pervade the collection. '[B]roken voices' and 'broken stones' reappear in 'On Hearing Irish Spoken' to become the 'stepping stones' of broken comprehension: 'An echo of technical terms, the one I know / Repeating itself at desperate intervals…across a river in spate.' The echo is picked up on in the movement of objects 'ferried' to and fro by the 'Spring Tide'. It is possible, also, to understand the recurrence of poems which in fact consist of several short, individually titled poems – 'Architecture', 'Entomology', 'Lore', 'Botany' – in this context too, all of which build their complete structure from identifiably smaller parts. But as with the earlier 'Edward Thomas's War Diary' and 'Granny', poems which point forward to *The Echo Gate*, the poet's more evident concern is to read fragments of the past, to try to understand and, if possible, heal, a broken inheritance. In the context of Northern Ireland in the 1970s, there are obvious socio-political implications to such a concern, although it is never reducible only to this.

The fragments of this book tend to be remains: the saint's 'bits and pieces' in 'Obsequies'; Oliver Plunkett's mummified head and his body 'divided into four'; Christ's teeth, and his father's 'false teeth…outside of his body', along with the 'spectacles, / Wallets, small change' of 'Wreaths'; the 'pocket watch and cigarette case' ('all he could salvage') in 'Last Rites'; the 'earthly remains, ghosts of skulls' in 'The Barber's Wife'. That these objects are, metaphorically or otherwise, relics is also worthy of note, since the ambiguous religiosity of *The Echo Gate* is, as will be seen, embedded in its recurrent tripartite structures.

More subtly, the fragmentation of *The Echo Gate* is also bound up with a fractured, or fragmented selfhood. As Peter McDonald has observed, 'There is nothing uniquely "shaky" about Longley's "identity"; instead, Longley is aware of how shaky a concept "identity" is in poetry.'[3] The barber's wife 'repeats herself / In one mirror after another', and the poet exists 'In the harem of her reflections'. In 'Self-Portrait', the speaker's 'eyes...reflect a foreign sky'. In 'Entomology', the dragonfly's eye is 'Like a stained glass window diminished / To a prism...'. The leaves in 'Botany' are 'Afloat on their own reflection'. Oliver Plunkett 'seems to be / Refracting the gleam in his father's eye / Like a shattered mirror in a handbag'.

Partly what we are seeing here is the idea of variant selves explored in earlier poems obliquely refracted through the imagery of *The Echo Gate*, imagery which renders the "placing" of self a complicated business – indeed, destabilises the notion of a centred subject altogether. As in the title-poem, the poet may be a repository for voices, objects, relics; but he is also the point of origin who reflects those voices back to the world. In 'The Echo Gate', the self along with history is remade as the 'skull between two ears...reconstructs'; but that self is unmade too, as if it repeats in one mirror after another shifting patterns 'at the speed of sound'.

In *The Echo Gate*, it is sometimes difficult to tell what is real or illusory, what is a reflection or what is the thing itself – and this, of course, is part of the point. 'Oliver Plunkett' is exemplary in this context:

> Your own face is reflected by the casket
> And this is anybody's head in a room
> Except that the walls are all windows and
> He has written his name over the glass.

This can seem straightforward, but there are shifting sands here: whose face is reflected? which head 'is anybody's head'? Plunkett's mummified head in a glass case slides into the face reflected in the glass, and both into the conceit of the space in one's head as itself 'a room', and so on. The relic becomes fluid, a motif repeating further and further from, or back to, its "origin".

It is also impossible to pin down the poet's "identity" in space and time: the 'simple question' in 'Alibis' is by this stage an intricate patterning across Longley's *oeuvre*. That the site for remembering and dismembering is the self is important: the poet is not a preacher on the subject of a history which does not directly implicate him; rather, to question assumptions about identity, language, and perspective is also to question assumptions about history. The echo of the title-poem runs between past, present and future; the mirror imagery of *The Echo Gate* is also a three-way echo – self, mirror, reflection – which centres none of the three, or at least never stabilises a centre. *The Echo Gate* is full of double-takes, poems that occupy more than one time and space, manipulate different angles of perception. In 'Dead Men's Fingers', 'The first time we meet is really the last time in reverse'; in Second Sight 'Flanders began at the kitchen window...gas...blew the wrong way from the salient'; 'The War Poets' travel back in time when 'shrapnel opened up again the fontanel'; there are frequent comings and goings into past and future; death intrudes upon life; seemingly rigid categories are rendered fluid and shifting.

Throughout the collection Longley manipulates perception, through middle distance rifle sights, through a lens inverting his surroundings. The poet works with mirror images, the shock-waves, or echo of the title-poem fed through the collection as a whole. Muldoon, echoing central concerns of *The Echo Gate* (a collection dedicated to him, and influential in his development), talks of writing about 'what is immediately in front of me, or immediately over my shoulder'.[4] But what one looks for, Longley implies in the title-poem, is a way of doing both simultaneously, and the way to do it, as Robert Graves once explained, is with mirrors: an 'intricate pattern' made by 'interlinked images of several round mirrors set at different angles to one another' is, Graves argues, a 'close enough metaphor for poetry'.

That also partly explains why intricate patterning across a collection is characteristic of Longley, as also later of Muldoon: it is, Graves stresses, 'the angle at which the mirrors are set that determines the final result'.[5] While such patterning – and the belief that a poetry collection should work as a book in its own right – has always been present in Longley's work, it is in *The Echo Gate* that the ambition realises itself fully.

II

The manipulations of time and space which are the subject of 'The Echo Gate' may be read, therefore, as an intricate pattern repeated across other poems: 'Ash Keys', 'Frozen Rain', 'Thaw', 'Spring Tide' and 'Bog Cotton' among them. 'Ash Keys' is in some ways the companion poem to 'The Echo Gate' (in the original collection, they are on facing pages). Its six stanzas, made up of three sentences, or three "movements", vary perspectives between past, present and future. Its speaker is himself an echo from, or back to, different time frames. Engaged in 'conversations' in 'a field / That touches the horizon' in the first two stanzas, by the final stanzas that perspective has been reversed: 'Far from the perimeter...In the middle of the field / I stand talking to myself'. It begins with boundaries in place, surrounded by 'Ghosts of hedgers and ditchers, / The ash trees rattling keys'; by its close these have given way: 'the ash keys scatter / And the gates creak open'.

Or, put another way, this poem may be read as both drawing everything inwards, and scattering everything outwards; it retrieves a past and dissipates it. It is about the recovery of 'long perspectives' (which look forwards to renewal as well as backwards to what has gone) and about decline. The 'talking to myself' is thus also a conversation with history, as the speaker imaginatively repeats through time:

> I am herding cattle there
> As a boy, as the old man
> Following in his footsteps
> Who begins the task again
>
> As though there'd never been
> In some interim or hollow
> Wives and children...

While the poem is about ageing and the passing of time, it is also about circularity and a return to origins, where past and future collapse into each other: 'the barbed wire rusts / To hay-ropes strung with thorns.' As with Edward Thomas's 'Old Man or lad's love', the 'boy' or 'old man' who 'begins the task again' finds his parallel in the cycles of the natural world: the autumnal scattering of the ash keys also contains within it the promise of spring's germination. But 'Ash Keys' too is a poem whose promise of renewal is never without its imaginative understanding of decline. Like Thomas's 'Old Man', 'Ash Keys' is concerned with the workings of memory, with both preservation and loss. When the 'gates creak open' at the close of the poem, we are in an imaginative territory that by now is familiar to Longley's readers, one which is not impervious to what lies outside it, which crosses and eliminates borders and boundaries, and which can encompass two worlds in one.

Partly this is to suggest that the poem subtly plays with its own reflections and repetitions. Here, as in 'The Echo Gate', syntax complicates sequence; the shifting position of the subject in each sentence echoes the speaker's shifts in time. Such complexities can also manifest themselves in miniature. The short poem 'Thaw' is a forerunner for the increasing number of densely layered short poems in Longley's later work. (It is the only poem in *The Echo Gate* – indeed, the only one in the first four books – that consists of a single quatrain; in contrast, there are ten such poems in *Gorse Fires* alone.) It also echoes, with a precision and tautness of imagery, the three-part structure of 'Ash Keys' or 'Spring Tide':

> Snow curls into the coalhouse, flecks the coal.
> We burn the snow as well in bad weather
> As though to spring-clean that darkening hole.
> The snow's a blackbird with one white feather.

In its final line, the poem realises the capacity to transform. Not merely an imagistic parallel, the shift from the opening to the closing line is also, by implication, a shift from winter to spring. But it runs a counter movement too, in the (ambiguous) 'darkening hole'. It is relatively unusual for a quatrain in having this kind of three-sentence structure, which, although it does not state a connective argument, implies a forward movement; at the same time, the rhyming cuts across the syntax to give a different effect of cyclical return. Its own 'thaw' comes partly, too, in the way it shifts between masculine and feminine rhyme to give a lightness of touch, almost a fragility, to the 'one white feather'.

Longley's concern, here and elsewhere, is with mutability and transience, an imaginative preoccupation with things that come and go (and come again), akin, in its way, to Yeats's 'Man is in love and loves what vanishes' in 'Nineteen Hundred and Nineteen'. The images of ice, water, and snow, prevalent in this book and culminating in his most recent collection *Snow Water*, like his footprints in sand, encapsulate precisely the ground traversed between fixity and fluidity, transformation and permanence, disappearance and survival. The natural world, with its continuities and its transformations, is thus a world of possibility and of poignancy, its cycles those of loss as well as gain. It is also, therefore, a world implicated in an understanding of self and society, not an inviolate realm beyond them.

As Neil Corcoran notes in relation to 'Spring Tide', 'a lyric subjectivity discovers itself only in the act of witnessing or recording its own vanishing'.[6] The poem's retrievals and vanishings also relate to the workings of history and memory. The tide, from one perspective, 'behaves like a preservative / And erases neither the cattle's / And the sheep's nor my own footprints'; but of course it does do so, and those 'hieroglyphics under glass…feathers that hardly budge' mutate into the 'Wet flowers' ferried by the tide, 'the zigzags I make', and the ambiguous and erotic loss of self in the 'Marsh helleborine waiting for me / To come and go with the spring tide'. The tide cleans and 'excavates…scapulae, tibias, / Loose teeth, cowrie…', the debris of history, objects reminiscent of the relics, or 'Broken voices' of other poems. In doing so, it places everything in flux, shifts the ground under our feet. Even the burial mound 'isn't really a burial mound / Reflected there, but all that remains / Of a sandy meadow, a graveyard'. It is a 'reflection' in more than one sense, since it is at one remove, a memorial for a memorial that was there once, and which is itself gradually being eroded by the tide. (The burial mound at Carrigskeewaun increases in symbolic significance in Longley's poetry as it also decreases in its physical form; its presence, in his most recent poems, depends, paradoxically, on its absence.) In 'Spring Tide', past, present and future revolve with the tide. The poem allows no single point of rest, its movement to and fro akin to the echoes and reflections elsewhere in *The Echo Gate*.

The play between absence and presence, preservation and erosion, connects these poems about the natural world to Longley's elegies and love poems; they share, also, the tentative wish that the 'art of losing' could become an art of healing. By implication, to re-construct is – or at least could be – also to heal: these poems seek, metaphorically, a 'thaw', a palliative for what Wallace Stevens terms 'a mind of winter'. Longley himself has quoted Don Shriver's suggestion that 'The cure and the remembrance are co-terminous',[7] linking the recovery of what has been forgotten or repressed with the process of healing. But healing through remembering is a complex, sometimes contradictory (in as much as it is also a healing through forgetting), and still controversial cultural project, particularly in Northern Ireland, one which Longley approaches with subtlety and caution.

The healing possibilities are present in the potentially redemptive 'thaw' as a 'blackbird', in burning the snow 'as though to spring-clean', or in the spring tide's 'cupfuls' poured 'into the lark's nests'. But that the nature poem can "heal" any more than the elegy can "console" is never something to be taken for granted. These are not poems that set out to affirm nature's capacity to heal; they are poems suggestive of the desire that it might be able to do so.

The possibilities implied by 'Thaw' and 'Spring Tide' are more directly the subject of 'Frozen Rain', a poem which, like 'The Echo Gate', gives some insight into what Longley sees as the role of the poet:

> I slow down the waterfall to a chandelier,
> Filaments of daylight, bones fleshed out by ice
> That recuperate in their bandages of glass
> And, where the lake behaves like a spirit-level,
> I save pockets of air for the otter to breathe.

Its first stanza here seems to make explicit a healing or restorative agenda, reminiscent of the earlier desire to give 'skin and bones' to his 'jewish granny'. It links preservation, holding a moment of stillness against the flow of time, with recuperation, as if in preparation for the thaw. But 'Frozen Rain' is also a poem aware of the contradictory pull between fixity and fluidity (even its title is an aporia), both of which can carry positive and negative connotations. The waterfall encompasses this duality – always moving, but always staying in the same place – even before it is slowed to a halt. Flesh as ice; bandages as glass: these contradictory images suggest atrophy and stasis, but also the fragility of the enterprise – bodies are things which can be broken.

'Frozen Rain', unusually for Longley, makes particular claims for what the poet is doing: 'I slow down...'; 'I save pockets of air...'; 'I magnify each individual blade of grass'. In a way, the poem shows the inside workings of an imagination that will make room, make time, and bring detail into focus. The enterprise is tentative in expression, but its implications are far-reaching. Finding space, time and perspective in a climate where they too readily disappear can be, in and of itself, a revolutionary undertaking.

Without wanting to over-interpret Longley's 'botanical explorations' in a Troubles context, it is still the case that their implications in this context have, as a rule, been under-interpreted: there is more at issue here than a celebration of the natural world. Neil Corcoran has rightly noted in relation to 'Finding a Remedy', from the sequence 'Lore', that while the poem is 'reticent about the actual source of the bleeding...in a poem from Northern Ireland in the 1970s, there is a political subtext'.[8] Similarly, a poem such as 'Self-heal', from the 'Mayo Monologues' sequence (like Muldoon's 'Anseo' later), carries implications for understanding a violent society. In 'Self-heal', brutality breeds brutality; mutilation begins to turn inwards on itself:

> I heard how every day for one whole week
> He was flogged with a blackthorn, then tethered
> In the hayfield. I might have been the cow
> Whose tail he would later dock with shears,
> And he the ram tangled in barbed wire
> That he stoned to death when they set him free.

The poem is about loss of innocence for both its protagonists – not so much in terms of a fall into sexual awareness, as in the discovery of violence and betrayal. Self-healing does not happen; Eden is not recoverable. The young woman who 'wanted to teach him the names of flowers' fails to do so: 'Each name would hover above its flower / Like a butterfly unable to alight'. This is the desire to return language to an illusory "unfallen" state, but with the knowledge that such a state does not exist: the disjunction between word and thing can never be healed; what is broken in this poem cannot be mended. It is, in that sense, a strictly anti-pastoral poem, which, not least through its portrait of the adult-child, violates expectations about childhood, language, innocence and the restorative qualities of the pastoral world.

As with 'Ash Keys', it is possible to detect Edward Thomas's presence behind the poem, whose reflections on memory, identity and language are brought into focus by the trauma of the First World War, as are Longley's by the Troubles. (Thomas's 'Old Man', where 'the names / Half decorate, half perplex, the thing it is', and which is preoccupied with the loss of childhood, is one precedent for 'Self-heal'.)

For Corcoran, botanical explorations in Longley can be a means of 'addressing' (although he notes this is 'altogether too emphatic a word') the Troubles. In the case of 'Finding a Remedy', it is done, he suggests, with a 'scrupulous hesitation…continuous with Longley's stated unease in *Tuppenny Stung*: "I find offensive the notion that what we inadequately call 'the Troubles' might provide inspiration for artists; and that in some weird *quid pro quo* the arts might provide solace for grief and anguish".'[9] It is notable, too, that 'Finding a Remedy', in its 'bringing together verse / And herb, plant and prayer to stop the bleeding', treats the wounds but does not presume to propose a 'remedy' for their occurrence: 'healing' is always an ambiguous art.

If, as Corcoran suggests, 'Finding a Remedy' has a political subtext, it may be inferred partly from the resonance the idea of wounding has in Longley's poetry as a whole, where it is to be understood emotionally and historically as well as literally. The poem is also one of a sequence of folklore sound-bites, insights into the myths and rituals by which a society once functioned and through which it tried to heal itself – a process not without relevance to contemporary society.

All these poems are, in different ways, haunted by preoccupations that emerge in one of the first poems in *The Echo Gate* to be written, 'Bog Cotton'.[10] Its different historical and geographical perspectives illuminate the poet's home ground; its structure epitomises the concern to 'make room'; its careful placing of the poet's enterprise in a tradition of First and Second World War writing –and the equally careful ways in which the poem is distinguished from that tradition – are key to understanding Longley's elegiac and pastoral modes. Like 'Spring Tide', 'Thaw', 'Ash Keys' and other poems, 'Bog Cotton' effectively works in three parts (which are also here three sentences). The first transforms bog cotton into a 'desert flower', its existence in the stony ground of the west of Ireland taking the poet back to the desert warfare of the 1940s:

Let me make room for bog cotton, a desert flower –
Keith Douglas, I nearly repeat what you were saying
When you apostrophised the poppies of Flanders...

The poem rewrites Keith Douglas's 1943 'Desert Flowers', itself a response to Isaac Rosenberg's 1917 'Break of Day in the Trenches'. In 'Desert Flowers', Douglas effectively acknowledges the 'tautological' nature of the war poet's role with his opening: 'Living in a wide landscape are the flowers – / Rosenberg I only repeat what you were saying – '. In Douglas's poem the 'body can fill / the hungry flowers', as in Rosenberg's 'Break of Day in the Trenches', with its 'poppies whose roots are in man's veins'; Rosenberg's rat has its echo in Douglas's jerboa, and so on. As Douglas writes of his own opening stanzas, 'that is not new' (although it should be said that his recognition of this is one of the reasons 'Desert Flowers' does 'make it new').

Longley both evokes this tradition and differentiates himself from it – and in two ways. First, by 'nearly' rather than 'only' repeating his predecessors, he denies for himself the experiential war poet status of Rosenberg and Douglas (both killed in action), and disallows any straightforward comparison between the world wars and the conflicts of his own ground. Inspired by a poetic tradition that runs from Owen, Rosenberg and Thomas through to Douglas, this is no assured claim on the part of the poet to a place in it, although his readers are more than likely to grant it to him. Second, although the claim to continuity lies in the evocation of the flower, Longley's bog cotton differs from the blood-red symbolic poppy of the Great War battlefields:

(It hangs on by a thread, denser than thistledown,
Reluctant to fly, a weather vane that traces
The flow of cloud shadow over monotonous bog –
And useless too, though it might well bring to mind
The plumpness of pillows, the staunching of wounds,

Rags torn from a petticoat and soaked in water
And tied to the bushes around some holy well
As though to make a hospital of the landscape –
Cures and medicines as far as the horizon
Which nobody harvests except with the eye.)

As Paul Fussell notes, red flowers are traditionally found in pastoral elegy, one reason why they became 'fixtures of experience' in the Great War.[11] Rather than symbolising death, or "feeding" on the corpses of the battlefield, Longley's white flower is associated with healing, innocence, beauty, femininity (in the 'Rags torn from a petticoat') and, despite its fragility, a certain tenacity for life. But it is also 'useless'. Even if it 'bring[s] to mind' comfort and healing, 'As though' to offer a cure, it cannot itself actually do any of these things. In that sense, this poem also relates to Longley's own recognition of what poetry (in its own way, 'useless') can and cannot do.

Yet 'Bog Cotton' is a poem whose structure is suggestive of a message at odds with its content. The middle section of the poem pushes outwards to create, in parentheses, a space which in itself may be seen as curative. In a symbolic gesture, it 'make[s] room' for what 'hangs on by a thread'. It deliberately protects what is fragile and – from some perspectives – 'useless', not least because the poem understands the importance of trying what may seem useless: the gesture, say, of Rosenberg's poppy 'safe' behind his ear.

As with Longley's other elegies (and this is, obliquely, also an elegy for its solder-poet subjects) it creates space – even if only space to mourn. Doubly scrupulous, 'the staunching of wounds', the 'landscape' as a 'hospital', are an almost parenthetical aside within the parentheses themselves, an illusion becoming grammatically more and more elusive. But this imagery is also at the centre of the poem; and to 'harvest with the eye' is, by implication, a more significant action in the context of this poem than bog cotton's failure to yield practical help might suggest.

'Bog Cotton' harvests history with the eye, with its perspectives on past and present. The poem brings the flower into detailed focus at its centre; in its final stanza it too sees 'beyond' the Second World War to the First; from the 'hundreds of thousands of poppy petals' it sees the 'blood stains' in the 'middle distance' and the 'one' poppy worn by Rosenberg. Where Keith Douglas, both killer and elegist, views his victim/subject through a 'dial of glass' in 'How to Kill', in 'Bog Cotton', Douglas's poems become the lens, the rifle sights, which can bring earlier wars – and the poet's own present – into and out of focus. Its perspectives on space – magnification, the middle distance, or the far horizon – are also perspectives on time, from Ireland in the 1970s to the Second World War in the Middle East to the 1914-18 Western Front.

Longley's "nature" poems in *The Echo Gate* have implications for understanding the more obviously political, or "public" poems in the book, because they are bound up with an understanding of the past, and with the ways in which identity is made and unmade. While this is at its most explicit in 'Bog Cotton', which places itself in a tradition of pastoral war writing, all these poems, though their concern is with the natural world, are implicated in the processes of history and memory as well. Like the objects ferried by the spring tide, the poems also 'come and go' between each other, part of the broader pattern of the book. Longley's "project" in *The Echo Gate* is, in the broadest sense of the word, a political one; his "pastoral" is always implicated in his understanding of his home of Belfast. To define that project in its simplest terms, his poetry reminds us that it is possible to look at the world from different, sometimes forgotten angles, to alter perspective, to make room for the unexpected and the extraordinary.

III

The tripartite structure of 'The Echo Gate' is oblique, since one of the ways it manifests itself is by utilising the space between stanzas; but it is echoed in many other poems. 'Oliver Plunkett', 'Wreaths', 'Spring Tide' and 'On Mweelrea' most obviously are triptych poems, structured in three interlinked parts (in the case of 'Oliver Plunkett', these are Soul, Head and Body). That structure is also, as has been seen, the more shadowy underpinning of 'Ash Keys', 'Bog Cotton' and 'Thaw'; and it is implied in the placing side by side of the three sonnets about Sulpicia, Grace Darling and Florence Nightingale. But given Longley's fascination with the Great War, and the debt owed by his elegies to the Great War protest elegy, there may be a more particular precedent for his tripartite vision.

As Paul Fussell has noted, 'Threes' are central to understanding the way in which First World War writing incorporates the structures of myth, ritual and romance. Longley's fascination with the Great War in *The Echo Gate* places him in a tradition of 20th-century war writing; one of the things he has absorbed from that tradition is the principle of threes that Fussell's work uncovers. The 'tripartite vision' is, Fussell notes, one whose origins are lost in antiquity, but its reverberations are many: it is the Pythagorean 'perfect number, implying beginning, middle and end'; it refers to the stages of human life (youth, maturity, age), as well as to mythical narratives of birth–death–resurrection, death–disappearance–revival or innocence–death–rebirth. He identifies other echoes of the principle: the three Christian virtues (Faith, Hope and Charity) and enemies

(World, Flesh and Devil); the three Furies; the three Graces; the three Harpies; and the Triple Goddess revered by Robert Graves. It is in this context that Fussell makes the important argument that the 'movement' of Great War literature was 'towards myth, towards a revival of the cultic, the mystical, the sacrificial, the prophetic, the sacramental, and the universally significant. In short, towards fiction.'[12]

The Echo Gate's 'Threes' are informed, consciously or otherwise, by the broader symbolic resonance of a tripartite vision. In 'The Echo Gate', the pattern of echo-self-echo paralleling past-present-future is a pattern repeated in 'Ash Keys' or 'Bog Cotton'; 'Oliver Plunkett''s Soul, Head and Body parts are evocative of the Trinity (father, son, spirit), a motif also present in 'Wreaths'. Partly this is to suggest that Longley's Troubles elegies, along with his First World War poems, owe a particular debt to the Great War elegists themselves, who abandoned belief in the (state endorsed) structures of Christian consolation as they simultaneously proposed mythic paradigms by which their experience could be rendered in language. The distinction is an important one for understanding the sacramental and mythic aspects of Longley's work. Religiosity is a vital element in Longley's imagination; at the same time, *The Echo Gate* is a collection which questions some assumptions about conventional religion as it is practised, and abused, in contemporary society.

'Wreaths' is a sequence of elegies for the Catholic greengrocer, James Gibson, murdered in his shop in south Belfast in December 1973, the civil servant Martin McBirney, shot at his home in September 1974, and for the ten protestant workers machine-gunned at Kingsmill in January 1976.[13]

The sequence is a triptych which also evokes 'Threes' in more elusive ways. In 'The Greengrocer', the 'three wise men' should buy three gifts 'at Jim Gibson's shop, / Dates and chestnuts and tangerines'; 'The Linen Workers' evokes father, son, and, by implication, spirit, and picks up on the Christmas killing in 'The Greengrocer' in its eucharistic imagery suggestive of the cycles of birth, death and resurrection. More obliquely, this is a poem in which Longley resurrects his own father in order to bury him 'once again' – and for the third time. The process begun in 'In Memoriam' and 'Wounds' becomes an imaginative cycle. At the same time, the poem is deeply ambiguous about the concept of a Christian resurrection: in 'The Linen Workers', Christ is 'fastened for ever / By his exposed canines to a wintry sky', in a failed – or at least only partial – ascension that is also a kind of permanent crucifixion. That the 'three wise men' in 'The Greengrocer' 'may shortly be setting out / For a small house up the Shankill / Or the

Falls' might suggest that a First Coming hasn't happened yet, as much as it projects forward to a Second one.

Throughout 'Wreaths' there is a tension between cycles of repetition as redemptive or destructive. His title suggests funeral wreaths: Longley has observed of his own elegies, written out of 'bewilderment and despair', that they are offered 'as wreaths. That is all'.[14] In 'The Greengrocer', the 'holly wreaths for Christmas' are meant to celebrate a birth, even though they end up commemorating a death. The eucharistic 'bread' and 'wine', symbols of the ritual sacrifice that is meant to bring about wholeness and redemption, are the 'Blood' and 'food particles' scattered on the roadside after the Kingsmill massacre.

Violence, disruption and death can never be kept isolated from the tranquillity of ordinary routine ('the death-dealers' found the greengrocer 'busy as usual / Behind the counter') or from the celebratory moments of life. As has already been seen, Longley's domestic space, his understanding of 'home', and his pastoral 'elsewhere', or home from home, are never remote from either the mundanities or the brutalities of everyday life in Northern Ireland in the 1970s. There is no inviolate space, even if there is the desire for one, a sensibility also at the heart of his elegies. 'Wreaths' brings life and death into collision. In 'The Civil Servant':

> He was preparing an Ulster fry for breakfast
> When someone walked into the kitchen and shot him:
> A bullet entered his mouth and pierced his skull,
> The books he had read, the music he could play.

Through the 20th century, lines between "front" and "home" have been gradually eroded: Ireland's civil wars, and the sheer scale of the world wars, have made such distinctions impossible to maintain. When the bullet pierces the civil servant's skull here, it does more than cause death: it invades his past as well as destroying his future; it crosses, or rather obliterates, the lines between war and peace, front and home; it violates what should be protected – and protective – domestic space; and it pierces, also, a collective consciousness. The shock violates the lyric poem too, which is rhythmically disruptive and musically discordant, as well as uncompromising in the plainness of its description.

The poem's "objectivity", indeed, is the real indictment it makes, since it is the treatment of the victim as object that is so profoundly disturbing in the aftermath of the killing:

> While they dusted the dresser for fingerprints
> And then shuffled backwards across the garden

With notebooks, cameras and measuring tapes.

They rolled him up like a red carpet...

In reporting the facts, it simultaneously points up the inadequacy of 'cameras and measuring tapes' to take the measure of the event, which is left unspoken, beyond words, an absent presence like the 'bullet hole in the cutlery drawer'.

The poem also reports what is not usually seen, and what is beyond comprehension: 'Later his widow took a hammer and chisel / And removed the black keys from his piano.' The action lies outside the normal codes of grieving because grief itself is not reducible to a formula. It has a ritualistic aura to it; but it is a "ritual" which has no meaning beyond its futility.

Yet as with many of the Great War poets, if myth and ritual cannot offer metaphysical consolation (the afterlife, the worthwhile sacrifice), they do have a symbolic value in terms of psychological transitions, as in 'The Linen Workers':

> When they massacred the ten linen workers
> There fell on the road beside them spectacles,
> Wallets, small change, and a set of dentures:
> Blood, food particles, the bread, the wine.
>
> Before I can bury my father once again
> I must polish the spectacles, balance them
> Upon his nose, fill his pockets with money
> And into his dead mouth slip the set of teeth.

The relics at the scene of the massacre are poignant, intimate details that contrast with the objects – 'notebooks, cameras and measuring tapes' – on the scene in 'The Civil Servant'; they are also, as the (failed) symbols of sacrifice, the dark underside to the three gifts – 'Dates and chestnuts and tangerines' – of 'The Greengrocer'. And they are remnants salvaged by the poet, not only through recording details.

The final stanza is a rite of passage, filling his father's pockets with money to pay the ferryman on the last journey across the River Styx to the underworld. His father's death is relived through the later killings; the metaphorical gathering up of 'small change' from the debris of the massacre enables the poet to inter his father 'once again'. As in 'Wounds', his death becomes symbolic of other deaths in the conflicts of the 20th century. The burial preparations do not provide solace for death; perhaps, in one sense, such gestures are 'useless too'. But in balancing the spectacles on his father's nose, and slipping in his mouth the set of teeth, the poet adds, in death, the personal touch missing from the civil servant 'rolled up like a red carpet'.

Christian resurrection is, or should be, the triumph of life over death, but the opening of 'The Linen Workers' projects only an incompletely resurrected Christ. At the close of the poem, the transition from life to death is also, in a different way, a sacrificial gesture, one which restores the dignity of wholeness. Yet, significantly, it is one without redemption inscribed into it: each burial of his father is also a bringing of the memory of him back to life, one which rather than healing the wound, reopens it each time, keeps it green.

The cycle repeats as long as the violence in Northern Ireland perpetuates itself: the socio-political critique implicit in this is that the conditions for "redemption", or for breaking the cycle, are not in place – not least of which is an acceptance of a shared guilt and responsibility. 'Wreaths', like Longley's nature poems, is about taking time (to 'pause' at Jim Gibson's shop); about seeing beyond 'cameras and measuring tapes'; about an imaginative identification with those who can all too easily become merely another statistic.

The continuity with the Great War protest-elegy implied by both the socio-political message and mythic techniques of 'Wreaths' is more broadly implicated in Longley's fascination with the Great War, and his explorations of the continuities and disjunctions between the earlier conflict in which his father fought, and the Northern Irish conflict with which he lives. It is also a concern with origins and ancestry – on personal, literary, and socio-political levels. Longley's autobiographical explorations are also explorations of his own time and place. His sense of himself from 'In Memoriam' as being 'held secure', remembered for the future, in the no man's land of the Great War implicates his origin in his aesthetic vision and in the origin of his home ground – the "birth" of Northern Ireland out of the events of 1914 to 1920. It is also bound up with his sense of literary tradition and inheritance. That is to say, family history, literary history, and political history are interwoven in poems that work more than one angle at once.

In a 1986 interview, Longley suggested that 'Looked at from the next century, we will be thinking in terms of the fifty or sixty years war that began in 1914.'[15] The perspective is more readily under-stood in Ireland than in England perhaps, where the Anglo-Irish War, the Civil War and the Troubles, in addition to the two world wars, have brought conflict "home" in a different way. That conti-nuity, a closed circuit of violence, is implied in 'The War Poets', where the armistice never comes: 'everybody talked about the war ending / And always it would be the last week of the war'. Terence Brown notes 'a buried allusion to MacNeice's "Carrickfergus", where

the Irish boy at school...thinks "the war would go on for ever"', an
allusion which makes 'the sense of the endlessness of the First World
War...a metaphor for the interminable nature of the Irish troubles'.[16]
    There are other continuities implied in the poem as well, in its
play on origins and destinations:

> Unmarked were the bodies of the soldier-poets
> For shrapnel opened up again the fontanel
> Like a hailstone melting towards deep water
> At the bottom of a well, or a mosquito
> Balancing its tiny shadow above the lip.

It is Edward Thomas's body which was 'Unmarked' on his death in
1917; and it is Keith Douglas's 1943 'How to Kill' which is alluded
to in this first stanza. In 'How to Kill', Douglas links the moment
of death, making 'a man of dust / of a man of flesh', with the
'weightless mosquito' who 'touches / her tiny shadow on the
stone'. In Longley's poem too, it is as if the soldier-poets are
returned to the element from which they came, ghosts, or shadows,
of their solid form. But death is also a travelling backwards
through time to birth: 'shrapnel opened up again the fontanel'.
    'Unmarked' thus becomes suggestive of innocence, as if death is
a new beginning, a restorative moment. Yet the birth is a birth into
nothingness, an ending not a beginning. In being unmarked – or
perhaps, like many nameless and faceless war victims, unremarked
– they are obliterated from history: the poem's subjects deliberate-
ly remain unnamed. The opening line also obliquely alludes to
those whose graves are unmarked, whose bodies were never found
(Rosenberg and Sorley are among the missing soldier-poets).
    On one level, then, the poem's continuity is the continuity of war
and death – an ever-repeating motif of endings. But in its allusions to
Irish and British poets of both world wars, it suggests, more positively,
a continuity of literary tradition, a survival of poetry against the odds.
In Longley's reading of literary history, the capacity of the lyric poem
to deal with the challenges the 20th century throws at it implicitly
validates his own response as a lyric poet two generations later:

> ...a brilliant generation of poets in the 30s – mainly MacNeice and
> Auden – showed by their practice that the lyric tradition was not
> exhausted. They went back via Edward Thomas and Wilfred Owen,
> both of whom were killed in the trenches, to Hardy and Keats and
> Donne. I see myself as doing that in a humble way as well.[17]

Longley's literary antecedents are bound up with his familial ones.
He draws on both English and Irish poetic traditions; the Great
War offers, poetically, both a way back and a way forward, an origin

for past and future. In a sense, Longley's metaphorical conception in the landscape of the First World War and actual birth on the eve of the Second World War enable him to traverse, imaginatively, a century's poetry and a family genealogy through some of the formative historical events that condition his own time and place.

In 'Second Sight', the poet is both setting out into his own future – 'A lover looking for somewhere to live' – and travelling back through his family history: 'A ghost among ghosts of aunts and uncles / Who crowd around me to give directions.' The poem collapses space and time. His grandmother's 'second sight' brings the landscape of war into the home: 'Flanders began at the kitchen window – / The mangle rusting in No Man's Land, gas / turning the antimacassars yellow...'. With his '*Pocket Guide to London*' and '*Map of the Underground*', this last evocative of the troglodyte trench world of the First World War, the poet's quest for 'somewhere to live' takes on symbolic resonance:

> Where is my father's house, where my father?
> If I could walk in on my grandmother
> She'd see right through me and the hallway
> And the miles of cloud and sky to Ireland.
> 'You have crossed the water to visit me.'

The question, 'Where is my father's house...?', works literally in the context of the poem, but it is also – and this is part of the deceptive simplicity of Longley's writing – metaphorical. (In the same way, 'She'd see right through me' works on several levels, one of which is a pun on the 'ghosts' of the previous stanza.)

The question is also a quest for selfhood, for understanding who he is and where he comes from, one that has spiritual echoes, in the biblical quotation 'my father's house'. He may be lost, but this is also about his own loss; once again, Longley is a son in search of a lost father. Crossing the water encompasses the desire to go back in time to his grandmother's England, to meet the paternal grandparents he never knew;[18] at the same time, the poem allows her, imaginatively, to 'see...through' to his Ireland. The final line consists, at first sight, of his grandmother's words; but they could also, from a reverse angle, be the poet's, whose imaginative recovery of his family history brings his ancestors into his own 'home'. The shift from conditional ('If I could...') to perfect tense ('"You have crossed..."'), is a shift into the illusion of actuality, as if the impossible connection across space and time can be made after all.

That sense of loss implied in 'Where is my father's house...?' is also at the heart of another poem about his father, 'Last Requests'.

But 'Last Requests', a poem which implicitly reflects on the nature of elegy, fails to connect across space and time. As with the earlier 'Wounds', death is the point where touch, the literal connection, is lost forever; but the failure to 'reach' his father in 'Last Requests' is symbolic too, and connects the poem in a different way to its Great War heritage. Jahan Ramazani points out that Wilfred Owen's statement 'My subject is War, and the pity of War. The Poetry is in the pity' only half-explains Owen's own aesthetic:

> 'Pity' is Owen's term for emotional identification with the victims of war. But Owen's poetry suggests that 'pity' cannot erase the boundary that separates victim from onlooker....His subject is also the incomprehensibility of war; the poetry is also in the alienation. Having roused pity, Owen often forces the reader back, warning that pity cannot bridge the chasm separating spectator and victim.[19]

Longley's poetry understands that alienation. It is the reason his elegies do not presume to console; it is why he carefully distinguishes his own writing from that of the soldier-poets; and it helps to explain why the element of private grief (as in 'Wreaths') is vital: the line between onlooker and voyeur can be a fine one.

In part 2 of 'Last Requests' the poet is himself forced back through incomprehension, the boundary between victim and onlooker a tangible barrier:

> I thought you blew a kiss before you died,
> But the bony fingers that waved to and fro
> Were asking for a Woodbine, the last request
> Of many soldiers in your company,
> The brand you chose to smoke for forty years
> Thoughtfully, each one like a sacrament.
> I who brought peppermints and grapes only
> Couldn't reach you through the oxygen tent.

That tangible barrier is also, metaphorically, the chasm between life and death that even love cannot bridge, and the failure to understand a gesture that belongs to a past, to an experience of the Great War, the poet cannot share. But in its failure to understand, the poem does, paradoxically, understand what it cannot know: its emotional identification is at one remove, and it comes through a recognition of what is incomprehensible, either to the onlooker, or, as is often seen to be the case with the Great War, in and of itself.

Thus, Longley's elegies – and Great War protest elegies – do not ascribe meaning to death or "sacrifice". Here, bringing peppermints and grapes is a futile gesture, although the futility becomes, in the poem, a measure of grief as well as guilt for what he cannot do. Perhaps the 'last request' in the poem is, strictly, a futile, useless gesture too. Nevertheless, as in 'Wreaths', such gestures, or rituals, may be positive as well as negative. Of the Woodbines his father smokes 'like a sacrament', each one is both a ritual com-memoration of the dead, and a last rite rehearsed over and over again. Yet the ritual is also an affirmation of life, reliving time after time the Great War survival against the odds in part 1 of the poem where, after being almost buried alive, his 'lungs / Surfaced to take a long remembered drag'.

This is to suggest that Longley, too, has mastered, at the deepest structural level and through a "sacramental" imagination, what Paul Fussell describes as 'the Great War theme' of 'the ironic proximity of violence and disaster to safety, to meaning, and to love',[20] a theme which the random killings in Northern Ireland rendered all the more urgent through the 1970s. The theme is at the core of his elegies and Great War poems; it is also present in the nature poems and love poems, which carry the burden of mortality and the memory of loss even in their celebratory moments. The handling of that theme is learned partly through the example of poets earlier in the century; its effect is heightened – as the theme itself is, in a way, validated – through the poet's invocation of his personal experience and family history.

While none of the poems in *The Echo Gate* renders the connec-tions suggested above between a literary-historical and personal inheritance explicit, the last poem to be written in the *New Poems* section of *Poems 1963-1983*, 'No Man's Land', is a self-conscious drawing together of familial and literary antecedents. Part I is a restructuring, and slight rewriting of 'Granny', from *Man Lying on a Wall*; in part II, Jessica's 'mislaid whereabouts' links her to Isaac Rosenberg, whose 'body was not recovered either'. As in 'The War Poets', this second section is also evocative of Keith Douglas, whose 'stars' as 'dead men in the sky' in 'The Offensive 2' become Longley's 'constellations of brass buttons, / Identity discs that catch the light a little' on the corpses of the battlefields of World War I.

In style and theme, the poem, in some respects, "belongs" with the war poems of *The Echo Gate*. For both Jessica and Rosenberg, the 'mislaid whereabouts' refers to a mislaid whereabouts in history, and the poem is an act of retrieval, one which attempts to 'pick out that echo of splintering glass / From under the bombardment', to reconstruct the individual histories lost in large-scale atrocity, to 'read' the fragments that survive. It is a reflection on the difficult aesthetic space the poet has tried to clear for himself somewhere between opposing sides, opposing histories, one which recognises that to do so may be a forlorn, perhaps unheard gesture: 'in No

Man's Land / What is there to talk about but difficult poems?'. And its 'shell-shocked carrier pigeon' that 'flaps behind the lines' of the battlefield implicitly suggests that the lines of Longley's own verse are themselves informed by a backdrop of historical trauma.

Yet whatever its merits as a poem, that 'No Man's Land' revisits, almost summarises, some of *The Echo Gate*'s preoccupations is suggestive, given the writer's block Longley experienced intermittently from 1979 to 1985 (and again in 1987 and 1988). 'No Man's Land', written in November 1983, does, in some ways, point towards *Gorse Fires* and *The Ghost Orchid*, but at the same time it draws perhaps an almost too convenient circle around work which precedes it. Such comments are, of course, speculative, and as discussed below, the reasons for the long gap between *The Echo Gate* and *Gorse Fires* are multiple and complex. Nevertheless, this poem might suggest one reason why the *New Poems* turn out to be a closed circuit for the poet, in as much as it is indicative of a self-consciousness, an unusual degree of knowingness, about what the poet has already done.[21]

IV

Throughout Longley's war poems and elegies, his father, and the paternal line, are an important 'taproot' into the history of the 20th century. Yet to say this is to show only one side of the coin in *The Echo Gate*. Paul Durcan rightly summarises Longley's themes in this book as 'Of Love and War'.[22] In the last third of the collection, Longley's fascination with the 'female principle' comes to the fore through his love poems. In the sonnets 'Florence Nightingale' and 'Grace Darling', the two women are redemptive figures. Florence Nightingale purges ugliness, the 'bad words...rinsed in your head like the smell of wounds'; beneath the surface, wounds are healing and 'maggots are stitching the scar'. She is both maternal figure and sexual temptation: 'The halo of your lamp, a brothel's fanlight / Or a nightlight carried in by nanny and nurse'. Grave Darling's rescue of drowning sailors is also symbolic, the 'small boats at sea, lifeboats, named after girls' in the closing couplet a saving legacy. The third sonnet in the book, 'Sulpicia', performs another act of rescue: the poem is spoken by a mythological female, a temptress 'dressed to kill'; but this is also a reconstructive process, as fragments of the Roman poet's work are brought back together in what Longley describes in the note to the poem as a 'collage of original lines and free translations of lines and phrases'.

It is significant that Longley's representations of women, even those instances which retrieve, without sentimentality, female histories, have strong mythological overtones. Derek Mahon has described Robert Graves (and it is a point which applies also to Mahon) as in some ways Longley's 'kindred spirit'; Longley himself writes that 'I suppose that my love poetry is addressed to what I grandiosely call the female principle, to the Gravesian notion of the Muse.'[23] Graves's goddess is, of course, threefold – bride, mother, layer-out. That conjunction of death and sex is also present in Longley's writing, as is the merging of mother, lover, and, sometimes, destroyer.

So in 'Peace: after Tibullus', the desire for 'a woman / To come and fondle my ears of wheat and let apples / Overflow between her breasts' transforms her into the epitome of the natural world's beauty and bounty, peace itself, an erotic ideal, *and* the maternal figure whose breasts overflow with nourishment. On a more sinister, if blackly humorous note, 'The Barber's Wife' is an 'interloper' who comes at the end of the day to 'sweep the presences, absences, // Earthly remains, ghosts of skulls / With graceful movements into the bin', and who seems to paralyse, and unsex, both poet and barber.

The Gravesian Muse, in other words, is never celebrated without the awareness of mortality. In one of the outstanding love poems of Longley's career, 'The Linen Industry', the way in which that awareness is implicated in the love-making of the poem gives it its poignancy, and its beauty. Many of Longley's love poems subtly merge the act of love with the natural world, a merging that brings both change and decay, and cyclical renewal, to human relationships. In 'The Linen Industry', the processes of love, nature, and linen-making are seamlessly interwoven. Consequently, as Neil Corcoran observes, there are multiple 'strands' which can be pulled in readings of this text – political, intertextual, botanical, erotic.[24]

It is a poem of expansions and contractions, decline and regeneration, from 'Pulling up flax' and 'laying...handfuls in the peaty water / To rot those grasses to the bone' to the 'combing out of fibres like hair / And a weaving of these into christening robes'; or from the 'fields...compacted' and the 'little room' which, once again, is transformed into an everywhere: 'in our attic under the skylight / We make love on a bleach green, the whole meadow / Draped with material...'. The poem also intertwines origins and destinations: the 'passion' that weaves 'christening robes' also makes 'garments for a marriage or funeral'. The process of linen-making is a 'dying trade' in more sense than one, the completion of the garments 'like a bereavement once the labour's done'; creation is also about

loss. The 'female principle' is both a stay against mortality, and the
holder of its secrets:

> Let flax be our matchmaker, our undertaker,
> The provider of sheets for whatever the bed –

> And be shy of your breasts in the presence of death,
> Say that you look more beautiful in linen
> Wearing white petticoats, the bow on your bodice
> A butterfly attending the embroidered flowers.

The lover is a bridal figure in 'white petticoats' here; but the white
clothing can be a shroud as well as a bridal gown. When the poet
is 'shy of your breasts in the presence of death', the female body
affirms life, love and (maternal) nurture.

The poet is, both here, and in the later 'Icon', from *Gorse Fires*,
reluctant to concede mortality to the loved one's breasts – in which,
as Peter McDonald notes, he develops an idea from Louis MacNeice's
'Mayfly'.[25] At the same time, death, like the body here, is itself
something to be 'shy of'. The metamorphosis in the final two lines,
of the linen bow into a butterfly, a transformation that gives the
impression the lover herself has become a landscape of flowers, is
delicately erotic. But the erotic imagery is fragile and ephemeral.
Perhaps it is also worth remembering a poem written two years
later, in October 1979, 'The White Butterfly', (from *New Poems*)
which is an elegy for Longley's mother, and which draws on a
legend that fascinated him at the time, where the butterfly 'may
become the soul of one / Who lies sleeping in the fields'.

Longley's metamorphoses – in this and other poems – tend to
merge death and desire. It is not until *The Ghost Orchid* that a
fascination with Ovid becomes a dominant trend, but that fascina-
tion is foreshadowed in the transformations of *The Echo Gate*,
particularly in the association of femininity with fluidity seen in
'Metamorphoses', 'Mountain Swim', 'On Mweelrea' and 'Meniscus'.
The association is sexual; but it is also more generally suggestive
of mutability and mortality.

As with much of Longley's imagery, the redemptive potential
lies in the capacity to transform; at the same time, the need for
something solid to contest what may become dissolution and loss
is present as a counter-impulse. As Peter McDonald points out, in
rendering the human body as flux, Longley then tends to bring it
together with landscape, 'the mortality of the one colouring, and
being coloured by, the resilience of the other'.[26]

'Meniscus' implicitly recalls Ovid's Cyane (who resurfaces in
The Ghost Orchid), the nymph who, with weeping, dissolves into

the waters of which she had been the presiding spirit. The poem plays on the title's several meaning, connecting to *The Echo Gate*'s concern with mirror images and differently angled perception; but this is a reflection into which things are 'dissolved'. Rather than, as in '*The Echo Gate*', providing a fixed point as conduit, if not origin, here the poem itself seems to be absorbed into flux: 'faces / Are reflected, then dissolved by swaying water'. In the same way, the lover on 'On Mweelrea' merges with the mountainside; or in one of the 'Metamorphoses' the female figure becomes 'water / Snuggling in its own embrace'.

'Meniscus' is one of several poems in *The Echo Gate* which stylistically point forwards to the longer, more fluid line Longley develops through the 1990s. It begins to push slightly beyond the confines of the pentameter line; other poems, such as the three sonnets, 'Peace' and 'Dead Men's Fingers' more obviously foreshadow the hexameters of much of *The Ghost Orchid*. But poems such as 'Meniscus' are also implicated, in a different way, in the direction taken in *New Poems*.

I suggested at the outset of this chapter that Longley's reconstructive project in *The Echo Gate* was also, inevitably, one of dismantling: the poems dissipate and fragment as they also reconstruct and reorder. Thus, as the 'small change' spills onto the roadside in 'Wreaths', the poet also gathers it up. But in the handful of *New Poems*, written from 1979 to 1983, what seems to be most in evidence is an urgently felt need for human beings to hold onto – and hold together – each other, in fear of things dissolving around them, or in fear that the loved one will fragment and disappear.

That fear is a new element in Longley's writing, at least to this extent; also more in evidence is the corresponding desire for the speaker to be himself hidden, protected, and comforted. Thus, in *New Poems*, the speaker in 'View' puts his 'arms around her skeleton / For fear that her forearms might unravel'; in 'Patchwork', it is as if the poem is a fragile as the 'ribbons that hold you together' in its 'Stitching together shirts and nightshirts'. 'Light Behind the Rain', although at times obscure, broods on these themes through its eleven short sections, in its desire to be 'collected...into your hand', in its speaker 'left...behind, trawling...for strands of your hair', in its fragmentation of the human body. More explicit, in 'Among Waterbirds', is the desire to 'use your body like a hide'.

The fear of loss and isolation, the awareness of the frailty and fragility of those who are loved is endemic to Longley's early 1980s writing. Most of these poems are love poems, trying to hold on to that 'one high room', as in 'Company', against the flow of time and mortality – almost, it seems, against the elements of water and earth into which the human body will merge and lose itself. In some ways, the longer line Longley returns to in the 1990s is a way of both containing and permitting such preoccupations: it allows fluidity and collapse within the form of the poem. But in *New Poems*, it feels, at times, as if the poetry is at risk of fragmenting too (in the structure, for example, of 'Light Behind the Rain'), the poems themselves 'markings' that 'almost disappear'.

The new poems are about being, literally and emotionally, orphaned: and it is possible to speculate that the sense of loss is implicated in – as if mirrored by – the loss of poetry through writer's block at the same time. For Longley, this period of writer's block, like the one in the 1960s, is about form, and the need to reinvent his forms; it is also bound up with what he calls, after MacNeice, 'the middle stretch' and its accompanying 'internal turmoil'.[27]

The first of these perhaps identifies symptom not cause. The second is more difficult to quantify. And writer's block may be, ultimately, inexplicable. Derek Mahon, too, published no major new collection in the 1980s. But I want to suggest here four reasons (there may be others) for the near-silence Longley experienced in the early 1980s, all of which are to greater or lesser degrees speculative, a matter of inference only: first, the death of Longley's mother in 1979; second, the conditions of his working life in the Arts Council in the early to mid 1980s; third, the sense that *The Echo Gate* was in some ways the culmination of particular techniques developed through the first four books; fourth, and related, the publication of *Poems 1963-1983*.

The last three are easily understandable. In 'Blackthorn and Bonsai', a lecture Longley delivered at Trinity College Dublin in 1992, and reprinted in *Tuppenny Stung*, he gives an insight into life in the Arts Council in the 1980s that, in terms of bureaucracy's stifling effect on the imagination, speaks for itself. Some of the particularly bleak years in terms of poetry writing (1981, 1982, 1987) coincided with exceptionally fraught, and unpleasant issues arising in the Arts Council.[28]

The very accomplishment of *The Echo Gate* is also significant: it received not inconsiderable critical attention; it was the Poetry Book Society Choice for Christmas 1979; and it may be read as a resolution of some of the problems evident in *An Exploded View* and *Man Lying on a Wall*. That explains Longley's own feeling, in the 1980s, of having left himself nowhere else to go. Revisiting all his poems (and making some very slight revisions in the process) in preparing *Poems 1963-1983* for publication may have compounded

the feeling, as it may also have introduced a (paralysing) self-con-
sciousness about his own *oeuvre*. Trying to understand the period
of writer's block from within it, Longley suggested that:

> It may have something to do – and this is an intuitive, mysterious thing
> – with the feeling I had when I was putting the four books together
> with the little coda of new poems, that I'd come full circle, that there's
> some kind of formal impasse and that I've got to break out of the circle
> that I've carefully, over 20 years, inscribed around myself. It might also
> have something to do with my job becoming more demanding. In a
> religious sense I believe that my present silence is part of the impulse
> and sooner silence than forgery.[29]

Retrospectively, in 'A Tongue at Play' from 1996, he reiterates these
ideas: 'My second crisis…could be explained in terms of the male
menopause and loss of bureaucratic innocence in an increasingly
fractious institution. In 1985 I had published *Poems 1963-1983…*
Perhaps preparing this premature "collected" made me too self-
aware.'[30]

But the first reason – the death of Longley's mother – is more
elusive, and it is not a reason the poet has himself suggested. To
begin to understand its significance for his writing, revisiting two
cryptic autobiographical moments in *The Echo Gate* may prove
helpful.

At the beginning of 'Housekeeper', one of the 'Mayo Monologues',
is a disguised reference to Longley's maternal grandfather George
and his second wife Maud: 'She burst out laughing at the interview /
Because he complained about his catheter.' At the close of 'Dead
Men's Finger's' is an oblique reference to events in Longley's own
mother's pregnancy: '…I feel like the ghost of a child / Visiting the
mother who long ago aborted him'. The second, unlike the first,
is cryptic even in the context of the poem; in both cases, their auto-
biographical relevance only becomes apparent a few years later, in
1985, when Longley was requested by Mick Imlah to write an
autobiographical piece, 'Tuppenny Stung' for *Poetry Review*. The
significant passage as regards Longley's mother is as follows:

> My mother died in April 1979. For about a year beforehand we both
> knew that she was going to die. I wanted to feel free to embrace her as
> I had embraced Lena [the nursemaid who Longley sees as the 'other'
> mother of his childhood], and agreed to call with her every day for
> five minutes or five hours – for as long as both of us could stand it.
> Over several tumultuous months we lived out her childhood and mine.
> She gave me X-ray pictures in which the shadowy shapes of Peter and
> me curl up and tangle about five months after conception. ('Tuppenny
> Stung for a penny bung,' my father had said.) She confessed that in
> the early days of the pregnancy she had attempted in an amateurish

way to abort us – or 'it' as we then were. I registered neither shock
nor pain. Somehow this knowledge made it easier for me to hug her
dying lopsided body. It was like a courtship, and I accompanied her
on my arm to death's door.[31]

This story haunts Longley's imagination towards the end of *The
Echo Gate* even if it remains, at this stage, unexplained to his
readers. That the progress towards death is a 'courtship' is also
significant, given the habitual conflation of mother/lover in his
writing of this period.

In 'The Third Light', from *New Poems*, an elegy for his mother
which is also a First World War poem, his mother's grave is a
marriage bed and her interment an act of love:

> The sexton is opening up the grave,
> Lined with mossy cushions and couch grass
> This shaft of light, entrance to the earth
> Where I kneel to marry you again...

In reuniting his mother with his father, the poet ambiguously
'marries' her himself; he becomes his mother's father, giving away
the bride into death: 'I have handed over to him your pain / And
your preference for Cyprus sherry...'. As in the earlier elegy for
his father, 'In Memoriam', the role assumed here is protective, a
generation reversal that comes from a belated understanding of his
mother's own painful childhood. As he writes later in *Tuppenny
Stung*, 'My mother's childhood was an unrelieved misery: daily
humiliations, mental and physical cruelty. My heart goes out to
the little girl cowering in a corner, sobbing at the top of the dark
stairs.'[32]

The fear and loneliness of some of the *New Poems* is thus, in
part, an imaginative identification with the maternal figure who is
understood as the defenceless child. The poems cross a generation
gap to make his mother, finally, a loved one for the poet, who meets
her on equal terms. Nevertheless, it is the poet's own sense of loss,
his own anxieties of origin, and his own feelings of neglect that
are at work in these poems too. Those feelings relate both to his
childhood, and to the more recent bereavement. 'Her moods', he
writes of his mother, 'changed unpredictably. It has taken me a long
time to forgive her that atmosphere of uncertainty, its anxieties, even
fears.'[33] She is recovered for him, emotionally, in their 'courtship'
– only to be lost again in death.

Part of Longley's concern in *Tuppenny Stung* is to affirm for his
childhood self the presence of compensatory maternal affection
from other women: the nurse maid Lena, who was 'a natural and

devoted surrogate mother'; his sister Wendy, who filled 'the emo-
tional gaps'. But Lena left too, and left him 'inconsolable'.[34] The
childhood hurt is replicated in the adult bereavement. The sense
of 'uncertainty' becomes implicated in his own origin. From being
'held secure' in the no man's land of the Great War, promised
existence through the paternal line, in 'Dead Men's Finger's – and
in 'Self-Portrait' – the poet is 'threatened' in the womb, first by
his own brother, then by the 'mother who long ago aborted him'.
It is possible to suggest that mythic autobiographical structures
come into collision at this point in ways which take some time to
work themselves out.

When asked about 'autobiographical verse' in a 1985 interview,
Longley's answer in this context is revealing:

> I do feel anxious about invading family privacies or about being private
> in public. When I write about my father I write about him because
> he's representative of a generation, the survivors of the trenches. My
> mother's more difficult. I've written a couple of elegies for her.[35]

Throughout the interview, Longley is perceptive and sensitive on
the subject of form, and what can go wrong in relation to form, as
he is also on his father's 'representative' role in his poetry. But the
fluency falters when it comes to the more 'difficult' subject of his
mother. His own arguments from the earlier *Causeway* are perhaps
relevant here: 'the artist needs time in which to allow the raw
material of experience to settle to an imaginative depth where he
can transform it.'

Those transformations occur a few years later, in 1989, when
some of the 'autobiographical' poems for *Gorse Fires* are written.
Among them are 'Anticleia', 'Eurycleia' and 'Laertes', poems which
transform 'raw material' about his mother, surrogate mother and
father through mythic structures. The search for the kind for
imaginative homecoming of these poems has its origins in the mid-
1970s. Fragments of 'Eurycleia' and 'Laertes' are traceable back to
attempts to retell the myths in the 1970s with an (unsuccessful)
trimeter line. (As suggested earlier, it is perhaps impossible to say
whether changes in form – notably Longley's use of the longer line
in *Gorse Fires* – allow the expression of what had been unsayable,
or whether such changes follow on inevitably from the emergence
of the subject at its proper time.)

A different version of an abandoned poem, 'Odyssey', from April
1975, is also suggestive as regards the imaginative quest for the
'female principle' underpinning Longley's late 1970s and early 1980s
poetry:

> The last piece of that sexual
> Jigsaw puzzle which includes
> Circe, Nausicaa, Calypso,
> Is not Penelope his wife
> Whose shadow had been embroidered
> On all those other nightdresses,
>
> But the old nurse who bathed him
> And touch-read his identity
> By the braille of a boyhood scar
> And said that he was the baby
> She hadn't recognised before
> Feeling her master all over.[36]

It is possible, in retrospect, to detect Longley's old nurse, Lena, behind Odysseus's nurse here. (The later 'Eurycleia' makes the connection explicitly.) Of more interest is the suggestion that the Odyssean voyage, with which Longley has been imaginatively pre-occupied since the mid-1960s, has at its core neither the search for father/son, nor the quest, through various sexual encounters for the 'last girl', but for a sense of self, an 'identity' that only truly comes into being through an unspoken maternal bond. The maternal principle seems to be the piece of the puzzle that is missing for Longley, one which he tries, repeatedly, to put in place. Furthermore, 'identity' is established only through the body's being 'touch-read'. Yet, as suggested earlier, 'touch' is the one thing lost forever in death. As the loved one slips out of the poet's grasp in the last poems of *The Echo Gate* and in *New Poems*, as she dissi-pates, melts into water, or back into the landscape, the maternal principle is lost as well. 'Homecoming', at this point, is still out of reach.

   Perhaps it is not too far-fetched to suggest that after ten years of imaginative preoccupation with the *Odyssey*, there is, at the end of the 1970s, a desire for a journey's end, one which brings Odysseus home; but the endings which colour the poet's personal history seem here to proscribe, rather than permit, that return, and it is deferred until *Gorse Fires*. In that respect, Longley's own feeling that he had come 'full circle' with *The Echo Gate* proves not to be the case. And it is, of course, twenty years not ten before Odysseus returns to Ithaca.

5

Between Hovers: *Gorse Fires*
1984-1990

> ... the seafaring ship drew near to Ithaca, to home
> And that harbour named after the old man of the sea, two
> Headlands huddling together as breakwater, windbreak,
> Haven where complicated vessels float free of moorings
> In their actual mooring-places.
>
> MICHAEL LONGLEY, 1990

I

It is now a commonplace to suggest that the publication of Longley's fifth collection, *Gorse Fires* in 1991, twelve years after *The Echo Gate*, marked an extraordinary resurgence of poetic energy, another turn in the gyre for which there are not many precedents: MacNeice in his last poems from the early 1960s; Yeats's reinvention of himself after 1910. *Gorse Fires* appeared as Longley took early retirement from the Arts Council of Northern Ireland, a coincidence of timing that brings a fairytale quality to an already extraordinary story of renewal. Variously described as a 'dazzling renaissance', a 'momentous return', *Gorse Fires* is the happy ending to a bleak period in the 1980s, when the muse was, if not entirely absent, only intermittently present. Longley's own renewal coincides, too, with a new decade that would bring extraordinary changes to Northern Ireland.

Unsurprisingly, the critical enthusiasm generated by the new poetry of the 1990s, together with the romance of the story itself, have encouraged some rhetorical flourishes on the subject. Comments about Longley's 'twelve year silence', 'ten year silence', or even, impossibly, his 'twelve year silence in the 1980s', give dramatic context to a critical appreciation of Longley's poetry from *Gorse Fires* onwards. The rhetoric of long silence and sudden renewal says as much, perhaps more, about the profound effect of *Gorse Fires* on a critical climate that was seemingly unprepared for it as it does about the workings of Longley's imagination. But it serves its purpose both in affirming that effect, and in bringing to public consciousness an awareness of the long publication gap between Longley's fourth and fifth books.

That gap has not been without its consequences. The absence of any new collection by Longley in the 1980s, a decade in which 'Irish Studies' was itself consolidated in the academy, may be seen as one reason for the comparatively limited critical attention paid to his work at that time, compounding the problems Longley's complex sense of identity had already caused for certain critical perspectives. (The 'twelve year silence' narrative can sometimes operate, not very successfully, as a kind of critical alibi for the delay in paying proper attention to his earlier work.) More importantly now, in terms of reading Longley's poetry, the long gap between collections has tended, in both practical and critical ways, to obscure the continuities between his 1970s poetry, and the work published in the 1990s. In that sense, describing the period as a 'twelve year silence' could be more misleading than helpful. Most of *Gorse Fires* was written in the late 1980s; the 'silence' relates predominantly to the years 1979-85, during which the fourteen *New Poems* were written, and to 1987-88, when only six poems were added to the by then half-completed *Gorse Fires*. In addition, that the only previous work by Longley in print at the point when *Gorse Fires* was published was the 'collected' *Poems 1963-1983* may have compounded the temptation to think of his career in two parts, under the first of which a line had been firmly drawn. (The 1998 *Selected Poems*, with its careful continuity of dating, has since encouraged a reading across the publication gap.)

Gorse Fires is on one level a break with the past, in so far as it finds a way of stepping outside the 'circle' the poet felt he had inscribed around himself with *Poems 1963-83*. The 'formal problems' Longley encountered towards the end of the 1970s are solved in *Gorse Fires* through what he describes as 'prosodic loosenings-up and an increasingly ambitious, even reckless, syntactical reach'.[1] Yet it is also very evidently a collection which develops not just from, but out of, his earlier work, one which has thematic and formal continuities not only with *The Echo Gate* but also noticeably with *No Continuing City*. In another sense, therefore, it revisits and broadens that 'circle' to become another turn in a widening gyre.

Although four of the *Gorse Fires* poems were written in 1984-85, the breakthrough for the poet, in terms of writer's block, came in early 1986. Longley's central involvement through the 1980s in the effort to develop Northern Ireland's cultural life – and its cultural tolerance – carried, as suggested in the previous chapters, certain penalties in terms of his own imaginative life, through what he describes as a 'loss of bureaucratic innocence'.[2] On 1 February 1986 he was granted a year's sabbatical from the Arts Council of Northern Ireland for the purposes of devoting 'time to creative work'.[3] At that point in time, Longley had written nothing at all since 'Remembering Carrigskeewaun' in April 1985, a silence which engendered 'an increasing sense of panic' in the poet.[4] At the beginning of March 1986 he left Belfast for a month-long sojourn in Carrigskeewaun, in the hope, as he put it, of the 'clouds lifting ... away from bureaucrats and Unionist politicians'.[5]

For the period 2 March to 5 April 1986, Longley kept a diary of his solitary stay in Carrigskeewaun, a foray into prose writing, which, like the autobiographical piece written for *Poetry Review* earlier, might be seen as a therapeutic enterprise, a way of facilitating the return of inspiration. In the earlier period of writer's block, in 1970, Longley retreated to Wicklow, but, as he notes in 'A Tongue at Play', on that occasion, 'My muse did not come on sabbatical with me. Dead silence.'[6] The memory of that failure haunts the early days in Carrigskeewaun, with Longley 'worrying that every day of my sabbatical should bear fruit of some kind'.[7] The first poem to be completed in 1986 – 'Sea Shanty' – is both a breakthrough poem, and, implicitly, a poem about how that breakthrough has been achieved. In the process of composition, it is worried over to an unusual degree, as the diary entries suggest:

> Monday 3 March...Read Sappho's fragments...guessing that I should approach her & feeling reassured when I spot the word 'samphire' in the commentary...
> Tuesday 4 March...Work all day, for many hours, on 'Sea Shanty II'. Feel I'm getting somewhere, though it isn't flowing easily like the first part...
> Wednesday 5 March. Started on 'Shanty II' as soon as I woke. After more hours, decided it's no good. Ah well. Full marks for effort. The first part is good enough as it stands.... [R]elaxed into realisation that the new lines don't work. Then, to my surprise, found myself re-jigging them substantially, so that the wound is either healed or suppurating....
> Thursday 6 March...Further bed-bound tinkerings. Decided to send the thing to Edna before it drives me mad. She at least will wring its neck for me, if need be.
> Sunday 9 March...Walked past the burial mound to the roaring breakers, & sat there on a spar from the old wreck. Part of me is a sailor....
> Monday 10 March...We discussed 'Sea Shanty', & I spent the evening working on it in light of her suggestions. God, you'd think it was 'Paradise Lost'. But I did feel pleased & relieved to have reached somewhere after my first week in Carrigskeewaun.

From this point onwards, the poems are written with a confidence and celerity that stands in marked contrast to these early days; the four lines of 'Insomnia', for example, Longley notes on 23 March, '[came] into my head quite effortlessly'.

'Sea Shanty' is, as Michael Allen notes, a poem in which 'the speaker circumspectly renounces the rather flamboyant Muse he "would have waited" for'.[8] The poem is about coming down to earth, about a rediscovery of perspective:

> I would have waited under the statue of Eros
> While the wind whistled in my bell-bottoms,
> Taken my bearings from the blink of daylight
> Her thighs and feathery maidenhair let through.
> But now from the high ground of Carrigkeewaun
> I watch Lesbos rising among the islands.
> Rain shivers off the machair, and exposes me
> In my long-johns, who dozed on her breastbone,
> On pillows of sea-pink beyond the shingle,
> Who mumbled into the ringlets at her ear
> My repertoire of sea shanties and love songs...

Its opening lines evoke the muse in the context of sexual desire, which is also a desire for poetry: her attempted seduction by the poet as courtier mumbling 'sea shanties and love songs' submerges him in a kind of romantic illusion, with only the occasional 'blink of daylight'. But he does not, in the end, get his 'bearings' from this too close – perhaps claustrophobic – devotion; rather, he is exposed, an unromantic, grumpy, and defenceless figure in his winter underwear, on the 'high ground' from which he obtains a proper perspective – on the muse and on himself. The poem confronts head-on the possibility that the muse might not have come with him; yet in abandoning what he 'would have waited' for, the wait itself is, in another sense, over.

In his newly exposed position, the Aegean island of Lesbos rises among the west of Ireland islands of Inishturk and Inishbofin, and represents, symbolically, the resurfacing of poetry. Lesbos was, in the early history of Greece, the home of Aeolian lyric poetry, and the home of Sappho, who is evoked again in the final lines of the poem. 'Sea Shanty' brings the Aegean to the Atlantic, and Greek myth to Ireland, as if returning the source of poetry to Longley's own home; it pre-empts the (Hibernicised) Homeric preoccupations of the volume as a whole. It is also, as with other poems in *Gorse Fires*, obliquely about being orphaned: 'I am making do with what has been left me'. In a sense, this is always what the poet has done: an idealised world is traded for the fragments of this world, which he then transforms imaginatively. But here, there is a more personal resonance, both autobiographically – since what has been 'left' him is also about being left himself – and as regards the poetic enterprise. Longley has never taken poetry for granted in any sense; but there is a maturity of vision here, a recognition that inheritance is about loss as well as gain. What is left to him – the symbolic 'saltier leaves of samphire' – may not be to his taste, but it is also resonant of preservation.

Like Edward Thomas, in 'Edward Thomas's War Diary', with his 'eye on what remained', the poet finds something to work with even in what seem to be the most difficult circumstances. If 'making do with what has been left me' suggests both a humility and a lack of confidence, the poem retains the former, but is about overcoming the latter. It validates Longley's contention that 'nothing remains ordinary if you look at it for long enough'.[9] By the close of the poem, the 'Pleiades' can be seen in the 'sparkle of sand grains on my wellingtons', the stars themselves momentarily reflected in the minutiae of everyday life.

II

Gorse Fires is thus a homecoming for the poet, because it is a return of poetry as the place where he is, elusively, always at home. It is also a homecoming in terms of style and theme, since in this volume Longley finds a form within which he is at ease, and mythic structures which resolve some of the issues raised by *New Poems*. At intervals through the volume, and stitching it together thematically, are the seven free translations, or versions, from Homer's *Odyssey*: 'Homecoming', 'Tree House', 'Eurycleia', 'Laertes', 'Anticleia', 'Argos', and 'The Butchers'. The abortive attempt to invoke some of those myths in the mid to late 1970s here finds its proper resolution; and it is in the working of these poems that the stylistic shift through the 1980s can best be understood.

Translating Homer brings with it multiple stylistic, more particularly metrical, problems for the writer in English, in the transition from quantitative to accentual measure.[10] Longley's flexible long line is one way of dealing with such problems; it has also become a characteristic of his late 1980s and 1990s poetry more generally. In the Homeric poems of *Gorse Fires*, that longer line can range between 11 and 16 syllables, with anything from four to seven stresses. It is, however, possible to suggest that the staple is a five or six-stress, roughly 14-syllable line; and some of the patterns of Homeric verse – both in its original, and in the traditional forms of translation which have followed – are traceable in these lyrics.

As Douglas Dunn notes, however, Longley's lines often 'resist scansion', and may be better 'measured by voice and temperament'.[11] Despite their regularity of appearance, the poems introduce an extraordinary degree of rhythmic flexibility. The closing lines of 'Laertes' may be taken as exemplary:

> Until Laertes recognised his son and, weak at the knees,
> Dizzy, flung his arms around the neck of great Odysseus
> Who drew the old man fainting to his breast and held him there
> And cradled like driftwood the bones of his dwindling father.

The loose iambic here is disrupted, and disoriented, with the trochaic reversal of 'Dízzy'. The stresses on 'óld mán fáinting' hold him fast against the falling rhythm (compounded in this line by the three unstressed syllables which follow) of the rest of the poem. And the last line shifts away from a loose iambic into a line that might be as easily be scanned as loosely amphibrachic: 'And crádled like dríftwood the bónes of his dwíndling fáther'. In doing so, the line introduces a musicality (its stresses are perhaps the least ambiguous of any line in the poem) that lulls, almost comforts, its listener, as Odysseus does Laertes. In paradoxical fashion, the five rather than six stresses, and the degree of regularity, give the effect of the line cradling itself; at the same time, the falling rhythm of 'dwindling father' with which it closes leaves the poem drifting and eluding closure, itself 'driftwood', as well as held intact. That is to say, the lines rhythmically encompass the conditions of both immediate recovery and imminent loss implicit in the Odysseus/Laertes encounter. Similarly, while no strict pattern of rhyme may be discernable, the poem does not abandon rhyme altogether, although the pattern is thematic and elusive. The off-beat half rhyme (there/father) of the closing couplet, for instance, where Laertes recognises Odysseus, has a reverse echo earlier in the poem where Odysseus first weeps for Laertes: 'Odysseus sobbed in the shade of a pear-tree for his father / So old and pathetic that all he wanted then and there / Was to kiss him and hug him...'.

Douglas Dunn's argument about Longley's style is pertinent here: 'no matter,' he writes, 'if he seems to have grown into a more spacious, freer range of styles. In fact, he hasn't; instead, he has achieved a truly remarkable formal control, the true spirit of which is ease'.[12] As these instances from 'Laertes' demonstrate, Longley has travelled some distance from the earlier stylised forms that forced a kind of serendipity – forms which in one way perfectly suited the 1960s concern with the divided mind – to a style which reflects, and derives from, the thematic preoccupations developed through the 1970s. While the relationship between freedom and constraint remains a central concern, it is also increasingly implicated in Longley's fascination with presence and absence, containment and dissolution, purity and impurity.

In terms of their formal properties, the *Gorse Fires* poems are themselves both free and not free: at the very least, in fact, a stylistic analysis throws such distinctions into question. What looks conventional once again breaks all the rules – but in a different way from the earlier poems. The formal structures of the 1960s poetry paradoxically imposed risk on the poet within that framework. *Gorse Fires*, in a more complicated fashion, plays it two ways simultaneously: on the one hand, the formal reins are drawn tight; on the other, the poems are allowed to run free. Syntactically and rhythmically resistant to the imposition of fixed patterns, the poems which incorporate the fluid, longer line also invent their own patterns.

It is this that makes the poems both resistant to scansion, and yet obviously implicated in particular metrical traditions and patterns. It is also, therefore, as will be seen, the longer line, with its correspondingly 'reckless, syntactical reach', that allows the simultaneous expression of both containment and loss (the paradox on which some of the *New Poems* foundered). In the forms and themes of *Gorse Fires*, in other words, it is possible to see the question Yeats once asked in 'Among School Children' – 'How can we know the dancer from the dance?' – as unanswerable.

It is significant that in the breakthrough poem 'Sea Shanty', the speaker identifies himself as a sailor. Through the Homeric poems which follow in *Gorse Fires*, Longley returns to the familiar conceit in his work (one that had been in abeyance during the late 1970s) of the poet-as-voyager; an imaginative identification with Odysseus haunts his first and fifth books to an unusual degree. Yet as with the style, the terms of the homecoming have changed. The first of the translations to appear in *Gorse Fires* (although one of the last to be written), 'Homecoming', which details Odysseus's return to Ithaca, suggests the complications inherent both in Longley's sense of place, and in poetic form as its own 'place':

> And the seafaring ship drew near to Ithaca, to home
> And that harbour named after the old man of the sea, two
> Headlands huddling together as breakwater, windbreak,
> Haven where complicated vessels float free of moorings
> In their actual mooring places.

Following on, obliquely, from the earlier 'anchored boat' of 'Letter to Derek Mahon', the poem finds its 'mooring place[s]', but it is,

simultaneously, 'free of moorings'. Perhaps this is itself the best
way to explain poetic form in Longley's later poetry – moored
without obvious moorings – particularly in those poems such as
'Laertes', 'Anticleia' or 'The Butchers' which comprise a single
long sentence.

In such instances, the fluid long line, with its syntactical twists
and turns, might seem to float free, but is invisibly checked by the
frame of the poem itself. Longley's translation also here encour-
ages a self-reflexive reading of the poem. His 'complicated vessels'
are unusual. In other writers' versions of this passage, they appear
as 'decked ships', 'large ships', 'well-bench'd galleys', 'well-built
ships'.[13] With 'vessels', Longley gives his own phrase an oblique
intertextual relation to the idea of poetry as a 'vessel', as a form of
containment; and with 'complicated' we see the first stirrings of
what becomes, in *Snow Water* (2004), a slightly mischievous if less
subtle reflection on his own style as a 'complicated recipe'.

'Homecoming' thus reflects on Longley's stylistic development.
But the harbour located between 'two / Headlands' and with 'two
ways in' is also typical of the betwixt and between sensibility of
Gorse Fires as a whole. The poem immediately preceding 'Home-
coming', 'Remembering Carrigskeewaun', describes home as 'a
hollow between the waves'. Habitually, in this collection, the poet
locates his place and time somewhere between: the snow in the
dedicatory poem falls 'Between now and one week ago'; the otter
is 'Between Hovers' or (in 'Otters') on 'wet sand in between' cur-
rach and wave. In the title-poem, the speaker is on 'the same train
between the same embankments'; in 'The Shack' he lies awake
'between the two sleeping couples'.

'Homecoming' is achieved for Longley after a long wait. But
while homecoming may be understood as the recovery of a secure
sense of place, in *Gorse Fires* is it, rather, a recovered confidence in
the poetic virtue of indeterminacy, in the idea of a space 'between'
as potentially redemptive. The harbour in 'Homecoming' is the
natural inheritor of the 'half-door' image – and all it implies –
recurrent in the 1970s. Its 'two ways in, one looking north where
men descend / While the other faces south, a footpath for the
gods', suggest the place of poetry as one in which the ideal and
the real, purity and impurity, meet each other, and in which there
is always – be it mundane or visionary – more than one outward
perspective. The 'mind dividing' of the early poems becomes, more
positively, the imagined space of poetry itself.

In 'Homecoming', as in virtually all of his classical versions,
Longley identifies and isolates a brief lyric moment from the epic

sweep of the source poem. In the process of translation, the Greek myths are reinvented as a response to his own time and place; they are also rendered intimate and, obliquely, autobiographical. If the 'complicated vessels' are one obvious Longley twist in the tale, also recognisably his is the choice of 'huddling' for the two head-lands, and it links this, the first Homeric poem in the book, back to the concerns of *The Echo Gate* and *New Poems*. The 'Headlands huddling together' transform the landscape into the embodiment of either two lovers protecting each other, or two nurturing parental figures protecting the harbour.

Odysseus's homecoming is a return to his wife – or, as in 'No Continuing City', to the 'last girl' – but it is also a return to origins. In that sense, the poem recovers imaginatively in its closing lines what could not be recreated in the late 1970s – a sense of security:

> ...they lifted Odysseus out of his hollow
> Just as he was, linen sheet and glossy rug and all,
> And put him to bed on the sand, still lost in sleep.

The war hero is transformed into the defenceless child 'put...to bed on the sand' in a lyric closure with an obvious personal appeal for the poet. The image we are left with – the childlike figure cradled in the cove, as if held secure between the headlands – interprets 'homecoming' with a particular emotional resonance, one that may be linked to the loss of the poet's own parents and the sense of being 'an orphan now' ('Icon'). Longley's preference for 'lost in sleep' over various other possible permutations (notably E.V. Rieu's 'fast asleep'), also continues a play on lost and found that has been present in his work from the beginning, as when the poet loses and thereby finds himself 'far from home' in 'The Hebrides'. Odysseus may be 'lost in sleep' but he is also, finally, found for those who have lost him, and has found his way home.

This is not, however, the last word, or the final resolution: 'home-coming', as the *Odyssey* itself makes clear, is also about the need to begin all over again, and Odysseus's voyage home is only half of the story. But once again, the transmutation of life into myth, and the distance, or perspective, this brings enables the expression of what had seemingly become for Longley, in the early 1980s, inex-pressible. Reading autobiographical elements in the Homeric poems is encouraged, implicitly, by their placing in the context of *Gorse Fires*. On the facing page to 'Homecoming' is 'Remembering Carrigskeewaun', where memory recreates a home from home. 'Tree House', which unites Penelope and Odysseus, is linked, through the 'ingenious' tree-bed and its 'imaginary branches' to the 'imaginary roots' of the 'glass flowers' that heal the 'broken marriages' in the previous poem 'Glass Flowers'. 'Laertes' is beside 'Northern Lights', a reminiscence of, and addressed to, Longley's own father; 'Anticleia', the story of Odysseus's meeting with his mother in the underworld, is the companion poem to 'The Balloon', which invokes Longley's mother Constance.

As Longley observes in the notes to *Gorse Fires*, 'Laertes' and 'Anticleia' are among those five poems which deal with the 'delayed recognitions and complicated reunions' between Odysseus and, respectively, his wife, nurse, father, mother, and dog. The theme of recognition (in Aristotle's term *anagnorisis*) is central – to the Odyssey, to Greek tragedy, to these poems, and to Longley's aesthetic more generally. The task of the early 'No Continuing City' was 'to recognise / This new dimension, my last girl'; recognition is part of the continuing concern to traverse that 'no man's land between one human being and another'; it is about the capacity to recognise – and confront – that which may be repulsive; and it is about self-discovery. Thus, in the encounter with Penelope in 'Tree House', recognition is about trust, about believing 'at last' in the Odysseus who is (in the final three lines which are Longley's addition to the original passage) 'love poet, carpenter'.

For Longley, the 'whole story' of the *Odyssey* is 'founded on the faithful wedded love of Odysseus and Penelope...reflected and amplified by filial affection'.[14] *Gorse Fires*, in that sense, is a reaffirmation in maturity of the 'recognitions' of *No Continuing City*. In 'Laertes', Odysseus imaginatively travels back in time to rediscover, from 'Evidence of a childhood', an earlier self, as Laertes also recognises Odysseus in the present time. Himself 'held secure' in 'In Memoriam', the poet now holds his 'dwindling father' in 'Laertes'. 'Eurycleia' returns to an earlier concern with touch: 'His wet-nurse cradled his foot in her hands and touched / The scar'. Touch is the moment of recognition, as it earlier rendered emotion tangible in the touching of 'Wounds'.

Conversely, like 'Last Requests', with its failure to connect, 'Argos' and 'Anticleia' are poems of recognition in which the physical connection is denied, and the barrier between life and death thrown up again. 'The Butchers', while not directly one of the sequence dealing with 'delayed recognitions', is nevertheless about recognising the other side of the 'love poet' – the killer – and about confronting an individual's, and a society's, capacity for brutality and evil.

The faithfulness which, for Longley, underpins the 'whole story' is self-reflexive too. What the *Odyssey* teaches is the importance of waiting, of fidelity to the idea of return however improbable that return might seem. To some extent, this is, as in 'Homecoming', about Longley's own trusting of silence – in contrast to those over-productive lyric poets who continue to write throughout what are, in effect, periods of writer's block – and trusting in poetry's eventual return. It is notable that Odysseus's indecisive musings on how to proceed in his meeting with Laertes in the *Odyssey* are discarded in Longley's 'Laertes', which opts instead for 'he waited for images from that formal garden'.

The reward of that patience is that these poems achieve what the poet attempted, and failed, with the abandoned *Odyssey* poems of the late 1970s. Significantly different in terms of style, they are also less self-conscious about the myth's relation to the pattern of Longley's own life, as if they are not so much trying to solve a 'puzzle' as simply to let its elements unfold.

'Eurycleia', the first of the Homeric poems in *Gorse Fires* to be written, is the exception, in that its leap from the mythic to the autobiographical, from Odysseus's Eurycleia to Longley's Lena, is at once too explicit and too obscure. Part II of the poem perhaps depends too much on knowledge of Longley's *Tuppenny Stung* if it is to yield its full meaning. 'Anticleia' and 'Laertes', however, do not suffer from that problem.

Those aspects of Homer which are more homely than heroic are the ones which chime most obviously with Longley's own imagination. The introduction of homely details into 'Laertes' enables the transition from Greek epic to contemporary lyric, in which process the poem is transformed into a lament for the poet's own father. The 'duds', the 'deep depression', and ('to cap it all') the 'duncher' (Belfast dialect for a flat cap) are all elements in a collo-quial, distinctively modern idiom that brings intimacy, poignancy and an affectionate humour to the encounter. The companion poem, 'Northern Lights', returns to the poet's childhood, with his father's 'hand on my shoulder', and metaphorically unites the two of them inside their own 'magnetic field'. 'Laertes' works a reverse angle, in which 'great Odysseus' has become the paternal figure, Laertes the childlike figure held at his breast. And where both poems are about uniting father and son, the mythic rather than autobiograph-ical poem is the one in which the poet confronts his personal loss directly.

The elegiac moments in 'Laertes' link it to Longley's earlier poems about his father, and to the problem of elegising more gen-erally. Odysseus's desire to 'blurt out the whole story' to Laertes is followed by a line which has no source in Homer, and which con-nects their meeting to the problem of language of which Longley's

poetry is always cognisant: 'But the whole story is one catalogue
and then another'. As with Edward Thomas, the child Odysseus,
'asking for everything he saw, the thirteen pear-trees, / Ten apple-
trees, forty fig-trees, the fifty rows of vines', likes the names. Yet
once again, as in Thomas's 'Old Man', 'the names / Half decorate,
half perplex, the thing it is'. In 'Laertes', the catalogue is a substi-
tute. Words replace the words that Odysseus cannot find; language
is an approximation. While the catalogues have their origin in
Homer's epic lists, they work rather differently in Longley's poetry
to point up the gap between feeling and language. The 'whole story'
becomes – as it is in 'Ghetto' and 'The Ice-cream Man' – the
problem of telling; language both reveals and conceals the truth.

A lament for his father, 'Laertes' is a poem that shows the inside
workings of Longley's later, more overtly political elegies, and
which has its own tradition behind it in the poet's *oeuvre*, since
elegising his father has always provided a 'taproot' into history.
'Anticleia', however, which might be described as a lament for his
mother, is comparatively, as might have been expected, a 'more
difficult' poem than 'Laertes'. This is, of course, to borrow Longley's
own phrase in relation to his mother from 1985. But there is also
a difference in 'Anticleia' in comparison with the earlier poems
implicitly about Constance Longley's death: if the difficulty – of
the mother-son relationship as well as of the bereavement – is not,
and cannot be, assuaged, it has at least found a form of expression
within which it can be accommodated.

'Anticleia', an 18-line poem, is poised as a single conditional
sentence which is also a question. This leaves the poem infinitely
suspended, as Anticleia herself repeatedly eludes Odysseus's grasp:

> And if, having given her blood to drink and talked about home,
> You lunge forward three times to hug her and three times
> Like a shadow or idea she vanishes through your arms
> And you ask her why she keeps avoiding your touch and weep
> Because here is your mother and even here in Hades
> You could comfort each other in a shuddering embrace,
> Will she explain that the sinews no longer bind her flesh
> And bones, that the irresistible fire has demolished these,
> That the soul takes flight like a dream and flutters in the sky,
> That this is what happens to human beings when they die?

The enjambment of the first five lines quoted here makes this
sentence equally elusive, slipping away unstoppably from the
reader's grasp. There is a personal hurt here too, as she seemingly
avoids his touch, and as at the point of being found ('here is your
mother') she is also once more lost to him.

The tentativeness which poses the poem as a question ('Will she explain...?') is, of course, Longley's own, since in the *Odyssey* Anticleia does explain to Odysseus why they cannot embrace, and it offers one means of expressing the emotional and practical uncertainties inherent in the encounter. If the meeting it describes is unsettling, so too is this poem's form. In one sense, Odysseus and Anticleia cannot meet, even when they do so. Similarly, the whole poem depends on the 'If' with which it begins; but the line lengths and sustained sentence encourage a forgetfulness of that conditional opening in the process of reading. As in 'Laertes', Odysseus recognises Anticleia first; she can see him only after the ritual in which she is 'given...blood to drink'. But unlike in 'Laertes', physical contact – touch – is irrecoverable in this poem.

It is easy to see why Longley is drawn to the Anticleia story. Her death (from grief) is bound up with Odysseus's long absence from her, literally and emotionally; at the point where they can recognise and understand each other they are separated forever. If there are echoes here of the hurt, and the 'courtship' to death's door described in Longley's autobiography, there are also, in the closing lines of the poem, oblique intertextual connections to 'The White Butterfly', 'View', 'The Third Light' and others of the *New Poems* which struggle with loss of the loved one. Hades, as the place of a shadowy, flickering, dream-like existence, is also a place where the earlier images of the butterfly, the smoke ring, or the unravelling skeleton find their 'home'. But where some of the earlier poems tried repeatedly to recover the maternal principle, 'Anticleia' instead dramatises the failure to do so.

Although its grammatical permutations give the illusion of a 'shadow or idea' vanishing, the single-sentence poem is also, in another sense, a 'complicated vessel' which contains that loss, its form a far cry from the brief 'markings' and stylistic fragmentation in some of the *New Poems*. If 'sinews no longer bind her flesh', the longer line in this poem does at least serve to bind its emotional difficulties together. While the final question mark leaves the poem open, the repetitions and perfect end rhyme of the last two lines of the poem counter that open-endedness with stability and a form of closure. In dramatising – at the level of form – rather than assuaging the difficulty of the encounter, 'Anticleia' thus also shows the other side of the coin to 'The Balloon'. Indeed, the difficulty of one poem seems necessary for the relative simplicity of the other.

'The Balloon' does what 'Anticleia' cannot do, and what Longley ten years earlier could not have done: it liberates the frightened child of his imagination; it heals his mother and sets her free, 'smiling and waving and running without a limp / Across the shallow streams and fields of shiny grass / As thought there were neither malformation nor pain'. It has its parallels with 'Anticleia', but they are also contrasts. In 'The Balloon' there are 'shallow streams' rather than 'resonant rivers'; Anticleia vanishes 'Like a shadow', but the balloon 'casts no shadow' between mother and son; the underworld is transformed to open fields; the 'soul' that 'takes flight' after death is now the child full of life and almost able to fly, as the poet exhorts her to '"Jump over the hedges, Connie, jump over the trees."'

III

'Laertes', 'Anticleia', 'Eurycleia' and 'Tree House' link the mythic to the autobiographical; their connection to some of the traumas of 20th-century history is also evident at an intertextual level. The child and mother of 'The Balloon' and 'Anticleia' resurface in Longley's holocaust poem 'Ghetto' as 'The little girl without a mother' who 'behaves like a mother / With her rag doll to whom she explains fear and anguish'; the 'whole story' as 'one catalogue and then another' in 'Laertes' is echoed in the 'choices', the 'list of your belongings' of the victims of 'Ghetto'. 'Argos' and 'The Butchers', however, reach more explicitly from the mythic to the socio-political. The *Odyssey* poems scattered through *Gorse Fires* thus form a narrative in their own right, one which progressively expands the historical resonance of the myth.

In 'Argos' Longley transforms the story of Odysseus's pet into a symbol of suffering. Mythic cycles of repetition become a continuity of suffering:

> ...like Odysseus
> We weep for Argos the dog, and for all those other dogs,
> For the rounding-up of hamsters, the panic of white mice
> And the deportation of one canary called Pepicek.

The source for these final lines is Helen Lewis's memoir of the treatment of the Czechoslovakian Jews during World War II, and of her own imprisonment first in the ghetto at Terezín, then in Auschwitz. The relevant passage is as follows:

> Even before 1942 Jews had to hand over to the German authorities not only their radios but jewellery and silver, furs, and anything of value. What else was there to take from them? Unbelievably, the

answer was their pets [...] To some, especially children and old people, this was the hardest blow. On the prescribed day, there they were in the trams, white-faced, choking back tears, clutching their pathetic little boxes, cartons or bundles, which were to be handed in at the reception centres: guinea-pigs and hamsters, white mice and tortoises, and of course caged birds. Dogs and cats were the worst, they cried aloud all the way, as if they knew. Paul's father, a tall, calm gentleman, always dignified, had to hand over his much loved canary, Pepicek. That evening he seemed smaller, shrunken and forlorn.[15]

The close of 'Argos', however, is transparent even without awareness of its "source", and that it does not explain itself is also a measure of anger. In its choice of 'rounding-up' and 'deportation', it takes us into the world of human atrocity, the 'panic' here pre-empting that of the people themselves who will, eventually, share the fate of their pets. The loss of human dignity is also implicitly the poem's subject: Argos, once 'A real thoroughbred, a marvel at picking up the scent' is now 'neglected on the manure-heap...flea-ridden, more dead than alive'. And 'neglected' is the poem's real indictment of society: it insists that we 'weep' for the details often forgotten, and in doing so for the atrocities they foreshadow, but always with the knowledge that those who weep in retrospect may also be those who permitted neglect or forgot those details in the first place.

'Argos' is as bitter as it is compassionate, and in this it paves the way for 'The Butchers', a poem which shows the brutality of the *Odyssey*'s hero, the love poet as the killer, and which therefore reflects back on the self – and on contemporary society – in even more disturbing ways. In 'No Continuing City' the poet, recognising a 'new dimension', undertakes a 'spring cleaning' of his own past, 'to set my house in order'. In 'The Butchers', Odysseus also sets his house in order, but here the more sinister reverberations of the phrase are in evidence, and 'his house' represents the state as well as the home. There are two forms of cleansing in 'The Butchers', the second of which, 'the need for whitewash and disinfectant', the fumigation of 'the house and the outhouses', is consequent upon the first – Odysseus's slaughter of the suitors and the 'disloyal housemaids'. That they can both be seen as a means of cleansing is profoundly unsettling, as if the desire for a surface order and purity is attainable only through atrocity. Stylistically, the unstoppable frenzy of the slaughter and the equally unstoppable cleaning up (the enjambment of 20 of the poem's 28 lines contributes to the effect of extraordinary compulsion, as if pushing beyond acceptable limits) can feel like the same thing, as they are also contained in the same sentence.

The historical nerves the poem touches upon are several. Its title is evocative of the Shankill Butchers, the loyalist gang who tortured and murdered many Catholics through the 1970s and 1980s. The close of the poem, which brings the souls of the suitors 'to a bog-meadow full of bog-asphodels', Hibernicises the myth ('bog meadow' evokes the west of Ireland, but the Bog Meadows is also an area in west Belfast), a tactic which might bring to mind Northern Ireland's many revenge killings, the competing territorial claims in Ireland more generally, and the concomitant urges to "cleanse" certain areas of certain people.

For Longley, 'The Butchers' has a personal resonance too. Although not explicitly autobiographical, the poem is bound up for him with the 'loss of bureaucratic innocence' suggested earlier, the sense, perhaps, of being corrupted by his working life. In an interview he explains:

> ...I had in the back of my mind the Shankill Butchers – I had in the back of my mind the sort of outhouses and smallholdings that would have been on Ithaca and which were reflected in the landscape of Ireland. [...] I wanted this headlong violent expression of something. [...] And when I'd finished, I was very frightened. I felt as though I had released something. And also, one of the things that bothered me about the poem was my hatred for various people on the Arts Council – this was how I would have liked to have behaved, to clean out the Augean stables. So there was a personal emotion in it.[16]

A personal emotion drives the poem; but its historical scope is still much broader than Longley's comments here – or the Hibernicisation of the poem – might suggest. 'The Butchers' raises questions about human capability – and culpability. Odysseus is 'like a lion dripping blood / From his chest and cheeks after devouring a farmer's bullock'; the dead suitors are 'heaped in blood and dust / Like fish... gasping for salt water'; the hanged women are 'like long-winged thrushes / Or doves trapped in a mist-net'; Melanthios's body parts – 'nose and ears and cock and balls' – are cut off to become, literally, a 'dog's dinner'; the suitors' and housemaids' souls are 'Like bats gibbering'. In 'Argos', the animals disturbingly evoke human beings; in 'The Butchers', human beings are equally disturbingly portrayed the other way around.

The poem raises questions about civilisation and barbarism, most tellingly in the contrast between the animal instinct of Odysseus's brutality, and the distinctively modern, "civilised" trappings of 'whitewash and disinfectant' which are needed in its service. The cleansing is also, in another way, a cover-up. As this poem shows all too clearly, to get rid of what is corrupt, to 'clean out the Augean stables', can be itself a form of corruption. The 'ethnic cleansing' of the Holocaust is implicitly evoked in 'The Butchers', in the bodies 'heaped in blood and dust', and in the appallingly clinical and efficient elimination of all traces of the carnage. The 'whitewash' of this poem has its echoes elsewhere in *Gorse Fires*, in 'the equalising lime' that 'has covered our excrement' ('The Shack'), in the 'sprinkle of snowflakes' covering the child in 'Ghetto'. Throughout the collection, the recurrent imagery of whiteness (something that can literally, of course, appal) is deeply ambiguous, redolent on the one hand of healing and purity, but on the other of deception and death, always carrying awareness of the underlying 'excrement' or corruption of the self that it hides.

For a writer, as Longley is aware, the Holocaust is 'dangerous territory'. Nevertheless, we are also, he argues 'duty bound to try and work out how we got there'.[17] The sense of a shared responsibility – not least in the creation of a civilised society capable of co-ordinating atrocity on this scale – is implicit in that idea. After the Holocaust, George Steiner questioned not only the supposed connection between literature and civilised values, but also raised the possibility that literary values could themselves be seen as deeply implicated in institutional acts of sadism. Language is implicated in those acts too. Steiner notes that 'It was one of the precise horrors of the Nazi era that all that happened was recorded, catalogued, chronicled, set down...The unspeakable being said, over and over, for twelve years. The unspeakable being written down, indexed, filed for reference.'[18]

As Longley has observed, 'The Final Solution happened to be, among other ghastly things, a bureaucratic triumph'; as such it raises for him the question of 'to what extent one would have been involved in it oneself, as a bureaucrat, as a station master'.[19] 'The Butchers' is effective partly because, as in earlier poems which probe beneath the surface to reveal uncomfortable depths, it is prepared to confront human atrocity without presuming such atrocity to be remote from or incomprehensible to the self. The poem generates an excitement, stylistically, by scarcely drawing breath, in a manner illustrative of Steiner's suggestion that 'literary imagination' could give 'ecstatic welcome to political bestiality'. But the compulsive, seemingly unstoppable natural force which is Odysseus in this poem is also, as the unsettling imagery of the poem suggests, a compulsion to be resisted.

The preoccupation with the Holocaust evoked in the Homeric poems is the subject of two of the most complex poems in *Gorse Fires* – the sequence 'Ghetto', and the couplet poem 'Terezín'.

(The fate of the Jewish children in the extermination camps also haunts 'The Cairn at Dooaghtry'.) The poems grapple with the problems inherent in imagining the Holocaust: how poetry can approach the subject; whether, or why it should do so; whether imaginative engagement may become presumptuous, or even self-indulgent. It is this last danger, for instance, that Geoffrey Hill acknowledges, as a way of trying to avoid it, in the wry aside of his Holocaust poem, 'September Song', '(I have made / an elegy for myself it / is true)'. Whether language should fall silent in the face of such atrocity remains a controversial point. Adorno's famous dictum 'No poetry after Auschwitz' implies the subject can never be grasped in words. Ionesco concluded, too, that 'words say nothing', that 'There are no words for the deepest experience'. George Steiner, on the other hand, with the awareness that 'so far as a model of language goes, silence is, palpably, a dead end', suggests that 'language...must not, indeed ought not, to fall silent at the boundaries of the monstrous'.[20]

'Ghetto', a sequence of eight short poems, draws its inspiration from Helen Lewis's memoir, from a journey by Longley across Poland in 1986, and from the children's drawings that survived the Terezín ghetto.[21] Its first and final sections were written in the spring of 1989, and sections II to VII between January and May 1990. That its different sections only came together belatedly, and out of sequence, is significant. One of the last poems in the book to be completed, 'Ghetto' also has a sense of being unfinished: it stops and starts abruptly; it denies narrative coherence or closure. Its multiple sections suggest a need to try again and again, but never with the presumption that a final word can be said. At moments seeming to come close to what he can 'imagine', the poet is also, as in section IV, 'transported / Away'. That closeness and distance works even at the level of the speaking voice, which shifts between first person (sections IV and V), second person (sections I and VI) and third person (sections II, III, VII and VIII), and shifts tonally between childhood and adult idioms, continually seeking different perspectives, never bringing the self to rest in one place.

Throughout, the poem struggles with permanence and imper-manence, how to fix its subject imaginatively when that subject is the disappearance of 'hundreds of thousands'. The 'heirlooms, perishables, worldly goods' of section I are all, like their owners, ultimately perishable. As Helen Lewis writes, the 50 kilos of lug-gage permitted to the deportees forced them to 'choose what would be indispensable for their future life', a 'harrowing task',

since they did not know what that future would be. 'In their fran-
tic efforts to make the right choices,' she continues, 'people used
up their precious physical and emotional energies'.[22]

In 'Ghetto', that future is, for most, non-existent: 'Because you
will suffer soon and die, your choices / Are neither right nor wrong...'.
At the same time, the list of 'Photographs, medicines, a change of
underwear, a book, / A candlestick, a loaf, sardines, needle and thread'
becomes the 'heirloom[s]', the inventory itself all that survives – 'Your
last belonging a list of your belongings'. The desire to be able to
'rescue from their separate rooms love and sorrow' in section III is
never one the poet claims to be able to fulfil; but in its recovery
of detail, these poems do, in another way, recover 'small fortunes'.

The difficulty inherent in the sheer scale of the Holocaust is
implied in section IV: 'From among the hundreds of thousands I
can imagine one...'. The 'one' is seen only fleetingly, 'for long enough
to catch the sprinkle of snowflakes / On his hair and schoolbag',
and the train transports the poet away. But 'transported' works in
another sense here too: while he has literally left the boy behind,
the sight of him gives him permanence in the imagination, like
the earlier children of 'Kindertotenlieder' who left 'teethmarks' on
the memory: 'He turns into a little snowman and refuses to melt.'
Typically, though, that imagery of permanence is the stuff of
impermanence too, the play between fixity and fluidity also encap-
sulating the problem of memory.

If the poem is about imaginative recovery, about the hope that
something survives the carnage, the poem's final section makes a
transition from crayon to ink – impermanence to permanence,
childhood to maturity – that also turns the seemingly positive, the
fact that something survives, on its head:

> There were drawing lessons, and drawings of kitchens
> And farms, farm animals, butterflies, mothers, fathers
> Who survived in crayon until in pen and ink
> They turned into guards at executions and funerals
> Torturing and hanging even these stick figures.

With 'even' here, the poem makes the point that nothing is invio-
late, nothing exempt from contamination. 'Ghetto' is profoundly,
if not obviously, a reflection on the status and function of art in
the face of atrocity; it finds no easy answers to the problems it
raises. In section VI there is 'time / To jump over a skipping rope',
'time to adjust / As though for a dancing class the ribbons in your
hair'; there is a moment (one reminiscent of T.S. Eliot) held,
seemingly indefinitely, against barbarism, and against the nature

seen so brutally in 'The Butchers': 'This string quartet is the most
natural thing in the world'. But the timeless quality here – as if
there is all the time in the world too – is about innocence, and
section VII fragments those civilities into brief, elusive 'harmonics...
between electrified fences'.

Section V is also a confession of inadequacy. Beginning in a
fashion reminiscent of the Audenesque social conscience poetry of
the 1930s ('For the street-singers in the marketplace, weavers, warp-
makers, / Those who suffer in sewing-machine repair shops...there
are not enough root vegetables') the poet quickly undercuts his
right to speak to or for them. The hungry people are:

> ...turning like a thick slice of potato-bread
> This page, which is everything I know about potatoes,
> My delivery of Irish Peace, Beauty of Hebron, Home
> Guard, Arran Banners, Kerr's Pinks, resistant to eelworm,
> Resignation, common scab, terror, frost, potato-blight.

'[E]verything I know' is, in effect, an admission of knowing nothing,
of being able to do nothing. The lines are deliberately clumsy; they
leave their readership uncomfortable with them, and with their
author. Yet this is also what they are meant to do. The poignant
catalogue of section I has its counterpart here, in the catalogue
which, with its 'Irish Peace' and 'Home / Guard' is ironic and self-
consciously inept. Listing may be consolation, or, in Greek epic,
celebration; here, it is a confession of inadequacy. 'Ghetto' is a
poem of checks and balances, constantly crossing out any claims it
might seem to have made, but never content to rest there.

In 'Ghetto', the link between silence and absence, and the para-
dox of trying to express either through poetry, is at the heart of the
difficulty in this 'dangerous territory'. That paradox is obliquely
encapsulated in section II:

> As though it were against the law to sleep on pillows
> They have filled a cathedral with confiscated feathers:
> Silence irrefrangible, no room for angels' wings,
> Tons of feathers suffocating cherubim and seraphim.

The 'Silence irrefrangible' here, a silence which cannot be broken
or violated, is not because of emptiness, but because the space is
full – too full to admit of sound. But this is also about absence, the
'confiscated feathers' another of the petty torments visited on the
people whose own absence is therefore present in these lines. The
poem creates its own suffocating silence, whilst it simultaneously
ensures the 'feathers' are always present and filling the poem,
through the repeated 's' and 'f' sounds which sound in almost

every stress in these lines, and which are refracted through later parts of 'Ghetto' – in the 'fear and anguish', the 'small fortunes', the 'sprinkle of snowflakes', and the world of 'silent toys'.

The attempt to bring absence into consciousness – into imaginative presence – and to remember silence through sound is always, in one way, doomed to failure. But Longley's elegies, which have always understood failure and paradox to be at the heart of the elegiac mode, tread the ground more sensitively than most. 'Ghetto' as a whole understands that its own subject is a form of 'Silence irrefrangible', one to be broached only on the understanding that artistic violations may be unforgivable. (Whether rightly or wrongly in terms of abstract aesthetic principles, it is one of the few poems of Longley's career which he has tested in experiential waters before publication.)[23]

The play on silence and absence in section II of 'Ghetto' is a theme which haunts many of the poems in *Gorse Fires*; but it finds its ultimate and most concentrated expression in 'Terezín'. The two-line poem functions as the closing couplet of an exploded, or split sonnet, following on as it does from the three quatrain poems 'Eva Braun', 'Geisha' and Blitz'. But 'Terezín' also stands alone, and is positioned so that the surrounding white space on the page is integral to its meaning (a technique retained, unusually, in the *Selected Poems* as well). In its evocation of the unmentionable, the poem is a stay against silence, but at the same time it seems almost to approach the condition of silence:

> No room has ever been as silent as the room
> Where hundreds of violins are hung in unison.

As Douglas Dunn has noted, the alexandrine is 'the metrical foundation of these lines'; but the necessary 'Where' of the second line 'forestalls the couplet's regularity', a technique which he sees as implicated in Longley's acceptance of 'the impure, the imperfect, as a necessity in the reflection of contemporary facts'.[24] The same may be said of its rhyming, which (as also in 'Blitz' with its soundless shockwaves) is imperfect, and slightly off-key: the couplet does not chime in unison; only the silence beyond the poem is capable of doing so. The poem evokes silence and simultaneously strikes a discordant note.

Longley has observed that 'I don't think there's anything one can do imaginatively with the photographs of the piles of bodies or the idea of the torture chambers';[25] but here, as with the feathers of 'Ghetto', the 'hundreds of thousands' are evoked through a kind of imaginative substitution. Like the catalogues of his poems, these

objects are substitutions that are, in the end, approximations: they
cannot replace, or even stand in for, the people themselves; but
they can stand in for the absence of those people. In that sense,
the violins here, like the 'Shockwaves...wrinkling the water that
isn't there' in 'Blitz', are the presence of absence.

IV

These are poems which bring to Longley's elegiac concerns, and
to the paradox of elegy itself, a new intensity, and a new level of
sophistication in the relation between absence and presence, remem-
bering and forgetting. Unsurprisingly, the poem in *Gorse Fires* which
has perhaps attracted the most attention since its publication is the
Troubles elegy 'The Ice-cream Man'. It was written following the
murder, in October 1988, of John Larmour, an off-duty RUC
officer shot by the IRA whilst looking after his brother's ice-cream
shop on the Lisburn Road in Belfast. The politics behind the killing
are invisible in the poem itself, as they are, of course, invisible to
the child – Longley's youngest daughter – to whom it is addressed:

> Rum and raisin, vanilla, butter-scotch, walnut, peach:
> You would rhyme off the flavours. That was before
> They murdered the ice-cream man on the Lisburn Road
> And you bought carnations to lay outside his shop.
> I named for you all the wild flowers of the Burren
> I had seen in one day: thyme, valerian, loosestrife,
> Meadowsweet, tway blade, crowfoot, ling, angelica,
> Herb robert, marjoram, cow parsley, sundew, vetch,
> Mountain avens, wood sage, ragged robin, stitchwort,
> Yarrow, lady's bedstraw, bindweed, bog pimpernel.

In its deceptive simplicity it has a claim to be considered one of the
outstanding elegies of Longley's career. It encapsulates perfectly
what elegy can and cannot do, how language is both meaningful
and, in another sense, meaningless. Longley himself offers two
interpretations of 'The Ice-cream Man' which encompass both
attitudes. First, that the flower names 'are turned into a wreath of
words'; second, that 'A catalogue like this one is meant to go on
forever'.[26] In the first of these readings, the flower names are heal-
ing and encircling. Like many of the poems in *The Echo Gate*,
'The Ice-cream Man' has a tripartite structure. The three points
of the poem are each, in their own way, acts of remembrance: one
is in advance of the fact – the rhyming of flavours unknowingly
foreshadows the poem's end; the standard ritual of laying flowers

takes place in the middle; and the flower wreath of the final lines seems to offer future consolation. The poem mourns both the death of the ice-cream man, and the child's loss of innocence; it mourns the laying of carnations even as it offers that gesture as its own consolation. The flowers and flavours circle the poem, and are woven around the killing at its centre so that it becomes, if read in its entirety, if seen whole at the one moment, an object, a memorial, a wreath that can be laid.

But 'The Ice-cream Man' is a more ambiguous poem than this reading suggests. That the catalogue is 'meant to go on forever' gives a clue to the ways in which the poem destabilises its own achievement. The listing, for a start, is rhythmically slightly unsettled, particularly in the penultimate line: it *looks* incantatory, but it *sounds* far more hesitant than that. That the list reaches further than the opening list of flavours marks its failure at consolation: one might list forever, but the death still occurred. The poem might create a wreath, might express a traditional need for flowers and incantations in the process of mourning, but it finds no totalising meaning in that creation. Notwithstanding its final full-stop, the poem questions any easy distinctions between the "closed" traditional lyric poem, and the open-ended, experimental poem. Rather than being read as circular, it may be read as linear, as projecting through time into a future beyond its own existence, as destabilising language and lyricism. Like 'Terezín', it reverberates beyond its own limits in the space outside. The flowers do not so much "mean" anything as they memorialise an absence of available meaning. The killing, rather than being contained in and by the flower and flavour lists, falls in the gap between them.

The longer the list goes on, the more it begins to unravel, to "unwrite" itself through implicit recognition of its own inadequacy. The paradox of elegy is also here a paradox of reading: as each word in the catalogue comes into view, so another disappears into the past. In Longley's list of flowers, the names become almost a list of the dead. (The ice-cream man himself is not named; in a way the flower and flavour names stand in for his absent name with another absence.) The flowers are recited, or inscribed, in order to remember, but with each name becoming present, the reader discards the presence of the previously present one. Hence the poem concerns the melancholy – and failure – of the act of remembering: memory can never really recover what has disappeared; remembering itself is something that can never be achieved in full; imaginative presence is always simultaneously the awareness of loss. (The same idea is present in 'In Memory of Charles Donnelly', where 'they accumulate for ever / The poems you go on not writing in the tree's shadow'.) The result is an inherent forgetting which forces us to go on remembering indefinitely. The paradox at the core of the poem is thus that remembering is about forgetting, that the presence of an object is also its immanent moment of absence.

The poem – like the killing which is its subject – falls between or beyond definitions. As with many of the poems in *Gorse Fires*, it is thematically and formally 'On home-made crutches and slipping all the tethers' ('The Velocipede'). The naming of flowers may be a Georgian convention; the wreath of words has a pedigree at least back to 'Lycidas'; catalogues have their origin in Homer's epics. But the conventions are used unconventionally by Longley. Paul Fussell notes that 'Pastoral reference…is a way of invoking a code to hint by antithesis at the indescribable; at the same time, it is a comfort in itself'.[27] 'The Ice-cream Man' is a pastoral elegy which works in some of these ways, and which draws on pastoral motifs of consolation. But it is also an elegy for the pastoral world. The flowers named from the Burren are almost impossible to see; they are also themselves under threat (the list is an attempted stay against that threat). The poem merges the poet's here and elsewhere – Belfast and the west of Ireland – always conscious that both worlds can be shattered in a moment. It is not a question of reading 'The Ice-cream Man' one way or the other – as consolatory or anti-consolatory, circular or linear, closed or open in form, traditional or experimental elegy; rather, it is a question of reading it both ways at once, of recognising that the poem works by hovering between possibilities and impossibilities, that it both meets and disrupts elegiac expectations.

The elegiac mode brings the relation of absence to presence into particular focus, but the theme runs throughout *Gorse Fires*, and is connected to the sense of being betwixt and between noted earlier. The sensibility that emerges is an elusive one, resistant to paraphrase. It is implied by 'Otters', where the otter is 'Tying and untying knots in the undertow / And wiring me like a harebell to the wind'. Similarly, in part II of the poem, the otter, in between holt and hover, 'Engraves its own reflection and departure'. As with Penelope's daytime weaving and night-time unravelling, what is caught here is the moment where time and timelessness, permanence and impermanence, movement and stasis intersect. Thus, the otter 'Engraves' what will disappear, marks its own absence; the poet freeze-frames the otter's moment between holt and hover – neither home, nor at a stopping place, but poised between them. And in the title-poem, the poet is himself caught in that moment, travelling 'from one April to another' in 'the same train between the same embankments'.

'Between Hovers' adopts that sensibility at the level of form as well as subject. The poem begins *in medias res*, as if 'between hovers' itself: 'And not even when we ran over the badger / Did he tell me he had cancer…'. Joe O'Toole's death is absent from the poem, but it is implied through the events that are present: running over the badger; the porch light O'Toole left burning to guide the poet home; sitting on the burial mound; and the dying otter of the final lines. The badger 'dragged…by two gritty paws into the ditch' subtly connects with O'Toole himself who is buried 'Close to the stony roads'. The car headlights, and the badger as 'a filament of light our lights had put out' pave the way for the 'porch light burning', with 'its sparkle / Shifting from widgeon to teal on Corragaun Lake', echoing the poem's own shifting in and out of different times and events. The badger is killed 'Somewhere between Kinnadoohy and Thallabaun; on the burial mound, the poet is 'Encircled by the spring tide and taking in / Cloonaghmanagh and Claggan and Carrigskeewaun'; and in the final lines:

> I watched a dying otter gaze right through me
> At the islands in Clew Bay, as though it were only
> Between hovers and not too far from the holt.

The insistence on naming runs along side an habitual placing 'Somewhere between' those names and places. That quality of being somewhere and nowhere is also present in the brief but telling sentence at the heart of the poem (with a poignant echo of Heaney's earlier elegy 'Casualty'): 'I missed his funeral'. Rendering the commonplace extraordinary, 'missed' works in at least two ways, encompassing both his own absence from the funeral, and the emotional condition of 'missing' something, which brings it back in memory. Missing the funeral is also about missing closure, or final definitions, in the series of parallels that constitute the poem. The ultimate finality is death – in which the poems are implicated, but against which they must always, by default, provide some resistance.

Implicitly, 'Between Hovers' links a return home (in this instance crossing the duach at night) with death, as suggested also by the 'dying otter…not too far from the holt'. The poem's subtle intertextual links with 'The Third Light' and 'Second Sight', also about death and a return to origins, contribute to that connection as well. 'Homecoming' is here, as always for Longley, an ambiguous act: it is about birth and death, return and departure. *Gorse Fires*, whilst

recognising the inevitability of death, also provides a stay against
it. Scattered through the book are the four-line poems which are a
new departure in Longley's writing. Where 'Thaw' is exceptional in
his earlier work, in *Gorse Fires*, *The Ghost Orchid*, and *The Weather
in Japan*, short poems (ranging between one and five lines) are in
abundance – there are eighteen such poems in *The Ghost Orchid*,
seventeen in *The Weather in Japan*. (The most recent collection,
Snow Water, however, breaks this pattern quite dramatically, marking
a further shift in style.) Variable in their nature and depth, they
are all nonetheless integral components in the aesthetic reshaping
of Longley's *oeuvre* through the 1990s.

One way of thinking about the emergence of the short poems is
to see them as a resistance to silence, in more ways than one. Or,
looked at the other way around, as 'a way of coming to terms with
the silence' ('Peregrine') – and thereby breaking it. In the late 1960s,
the short, spare poems of *Secret Marriages* led towards the 'blank
page and dead silence' that *Gorse Fires* – at the deepest level –
struggles against. To some extent this is personal, in Longley's
own emergence from the "silence" of the early 1980s; it is also, as
seen in relation to the Holocaust poems, deeply political, bound
up with responsibility towards language and history. Where the
Secret Marriages poems seemed to be part of a 'logical progression'
towards silence, the short poems of *Gorse Fires* might be read rather
as a progression out of silence. (It seems to be no coincidence that
the number of short poems has decreased so considerably in the
most recent collection, *Snow Water*, which stands at an almost 20
year distance from that silence.) Many of them are single sentence
quatrains (as in 'In Aillwee Cave', 'Geisha', 'Eva Braun', 'The
Hip-Bath' or 'The Fireplace'); where they are not, they tend to be
two sentences comprising two connected images (as in 'Phosphore-
scence' or 'Insomnia'). Where they are rhymed (as in 'Insomnia',
'Blitz', or more elusively 'Quails' Eggs'), the rhyming is an un-
obtrusive half-rhyme that resists finality. In all instances, they are
a far cry from the brief, claustrophobic couplets of the 1960s and
early 1970s, and they all use the longer line that allows them fluidity,
and room to breathe.

'Phosphorescence', read self-reflexively, gives some insight into
the working of these short poems across the collection as a whole:

> There was light without heat between the stepping stones
> And the duach, at every stride the Milky Way.
> Her four or five petals hanging from an eyelash,
> Venus bloomed like brookweed next to the Pleiades.

In its placing of 'Venus...next to the Pleiades', with its 'stepping stones' and 'petals' side by side, 'Phosphorescence' illustrates in miniature the way the poems themselves work as stepping stones through the book, sometimes evidently linked, sometimes arranged in sequences (as in 'Trade Winds', 'Otters' or 'Ghetto'), and sometimes simply 'hanging' together (many of the short poems are paired on the page) without explanation.

The next poem in the book, 'Insomnia', makes the connection explicit, in closing with 'the stepping stones' that open 'Phosphorescence'. But it is possible to read all the quatrain poems which capture (or sometimes miss) brief moments in time as 'hovers', strung across the gaps and silences. As in 'Washing', it is as if the poet has left these poems 'pegged out at intervals' to create 'Gaps in the dunes, a sky-space for the lapwings'. They use the space between them; they are also themselves the in-between spaces, the stopping-places on the to-and-fro journey between origins and destinations.

What was once, in 'Alibis', a 'simple question / Of being in two places at the one time' seems to have become, in *Gorse Fires*, a simple question of being and not being in one place at the same time. *Gorse Fires* is an extraordinary accomplishment, a book whose subject is, in part, its own emergence after a period of silence, but which transforms that subject into a much broader reflection on some of the fundamental issues to have surfaced, 'after Auschwitz', in the latter half of the 20th century. Longley's care with words, his precision, his sense of responsibility towards what he says, and how he says it, are qualities much-vaunted by his critics, if seldom explained in any detail. It is possible to see in *Gorse Fires* wherein that sense of responsibility lies – in the acceptance of collusion in the language of barbarism as we have made it; in the desire to reinvent language as a means of resistance to atrocity; in the acknowledgement of limitation in relation to what words can and cannot do; and yet in the refusal to fall silent.

6

Metamorphoses: *The Ghost Orchid*
1991-1994

One drop too many and the whole thing distintegrates
In this humidity your watercolour will never dry.
MICHAEL LONGLEY, 1991

I

In June 1992, the poet Michael Hofmann wrote to Longley to ask if he would be interested in translating a section of Ovid's *Metamorphoses* for Hofmann and James Lasdun's anthology *After Ovid: New Metamorphoses*, published in 1994. Some weeks later, the Baucis and Philemon story was offered to Longley, and the poem written by early September 1992. The timing of the request was propitious for Longley, since the Ovid poems which followed 'Baucis and Philemon' brought the themes of his next book, *The Ghost Orchid* (1995), already in evidence in embryonic form through 1991 and early 1992, into focus. As Hofmann and Lasdun note in their introduction, Michael Longley and Ted Hughes were the two most prolific contributors to *After Ovid*. Retrospectively, Hofmann noted that the singular virtue of their Ovid commissions was to have seeded what he takes to be some of Hughes's and Longley's finest work.[1] Commissioned to write 'Baucis and Philemon', Longley also added a version of 'Perdix', and in a month-long Ovidian out-pouring in the autumn of 1993, five more *Metamorphoses* poems: 'Spiderwoman', 'A Flowering', 'Ivory & Water', 'Phoenix', and 'According to Pythagoras'.

These excursions into the *Metamorphoses* give metaphoric coherence to *The Ghost Orchid* as a whole. They extend the formal pre-occupation with change and mutability, as seen in such poems as 'Watercolour' and 'Form', complement a long-standing fascination with nature's capacity to transform, and connect to the poet's concerns with truth, fiction and storytelling. Not least, Ovid's strong pictorial sense strikes an obvious chord with Longley's own fascination, in

The Ghost Orchid, with painting, word-painting, and with the process of painting/writing as a process of transformation.

'My purpose,' Ovid writes at the opening of the *Metamorphoses*, 'is to tell of bodies which have been transformed into shapes of a different kind.'[2] The theme of metamorphosis manifests itself through *The Ghost Orchid* in all its different shades of meaning as the source of the collection's 'fundamental interconnectedness' ('According to Pythagoras'). It encompasses shape-shifting, the transformation of (and by) form through supernatural, or imaginative means, as well as the natural process of growth and change in humans and animals and, more obliquely, the possible changes in a society's condition and character. Metamorphosis is also to do with translation, which is always, as Longley is aware, about transformation into and out of another language, time, and place, about taking on the shape of another and simultaneously reshaping it oneself.

Almost a third of *The Ghost Orchid* poems are free translations, versions, or part borrowings. After his immersion in Ovid, Longley reverted to his long-standing interest in Homer, mostly in the spring and summer of 1994, in the Homeric poems 'Phemios & Medon', 'The Helmet', 'The Parting', 'The Campfires', 'The Scales', 'A Bed of Leaves', 'The Oar', and 'Ceasefire'. There are also borrowings from Virgil ('Hippomanes' draws on the book III of the *Georgics*, *l.* 270-81), Horace (in 'After Horace'), as well as translations from Marin Sorescu, Hendrik Marsman, and Karel van de Woestijne. The Ovid poems are the vital beginning of what is a more sustained interest in translation than is seen in any other of Longley's collections, an interest which, in the challenges it poses in terms of style and form, is central to his aesthetic development in the early 1990s.

As John Kerrigan has shown, Ovid has been an influential presence in Northern Irish poetry for many years, a kind of 'Latin Ulsterman' whose appeal lies both in his early 'metamorphic imaginings' and in his later forced exile from Rome.[3] Mahon's restless pacing of a 'benighted coast' is one manifestation of a condition of psychological displacement, an exile of the mind; Heaney's weighing of his 'responsible *tristia*' in relation to Northern Ireland from the vantage point of the Republic is, more literally, another. For Muldoon, his 'attention to change' leads him eventually, Kerrigan notes, into 'equivalents of *Metamorphoses*' in the long poems 'Immram' and 'The More a Man Has the More a Man Wants' in which 'Plot-lines melt and diverge; we are distracted by embedded tales' and 'There is a cascading lucidity of detail which recalls Ovid's fluid precision'. Muldoon's 'pleasure in aetiological narrative' is also identified as an Ovidian trait.[4]

Kerrigan's essay remarks the coincidence of interest in Ovid on the part of Northern Irish poets in the 1980s. His work predates Longley's own Ovid poems, but Longley's emergent interest in Ovid is also seen in the late 1970s and in the *New Poems* of the early 1980s, and the metamorphoses of an earlier poem such as 'Alibis' are significant in their influence on Muldoon's own fascination with change. Kerrigan's work is thus suggestive when it comes to comparing Longley's Ovidian fascination with that of his contemporaries. It is, most evidently, the Ovid of *Metamorphoses*, a book barely completed before the poet was expelled from Rome, who appeals to Longley, rather than the Ovid in exile, post-*Metamorphoses*, who speaks so poignantly to Mahon's imagination. Although both poets are drawn to the Pythagorean philosophy which dominates book XV of *Metamorphoses*, for Mahon the philosophy wherein 'Everything is susceptible' ('The Mute Phenomena') is given a Beckettian twist in which 'Our hair and excrement // Litter the rich earth, / Changing, second by second, / To civilisations' ('An Image from Beckett'). Change and mutability are about decline and loss, but there is also, as in Beckett, a pessimism which simultaneously implies a latent optimism: as Mahon puts it, 'Having hit rock bottom as you do with [Beckett], you know there's nowhere to go but up'.[5]

For Longley, the charm of Pythagoras's teachings in *Metamorphoses* lies in the perceptive detail on the natural world, with its cycles of renewal, and its extraordinary possibilities ('did you know that / Hyenas change sex?'), as it is also Ovid the nature poet and love poet who is brought out in Longley's versions of the *Metamorphoses*. In that sense, 'According to Pythagoras', with its assumption that 'Any farmer knows that', and its (often mischievous) enjoyment of 'scientific facts' marks a natural continuation of such poems as 'Lore' from *The Echo Gate*. The common denominator of transformation in the *Metamorphoses* is also, in other words, transformed into something different by every contemporary poet who encounters the tales.

Unlike Muldoon, Longley is not a narrative poet – or only very rarely so. That said, it is, in the stylistic terms outlined by Kerrigan, Muldoon who perhaps comes closest to Longley's own divergences, distractions, detours, and temporal distortions in the Ovid poems – and this despite their surface differences. It is unsurprising that Longley is drawn, for instance, to the story of 'Perdix', an addendum to the better known story of Daedalus and Icarus. Habitually, as seen most notably up to this point in *Man Lying on a Wall*, the poet is preoccupied with the dramas played out in the wings rather than centre stage, with the often forgotten asides and detours that are then given their own integrity as lyric poems, Longley's 'Perdix'

is written 'In the wings of that story about the failure of wings'.
In miniature, here and elsewhere, he adapts Ovid's rhetorical and
narrative strategies to his own capturing of lyric moments. Ovid's
Metamorphoses takes the reader through two hundred and fifty stories
from Greek and Latin myth, stylistically and thematically woven
together in such a way that the joins are scarcely visible. The tour
through the myths in fact comprises multiple detours, in which a
narrative cause and effect sequence is often discarded in favour of
a more imagistic linkage of events.

The first of Longley's Ovid poems, 'Baucis & Philemon' follows
the remit given by Hofmann and Lasdun of telling the story in its
entirety. With a freer hand in those poems which followed, his more
usual practice of selecting, editing and highlighting lyric moments
from longer passages – and, indeed, selecting and linking passages
from different books (as was earlier the case with the close of 'The
Butchers' for instance) – is to the fore. 'Baucis & Philemon' is thus
unusual in Longley's *oeuvre*, since it is a narrative poem, comprising
18 five-line stanzas in loose hexameters.

In the *Metamorphoses*, the story of Baucis and Philemon, from
Book VIII, is told by the hero Lelex in order to convince Ixion's
doubting son of the power of the gods. The inventive reasons for
storytelling in the *Metamorphoses* are, of course, a means of con-
necting material that lacks the usual kind of unity to be found in
a poem on an epic scale. But they are suggestive in another way
too. The stories in *Metamorphoses* seem only to be passing through
the hands of the teller, with "ownership" an ambiguous issue. That
ambiguity is central to the style of Longley's Ovid versions. 'Baucis
& Philemon' introduces the first person singular in its first stanza;
it is also to be found in 'According to Pythagoras', 'Spiderwoman',
'A Flowering' and 'Phoenix'. The 'I' voice is thus far more prominent
in Longley's Ovidian as against his Homeric poems (where, in *Gorse
Fires*, it appears only in 'Eurycleia'), but it is also an elusive voice
in ways which reflect on the processes of translation and storytelling.

The opening of 'Baucis & Philemon' seemingly draws on Lelex's
introductory speech to the tale in *Metamorphoses*:

> In the Phrygian hills an oak tree grows beside a lime tree
> And a low wall encloses them. Not far away lies bogland.
> I have seen the spot myself. It should convince you
> – If you need to be convinced – that the power of heaven
> Is limitless, that whatever the gods desire gets done.

But the poem never tells us who is telling the story, and this first
stanza is already indicative of the slipperiness of "voice" in the

poem. The claim to "truth" telling in this stanza, which tinkers with the original, implies more the impossibility of "authenticity" than otherwise. Material is shifted around in Longley's version so that the power of eye-witnessing becomes, implicitly, a measure of credibility: 'I have seen the spot myself. It should convince you…'.

The ironies, however, are mischievous: to have 'seen the spot' is not, cannot be, "proof" of what once happened there; to a contemporary audience, well-versed in Christian culture, to see for oneself is the proof one should never, as a matter of faith, demand. Lastly, since that 'I' voice is evidently a merging of 'Lelex' and 'Longley', *and* of 'Ovid', of different times and perspectives, it is also conscious of itself as, impossibly, the eye-witness at several removes. That is, the story of Baucis and Philemon, like the Gospel stories of Christian myth, has passed through multiple hands before, as well as after, the first "authentic" telling. The overlap evident in the poem between Biblical and Classical myth – the search for lodgings, where only 'one house took them in'; the 'wine jug' which mysteriously 'Filled itself up again'; the corrupt 'townland flooded' with only the virtuous two saved – is itself indicative of the metamorphosis of one religion into the other, of a process of translation and inter-pretation that denies a stable textual resting-place for any of these tales.

The interweaving of past and present is there also in the language of the poem. 'Baucis & Philemon' has its demotic elements: the 'tightfisted neighbours', Jupiter addressing Philemon as 'Grandpa', the goose that was 'too nippy for them', the immortals taking time to 'freshen up' and so on. It also draws on a vocabulary whose archaic quality sends us back through time: the 'skillet', the (Old English) 'flitch', the 18th-century slang of 'flabbergasted'. One senses Longley is happily trawling the English language for all the richness – colloquial, archaic, poetic – that it has to offer, flitting from 'raked' to 'hoked' to 'poked' in one stanza; punning on 'home-cooking' where its positive contemporary resonance collides with Baucis and Philemon's apology; introducing the gods as 'sky-dwellers' – a phrase evocative of LSD trips as well as of the immortals.

For Hofmann and Lasdun, Ovid is unequivocally a poet of 'contemporary values', with 'qualities of mischief and cleverness… not always relished in the past'. His themes – 'rape, incest, seduction, pollution, sex-change, suicide, hetero- and homosexual love, torture, war' – are, they claim 'peculiarly modern'.[6] Peter McDonald takes issue with this kind of over-simplification and with the complacency that 'turns Ovid into a contemporary poet who has waited all these centuries for his moment to come'. It is not, he notes, Longley's own practice.[7] 'Baucis & Philemon' bears this out.

The choice of language never forces the story out of the ancient world and into contemporary Ireland or Britain, but it allows it to exist there too. It is possible to read the poem as subtly Hibernicised: the bogland, the cottage with the always-burning open fire, and its blackened rafters may all be evocative of the simple, often harsh, living once eked out from the land in the west of Ireland. The details, however, are all from Ovid, and the link a happy coincidence rather than an outside imposition. Similarly, the theme of the story, with its celebration of a married love that sustains itself over several decades, resonates implicitly in Longley's own autobiographical concerns, thereby linking the tale not only to the earlier Homeric poems, but also to other mature love poems in *The Ghost Orchid* such as 'The Scissors Ceremony' or 'The Kilt'; but it is a theme that belongs, like all Ovid's themes, as much in the first as the 21st century.

The poem "belongs", in the end, in both times and places, the story to no one and everyone. Longley's 'Baucis & Philemon' is an extraordinarily faithful version which nonetheless has embedded within it an alertness to such complexities. The sensitive crossing-over between the ancient and the contemporary, the manipulation of the narrative framing device, and the presence of the ambiguous first person speaker, converge on the last stanza of the poem, which may be read both as translation – as Lelex's final words [8] – or as a self-reflexive commentary on the process of translation:

> Two trees are grafted together where their two bodies stood.
> I add my flowers to bouquets in the branches by saying
> 'Treat those whom God loves as your local gods – a blackthorn
> Or a standing stone. Take care of caretakers and watch
> Over the nightwatchman and the nightwatchman's wife.'

The image of the Baucis and Philemon trees 'grafted together' mirrors the way in which these final lines marry monotheism and polytheism all in the service of a benevolent humanism. This last instruction is close to, but, crucially, not the same as, the "moral" drawn from the tale by its original teller in *Metamorphoses*. It shares the Pythagorean view, which appeals also to Mahon, that the inanimate is imbued with a hidden life and spirituality. The 'blackthorn' and 'standing stone' are Longley's details, and serve to evoke an Irish context as well as reaching out to recurrent images in his own *oeuvre*. '[L]ocal gods' irresistibly takes us back to a Kavanagh-esque parochialism and an Irish poetic tradition, with its echo of Kavanagh's 'Epic' in which 'Gods make their own importance.' The injunction to 'Take care of caretakers', to 'watch / Over the nightwatchman' is not from *Metamorphoses* but is a borrowing from Juvenal (*'quis custodiet ipsos Custodes?'*) typical of Longley's own aesthetic. 'I add my flowers to bouquets in the branches' is a line which is faithful to the source, and which multiplies its implications. It is impossible at this point to define who is speaking, or when: Lelex laid wreaths on the trees in Ovid's version; Ovid, too, in re-telling the tale, metaphorically does so once again himself; Longley adds an extra injunction at the close of the poem; the line affirms his own poem as a further tribute to Baucis and Philemon; the poem is also, of course, an addition to a long line of translations of the tale; and it is conscious of itself as an anthology piece, playing on the meaning of 'anthology' as derived from the Greek word *anthos*, or 'flower'. Longley, in other words, along with the other 41 poets in *After Ovid*, has added his poem to help make up the whole picture.

That same ambiguity of voice and persona is present in 'Spider-woman', based on the story of Arachne from book VI of *Meta-morphoses*. Its opening line – 'Arachne starts with Ovid and finishes with me' – once again raises the question of where, and to whom, the story belongs. In its simplest interpretation, it means that Arachne's story was told first by Ovid, and has then finished up, much later, in the hands of 'me', being the poet Michael Longley. But equally, it may be read the other way around as Arachne starting with 'Ovid' after having finished with 'me', and the implications of that are very different.

In one sense, the poem has its tail in its mouth even before it gets underway. It directs us back to the "source" in advance of its own "translation". The ambiguities here are also bound up with questions of authorial control – or lack thereof. As much as Arachne's story is in the hands of her authors are they in their turn caught in her spider's web, the subjects, not the authors, of a story she weaves herself. The voice of the two middle stanzas of the poem is equally elusive. 'Enticing the eight eyes of my imagination', smiling 'behind her embroidery', Arachne is both the woman before her metamorphosis, weaving her tapestry, seducing her poet-lovers, and she is the metamorphosed spider with her 'lethal doily'. The poet's 'imagination' thus transforms the 'I' voice through the poem from her human chronicler to her spider-lover/victim. The enticement is also the compulsion to tell her story over again; the poem itself, with its complex syntactical permutations across the two stanzas, weaves a stylistic web of its own.

The fluidity of style in this, and others of the Ovid poems, notably 'Ivory & Water', enables the lyric poem to catch, and seemingly hold, the impossible – the moment of transformation itself. 'Spider-woman' resists the conventions of beginnings, endings, of chrono-logical cause and effect sequences. To borrow the idea expressed at the close of 'Watercolour', of which more anon, it is as if Longley is striving, stylistically, towards the poem as an art form in which the ink will never quite dry on the page. From his first collection onwards, he has been drawn to the myths which simultaneously make and unmake, Penelope's weaving and unravelling the perfect example. In the syntactically fluid longer line developed from *Gorse Fires* onwards, that theme is expressed indirectly in the rhythm, texture and rhetoric of the poetry. In 'Spiderwoman', Arachne both disintegrates – 'Her hair falls out and the ears and nostrils disappear / From her contracting face' – and 'manufactures gossamer' to recreate herself and reproduce her kind with a 'widening smile'; the form itself permits both contracting and widening.

Longley's love poems, such as 'The Kilt' or 'The Scissors Cere-mony', play with the same idea, though without the sinister over-tones of 'Spiderwoman'. In 'The Kilt', for instance, the re-enact-ment of his father's kilt unravelling as he advances in battle is simultaneously an imaginative stitching together of the threads: 'You pick up the stitches and with needle and thread / Accompany him out of the grave and into battle...'. The poem's repetitions and reversals, and Longley's mastery of the chiasmus – 'He had killed him in real life and in real life had killed' – enact the process rhetorically as well as thematically.

In 'Ivory & Water', various different moments from Ovid are merged to give concentrated expression to the theme of metamor-phosis in its various manifestations. The poem combines the stories of Arethusa, transformed into a stream, and Cyane, who wept until she dissolved into water (both from book V) with that of Pygmalion (book X) who, revolted by ordinary women, carved a perfect statue of a maiden out of ivory and fell in love with his creation. Venus, taking pity on him, brought the statue to life. Longley's 'Ivory & Water' has its obvious precursors in his own work: it echoes Odysseus's failure to grasp Anticleia in *Gorse Fires*, as well as the dissolutions and fragmentations of the early 1980s *New Poems*; it takes its place in a line of formal development that can accommo-date contradictory impulses. By mixing the elements from Ovid, Longley once again brings a personal sense of mortality and loss to bear on the translation/transformation:

> If as a lonely bachelor who disapproves of women
> You carve the perfect specimen out of snow-white ivory
> And fall in love with your masterpiece and make love to her

(Or try to) stroking, fondling, whispering, kissing, nervous
In case you bruise ivory like flesh with prodding fingers,
And bring sea-shells, shiny pebbles, song-birds, colourful wild
Flowers, amber-beads, orchids, beach-balls as her presents,
And put real women's clothes, wedding rings, ear-rings, long
Necklaces, a brassière on the statue, then undress her
And lay her in your bed, her head on the feathery pillows
As if to sleep like a girlfriend, your dream may come true
And she warms and softens and you are kissing actual lips
And she blushes as she takes you in, the light of her eyes,
And her veins pulse under your thumb at the end of the dream
When she breaks out into a cold sweat that trickles into pools
And drips from her hair dissolving it and her fingers and toes,
Watering down her wrists, shoulders, rib-cage, breasts until
There is nothing left of her for anyone to hug or hold.

At the point when Pygmalion's dream, in the original myth, comes true, the merging of myth, and the transformation of the statue into Cyane/Arethusa, also, in Longley's poem, marks the dream's end. The poem's catalogues and elaborations – 'sea-shells, shiny pebbles, song-birds...wedding rings, ear-rings, long / Necklaces' – and its clausal accumulations build to a climax that melts away at the moment of its attainment. The insistent repetitions – 'And she warms and softens...And she blushes...' – seem to be part of the gathering momentum that brings the statue to life, the rhythms here like the 'veins' that 'pulse under your thumb'. But the poem is deceptive. It thwarts the expectations raised by its own syntactical logic. The sequence 'If...You carve the perfect specimen...And fall in love with your masterpiece...your dream may come true' is coherent in itself; but the seven lines which follow unravel that meaning, and the climactic eroticism of the statue's burgeoning life is also the start of dissolution. An insistent repetition, a force of will that brings life, is simultaneously the futile attempted stay against the inevitability of loss. This is the illusion of one "closure" on top of another, "resolution" only the beginning of another transformation. The clausal logic of the poem itself slips away from the reader's grasp until 'There is nothing left...to...hold'.

'Ivory & Water' is a poem about mortality and creativity, and about the tension between the two. The original story of Pythagoras brings the statue to life, and in doing so renders the timeless masterpiece mortal; Longley's poem takes the implication of that mortality to its inevitable conclusion and in doing so reflects on the act of creation. The 'snow-white ivory...masterpiece' is a remote and, ultimately chilling ideal: as with Mahon's 'cold dream / Of a place out of time, / A palace of porcelain' ('The Last of the Fire Kings') its perfection is, paradoxically, its limitation. Rather, the poem implicitly suggests that art is about change and mutation, about bringing colour, difference and, in effect, compromise, to the 'perfect specimen', even if to do so is to forfeit the claim to permanence. (As Longley noted in the early 1970s, 'who's interested in pure art anyway?')[9] Like the earlier 'Anticleia', the poem is conditional. The possibility of what might be created is infinitely suspended. At the same time, the poem is itself that creation, a word-sculpture in which the texture of the language is redolent not just of bringing the statue to life, but of carving it in the first place: 'stroking, fondling... nervous / In case you bruise ivory like flesh with prodding fingers'.

There is something of a nervousness here about how the poet shapes his own subject, and it is implicated in what has always been, in Longley, a precision and care in the way words – by no means harmless – are used. Increasingly, through the 1990s, the self-reflexivity of the poems suggests the process of composition as one in which material is shaped and fined down rather than developed, more laboriously, from scratch. Longley himself describes it as a shift in which he has now 'to let the poems happen.... It's the difference between trimming a hedge and building a wall'.[10] The density of meaning compressed into the later short poems affirms the maturity of vision and style that shifts the emphasis in this way.

Both 'Ivory & Water' and 'Phoenix' are fascinated with the link between words and the plastic arts. 'Phoenix', too, is a poem about form, about recreating, in its own form, the 'beechwood bowl Ted O'Driscoll turned', which will contain 'six duck eggs', 'a double-yolk inside each shell / Laid by a duck that renovates and begets itself / Inside my head...'. It's a 'double-yolk' poem. The story of the phoenix of *Metamorphoses* is folded inside the poet's promised visit to Baltimore, Co. Cork, that begins and ends the poem. As with the structure of the *Metamorphoses* as a whole, one story begets the other inside his head. The phoenix's 'heavy nest' is, in a typical Longley dualism, both 'His cradle, his father's coffin', and it echoes the 'nest / Jiggling eggs' the poet will bring. The poem "turns" to come full circle, following the pattern of the phoenix's cycle of death and renewal as well as the shaping of the bowl, closing where it began, with the promise to 'put down the eggs Orla Murphy gave me / In a beechwood bowl Ted O'Driscoll turned for her'. But as with the conditional sentence that comprises the whole of 'Ivory & Water', this echo of the wood-turning in the structure of the poem sits more ambiguously alongside the poem's simultaneous claim that this is a future promise not a present achievement: 'I'll hand to you...I shall put down...'.

II

What 'Ivory & Water' and 'Phoenix' have in common with each other, and with many other poems in *The Ghost Orchid*, is their quality of both being and becoming. These are poems poised on the verge of what might be, or could have been. One way of capturing that quality is through poems as questions – 'Autumn Lady's Tresses', 'Sorescu's Circles', 'Sun & Moon', 'Sandpiper' – as if what they finally become is only the beginning. Another is in the tension between a source text and a free translation that informs so many of the poems in this book. The quality is embodied in Longley's forms themselves, in the way he plays nature and art alongside each other, and merges them to confound easy distinctions between seemingly fixed forms of representation and natural processes of growth, change, and decay.

The title-poem, 'The Ghost Orchid', encapsulates, in highly concentrated form, that ambiguous relation, a poem which looks outwards to the several poems in *The Ghost Orchid* which are directly preoccupied with painting (among them 'Watercolour', 'Sitting for Eddie', and 'Gretta Bowen's Emendations'), and those whose concern is with nature's metamorphoses. Put the other way around, the poem is a site on which both preoccupations converge.

'The Ghost Orchid' equates the flower with the poem to transform the work of art into one of nature's 'few remaining sites':

> Added to its few remaining sites will be the stanza
> I compose about leaves like flakes of skin, a colour
> Dithering between pink and yellow, and then the root
> That grows like coral among shadows and leaf-litter.
> Just touching the petals bruises them into darkness.

As with 'Ivory & Water', the poem reaches, in its first four lines, the end of one sense unit that is then, unexpectedly, extended. It illuminates, in concentrated form, the manipulation of space and time found in many of Longley's poems, (and brought into particular focus in *The Ghost Orchid* by the process of translation). The poem is, paradoxically, like the ivory statue which dissolves, a perfected instability held and dissipated across different temporal spheres. Like the 'Watercolour' that will 'never dry', the colour here misses a final definition, 'Dithering between pink and yellow'.

'The Ghost Orchid' both weaves and unravels, writes and unwrites itself. Its central contradiction is unresolved: is this the stanza itself or only a stanza about the stanza that will be composed? Are we witnessing the work of art in the process of creation, or only the prelude to something that never actually appears? There is no confident assertion as to what the poem does, only what it might do. Realisation of the object (which is both poem and orchid) is infinitely deferred. Yet the poem, a 'site' which returns the orchid to imaginative presence, is already what it claims it will become, thereby encompassing both decline and regeneration. The 'few remaining sites' imply the flower's rarity, its gradual disappearance. 'I compose' is projected into the future as a potential renewal which will counter that movement: the flower will increase, will be 'Added to'. At the same time, the lines themselves, in working backwards from the leaves to the root, suggest the decomposition, the deterioration of the flower (and of memory) that the poem's desire to 'compose' simultaneously works against. That ambiguity repeats itself in miniature in the poem's final line, where 'Just touching the petals bruises them into darkness'.

The future projection has here been imaginatively realised in the present moment, a realisation which encompasses both poem and flower (one ghost-writing the other). But since the petals are bruised 'into darkness', they disappear at the moment they appear. As with Pygmalion's statue in 'Ivory & Water', a poem with which 'The Ghost Orchid' shares a notable intertextual relation, the erotic climax – 'touching the petals' – is simultaneously the moment of loss. This poem also, obliquely, has its tail in is mouth, since the disappearance of the petals takes us back to the moment where they become future projection. We are left with the sense that both poem and flower are existent and non-existent, absent and present, remembered and forgotten. The poem collapses itself to become an object of instability; it is also the finished, perfected work of art, even if, like the petals in one of his Ovid poems, 'A Flowering', it can only 'hang on and no more'.

Such reflections on art and nature are by no means apolitical in their implications. 'The Ghost Orchid' is most evidently concerned with ecological threat; but the 'leaves like flakes of skin' encompass human disaster too. The poem's eroticism also blurs distinctions between two worlds. 'The Ghost Orchid' is, among other things, a reminder not to forget, a poem which understands that acts of recovery are sometimes as traumatic and difficult as they are necessary. It exemplifies a political and aesthetic vision that seeks to recover what is easily overlooked or forgotten, growing 'among shadows and leaf-litter', and which celebrates the unexpected detail too often over-shadowed by what seems to be more important.

Yet it also exemplifies an aesthetic always conscious of the imminence of failure, of there being 'nothing left...for anyone to hug or hold'. Ecologically – and politically – the poems seek a balance between preservation and development. Bold colours and broad brush-strokes paint one kind of picture; but what they leave out may be precisely the details and shades of difference – 'Dithering between pink and yellow' for instance – that could prove redemptive. The relevance of the point, in Longley's own Northern Irish society, is all too evident, given that the society polarised into increasingly antagonistic positions through the 1970s and 1980s, rendering the space 'between' such positions something to be affirmed and protected. In a context where (media) representations of the Northern Irish conflict have assumed it to be black-and-white, static and unchanging, Longley's poetry has been, Paul Muldoon suggests, 'emblematic' of 'an imaginative domain in which we can all move forward'.[11]

This is a powerful claim to make for a poetry which consistently refuses to promote itself in such terms. But it is that very tentativeness, the realisation that words cannot grasp the world, which makes the claim possible. Longley's 1990s poems are suggestive of the capacity to transform, partly because they don't presume to possess any final answers; the process is what matters. The last word – as the act of translation itself implies – is never said. (It is worth noting, too, the relevance of that aesthetic in the context of the Northern Irish peace process in the 1990s. While there might be an instinctive desire for closure, as if a society's problems can be finally resolved, the point rather is that the 'process' should never cease.)

It is typical that in a poem such as 'The White Garden', where, in a moment of lyric intensity, the poet asks the seemingly fundamental question 'For whom do I scribble the few words that come to me / From beyond the arch of white roses as from nowhere, / My memorandum to posterity?', the conclusion is at once mysterious and mischievous, no answer at all and, in being so, the only possible answer: 'Listen. "The saw / Is under the garden bench and the gate is unlatched."'.[12] This is a 'memorandum to posterity' which lets you go where you want. Probably the only thing it disallows is the idea that any poet can decide the terms – or even presume the eventual existence – of his own 'posterity'. That form of modesty is far from being a given in contemporary poetry; but it is a necessary effacement in an aesthetic that seeks to evoke what is elusive, fragile, shadowy, or 'In the wings', and which often subordinates a poem's status as the finished work of art to a delight in the process of creativity – in all its manifestations.

What nature and art have in common is the capacity to create and transform. One of the ways in which they are linked in *The Ghost Orchid* is through Longley's explorations of the paradox of the 'still life'. Painting, like sculpting, provides for Longley a subject within a subject, a means of creating a double reflection on the workings of the imagination. (It is not coincidental that at the point in the late 1980s when his own poetry returns, he finds himself 'in love with painting again'.)[13] The still life also evokes the idea of a 'still', holding movement in a moment of stasis. As the poems are in a state of both being and becoming, the 'still life', as it is painted, is changing all the time, a process which makes the inanimate animate and vice versa.

In 'Sitting for Eddie', an elegy for the painter Edward McGuire who painted Longley's portrait in the late 1980s, the poet is 'turning into a still life whose eyes are blue'. Part of the joke here is Longley's own sense that as a sitter he is, if not quite an inanimate object, the closest thing a painter might get to an actual still life (traditionally the dead pheasant, the bowl of fruit). That aside, the painter's 'strange mistake' (the poet's eyes are brown) is a fortuitous one, at least for the purposes of the poetry, a symbol of painting or writing as a transformation of self and subject. Obliquely, it is also a natural process, a reversal of time back to origins when, so the story goes, all children's eyes are blue. The still life mutates even as it is seemingly captured in space and time.

Longley himself plays the reverse trick on the photographer Robert Mapplethorpe, whose 1976 photograph 'Mark Stevens (Mr 10 $\frac{1}{2}$)' is an image of a male torso displaying a penis of remarkable size. In Longley's 'Mr 10 $\frac{1}{2}$':

> When he lays out as on a market stall or altar
> His penis and testicles in thanksgiving and for sale,
> I find myself considering his first months in the womb
> As a wee girl, and I substitute for his two plums
> Plum-blossom, for his cucumber a yellowy flower.

Among other things, the poem is a transformation of male genitalia into a cross between produce on a fruit-stall, and offerings for the harvest festival (a 'thanksgiving' for nature's bounty in scattering good seed on the land – in more ways than one).

Neil Corcoran's illuminating reading of the poem notes that Longley's concern is to reduce 'male presumption and arrogance' in reminding us of 'the instabilities of gender differentiation'. The poem is, he writes, 'physiologically knowledgeable here in a way that people are, sometimes, surprisingly, not'.[14] Reverting to the time in the womb when clitoris and penis are as yet undistinguishable,

Longley's substitution of female for male genitalia goes behind the
fixed image (its solidity associated with masculinity) to the fluid,
natural processes which led to its creation. Like the still life which
mutates in the act of painting, what begins as one thing is trans-
formed by nature to end up as another.

The transformation of 'Mr $10\,{}^{1}/_{2}$' makes it one of several poems
in *The Ghost Orchid* which delight in this kind of gender subversion.
In 'Sheela-na-Gig', the poet blends art, nature and sexuality in a
way which enables the poem to slip the net of typical gender-based
criticisms even though its subject-matter takes risks. The stone
carving is brought to life – 'She pulls her vulva apart for everyone
to look at' – as if the Sheela-na-gig is the author of her own image:
not she is made thus, but 'She behaves thus'. The carving mutates
into the 'orchids' which 'have borrowed her cunty petals'. The
'stonemason deflowering stone' is a pun which wryly acknowledges
masculine culpability; on the other hand, the fluidity of the 'proper
libation' of 'sperm and rainwater' counters the association of mas-
culinity with hardness: sperm, rainwater, petals, and stone inter-
mingle in ways which begin to merge male and female sexuality.

The fluidity that enables a process of transformation is a far cry
from the artistic attitudes mocked in 'After Horace', a poem that
plays on Longley's fascination with versions and translations to mock
the serious-minded postmodernism which, for all its theoretical
interest in "play", has perhaps lost its sense of humour. 'After
Horace', like 'The Mad Poet', encodes a covert literary criticism
in the translation from, and transformation of, its source to make
explicit the distinction between an imaginative metamorphosis
attained through formal accomplishment and the illusion of change
that comes only, so to speak, from dressing an object in different
clothes – 'the plastering of multi- / Coloured feathers over the limbs
of assorted animals'. The difference is between 'After Horace' in
the sense of acknowledging an indebtedness to, whilst reinventing,
the past, and, more literally, 'post-Horace', wherein traditional
forms are abandoned in the interests of an apparent, if not real,
"newness". The poem is interested in the relationship between the
abstract and the real; but its target is not so much "theory" as
technical ineptitude:

> Since our fertile imaginations cannot make head
> Or tail of anything, wild things interbreed with tame,
> Snakes with birds, lambs with tigers. If a retired sailor
> Commissions a picture of the shipwreck he survived,
> We give him a cypress tree because we can draw that.

This indicts a technical inadequacy that wears theory to disguise itself. Contrast Perdix's 'capacity / To look at the backbone of a fish and invent the saw...to draw conclusions / And a circle with the first compass, two iron limbs, / Arms, legs tied together, geometry's elbow or knee' ('Perdix'). Perdix, a different kind of artist, possesses the 'fertile' imagination that can make extraordinary conceptual leaps, transforming one thing into another with technical accomplishment and clear-sightedness. To borrow E.M.Forster's distinction, for the artist-figures in 'After Horace', the world is a muddle; for the artists celebrated in *The Ghost Orchid*, and in Longley's own aesthetic, the world is a mystery in which arbitrary connections potentially have meaning, even if that meaning remains hidden from view.

Longley's poems do not seek a "closure" that would simplify, or seem to solve the contradictions of the world around him – far from it. But the resistance to closure in his poems is far more sophisticated than that of the pseudo-craftsmanship of the 'Ultimate post- / Modernists' in 'After Horace' whose work 'ends up as a po'. 'Gretta Bowen's Emendations' makes the point that the work of art is, in one sense, never 'finished': multi-layered, the paintings are 'created' then re-created. Gretta Bowen, he writes, 'Postponed the finishing touches, and then in her nineties / Emended her world by painting on the glass that covered / Children's games, fairgrounds, swans on a pond...additional leaves and feathers falling on to ice'.

As with the stories that beget stories, these are paintings that beget paintings – and beget the word-painting of the poem itself as a further emendation. Similarly, in 'Watercolour: for Jeffrey Morgan', the poem word-paints Morgan's portrait of Longley as one in which solid objects break their bounds and melt into one another: 'My pullover a continuation of the lazy-beds...my shirt a running / Together of earth-colours...'. The fluidity of the image is epitomised by the final line: 'In this humidity your watercolour will never dry'. The close of the poem works against itself to leave the work finished and unfinished, as if the painting and poem will be 'emended' every time they are seen and read thereafter.

The aesthetic vision in the poems about painting seeps out into the intertextuality of *The Ghost Orchid* as a whole. This is a collection which works cumulatively to an extent not seen since *Man Lying on a Wall*. *The Ghost Orchid* is, overall, a stronger book than *Man Lying on a Wall*, not least because individual poems are rarely dependent for their effect on that cumulative development. One exception may be 'River & Fountain' which, commissioned by Trinity College Dublin, is perhaps too nostalgic about the poet's past, and too overtly autobiographical, fully to transcend the occasion of its composition. The preciosity of 'A Gift of Boxes' and 'A Grain of Rice' is also on a knife-edge between what is affecting or affected. Yet even in such instances, the intertextual links between the poems are still significant. It is as if the poems in *The Ghost Orchid* are over-spilling their own bounds, running one into the other even as they possess their own integrity.

The tension between fixity and fluidity found in so many of these poems is thereby embodied in the collection as a whole. The imagery of petals, snow, feathers, silk, glass, ivory, leaves, ivy, ice and water is pervasive; the collection's delicately implied colouring throughout of white, red, yellow and purple makes the richly evocative language of the poems a sensual experience. The story of 'Perdix', for instance, obliquely evokes the close of 'River & Fountain', with its snowfall as 'feathers from the wings of Icarus', as well as the 'leaves and feathers falling' of 'Gretta Bowen's Emendations', other origin poems such as 'Oasis', and even the love poem 'Snow Hole' in which Perdix's 'tumble' becomes 'Falling asleep in the snowscape of the big double-bed...we sink down and down'. The 'snowscape' of the bed is transformed into Odysseus's 'mattress of leaves...enough to make a double-bed' in 'A Bed of Leaves', the leaves which 'fall over him' evocative of falling feathers.

Poems not directly concerned with painting create their own tableaux, delighting in their pictorial effect, their appeal to the senses. In 'Baucis & Philemon', the table laid for the guests is itself a work of art: 'nuts / And figs and wrinkly dates, plums and sweet-smelling apples / In a wicker basket, purple grapes fresh from the vines. // The centrepiece was a honeycomb oozing clear honey...'. The colours mirror 'Ovid's lovely casualties' in 'A Flowering': 'flowers, purple, / Lily-shaped...Blood dosed with honey'. 'Blackbird' works as a mirror of 'Watercolour', in its picture of the bird with 'twiggy / Toes, crisp tail-feathers / And its wings wider than / The light from two windows' (Morgan's portrait of Longley is entitled 'Light from Two Windows'). Or in 'Lizard', the moment of heightened perception held for a split second, of nature as artifice, the lizard as 'a brooch that you / Could wear next to your skin', gives way to movement as 'It skittered...Over your shoulder'.

The tension between movement and stasis, solidity and fluidity, has always been present in Longley's work. In *The Ghost Orchid* it comes into particular focus through the book's concentration on the question of art – and the artist – as medium. The fascination with painting, sculpting, and transformation is bound up with an understanding of poetic form. *The Ghost Orchid* explores what form can achieve through marrying seemingly contradictory elements.

In Longley's writing, form embodies memory, with the implication of continuity and permanence; at the same time, his forms never claim to "hold" their object in words, since what is realised simultaneously vanishes. Hence the particular appeal of Ovid's transformation of shapes, sometimes into stone, sometimes into water. It is, as Neil Corcoran points out, 'a conception of poetry as the missing rather than the marking of its occasion'.[15]

The four-line poem 'Form' which opens the book is a concentrated probing into what the poems in *The Ghost Orchid* formally enact on so many different levels:

> Trying to tell it all to you and cover everything
> Is like awakening from its grassy form the hare:
> In that make-shift shelter your hand, then my hand
> Mislays the hare and the warmth it leaves behind.

As Brian John notes, 'Form' is implicitly an instruction on 'how to read'; a reminder that we should never confuse 'brevity with inconsequentiality'.[16] 'Form' is about missing and marking the occasion, even down to its elusive closing half-rhyme. At the point of 'Trying to tell it all to you', the hare, awakened, is mislaid: telling 'it all' is once again rendered impossible at the moment it is achieved.

As in 'Ivory & Water', bringing to life here – 'awakening…the hare' – is also about loss, since the object disappears almost at the same moment. But when 'your hand, then my hand / Mislays the hare', the lovers physically connect: the moment of loss is also one of gain; the 'warmth' left behind is, paradoxically, both lost and found. There is a sense here of the poet as the priest-like figure who breathes life into the inanimate, and who brings movement to stasis. It is significant that he does so in a poem whose self-reflexive title might seem to evoke the idea of poetic form as something traditionally unyielding and fixed. But while poetic form is a preservative, Yeats's 'ancient salt', it is also, Longley's 'Form' suggests, something else too – a medium for change.

The hare's (or the lovers') 'make-shift shelter' is one way to understand this. As in *Gorse Fires*, where the poet is 'making do with what has been left me', the 'make-shift shelter' is suggestive of a poetic inheritance, of being left something to work with; but it is also suggestive of the need to create anew different shapes and forms from those remains. In doing so, there is no claim that 'Form' will preserve beyond the moment of immediate need, as if the poem is the 'make-shift shelter' for the words that will ultimately give it the slip.

The multiple layers of meaning in 'Form' are implicated in the paradox of form itself. Longley's 'Form' understands memory, embodied in form, as a fluid, constantly mutating process, one which unceasingly reinterprets and therefore transforms the past; at the same time memory preserves that past from forgetfulness. The precursor to 'Form', a poem on which it takes a reverse angle, is Yeats's 'Memory', which, read self-reflexively rather than auto-biographically, is a poem about Yeats's use of traditional form: 'the mountain grass / Cannot but keep the form / Where the mountain hare has lain'.

Both are also love poems which find the presence of the loved one through absence: Yeats's poem is easily read in terms of the sexual act (the memory of the true love, presumably Maud Gonne, is forever imprinted on the poet). Longley's 'Form' also puns on 'Trying to...cover everything'. On the surface, the poet's concern here seems to be comprehensiveness. But covering also evokes the act of love, and this poem is about the way in which two lovers communicate, about the way in which words try to capture, but always stand at one remove from, the emotion, or the physical closeness, they seek to express.

This is not a poem that tries to 'tell it all'; it only tries to tell what the impossibility of ever doing so is like. As such, the desire to 'cover everything' resonates in a different way throughout *The Ghost Orchid* as a whole, where the need to shield, protect and shelter runs alongside the need to ensure that what is most in need of protection is never concealed or covered over from view.

III

The tensions at work in this poem, between the need to conceal and reveal, preserve and transform, as with the tensions between stasis and fluidity in art and nature in *The Ghost Orchid* as a whole, are paradigmatic of the broader social and political concerns of the book. The colours of red, purple and white evoked in *The Ghost Orchid* are also, significantly, the colours of remembrance and of sacrifice, both in social-political and religious terms. As 'The Ghost Orchid' and 'Form' implicitly suggest, memory can be an act of recovery fraught with complications. Central to the collection are the poems about war, violence, and remembrance that manifest, in a particularly acute form, the struggle between a history repeating itself, and a history open to change. It is a struggle which, seen even at the level of style and structure in such Ovidian poems as 'Ivory & Water' or

'Spiderwoman', takes on broader political resonance in the Homeric versions written some months later. As Longley has observed, 'resurrecting and distorting the past' may be a way of evading the present. '[W]e must', he continues, 'break the mythic cycles...'.[17]

In *The Ghost Orchid*, Homer's *Iliad* largely replaces the *Odyssey* as the source of Longley's inspiration and as the imaginative trigger for the more overtly political poems in the book. Broadly, one might say that the *Odyssey* provides a framework for poems that illuminate a personal journey, the *Iliad* for poems about social conflict. This is to over-simplify, in that Longley's *Odyssey* poems have always reverberated on a social-political as well as autobiographical level. Nevertheless, there is a shift in emphasis in *The Ghost Orchid*, and its timing is significant.

One might expect that the *Iliad*'s ten year war of attrition would speak more immediately to the poet at a time when Northern Ireland's own conflict seemed to have no end in view – that is, during the 1970s and 1980s. But the shift towards the *Iliad* at a point when a ceasefire is imminent relates to Longley's sense of how the poet's negotiations between public and private have to be acutely sensitive to context. If the *Iliad* were to serve, in Longley's poems, merely as a reflection of one war in another, it might prove more problematical than helpful. To transmute the Northern Irish conflict into a mythic pattern is to run the risk of attributing to that conflict precisely the kind of inevitability and inescapability that the poetry should, in Longley's terms, work against. But in *The Ghost Orchid*, the *Iliad* points up differences and possibilities; it works as a vehicle to illuminate change as well as repetition. Indicative of stasis on the one hand, the *Iliad* is also, on the other, the paradigmatic text which shows how attrition may be overcome.

It is hardly surprising that 'the fluidity of a possible life' which Derek Mahon hoped to see back in 1970 is central to a book coincidental with the emergence of significant changes in Northern Irish society. Yet it is equally unsurprising that Longley's awareness of the possibility of change carries within it awareness of the possibility of failure and stagnation. However much the ceasefires of 1994 transformed Northern Irish life, it is also the case that the lead up to those ceasefires was marked by a series of tit-for-tat killings, and that 'post-ceasefire', as will be seen, is a term which denotes neither a happy ending, nor even an end to violence. *The Ghost Orchid* is in many ways an aspirational book; but it is never a complacent one, and the poet never assumes the last word has been or even can be said.

In what might be termed the war poems in *The Ghost Orchid* – 'The Kilt', 'Behind a Cloud', 'A Pat of Butter', 'The Camp-fires', 'The Helmet', 'The Parting', 'Ceasefire', 'Poppies', 'Buchenwald Museum', 'The Fishing Party' and 'The Scales' – a complex network of parallels and contrasts enables the poet to hold the delicate balance between the desire for that 'possible life' and recognition of what Mahon termed 'the *rigor mortis* of archaic postures'.[18] It is also, implicitly, a balance between forgiveness and forgetfulness, past and present.

The oblique Troubles elegy 'The Fishing Party', for instance, acknowledges that Christ 'loves off-duty policemen and their murderers'; but in the next poem in the book, 'The Scales', Christian forgiveness is balanced by the terrifying day of judgement when 'God the Father...Adjusted his golden scales, and in them weighed / Death sentences'. In 'The Helmet', (an imagined footnote to the *Iliad*), a cycle of violence, repeating itself generation after generation is given a demotic touch through which the poem reverberates in the present day:

> His daddy laughed, his mammy laughed, and his daddy
> Took off the helmet and laid it on the ground to gleam,
> Then kissed the babbie and dandled him in his arms and
> Prayed that his son might grow up bloodier than him.

That the 'wean', in the first stanza, is 'terrorised by his father', is pointed in a contemporary Irish context too; the poem is alert to the possibility that the terrorised may grow up to become the terrorist.

In contrast, the poem on the facing page, 'Ceasefire', transforms parental inheritance into a mode of forgiveness: Achilles is 'Put in mind of his own father and moved to tears'. In a generational reversal, it is as if Priam, 'the old king', becomes the child 'curled up at his feet'. Where the child is 'dandled' in Hector's arms in 'The Helmet', Achilles takes 'Hector's corpse into his own hands' in 'Ceasefire', as if to transform him back to the innocent child. The two poems, side by side, show the cycle of violence as perpetuated and as broken. Other contrasts are at work too: the macho ideology parodied in 'The Parting' – 'He: "Leave it to the big boys, Andromache." / "Hector, my darling husband, och, och," she.' – finds its opposite in the encounter between Achilles and Priam in 'Ceasefire' where they weep together, and 'stare at each other's beauty as lovers might'.

A similar counterpointing is at work in the poems explicitly concerned with remembrance, 'Poppies' and 'Buchenwald Museum'. Longley's interest in the politics of remembrance is evident in his prose writings of the 1990s and it is a preoccupation that looks forward to several poems in both *The Weather in Japan* and *Snow Water*.[19]

In 'Poppies', Longley focuses on the controversy which surrounded – and still surrounds – Irish remembrance of the Great War:

> Some people tried to stop other people wearing poppies
> And ripped them from lapels as though uprooting poppies
> From Flanders fields, but others hid inside their poppies
> Razor blades and added to their poppies more red poppies.

In the post-war years in Ireland – and particularly in Belfast – those whose remembrance poppies were torn off in this way did sometimes resort to the tactic described in part I of 'Poppies', causing the shedding of yet more blood. Remembrance becomes a self-perpetuating blood-feud in the poem, as 'poppies', by the final line, translates as 'blood' both literally and symbolically. There are competing histories – unionist and nationalist – at work here. The poem's real indictment, however, is implied in the essential sameness of 'Some people' and 'other people' who, whatever their different versions of history, are all trapped in an escalating cycle of violence.

Part I of 'Poppies' is an uncomfortable quatrain, thematically and stylistically. The monotonous rhyming of 'poppies' with 'poppies', and its repetition in the fourth line, is evocative of the deadly repetitiveness of a history in which violence breeds violence, in ever-increasing circles. Its opening line is rhythmically awkward, deliberately so, as far removed as it can be from the rhythmical fluidity and seductiveness of other poems in the book. Its simplicities, tonally and linguistically, are reflective of the black and white political attitudes that feed into a kind of remembrance stand-off. The word 'poppies' itself becomes progressively more difficult to tolerate in the poem, as if the reader is willing the poet to do something different. That is to say, the style of this poem is part of its point: in exposing stasis and repetition at the level of form and language, what it also engenders is, implicitly, the desire for change.

If 'Poppies' is indicative of remembrance gone wrong, a remembrance that is simultaneously a wilful forgetfulness of complexity, 'Buchenwald Museum' reworks some of the same imagery to argue for a remembrance that unsettles, rather than endorses, simplified versions of history. Like 'A Pat of Butter', in which 'The doddery English veterans are getting / Fewer', 'Buchenwald Museum' implicitly worries about forgetting to remember, about what the passing of time, in the image of the snowfall, will obscure. As the 'official apology for bias' in the poem suggests, even recovery of the past may serve as a mode of forgetfulness.[20]

Once again, therefore, this is a poem about the recovery of detail: 'Although a snowfall had covered everything / A wreath of poppies was just about visible'. As with the 'disinfectant and whitewash' of 'The Butchers' in *Gorse Fires*, the snowfall may be a cover-up, one that sanitises the landscape of the past. To 'cover everything', as in 'Form', is here seen in its potentially negative sense of concealing rather than revealing truth. To 'allow the snow to wear a poppy' is to protect, and in effect to uncover, a past that is difficult to conceive of, or apprehend. To allow difference makes this (unrhymed) poem a subtle counter to the crude certainties of 'Poppies', whose insistent repetitions are transformed, in 'Buchenwald Museum', into delicate echoes ('snowfall' to 'snow', 'poppies' to 'poppy').

The intertextual links between these poems, and Longley's own consciousness of the ways in which they work cumulatively – he describes, for instance, an unpublished poem 'The Stone Garden' as 'a strange companion for "Sheelagh-na-gig" as well as for the Japanese poems'[21] – have particular implications for reading the poem whose publication outside the collection was notably high-profile.

'Ceasefire', the last poem written for *The Ghost Orchid*, and finished on 26 August 1994, was published in the *Irish Times* on the Saturday following the IRA's declaration of a ceasefire from midnight on 31 August 1994 (this was followed by a Loyalist ceasefire in October of the same year). The context of its publication inevitably affected the terms in which the poem was read. Unlike other Homeric poems by Longley, there is nothing in terms of style and idiom which explicitly Hibernicises the poem, although its title gives it some contemporary resonance, and as Peter McDonald observes, 'the poet's ability to keep at a distance from the parallels which his material suggests is crucial to the poem's success'.[22]

'Ceasefire' draws on the encounter between King Priam and Achilles in book XXIV of the *Iliad*. The meeting, which takes up more than two hundred lines of the original poem, is condensed by Longley into a sonnet that draws on four of the key moments from the narrative:

I

Put in mind of his own father and moved to tears
Achilles took him by the hand and pushed the old king
Gently away, but Priam curled up at his feet and
Wept with him until their sadness filled the building.

II

Taking Hector's corpse into his own hands Achilles
Made sure it was washed and, for the old king's sake,
Laid out in uniform, ready for Priam to carry
Wrapped like a present home to Troy at daybreak.

III

When they had eaten together, it pleased them both
To stare at each other's beauty as lovers might,
Achilles built like a god, Priam good-looking still
And full of conversation, who earlier had sighed:

IV

'I get down on my knees and do what must be done
And kiss Achilles' hand, the killer of my son.'

Omitted is the extensive discussion and negotiation in the *Iliad* through which Achilles agrees to return Hector's body to Priam. Rather, 'Ceasefire' highlights and intensifies the lyric moments of the source text to transform epic into sonnet.

The poem is illustrative of Longley's belief, affirmed for him through the work of the war poets earlier in the 20th century, that the lyric has the capacity to accommodate what was once seen as "epic" subject-matter. The poem marks, as McDonald notes, 'the most successful point in Longley's distillation process of Homer from narrative into contained and self-sufficient lyric form', and it is, crucially, a form which 'takes the measure of seemingly unstoppable emotions'.[23]

Longley begins not with debate, nor with the first detail of the meeting – where Priam kisses Achilles' hand – but with shared grief. Syntactically, the poem displaces the individual ego to the margins. The restructuring of events – which turns the opening gesture of the meeting the closing gesture of the poem – renders the poem's "closure" ambiguous. The final rhyming couplet of the sonnet, which echoes the close of Wilfred Owen's 'Strange Meeting', is suggestive of resolution; but part IV of the poem is also the 'earlier' gesture which predates part I. It is not an ending, in that sense, so much as a beginning. Whether this is a gesture of forgiveness or conciliation – two very different things and with very different resonance in the context of the Northern Irish ceasefires – is open to interpretation. Its powerful emotive pull may be precisely that sense of both difficulty and possibility, of a self-discovery that can break a cycle of hatred only through self-abnegation.

On its publication in the *Irish Times*, 'Ceasefire' caught the public imagination. The timing of composition and publication, coincidental with political developments of the time, make 'Ceasefire' one of the few poems written in Northern Ireland over the last 35 years that speaks to, and from, a particular occasion at the very moment of its occurrence. The temptation has been, therefore, as McDonald points out, 'to see the occasion as an integral (and perhaps primary) part of the poem's meaning', even though such a reading must always be 'a more contingent...even a lesser thing' than the poem itself.[24]

Longley's own observations on the poem, in the years immediately following its publication are indicative of the tensions in *The Ghost Orchid* as a whole. In a talk given in 1995, he reads the poem very much in the context of its first publication:

> Because at that time we were praying for an IRA ceasefire, I called the poem 'Ceasefire' and, hoping to make my own minute contribution, sent it to the *Irish Times*. It was the poem's good luck to be published two days after the IRA's declaration. Almost always a poem makes its own occasion in private. This was an exception, and I still find warming the response of several readers, some of them damaged or bereaved in the Troubles.[25]

This is a more direct articulation of Longley's desire that poetry should make something happen than is ever found in the poetry itself, or than is found in 'Ceasefire'. It is the aspirational Longley talking here, the poet as 'priest of the muses' who believes – or want to believe – in 'poetry's possible power of ministration'.[26] But it is not his only reading of the poem.

Some months later, in a speech made at the American Ireland Fund Literary Awards on 19 June 1996, he is more cautious:

> Since August 1994 I have read 'Ceasefire' many times in public. But only once or twice have I pointed out that the truce is temporary, that after the ceasefire the Trojan War is resumed and Achilles himself is killed. I suppose I was trying not to tempt fate.
>
> I did certainly have misgivings. In my poem as in my political attitude, was I pressurising those who had been bereaved or maimed to forgive before they were ready to forgive? Was I in my presumption suggesting that widows, widowers, orphans might kiss the hands (as it were) of self-appointed murderers and torturers?
>
> I was also sickened by the so-called punishment beatings. (The 400th took place in Belfast 2 weeks ago.) So last December I wrote a lopsided eleven-line poem to accompany my sonnet 'Ceasefire' – an amplification; a qualification.[27]

There is an awareness here that the 'warming' response from some readers to the poem is not the whole story: others were not ready to accept the necessity that seemed to be implied by 'Ceasefire'. But because the poem made its occasion in public, it was too readily understood as the last, or at least the only, word – something to

which Longley's aesthetic, as with as the political situation itself,
is always resistant. The end of the *Iliad* is not the end of the story.
The publication and reception of 'Ceasefire' might now be seen in
miniature, like the poem itself, as a cautionary tale as well as a
cause for celebration. The possibility of transformation carries
with it the possibility of failure; a story once told can always be
retold. To read 'Ceasefire' in such terms is to recognise the ten-
sions that *The Ghost Orchid* as a whole understands at the deepest
structural and thematic levels.

7

Outwitting Winter:
The Weather in Japan
1994-1998

> Two thousand petals overlapping as though to make
> A cape for the corn goddess or a soldier's soul.
> MICHAEL LONGLEY, 1997

I

The dedicatory poem to *The Weather in Japan* (2000), 'For Ronald Ewart', is about what appear to be two very different ways of living:

> In my ideal village the houses lie scattered
> Over miles and are called a townland, while in yours
> Neighbours live above and below, and a nightcap
> Means climbing up steps in the direction of the stars.

Perhaps it is not too far-fetched to suggest that the difference here might also be understood as suggesting two different ways of writing and reading, with the proviso that both are still neighbouring 'ideal[s]'. The distinction Longley makes, as discussed in the previous chapter, between poetry as building a wall, and poetry as trimming a hedge is one that is evident in the changes in his style through the 1990s. Where the early poems constructed complex stanza upon stanza, he inclines, from *Gorse Fires* onwards, more towards short poems, with intertextual links. Occasionally they may appear in sequences; but far more often, the connections are left unspoken, and the short poems scattered through the book. It is a different way of shaping poems and collections, and one more akin to his own 'ideal village' than 'climbing up steps' to the stars.

In *Gorse Fires* and *The Ghost Orchid* the interlinking of short poems and motifs is at work to a greater extent than in the earlier books. *The Weather in Japan* takes the idea a stage further – perhaps, even, as far as it can go. Its connecting motif is the patchwork quilt. There are precedents for the image, such as 'Patchwork' and others of the *New Poems*, or 'The Kilt' from *The Ghost Orchid*, and in 1998, Longley published a pamphlet of 17 poems, 15 of them elegies, under the title *Broken Dishes*, the name of an Amish quilt design, *c.* 1930.[1]

The quilt is a dominant motif in the pamphlet, one which becomes a metaphor for Longley's elegiac practice in the poems. With the exception of 'Somewhere in Transylvania', all the poems are later stitched into *The Weather in Japan* (the opening and closing poems, untitled in *Broken Dishes*, appear as 'The Design' and 'Found Poem'). By the time *The Weather in Japan* is complete, the metaphoric resonance of the motif is expanded far beyond its earlier manifestations to accommodate the central preoccupations of the book.

The quilt is evoked directly in seven poems in *The Weather in Japan*, and indirectly in many more. In so far as it is a motif for understanding the collection as a whole, indeed, it permeates every poem in the collection. It works self-reflexively, as an oblique indicator of how to read the poems one against the other, and symbolically, as a means of understanding the world around us. It appears in various guises – as a quilt, an altar cloth, a handkerchief, a cape, as sheets and blankets.

In 'A Linen Handkerchief', the embroidered handkerchief is a symbol of survival and fidelity, as it is also the sail that guides Helen Lewis – 'Odysseus as a girl' – home after Auschwitz. In 'Found Poem', the quilt pattern echoes 'the wild flowers that grew in the wood'; at the same time, the laying out of the poem – which versifies lines from Ann Petry's *Harriet Tubman* – transforms its prose source into a kind of 'quilt pattern' of its own, restructuring the words as the 'oblongs and squares', in Auden's phrase, of poetry. More obliquely, the quilt returns in 'A Poppy' as the Remembrance Day poppy petal shower imaginatively stitched together to make 'A cape for the corn goddess'. It also resurfaces in several of Longley's evocations of the natural world: the 'raggedy rainbows' of the waves in 'The Comber' are suggestive of the scraps of fabric that make up a quilt; in 'Burren Prayer', 'Gentians and lady's bedstraw embroider' the ground. The snowy landscapes of 'The Snow Leopard' or 'Maureen Murphy's Husband' subtly link to the quilt in 'The Design', where 'Sometimes the quilts were white for weddings'.

The reverberations of the motif are seen in other ways too. In 'Sweetie Papers', the 'Tinfoil and cellophane' are 'Pinned to the wall', 'squares' to gaze through 'as through a stained glass window'. Each square in the poem is a 'light-conductor[s]' which offers an insight into a traumatic past, and reflects back a self-portrait. Or in 'Scrap Metal', the sculpture of a raven works as a form of patchwork: it is put together from the bits and pieces of 'old iron...the

brake shoes from a lorry, nuts / And bolts…engine mountings…
Sprockets, plough points, clutch plate…', recycled and reassembled
to make the work of art.

In a way, *The Weather in Japan* is all about things coming apart
and being put together again. This is the principle behind making a
patchwork quilt, but it has in these poems a much deeper significance.
The sculpting celebrated in 'Scrap Metal', or the delight in his
father's own method of 'mending things' (which is also a process
of self-healing) in 'The Branch', are paradigmatic of Longley's
own ambitions, formal and political. The motif, and the work of
art it comes to represent, are more than merely decorative. To
recycle has virtues on more than one level. The patchwork quilt
has history inscribed within it, the remnants of a past retrieved
from forgetfulness, as if each square tells its own story.

In 'The Sewing Machine' the retired sailor and quilter George
Fleming 'is making out of sailors' collars / A quilt that will cover
the sea bed and the graves / Of submariners'. The making of the
quilt is a commemorative gesture, literally inscribed with historical
detail: 'his sewing machine cruises among the flotsam / And picks
up hundreds of waterlogged cap tallies', gathering together the
names of lost submarines. It is as if something, at least, has been
saved from the water, even though at the same time the names are
a poignant reminder of the sailors who were not picked up. In
listing those names in its final lines, the poet's naming imitates
the quilter's stitching together of fragments.

The conceit of naming/quilting is evoked again in 'The Yellow
Teapot'. Responding fiercely and protectively to the hurt and betrayal
of a loved one, the poet 'stitched together this spell, / A quilt of
quilt names to keep you warm in the dark':

> *Snake's Trail, Shoo Fly, Flying Bats, Spider Web,*
> *Broken Handle, Tumbling Blocks, Hole in the Barn*
> *Door, Dove at the Window, Doors and Windows,*
> *Grandmother's Flower Garden, Sun Dial, Mariner's*
> *Compass, Delectable Mountains, World without End.*[2]

This is a list of quilts, and a quilted list, one whose overlaps and
its moments of enjambment wrap it around itself and its recipient.
As is the case with others of Longley's lists, the names here are
not "meaningful" in any straightforward narrative sense; but they
accumulate meaning in a different way as the list progresses, mov-
ing from the slightly more sinister snakes, bats, and spiders to the
healing flower garden, the mountains, and, finally, with its reli-
gious and consolatory overtones, the 'World without End'. It is

typical, too, that the close of the list thereby opens it up to infinity.

Given the reverberations of the motif throughout *The Weather in Japan*, it is hardly surprising that when 'The Quilt' earns its own poem, it symbolises life itself. In the opening lines, the speaker's fleeting visit, passing through Amherst, allows only a partial picture:

> I come here in the dark, I shall leave in the dark –
> No time to look around Amherst and your little house,
> To talk of your ill father, my daughter's broken – no,
> There isn't time – tears in the quilt, patterns repeating.

For the poet to go as he came, in the dark, reverberates beyond the immediate occasion: in the space between birth and death, the narrative of life is 'the quilt', with its occasional 'tears' (in both senses) of bereavements, broken marriages, gaps in perspective, and its 'patterns repeating'. The lines themselves mirror the life/ the quilt, with their repetitions and the tear in the narrative. The fragmentations of style in 'The Quilt' are suggestive of what it is difficult to say, of linguistic stops and starts, of circling subjects that won't accommodate themselves in words – an imminent death, a broken marriage. But what cannot be seen beyond one's own life can, the poem suggests, be imagined.

This one brief encounter is part of a pattern; it is also a human contact and, as such, a stay against the darkness which is death, nothingness, absence: 'we / Stitch a square of colour on the darkness, needle- / Work, materials and words...'. In the end, the poem is not 'in the dark'; more than this, it has suggested a healing through imagination in a manner which transcends the brief visit that is its ostensible subject. If the quilt is a measure of life, it is also a measure of poetry, or of what the poet hopes poetry can do, another way of 'mending things'.

> ...in your neighbourhood instead of snow the bushes
> Wear quilts left out all night to dry, like one enormous
> Patchwork spring-cleaned, well-aired, mended by morning.

The patterns created here, and in the other quilt poems, reflect the composition of *The Weather in Japan* structurally as well as thematically. In 'The Quilt', each quilt becomes a patch in 'one enormous / Patchwork'.

What is complete in itself is also part of a greater whole; it is that idea which *The Weather in Japan* strives towards through its complex intertextualities. This is not to say that the poems have to be read through each other; as in *The Ghost Orchid*, each stands on its own. But to read them together is also to see the pattern

differently from different and multiple vantage points. The making
of a quilt – fragments, odds and ends stitched together to make
the whole work of art – is thus paradigmatic of the overall struc-
ture of the collection. The quilt image holds significance for read-
ing individual poems too.

In 'The Sunburst' the quilt is 'Made out of uniforms, coat linings,
petticoats, / Waistcoats, flannel shirts, ball gowns' with 'twenty
stitches to every inch'. The detail of those stitches complements
Longley's own arguments about miniaturism in poetry, of the
capacity of the couplet or quatrain poem to contain an extraordi-
nary degree of complexity. (Later, in *Snow Water*, the poem
'Taxonomy' makes the same point explicitly in relation to poetry,
mirroring the 'twenty stitches to every inch' with 'I have fitted a
hundred wing-glints into this one line.') 'The Sunburst' is also
about how one 'square' – or, if you like, one poem – might reflect
and absorb what is around it, both in terms of other poems in the
book, and as a brief window onto, or out of, a world beyond the
text: 'a diamond pattern / That radiates from the smallest grey
square / Until the sunburst fades into the calico'.

In the patchwork quilt, in other words, Longley has found an art-
form – an endearingly domestic one for a poet preoccupied with
'home' and 'snoozing' – which is also a metaphor for poetry, one
which marries itself perfectly to the expression of his own aesthetic.
It is possible to see *The Weather in Japan* as a culmination of some-
thing Longley has been striving towards since the early 1980s. As
with the merging of the fluidity of writing and painting in *The Ghost
Orchid*, it is as if making a quilt, making a poem about a quilt,
and making a collection of poems, are almost indistinguishable;
stitching and writing and patterning go hand in hand.

More than any other of Longley's books, *The Weather in Japan*
is an extraordinarily unified collection. This is partly because the
fascination with the motif serves him so well; it is also because by
the time of *The Weather in Japan*, Longley has begun to develop,
and articulate, a conscious sense of what is happening in the later
books. In a 1998 interview he says:

> In my first four books I had indulged a tendency to write short intense
> lyrics and then arrange them in sequences. Something different began to
> happen in *Gorse Fires* – some kind of involuntary denial of the urge to
> string poems together in rosaries. The book emerged like a big patch-
> work. I wanted any given poem to draw resonances from other poems
> ten or twenty pages in front or behind. I was aiming for a deeper
> cohesiveness. In more confident moments the book looks to me like
> one big poem, although each piece has its own title and independence.
> This process was taken further in *The Ghost Orchid*.[3]

And, it is tempting to add, it culminates in *The Weather in Japan*. At the point the interview took place (22 May 1998), the collection was three-quarters complete, and the imagery used here of a book like a 'big patchwork' suggests that the process of writing and structuring *The Weather in Japan* offered a way for Longley to interpret his own work post-*The Echo Gate*. Although he is talking of *Gorse Fires*, it is, on the surface at least, *The Weather in Japan*, more than any other collection, that fulfils his aim as expressed here.

But it is not as simple as that. In *Gorse Fires*, that 'deeper cohesiveness' is latent rather than manifest in the collection's structure; by *The Weather in Japan*, Longley's fascination with his quilt motif offers a means of rendering the 'cohesiveness' a surface, as well as deeper, phenomenon. The later collection may therefore be read as a more deliberate reflection on, as well as of, the concerns he outlines here in interview, a more transparent rendering of an aesthetic ideal than is seen in the two previous books.

There are, of course, risks attendant upon this degree of self-analysis, of which Longley, with the memory of the problems caused by the circle he inscribed around himself in *Poems 1963-83*, is aware. If *The Weather in Japan* exemplifies an aesthetic ideal, where does the poet go next? While the temptation to see Longley's first four books as creating a kind of narrative in their own right is understandable, one might as easily see the four books from *The Echo Gate* onwards as drawing their own 'circle' around the poet, since *The Weather in Japan* has probably a closer relation to *The Echo Gate* than to any other of Longley's books.

In *The Weather in Japan* he retreads much of the ground of *The Echo Gate* – its pastoral, elegiac, and historical preoccupations – with greater confidence and (paradoxically a measure of his development) with an increased tendency to destabilise what that aesthetic confidence might achieve. The interview quoted above took place not long after Longley arranged his own *Selected Poems*. As a result, his realisations about his own practice – and anxieties about such realisations – are more than usually in evidence: 'Arranging the Selected, I realised how many of my poems are two stanza jobs. Quite a few sonnets, for instance. The stanzas can be very long as in "Wounds" or "Company", but that's unusual. The single four-line poems and lone couplets are meant to be just as roomy in their way.'

The interview is, overall, a masterly piece of extended paradox, in which the poet is self-consciously aware of the need to avoid self-consciousness; reluctant to admit to critical acumen as regards his own work, but urgent in the desire not to be misunderstood. Acknowledging that 'as you grow older some sense of an accumulating *oeuvre* is unavoidable' he also notes that 'There's always a danger of writers believing their own publicity'. Hoping that 'echoes and connections' will be found in a book, at the same time he says that he 'wouldn't plant them deliberately'; he also observes later on that 'A truly imagined arrangement will indicate gaps and generate new poems', and re-reads the new poems in his folder 'in the hope that this might happen'. On the one hand willing to offer subtle inter-pretive details on 'The Parting' and the Ovidian poems, on the other, he admits to being 'suspicious about being too self-aware'. 'Even giving an interview' is, he suggests, towards the close of the interview, a suspect activity: 'how many interviews did Beckett or Yeats give, or George Herbert? You live your life and you write your poems.'[4]

Since Longley is rarely coaxed by his interviewers outside the bounds of familiar comments, many of his interviews – as with his short critical pieces – rework the same ideas for different audiences. That practice is part of his avoidance of an unhealthy critical intro-spection that could compromise the writing of poetry, and of an understandable resistance to (political) pressure. His 1998 inter-view with McDonald contains some of those familiar comments; but it also proves more than usually revealing. One reason is the interviewer's skill; another is the interview's timing.

Longley's poems have always walked a line between hope and despair, their politics no less complex than, sometimes barometric of, the society in which he writes – a society whose self-awareness, even about the language of self-description, has developed in important ways over the last two decades. *The Weather in Japan* is Longley's first book in a new millennium, one which looks forward to change. Yet it is also affected by the *fin de siècle* climate in which it was written, as evidenced in its more cautious retrospections. The col-lection was finished only a few months before his sixtieth birthday, a point in a career where "taking stock" might be something to be expected. That coincidence of timing brings a personal focus for Longley to the *fin de siècle* sensibility evident in western culture more generally, and to post-ceasefire developments in Ireland in particular.

If he is unusually self-aware in talking about his poetry at this point in time, in other words, it is hardly surprising; nor is it sur-prising that *The Weather in Japan* manifests some millennial self-consciousness. Longley is not alone in this. In the cases of his contemporaries Mahon and Heaney, both stage of career and moment in history inform the work published at the end of the last century.

'To live in a decadence,' runs the epigraph to Derek Mahon's 1997 collection *The Yellow Book*, 'need not make us despair; it is but one technical problem the more which a writer has to solve.' By implication, the same problem confronts Mahon in the 1990s, and the changes in his style are consequent upon the need to rethink his past and future. *The Yellow Book*, whose title looks back to the 1890s *fin de siècle*, and whose first poem is written 'after Baudelaire', is at times in an intertextual dialogue with Mahon's earlier poetry as well as the 1890s, its self-consciousness about and implicit dissociation of the poet from the past allied to a *fin de siècle* weariness about the present.

Rather more energetically, if no less self-consciously, Heaney marked the end of the 20th century by wielding his heroic pen/spade/Beowulfian sword to slay monsters and mothers, and to make his epic mark on the second millennium with the translation, and Hibernicisation, of an Anglo-Saxon poem of the first millennium. Both Heaney's *Beowulf* and Mahon's *The Yellow Book* take their place in each writer's grand narrative as their final curtain calls to a century notable in its last decades, as it was also in its first, for the high profile of technically accomplished, aesthetically tormented Irish poets. They are enterprises which belong in, and emerge out of, a Janus-faced *fin de siècle* sensibility, in as much as they incline towards looking back – at history, at their own work – as well as forwards. The closing poem of Mahon's *The Yellow Book*, 'Christmas in Kinsale', epitomises that sensibility, its 'come on' into the future also evocative of a lost civilisation:

> I dreamed last night of a blue Cycladic dawn,
> a lone figure pointing to the horizon,
> again the white islands shouting, 'Come on; come on!'...

The Weather in Japan is also a collection haunted by a sense of endings, in which it is very much of its time. From the sensibility evident in its opening poem, 'Water-burn' ('Yes, we should have been doing more with our lives'), *The Weather in Japan* both evaluates, and questions, a 40-year writing career. Longley's concern, in such reflections, is not to transform his style, even themes, to the extent that divided opinion among Mahon's critics after publication of *The Yellow Book*. Rather, his hope, as he explained in the *Poetry Book Society Bulletin*, is that the book may be seen 'to deepen the preoccupations of forty years'.

Nor does he succumb, or at least not directly, to Mahon's inclination for what may be perhaps be seen as an uncomfortable degree of self-reference. Yet the collection more than once reminds us of

the 'Forty years I've been at it' ('Fragment'), of 'the poet who re-
collects his younger self' ('The Beech Tree'), and of a conscious-
ness that what now exists as a body of writing is a 'life's work' ('The
Waterfall'). In the hidden poem at the close of the book, the quilt
motif has been seamlessly woven into the poet's anticipation of his
own end, as it has also become, by implication, his life's work: '...on
the last morning / Tuck me in behind our windbreak of books'.

The buried allusion here to 'Company', from *Man Lying on a
Wall*, with its 'only surviving copies / Of the books that summarise
my lifetime', is also telling. *Man Lying on a Wall* projected a rather
tormented poet-figure, exploring the disjunctions between the
domestic figure, the artist, and the bureaucrat, and with a sense the
poet might disappear down the cracks. More than 20 years later,
The Weather in Japan comes closer to providing the affirmations
and to projecting a sense of wholeness that were once inconceiv-
able. It is as if maturity, and taking stock, have brought about a
kind of reconciliation, even if that reconciliation is, in these later
years, about embracing the 'immaculate sand that awaits our foot-
prints' after death ('Björn Olinder's Pictures').

In the context of *The Weather in Japan*'s introspections and retro-
spections, the quilt motif is more than a metaphor for the structure
of the book; it has also become an appropriate symbol of Longley's
oeuvre to date, a motif paradigmatic of 40 years of writing. It is
partly for this reason that the strategy of stitching together has
become manifest rather than latent; it is also for this reason that it
cannot thereafter repeat itself in quite the same way. To see 'tears
in the quilt' and 'patterns repeating' across his career implies an
emergent unity of thought, as if not only the poems, but even all
the books Longley published up to the end of the 20th century
make up their own 'big patchwork'.

II

Yet as with any *fin de siècle* sensibility, endings carry within them
implied beginnings, and things cannot end here, on what could
only be a dying fall, a closure to which his aesthetic has always
been resistant. Longley's 'Forty years I've been at it' is also a con-
fession of the inadequacy and wonder with which he began, as if
the challenge of words and the world is always felt anew: 'A poetic
pro' maybe, but still one who 'can't find the words for this starry
night' ('Fragment'). The 'last morning', imminent though it may
be, is always not here, not yet. The pattern is never complete.

That sensibility has a personal as well as millennial impetus behind it. But the timing of *The Weather in Japan* is of particular significance in the context of Northern Ireland. Longley subtitled his first four books 'Poems 1963-1968', 'Poems 1968-72', 'Poems 1972-75' and 'Poems 1975-79' respectively; but the practice ceased with *Gorse Fires*. *The Weather in Japan*, however, contains within it some careful dating – the elegies for Seán Dunne, Catherine Mercer and Fiona Jackson, all elegies for those who died young, give the birth and death dates of his subjects; the poet's own age is easily inferred from various poems, as in the 'bouquet for my fifties' in 'The Blackthorn'; the poem 'January 12, 1996' marks what would have been his father's hundredth birthday, and 'At Poll Salach' is subtitled 'Easter Sunday 1998'.

This is something rarely seen in his earlier books (the only exceptions are 'In Memory of Charles Donnelly' and 'Edward Thomas's War Diary'), not even – as in a poem such as 'Ceasefire' – where we might most expect it. In the elegies, it serves to point up the contrast between the poet's own maturity, and the lives cut short, a contrast which has become, for the elegist, more acute. But beyond this, it also serves to place the collection with unusual specificity in a particular historical moment, and in the case of 'At Poll Salach', in relation to key historical events.

The Weather in Japan was written between October 1994 and October 1998.[5] That is, broadly speaking, from the 1994 ceasefires, through to the April 1998 Good Friday (Belfast) Agreement and its immediate aftermath. It is a period in which an upwards trajectory, a growth of optimism, seems to be the order of the day. Not until July 1999 did the optimism generated by the Good Friday Agreement give way to a political stalemate over decommissioning from which it has yet, at the time of writing, to emerge. Yet it is also a period which encompasses some of the worst atrocities seen in Northern Ireland's 'Troubles' history, with sectarian murders and beatings, and the Canary Wharf (1996), Manchester (1996) and Omagh (1998) bombings, in which last 29 people, as well as unborn twins, were killed.

So is *The Weather in Japan* a 'Cycladic dawn' or a 'last morning'? In a sense, it is both, and its mood is, as Longley himself describes it in the *Poetry Book Society Bulletin*, one of 'embattled celebration': 'the great nature writer Michael Viney,' he writes, 'once said to me that poetry gives things a second chance. I am trying to believe him…'.

'At Poll Salach', an oblique response to the Good Friday Agreement, captures precisely that mood:

> While I was looking for Easter snow on the hills
> You showed me, like a concentration of violets
> Or a fragment from some future unimagined sky,
> A single spring gentian shivering at our feet.

This short poem concentrates and interweaves aesthetic, political, and ecological principles. Its speaker is, significantly, looking at first for the wrong thing in the wrong place – the broad panoramic vision – at the expense of the tiny detail of the here and now. Only by seeing that detail – not a blanket of snow but a 'single spring gentian' – is 'some future unimagined' rendered possible.

The need to look downwards and inwards, if not rather than, at least as well as, lifting one's eyes to the hills is one implication of the poem. (In 'Pale Butterwort' that warning is reiterated: 'with so much happening overhead / I forgot the pale butterwort there on the ground'.) The gentian in 'At Poll Salach' – fragile, 'shivering' (compare the 'shivering boy' of 'Wounds'), and by implication easily trampled underfoot – functions as a potentially healing symbol, given the political context of the poem; but it is also, literally, rare and endangered. The West of Ireland, more particularly the Burren, where the flower is found, is a landscape 'increasingly menaced'.[6] The poem's desire to protect the flower's symbolic status is allied to a desire to protect it from a very real ecological threat. In both cases, it is, like the patchwork squares of other poems, both fragment and concentration, the part and the whole.

In 'At Poll Salach', as in other poems, the desire to mend, protect, and stitch together goes hand in hand with a recognition that such work might easily come unravelled. '[T]rying to believe' is a recognition that complacence doesn't generally allow for second chances. In its double-vision of the part and the whole, the poem also makes what is for Longley a vital point of principle. 'The Waterfall' asks for his poems, his 'life's work', to be read 'here by this half-hearted waterfall / That allows each pebbly basin its separate say'. The absence of a voice that places itself – and selfhood – at the centre of the poem, or that claims to speak for "history" or "community" is a hallmark of Longley's later work.

In *An Exploded View* we find a not entirely successful attempt to speak for and from a specific community (of poets). The strategy is not attempted again; more than that, Longley's "voice" has moved progressively further and further to the margins, clearing the space of the poem as one in which each element is allowed its 'separate say'. 'At Poll Salach' traces, in miniature, that displacement of self, from 'I' to 'You' to 'A single spring gentian'. It is by doing so that the poem achieves its own form of 'concentration', a vision that reverberates beyond, by working through, a different kind of singularity than that which places the lyric 'I' at the centre of the poem.

In *The Weather in Japan*, this kind of 'lateral move' of the self is increasingly in evidence. It is, for Peter McDonald, reminiscent of Larkin's 'something is pushing them / To the side of their own lives' in 'Afternoons'.[7] As Longley's anxiety over ecological threat meets a new sense of political optimism, the aesthetic principle at work – to let speak rather than make speak – cuts across both pre-occupations. An ecological conscience becomes a paradigm of political responsibility; the two agendas are not separable, and they both shift the poet into the wings of multiple stories.

'The Comber', the first poem written for *The Weather in Japan* in October 1994, epitomises that fundamental aesthetic principle:

> A moment before the comber turns into
> A breaker – sea-spray, raggedy rainbows –
> Water and sunlight contain all the colours
> And suspend between Inishbofin and me
> The otter, and thus we meet, without my scent
> In her nostrils, the uproar of my presence,
> My unforgivable shadow on the sand –
> Even if this is the only sound I make.

Humanity is pushed to the side of an arena in which it does not belong. The poet is not the conduit through which nature's immanence makes itself felt, but the trespasser whose presence creates an 'uproar' in the scene, the 'unforgivable' intruder who contaminates, even as he celebrates, the natural world.

The human subject is subordinated in the form itself of the poem, where the four lines through which we wait, suspended, for the 'I' finally introduce it only to place 'The otter' in the poem's centre, between the self and the distant island of Inishbofin. Celebrating, as he so often does, the space between, Longley is also concerned to vacate himself from it. Each first person singular reiteration after that point is a reiteration of absence – 'without my scent…My unforgivable shadow' – which still acknowledges the culpability of presence. In the final line, even the poem itself may be an act of trespass. Yet while it is concerned to distance the self from an element not its own, the poem simultaneously, by capturing in a split second the 'moment' of transition before the breaker, holds multiple elements together, elements which themselves 'contain all the colours'.[8] As with 'The Waterfall', always moving, always in the same place, a single entity made up of multiple components, or the 'single spring gentian' that is also a 'concentration of violets', or the quilt motif itself, 'The Comber' creates its symbol of wholeness through an anxiety not to compromise the integrity of its constituent parts.

As suggested earlier, the 'separate say' given to different elements in a spirit of ecological preservation reverberates in an understanding of history. The individual work of art may be the site on which multiple histories converge. Longley's abandonment of the collective voice of a specific community of poets in the mid-1970s is far from being the abandonment of a sense of community *per se*. *The Weather in Japan* contains a number of poems which celebrate personal friendships and kindred spirits: its 'sodality of the imagination' crosses space and time to encompass not only his friends and contemporaries (as in 'The Well at Tully', 'The Rabbit', or 'The Factory') but also such figures as Edward Thomas, Keith Douglas, Pierre Bonnard, even Homer and Virgil.

In 'Poetry', imagined and real connections link John Keats, Edmund Blunden, Edward Thomas, and Thomas Hardy; in 'The Moustache', an image of Edward Thomas recalls the poet's own father; in 'Sweetie Papers', it is 'Mrs Parker's shop' in post-war Belfast that connects us to the art of Pierre Bonnard. The imagined community, and the "family" implied in this book are more expansive than they once were (which is itself one reason why betrayal, as in 'The Yellow Teapot', is so deeply felt).

Community is understood in *The Weather in Japan* with a subtlety that makes it both the whole and its individual parts – 'I' encompassed in 'we' and vice versa. Vacating the poems of the self allows both to co-exist. The 'lopsided' poem that qualifies and amplifies the earlier 'Ceasefire' is a case in point. 'All of these People', written in December 1995, deliberately avoids the shapeliness of 'Ceasefire', but its insistence on a community's collective responsibility for individual histories demands that we look within an aspirational political narrative to the details it must still contain:

Who was it suggested that the opposite of war
Is not so much peace as civilisation? He knew
Our assassinated Catholic greengrocer who died
At Christmas in the arms of our Methodist minister,
And our ice-cream man whose continuing requiem
Is the twenty-one flavours children have by heart.
Our cobbler mends shoes for everybody; our butcher
Blends into his best sausages leeks, garlic, honey;
Our cornershop sells everything from bread to kindling.
Who can bring peace to people who are not civilised?
All of these people, alive or dead, are civilised.

Talking of the poem in a 1996 interview, Longley explains: 'Peace is just the absence of war; civilisation is the impossibility of war. In order to bring about civilisation, we really do have to imagine the nightmare backwards, imagine every last bit of it, and try to make sure it won't happen again. [...] it's terribly important to remember in detail, to make one's testimony and listen to the testimony of others...'.[9]

The immediate message of the poem as regards the accommodation of (political and religious) difference is sufficiently pointed: the Catholic dying in the arms of the Methodist; the shoes mended 'for everybody'; the butcher's blending of different ingredients to make the 'best sausages'; the shop that sells 'everything'. More than this, in implicitly directing its reader out towards earlier poems – 'Wreaths' and 'The Ice-cream Man' – 'All of these People' suggests a way to read a life's work which may also be a metaphor for understanding, or "reading", history. The insistent repetition of 'our' in the poem is about belonging in a community of 'everybody'; it is also about 'our' responsibility towards, and ownership of, the past. It is even, perhaps, an acknowledgement that in different ways the past is as much 'our' fault as the future is ours to transform. As with the poems' relations to each other, the multiple narratives or testimonies that have to be known in order to create a civilised world are checks and balances, complicating, qualifying, or amplifying the whole picture.

In 'All of these People', a self-reflexivity – how to read Longley's poems as a 'big patchwork' – is also a particular kind of historical imagination at work, one that accommodates 'All of these people' in stark contrast to the rigid exclusivities exposed in the earlier poem 'Poppies' with its 'Some people' and 'other people'. In a 'continuing requiem', one poem does not displace another, and traumatic histories are not forgotten: rather, the poems, like the flavours, are held together 'by heart' and those histories taken to heart.

III

The effacement of the lyric 'I' in Longley's poems can thus serve a dual purpose, allowing for communal empathy, and creating space for the individual voice. To tread this ground has always been one of the most difficult tasks confronting poets in Northern Ireland. The political complexities implicated in the relation of self to society manifest themselves in formal challenges for the lyric poet – and for what we understand by lyric poetry. As so often, it is the elegiac poems, or the poems which create and recreate *lieux de mémoire*, which bring those challenges into focus. 'All of these People' evokes earlier elegies for particular individuals in order to project communal memories into the future. In that sense, it crosses deliberately from the personal into the political, from 'I' to 'our'. Yet that negotiation, if less transparently, troubles even the most intimate poems in a collection which is more elegiac than any other of Longley's books to date.

Elegies tend to involve a peculiarly fraught negotiation of the distance and/or closeness between their author, subject and audience. The authority to speak in memory of the dead, and for that memorialising to speak to an audience beyond the instance of private mourning, is by no means a given; rather it is earned by the poet in the process of elegising. This remains the case even in those instances where personal contact is the trigger for imaginative contact – in the elegies for friends, family, and neighbours which, in contrast to the Troubles elegies of *The Echo Gate*, dominate *The Weather in Japan*.

The poet's authority may stem partly from his own grief or anger, although it can never rest on that alone. In one sense, "authority" is itself a problematic term to describe Longley's elegiac practice, since his habitual *modus operandi* in this volume, which is to push the self to the margins, is implicated in a recognition that elegy too – like the human presence in 'The Comber' – may be an act of trespass on privacies even if such privacies are essential to the ways in which the poems reverberate publicly. To question poetic authority, in other words, even when private experience underlies the poem, may be essential to the finding of it. Put the other way around, finding an elegiac "voice" may be a discovery not of its capabilities, but of its culpabilities, not of its authority, but of its lack of authority.

Longley's most deeply affecting elegies tend to be those which recognise their own potential for emotional trespass alongside their failure to 'reach' their subject. As with the earlier 'Last Requests', and as we might expect from his aesthetic preoccupations more generally, what he captures most poignantly in *The Weather in Japan* is a moment of transition.

Some of the most successful "elegies" in this volume are in fact elegies-in-waiting, poems not for the dead but for the dying. Such elegies-in-waiting – 'Broken Dishes', 'The Daffodils', 'The Mustard Tin' – tap into fears evident elsewhere in the book for a world 'increasingly menaced', for that which is about to disappear. They also complicate ideas of beginnings and endings, presence and absence. 'Broken Dishes' ambiguously records the moment where 'you start to die'. It also records its own inadequacies and strengths in one concentrated image: 'All I can think of is a quilt called Broken Dishes / And spreading it out on the floor beneath his knees.' This both offers the quilt as imaginative consolation and deliberately registers, in 'All I can think of', imaginative failure. In 'The Mustard Tin', the poem itself is like the 'three of us standing / For a few seconds between you and the darkness', poised before its own disappearance into the 'total absence of the oval mustard tin' it brings into imaginative presence.

In 'The Daffodils', the elegiac 'art of losing' is an art of simultaneously forgetting and remembering, a play of absence against presence on which elegy's success and failure are predicated:

Your daughter is reading to you over and over again
Wordsworth's 'The Daffodils', her lips at your ear.
She wants you to know what a good girl you have been.
You are so good at joined-up writing the page you
Have filled with your knowledge is completely black.
Your hand presses her hand in response to rhyme words.
She wants you to turn away from the wooden desk
Before you die, and look out of the classroom window
Where all the available space is filled with daffodils.

The recitation serves a mnemonic purpose, in more ways than one. Since the poem is about a woman who, in later years, has suffered a gradual loss of memory, the reiteration 'over and over again' is each time a new beginning.

This poem also carries within it the memory of Wordsworth's poem, itself famously an emotion 'recollected in tranquillity'; the 'joined-up writing' encompasses a literary tradition, poetry as memory at work. The life drawing to its close is also given a (Wordsworthian) childlike quality of innocence, in which everything that is lost is there to be discovered anew. The accumulation of memory makes the page 'completely black'; yet this is also an accumulated forgetting, since the script of the subject's own life is one she can progressively no longer read. Knowledge is forgetfulness; presence is absence.

Like 'Broken Dishes' and 'The Mustard Tin', this is a poem addressed to the person dying. Yet its final lines render the distinction between its subjects, and therefore its own suggested consolation, subtly ambiguous: the obvious interpretation – the desire for the mother to look away from that 'completely black' page to the colour outside, from what is forgotten to what is present – is shadowed by its alternative – that the daughter herself should look beyond the traumatic memories implied by the events of the poem and gradually learn to forget grief.

All three poems register, in different ways, the failure of communication. In 'Broken Dishes', words have become staccato and inadequate ('You love your body. So does Sydney. So do I') to be smoothed over by linguistic absence, and a shared spiritual presence ('Communion is blankets and eiderdown and sheets'). In 'The Daffodils', the problem of language centres on the problem of memory versus forgetfulness, which is literally manifested in the relation of mother and daughter.

The real connection here, as in the earlier 'Wounds', is tactile not verbal ('Your hand presses her hand...'), thereby recording what can never be recaptured after death, and which words themselves – all the elegist has to work with – can never reach. The poet's fascination with a moment of transition in these poems relates to the ways in which they question language itself, as no more fixed and stable than what it tries to contain, as destined always to miss rather than mark its object.

Other elegies in *The Weather in Japan* rethink the relations between self, subject and audience in ways which may also unsettle audience expectation. In 'A Sprig of Bay, 'The Snow Leopard', and 'The Altar Cloth', the subject of the elegy is in each instance addressed directly, and intimately named in the process: 'Sean, / Wear like a gigantic bangle the cracked millstone'; 'there, Fiona, you would still be you...'; 'Marie, I only know this in retrospect'. To address one's subject in this way integrates the self into the poem to a greater extent than omitting to do so; the person naming is as much of a presence here as the person named. It is as if pushing a life to the centre has brought the speaker into the centre along with it.

If it is, as Yeats said, the elegist's part to 'murmur name upon name', the process of doing so may bring into play a tension between the 'I' who 'write[s] it out in a verse' and the subject, as in Yeats's own controversial 'Easter 1916'. In Longley's poems, naming through direct address works differently to establish an extraordinary degree of closeness between author and subject, to the extent that the audience are the trespassers, rendered uneasy by an intimacy which risks their alienation from the subject-matter. That alienation – as if the reader is eavesdropping on an essentially private conversation – may be seen as part of the effect of these poems, forcing the reader to see their own shadow as 'unforgivable'. Yet it is also a risky strategy, one that might limit these poems' emotional resonance in the public sphere where they must ultimately come to rest.

One of Longley's outstanding elegies, however, 'The Evening
Star: in memory of Catherine Mercer, 1994-96', undertakes the
most difficult task of all – to elegise a child. In doing so, it posi-
tions the speaker's voice relative to the child, the community, and
the poem's audience, in more elusive ways:

> The day we buried your two years and two months
> So many crocuses and snowdrops came out for you
> I tried to isolate from those galaxies one flower:
> A snowdrop appeared in the sky at dayligone,
>
> The evening star, the star in Sappho's epigram
> Which brings back everything that shiny daybreak
> Scatters, which brings the sheep and brings the goat
> And brings the wean back home to her mammy.

This poem works so well partly because of its careful simplicities
of tone and diction. It implicitly mourns the death of a child; it
also speaks to that child, but at several removes from the kind of
direct address seen in other poems. Its poignancy lies in the fact
that it may be read as a poem which seeks to console not the living
but the dead, as in the earlier 'In Memoriam' of *No Continuing City*.
But does this voice try 'to isolate...one flower' for the child, for
those who mourn her, for the speaker himself, or for his reader?

'The Evening Star' is a more ambiguously subtle poem than it
might appear at first sight. Its speaker is part of, but never directly
speaking for, the collective grief of 'we' who 'buried' the child.
The community who share that grief are also the 'crocuses and
snowdrops' that 'came out for you', both the mourners and the
consolation. Yet 'So many' is also indicative of what lies beyond
comprehension or containment. The 'I' who tries to 'isolate...one
flower' is a voice conscious of its own limitations, and conscious
too that imaginative realisation must come through detail. 'From
among the hundreds of thousands I can imagine one', as he writes
in 'Ghetto' (*Gorse Fires*); in another Holocaust poem from *The
Weather in Japan*, 'The Exhibit', the 'grandparents...Rummaging
in the tangled pile for their spectacles' also seek the one from the
many; from the 'millions' killed in the Great War, 'A Poppy' finds
'an image in Homer' that 'picks out the individual / Tommy'.

In 'The Evening Star', the translation from Sappho which makes
up most of the second stanza, and is extraordinarily faithful to, whilst
Hibernicising, its source, reunites, across space and time, mother and
child and, through the act of translation itself, past and present
lyric poetry.[10] The poem as a whole sets poetry as a vehicle for
remembering – the longevity of a poetic tradition manifest in its

intertextualities – against the tragic shortness of the life remembered, reiterated through 'two years', 'two months', two stanzas. At the same time, what the voice of the poem tries to do is never directly claimed as achieved consolation since the voice is heard, through the translation of the closing lines, at one remove from itself. For all its tonal simplicities, 'The Evening Star' negotiates the complex relations between 'I', 'we' and 'you' with an exemplary subtlety and tact.

Longley's interest in Sappho is a long-standing one.[11] In the late 1990s, however, her work strikes an obvious chord with his own concerns. As Josephine Balmer observes, Sappho's importance lies both in her assertion of the 'value of individual women' and in her establishment of a 'collective history'. The 'special distinctive-ness' of women's classical poetry more generally, she argues, is bound up with the ways in which such poetry 'recorded, reflected and also revised individual, collective and communal memories' and articulated 'the tensions inherent in such a task'.[12] This may serve also as a description of Longley's own distinctiveness in the 1990s, and in a context in which tensions about the politics of memory are more than usually apparent. 'Healing through Remembering' is one of several post-ceasefire projects in Northern Ireland that seek to recover aspects of the past erased from memory; but their necessary counterpart is a healing through forgetting, since "recovery" must also involve a willingness to let go of potentially reductive versions of history.

This brings poetry up against a paradox. The hold on reductive versions of the past has been a tenacious one, and as argued earlier, poetry might be seen to offer a rather more fluid alternative to such histories; but poetry as a vehicle for remembering makes it also a means of preservation, of holding in place that which might otherwise be lost. The paradox is at the heart of the politics of memorialising more generally, and at the heart of debates about poetry and monumentality. Give the (possibly premature) pre-occupation with memorialising in Northern Ireland after the 1994 ceasefires, it is not surprising that *The Weather in Japan* is full of memorials, not just in the form of elegies. Poems about memorials, and about their own capacity for remembering and forgetting, play out a sophisticated debate about the politics of memory even as they are themselves, like elegies, acts of remembrance. As Guy Rotella observes, 'when poetry addresses monuments it also addresses itself and its own claims to monumental persistence'.[13]

In 'The War Graves', Longley refers to 'Charles Sorley's mon-umental sonnet'. Sorley's 1915 sonnet, 'When you see millions...', is, of course, in one sense anti-monumentalising:

> When you see millions of the mouthless dead
> Across your dreams in pale battalions go,
> Say not soft things as other men have said,
> That you'll remember. For you need not so.
> Give them not praise. For, deaf, how should they know
> It is not curses heaped on each gashed head?
> Nor tears. Their blind eyes see not your ears flow.
> Nor honour. It is easy to be dead.
> Say only this, 'They are dead.' Then add thereto,
> 'Yet many a better one has died before.'
> Then, scanning all the o'ercrowded mass, should you
> Perceive one face that you loved heretofore,
> It is a spook. None wears the face you knew.
> Great death has made all his for evermore.

'Say not soft things' indicts forms of remembrance akin to, and as culpable as, forgetfulness. Longley too has protested against a 'cult of remembrance' in relation to the First World War, one which, he argues, 'encourages us not to remember how shrapnel and bullets flay and shatter human flesh'.[14]

Sorley's poem negotiates with Shelley's earlier reflection on monumentality in 'Ozymandias'. With its 'Nothing beside remains', 'Ozymandias' obliquely casts doubt on the poem's own survival as a testament to decline; for Sorley too, a recognition of the mnemonic power of 'soft things' implies that his own poem may not be what 'you'll remember'. That the fourth stanza of Laurence Binyon's 'For the Fallen' ('They shall grow not old, as we that are left grown old…') has a place in cultural memory his own poem lacks may prove his point. But Sorley's sonnet is, as Longley describes it, 'monumental' in a different way, in terms of its historical and aesthetic significance, and in the vastness of its scope. (It is worth noting that Longley pays tribute to its 'monumental' scale in a poem – 'The War Graves' – which is unusually long for him, but knowingly belittled by the evocation of Sorley's short poem.) Even as he questions monumentality, Sorley creates the poem-as-monument, although, paradoxically, his legacy may be a hostility to the idea that the poet can ever do any such thing.

In 'A Poppy', Longley follows a pattern already established in his own poetry – as seen in his responses to Douglas and Rosenberg – by responding to, and shifting the emphasis of, the earlier poem by Sorley. Its uncomfortable opening line, 'When millions march into the mincing machine', places the two poems (of which Longley's, at 12 lines, is not quite a sonnet, itself notable given the increasing number of sonnets he has written in the last ten years) in dialogue with each other.

Sorley's 'one face' among the 'o'ercrowded mass' becomes, in
'A Poppy', the 'image from Homer' of Gorgythion, son of Priam,
who is caught in the crossfire and dies from an arrow aimed at
Hector.[15] Gorgythion's innocence and his death's arbitrariness
reverberate in Longley's understanding of the Great War soldiers
(the UK 'Tommy' and the US 'doughboy') as youthful victims.
The poppy is both the image of Gorgythion's death, 'Lolling to
one side like a poppy in a garden', and the symbol of death in the
Great War. It is also a token of remembrance, and at the close of
'A Poppy', its (ambiguous) monumental status has obliquely become
the poem's subject:

> And the poppy that sheds its flower-heads in a day
> Grows in one summer four hundred more, which means
> Two thousand petals overlapping as though to make
> A cape for the corn goddess or a soldier's soul.

The proliferation of flower-heads is as suggestive of an escalating
scale of casualties, from that one death in Homer to the 'millions'
of the poem's opening, as much as it suggests life's natural repro-
duction, its regenerative force. That the poppy grows 'four hun-
dred more' says something, too, about poems as acts of remem-
brance, about an inherited memory (through Homer, Virgil, and
Sorley) that continues to reproduce itself, in part through these
kinds of intertextual overlappings. After all, 'A Poppy' makes
Homer the elegist of Great War soldiers as well as the chronicler
of the Trojan War. The symbol of remembrance, in the poppy
petal shower that makes a 'cape for...a soldier's soul' is also a
symbol of renewal and change: 'A cape for the corn goddess'. If
this is healing through remembering, it looks forwards as well as
back; what may be fragile, or ephemeral (including the poem itself)
is also, the poem implies, irrepressible.

Several of the war poems in *The Weather in Japan* made up a
radio programme entitled *Cenotaph of Snow* in August 1998; that
is also the title for a later collection of 60 war poems from across
Longley's career published in a limited edition by Enitharmon Press
in 2003. The phrase comes from the poem, 'The Cenotaph', which
concentrates, in its reflection on the poem-as-monument, some of
the aesthetic, political and cultural issues inherent in the creation
of *lieux de mémoire* more generally.

In 'The Cenotaph', the snowman of earlier collections, in the
various guises of ghetto child (who 'turns into a little snowman
and refuses to melt') and ice-cream man is re-imagined as a ceno-
taph snowman built by Great War veterans:

> They couldn't wait to remember and improvised
> A cenotaph of snow and a snowman soldier,
> Inscribing 'Lest we Forget' with handfuls of stones.

The story is a true one. In Newtownards, some years after the First World War, ex-soldiers, frustrated by what they saw as unnecessary delays in erecting Great War memorials, built their own snowman memorial. A photograph of that "memorial" has survived, a tangible object which inspired the poem, and which is itself now a memorial of the event.[16]

In contrast, the poem – and the original memorial – attempt the impossible, inscribing permanence on impermanence, stones on snow. The opening line – 'They couldn't wait to remember' – acknowledges the need for acts of commemoration as part of a healing process. These are, however, Great War veterans, and the need for such commemoration is, of course, to be able to leave the past behind. Shadowing this line is therefore its echo 'They couldn't wait to forget'. Consequently, while they create their own memorial, they also create an object that is both solid and fluid, whose inscription, like the process of writing – or reading – itself won't survive the thaw. The stones will become, beyond the limits of the poem, unintelligible. This is the *lieu de mémoire* melting before our eyes. (We might remember, too, that in 'The Horses', Longley finds 'the best war memorial...in Homer: two horses that refuse to budge...Immovable as a tombstone' and yet who weep, 'Hot tears spilling from their eyelids'.)

In one sense, the poem is itself the site of memory since it inscribes, for posterity, what has long since disappeared. Yet it is also a cenotaph of snow which melts into the white space beyond its close. The inscription of the poem is no less stable than that which it commemorates; at the same time, to enshrine in the poem the foreknowledge of its disappearance is, paradoxically, a way of ensuring its survival. In one sense, memorialising always strives for the impossible – to recapture what is lost. But because the fulfilment sought through remembrance is never attained, the processes of remembrance – memory as desire – continue to prevent our forgetting.

To see beyond the political whitewash of historical grand narratives into the fragments of individual lives, and to draw those lives into the pattern of memory is – and has always been – the impetus behind Longley's historical imagination. Throughout, *The Weather in Japan* is characterised by the desire to place the small, the apparently significant, the singular, against the blanket sameness of a destructive past and present, and against an equally destructive forgetfulness. It is by no means an uncomplicated task. For the poet to recover what is lost, to provide a record of people or events past or forgotten, to create sites of memory, might seem to make claims for poetry as an immortalising or solving force. Yet the characteristic self-reflexivity, self-effacement and profound scepticism about the capacity of language to contain its subject found in these poems together provide a destabilising counter-force to such claims. It is in the tension between obliteration and survival, past and future, that tentative memorialising gestures may be found.

The longest poem in *The Weather in Japan*, 'The War Graves', struggles throughout with a monumental scale of suffering: 'headstones' that 'wipe out the horizon like a blizzard' and 'mine craters so vast they are called after cities'. The poppy, that 'symbolic flora', is no longer visible in 'The War Graves', only 'the tiny whitish flowers / No one remembers the names of in time'. Yet Longley does name them in the poem – 'brookweed / And fairy-flax, say, lamb's lettuce and penny-cress' – as he also names forgotten casualties, 'Rifleman Parfitt, Corporal Vance, / Private Costello…'. In naming names, in detailing minutiae, the poem refuses to allow the past to be wiped clean. In the honesty of that refusal, it also finds, at least for the moment, a different monument and a possible future: 'we pick from a nettle bed / One celandine each, the flower that outwits winter'.

8

A Complicated Recipe: *Snow Water*
1999-2003

There's no such place as heaven...
MICHAEL LONGLEY, AUGUST 2001

I

There is, as one reviewer remarked, 'something new' about Longley's voice in *Snow Water*.[1] Despite the book's obvious thematic continuities with his earlier work, it also marks out a different territory for itself. Some stylistic and formal changes are notable. Longley may have taken the short poem as far as it can go in *Snow Water* (with the one-line poem 'Lost'); but the quatrain or quintain poems so prevalent in *The Weather in Japan* (where they number fourteen) have almost disappeared. Instead, the form that dominates *Snow Water* is the sonnet.

Almost a fifth of the poems in this book are (usually unrhymed) sonnets, culminating in the sonnet-sequence 'Woodsmoke'. That 'reckless syntactical reach' which liberated the poet in the 1980s is still in evidence in some of the sinuous single-sentence poems in the book – among them 'Above Dooaghtry' and 'The Pattern'. Yet also in evidence is a new fascination with syntactical simplicity, with short, seemingly transparent phrases and sentences played off against each other within grammatically contained stanzaic shapes. For the reader acclimatised to the long, fluid, five- or six-stress unrhymed line that has been the staple of Longley's work over the last fifteen years, there may be one or two other surprises; the tetrameter stanzaic poem 'Owl Cases', for instance, or the rhyme scheme employed in 'The Last Field'.

This is not to suggest that *Snow Water* marks a dramatic shift in style; it does not. But it is worth noting that these poems are written at more than a decade's distance from the silence of the early 1980s, and that the short poems' relation to, and emergence out of, a period of writer's block, as with the poet's need of the longer line, are no longer strategies immediately haunted by that silence.

In a 2003 interview, Longley quotes Yeats's 'As I altered my syntax, I altered my thought.'[2] Subtle shifts in style in *Snow Water* are indicative of subtle shifts in perspective. While the poems of *Snow Water* are not haunted by a previous silence, the newness of voice in this collection comes partly from the anticipation of a future silence, and from a changing perspective on death. As with Yeats's later poems, newness may be directly related to an increasing sense of maturity. Always an elegiac poet, in *Snow Water* Longley is frequently self-elegiac, never taking it for granted he will write more poems. He describes himself as living 'from poem to poem, from hand to mouth'.[3] Perhaps some of the more expansive structures in the volume have an element of *carpe diem* about them, for which the spur is not so much a Yeatsian 'lust and rage' as the question posed in the last poem of the book, 'Leaves', 'Is this my final phase?'

The question may be premature, since by its close 'Leaves' itself suggests a mood of vibrant imaginative confidence ('I can imagine foliage on fire like that') more than a peaceable 'hanging on'. There is an echo here of the persona of 'Alibis' thirty years earlier, 'Tattered and footloose in my final phase', a poem which also marked a resurgence of confidence, a beginning not an ending. Yet the perception of what 'I can imagine' in many of these poems is accompanied, even inspired, by a heightened sense of the poet's own mortality, and the obvious influence here is Yeats's self-elegy, 'The Wild Swans at Coole'. For Yeats, the autumnal 'count' of the 'nine-and-fifty swans' is also a count of the years through which 'All's changed'. Those changes, consequent upon his own ageing, are implied through contrast with the swans who remain 'Unwearied still', whose 'hearts have not grown old', and for whom 'Passion or conquest…Attend upon them still'.

The final stanza, which anticipates the poet's own end through the swans' departure, is also a celebration of the present moment, one which transforms the swans into a symbol of a still to be imagined future:

> But now they drift on the still water
> Mysterious, beautiful;
> Among what rushes will they build,
> By what lake's edge or pool
> Delight men's eyes when I awake some day
> To find they have flown away?

Longley's 'Arrival', in concentrated form, also treads some of this ground:

> It is as though David had whitewashed the cottage
> And the gateposts in the distance for this moment,

> The whooper swans' arrival, with you wide awake
> In your white nightdress at the erratic boulder
> Counting through binoculars. Oh, what day is it
> This October? And how many of them are there?

'There is no need,' Michael Allen suggests, 'to rake over distant memories of "The Wild Swans at Coole"' in reading 'Arrival', since what 'attracts us to the poem and the situation is the difference from Yeats, the absence of that slightly haughty poetic self-importance'.[4] But perhaps Longley is drawn to 'The Wild Swans at Coole' as one of the (rare) occasions on which Yeats's haughty self-importance – if not selfhood – is in abeyance. The elegiac tone of one poem finds parallels in the other. They both have the symbolic autumnal setting; it is 'now', or in 'this moment' that what is 'Mysterious, beautiful' resonates; and not least, the questions which close both poems share more than might at first appear.

It is hard not to see 'Arrival' as transforming 'The Wild Swans at Coole' into more than a distant memory for both poet and reader. The reversals of imagery are also similarities. For Yeats, to 'awake some day' is the conceit for death and departure; for Longley the lover is 'wide awake' at the swans' arrival, the eroticism of the moment suggestive of the flowering of marital love. Yet arrival and departure work two ways, since one is inherent in the other, to suggest the passing of years. The swans, for both poets, become a symbol of their own consciousness. For Yeats, there is some fear about what is lost of the self, when they have 'flown away'. For Longley, 'what day is it / This October?' captures, through the line-break, not merely 'This October', but those already gone, leaving the final question – 'And how many of them are there?' – finely ambiguous, rendering the present moment infinite, while anticipating his own time as finite: how many swans? days? years? This October, or in the future?

The unobtrusiveness of the speaking voice in 'Arrival' does, of course, distinguish Longley's style from Yeats's placing of himself at the centre of the scene/poem in 'The Wild Swans at Coole'. 'Arrival', along with several other poems in *Snow Water*, celebrates and centres marital love not the self. But its celebration is also tinged with fear. For the poet to entwine his own consciousness with the scene before him, to implicate a form of self-elegy with the landscape, suggests an indebtedness to the maturity of vision in Yeats's elegiac pastoral, in which a timeless beauty is qualified by time passing.

The whooper swans in Longley's poems may be an aesthetic symbol, but they also bring to the poet an awareness of mortality.

In 'Echoes', 'Forty-two whoopers call, then the echoes / As though there are more swans over the ridge.' The echo is suggestive of infinity, of something beyond the here and now: the poem as a whole complicates where things begin and end, what constitutes growth or decline. In 'Robin', a poem about leaving the cottage at Carrigskeewaun, the 'watery sun-glare is melting' the poet's vision of the swans, their disappearance from view mirroring his own departure – and, implicitly, his own emotion: 'I would count the swans but it hurts my eyes.'

If the swans are one symbol of arrival and departure in *Snow Water*, the Carrigskeewaun burial mound is another, and it too is implicated in the poet's own sense of growth and decline. As discussed earlier in relation to 'Spring Tide' from *The Echo Gate*, the burial mound is not actually a pre-historic burial mound, but is 'all that remains / Of a sandy meadow, a graveyard' from the nineteenth century. As the sea reclaimed the area around it, it became a mound which was, when Longley first visited it in the early 1970s, 20 feet high. Gradually eroded by the tide, it consists now only of a single, almost flat layer of stones, still shaped in a circle. It has become almost a memorial to the original graveyard, a commemoration of what was once there, but has now gone.

The erosion of the burial mound haunts the poet in *Snow Water*. 'Flight Feathers' is a sonnet which sets the 'wheezy epithalamion' of the nesting blue tits against 'all the birds that have disappeared'. Like 'Arrival' it is a love poem, itself a 'wheezy epithalamion', thirty-five years after the original 'Epithalamion', for a long marriage – and one of the few later poems in which the poet returns, perhaps with some nostalgia, to the rhyming characteristic of his early years. (Longley has said he would 'like every line in the last book to rhyme, as in *No Continuing City*', thus bringing him full circle.)[5] Yet once again, its final couplet complicates its celebratory mode, implicating the self with the landscape: 'The tide-digested burial mound has almost gone. / A peregrine is stooping high above my breastbone.'

In 'Above Dooaghtry', the site has been 'erased by wind and sea', pushing the poet's anticipated final resting place up on to the 'small plateau'. In 'Petalwort', the 'burial mound's wind-and-wave inspired / Vanishing act' is the inspiration for 'Self-effacement', for merging invisibly into the landscape after death. In 'Shadows' it has become a shadow of what it once was, another echo like the swans over the ridge: 'A flat circle of flat stones, anonymous / Headstones commemorating the burial mound'. 'Shadows' and 'Echoes' both raise questions about continuity after death, about what will survive of us, the burial mound a symbolic site onto which such concerns are projected.

In the final section of 'Level Pegging', its disappearance resonates with particular poignancy:

> Rubbed out by winds Anaximines imagined,
> The burial mound at Templedoomore has gone.
> Locals have driven their tractors along the strand
> And tugged apart the wooden wreck for gateposts.
> There are fewer exits than you'd think, fewer spars
> For us to build our ship of death and sail away.

The poem, dedicated to the critic Michael Allen, is a testament to friendship. It sets the longevity and consistency of that friendship against a world rapidly changing, and not always for the better. The short-sightedness and self interest behind the dismantling of the old shipwreck and the intrusion of the mechanical into the scene are implicitly rebuked. The sheer force of nature also erodes a once familiar landscape.

Holding on to one's own integrity and sense of self is, the poem suggests, increasingly difficult in the face of seemingly unstoppable forces; both figures are alienated from the supposed "values" of the contemporary world. This is, of course, about the passing of the years, measured against the disappearing burial mound: the accumulation of a life is also its erosion. It is also about a landscape itself under threat: as Longley has pointed out, 'The most urgent political problems are ecological', a reminder that his nature poems are his most political poems.[6] And it is about the imagination. To 'build our ship of death and sail away' is another version of 'making do with what has been left me', an imaginative quest that might, of necessity, begin only with fragments, odds and ends. ('I subsist', he writes in 'Praxilla', 'on fragments and improvisations.')

The burial mound has dwindled as the poet has aged, but it has also, as these poems suggest, increased in symbolic significance. It is barometric of the poet's shifting sense of self, and of the relationship between agency, nature and art. As 'tide-digested', the burial mound is subject to the forces of nature, but in a fashion reminiscent of Longley's own earlier fears of devouring and being devoured by others. '[E]rased by wind and sea', it is evocative of his own vanishing lyric subjectivity in earlier poems, of the scene erased in 'In Mayo', or of the self 'unclothed' in 'Landscape'. That it is 'inspired' to undertake its own 'Vanishing act' displaces agency onto the burial mound itself, although 'Vanishing act[s]' have more sinister overtones in Longley's poems too.[7]

The 'act' also has its performative and artistic element (as in the

earlier vanishing act of 'Fleance' in *Man Lying on a Wall*, or of
the poet in 'The Third Light') making the burial mound one of
several images that explore agency and selfhood. Yet its disappear-
ance is also something 'imagined' by the winds of Anaximines,
and in being so the burial mound is implicitly recreated in the
poems themselves as a different kind of memorial, brought back
into imaginative presence each time its absence is recorded.

'Level Pegging: for Michael Allen' is one of several poems in
Snow Water in which the poet's reflections on mortality have inspired
tributes to friendship and gestures of reconciliation. Peter McDonald
has noted moments where the 'camaraderie' seems slightly forced,
and where there is 'more than a hint of sentimentality'.[8] Perhaps
the self-consciousness in a poem such as 'The Pear' about Longley
and Montague as poets generates that feeling of unease, as it did
earlier for the recipients – and readers – of the 'Letters' sequence.
Its biblical references resonate with rather more dramatisation than
the situation of the poem demands: 'We have betrayed each other,
we agree. / Like Peter, I suggest, not like Judas – no.'

Poems such as 'The Last Field' or 'A Norwegian Wedding',
however, are exemplary in their treading of some of the same
ground, and the more oblique religious imagery which pervades
Snow Water is implicated in the book's celebration of friendship
and reconciliation in both subtle and moving ways. In 'A Norwegian
Wedding', the observation 'How few friends anyone has', tonally
both lament and celebration, takes us into the brief and poignant
lament for the crucified Christ (Oh, / His sore hands'), and to the
question which gives this 'epithalamion' its darker, more probing
side: 'How many friends does a leper have?' In 'The Last Field',
the poem's reconciliation is embodied in its rhyme, and in the
incantatory quality of its lilting repetitions: 'We who have fought
are friends now all the time.' The friendship with Medbh McGuckian
celebrated in 'Owl Cases' is one in which the two poets are tuned
into each other, as the 'owl that is all ears' is 'tuning in with its
feathers / To the togetherness of our heads'. The poem is also
attuned to the 'wavering hoot...which is the voice of God', its
'otherworldliness' not simply the other world of nature, but a world
of the imagination.

'You can be religious,' Longley has said, 'without believing any-
thing.'[9] In *Snow Water*, religious imagery and biblical echoes affirm
a religious sensibility, although not a religious belief system. 'House
Sparrows' quotes Psalm 84 ('Yea, / The sparrow hath found her
an house') and grounds the answer to its question 'But where?' in
the quotidian: 'At a water trough surrounded by sparrows / That

bicker and pick up the falling grains.' The one-line poem in the book, 'Lost' ('my lost lamb lovelier than all the wool'), has its obvious affiliation to the parable of the lost sheep, yet is also obliquely a love poem to a lost girl. 'Heron', an elegy for the American poet Kenneth Koch, borrows from Psalm 22 ('I didn't know you were "poured out like water / And all your bones were out of joint". I didn't know.') but without offering traditional Christian consolation. Instead, Koch is imaginatively transformed into the heron who 'take[s] to the air above a townland / That encloses Carrigskeewaun and Central Park'.

The naming of places here is also significant. In *Man Lying on a Wall*, 'There's no such place as home' encapsulated the poet's fraught relation to everyday life, and with one or two exceptions, place names in *Man Lying on a Wall* are notable for their absence. In relation to *Snow Water*, the comments Douglas Dunn made about *Man Lying on a Wall* seem now more apposite: 'the affectionate little details of life are seen to be as awe-inspiring as profounder designs, larger intentions....He seeks to affirm where he can. He makes ordinary endorsements and hallows the world.' Koch's after-life is imaginatively created in this world, as is the poet's projected afterlife in 'Above Dooaghtry': 'Our sandy dander to Allaran Point / Or Tonakeera will take for ever.' In 'Ceilidh', the thirteen O'Tooles are also, after death, still 'singing about everything', their coffins 'shouldered', 'Through the tide and over the Owennadornaun'. And the comment 'There's no such place as home' in *Man Lying on a Wall* is countered in 'Petalwort' by 'There's no such place as heaven, so let it be / The Carricknashinnagh shoal or Caher / Island...'.

This is to hallow the world, the equivalent of Praxilla's desire to 'set her groceries alongside the sun and moon'. The naming of places in these poems creates an imperfect Eden of this world. It is also to bring into the world, as Chris Agee observes, a 'note of...ceremon-iousness'.[10] The later Yeats is once again example and influence, for all the differences between the two poets. In 'A Prayer for My Daughter', Yeats's form of 'prayer' is for this world, this civilisation, this life: the 'soul' is 'self-delighting, / Self-appeasing, self-affrighting'. His rhetorical question – 'How but in custom and in ceremony / Are innocence and beauty born?' – also strikes some chords with Longley. There is an (oriental) ceremoniousness, a deliberate exquisiteness, about poems such as 'Moon Cakes' or 'Snow Water' – of which more anon. The quotidian, in a poem such as 'Robin', is also rendered ritualistic, a Carrigskeewaun leaving ceremony ('wiping wet windows / For Venus...'). Seven of the poems in this book are concerned with the ceremonies that surround death, others with marriage.

In 'Sleep & Death', which draws on a passage from book XVI of Homer's *Iliad*, the ritual preparation of the corpse is also about writing as ceremony:

> Zeus the cloud-gatherer said to sunny Apollo:
> 'Sponge the congealed blood from Sarpedon's corpse,
> Take him far away from here, out of the line of fire,
> Wash him properly in a stream, in running water,
> And rub supernatural preservative over him
> And wrap him up in imperishable fabrics,
> Then hand him over to those speedy chaperons,
> Sleep and his twin brother Death, who will bring him
> In no time at all to Lycia's abundant farmland
> Where his family will bury him with grave-mound
> And grave-stone, the entitlement of the dead.'
> And Apollo did exactly as he was told:
> He carried Sarpedon out of the line of fire,
> Washed him properly in a stream, in running water,
> And rubbed supernatural preservative over him
> And wrapped him up in imperishable fabrics
> And handed him over to the speedy chaperons
> Sleep and his twin brother Death, who brought him
> In no time at all to Lycia's abundant farmland.

As Peter McDonald notes, 'The close repetition is there in Homer, but in Longley's poem it is all there is, and the effect is one of eerie doubling...Care takes over where carnage has left off – but twice, and with a ritualistic attention to particulars mirrored in the act of verbal repetition.' [11] The poem's structure uncannily evokes the two chaperons, Sleep and Death, an effect compounded by its other subtle doublings: cloud and sun, fire and water.

The process of writing is itself a ritual, one that is undergone in order to make poetry, in Longley's phrase, 'experience transfigured'.[12] These careful preparations, for instance, are akin to the poems 'comfortlessly constructed' in 'An October Sun: in memory of Michael Hartnett', with 'Each sod handled how many times'. That handling – the process of writing, rewriting and crafting – produces the poem wrapped in its own kind of 'imperishable fabrics', the 'preservative' of its form. As Longley notes of Hartnett's poems in 'An October Sun', they 'endure the downpour like the skylark's / Chilly hallelujah, the robin's autumn song'. Perhaps it is not too far-fetched to find a religious echo in the endurance of poems too, although with a Gravesian, non-believer twist. As Graves writes at the close of his war memoir, *Goodbye to All That*, 'I no longer repeat to myself: "He who shall endure to the end, shall be saved." It is enough now to say that I have endured.' [13]

II

Such reflections on the self and mortality, the benevolence towards friends and fellow poets, and the fascination with 'custom and... ceremony' do to some extent show Longley in the mode of the 'grand old man of poetry'.[14] But to say only this is to miss the mischievousness and self-deprecating ironies also at the heart of *Snow Water*. Through the 1990s, Longley has been increasingly viewed as master elegist and concerned naturalist, sometimes to the exclusion of other readings of his work. His own consciousness of this kind of public profile may be sufficient reason to tread with some tonal caution as regards certain poems in *Snow Water*. (Muldoon perhaps suffers from the reverse response, habitually read as the poet of ironic "play".)

Are we to read the title-poem, 'Snow Water', for instance, as one in which 'the ceremonial brewing of "a gift of snow water" (reality) scalds into life a transformed "crock of snow water" (art's teapot: a second reality)'?[15] Or is it a poem which wryly undercuts expectations as regards its significance and/or its seriousness?:

> A fastidious brewer of tea, a tea
> Connoisseur as well as a poet,
> I modestly request on my sixtieth
> Birthday a gift of snow water.
>
> Tea steam and ink stains. Single-
> Mindedly I scald my teapot and
> Measure out some Silver Needles Tea,
> Enough for a second steeping.
>
> Other favourites include Clear
> Distance and Eyebrows of Longevity
> Or, from precarious mountain peaks,
> Cloud Mist Tea (quite delectable)
>
> Which competent monkeys harvest
> Filling their baskets with choice leaves
> And bringing them down to where I wait
> With my crock of snow water.

This is whimsical and elegiac. Like its companion poem 'Moon Cakes', it is a poem about art and ageing. Yet it is also tempting to read it as possessing an ironic consciousness of the ways in which Longley's poems are habitually read. '[F]astidious', for instance, reverberates in what has been, from the 1960s onwards, a perception of Longley's style as one of precision and control; with a careful measuring out of language rather than emotional and verbal excess. One reviewer of *Snow Water* observes that 'a

Longley poem that has lost all self-control is quite unimaginable'.[16]
The comment, however, may be misleading: a poem such as 'The
Butchers' both explores, and structurally embodies, a loss of self-
control; a loss of self-control need not equate to a breakdown of
form; it is also possible to argue that a poem which loses all self-
control is unimaginable as a poem.

Perhaps there is, in 'Snow Water', a knowingness about the
ways in which Longley's views on poetic form ('If it's not well
made, be it in strict stanzas or in Lawrentian free verse, then it
isn't a poem')[17] and the extraordinary formal control with which
he began his writing career, have been the subject, and the cause,
of some misunderstanding as regards the full implications of his
poems, particularly given the changes in his style through the 1980s.
That the 'gift' of snow water is 'modestly' requested has a self-
reflexive shrewdness about it too, as if the effacement and modesty
which characterise Longley's own lyric subjectivity are parodied
with a deliberateness that here creates their opposite. In another
sense, of course, there is nothing 'modest' about his poetic gift;
and the 'gift of snow water' is also the book itself as given to the
reader. That he makes his tea preparations 'Single- / Mindedly'
might serve as an ironic reference to the poet's own vocational
single-mindedness about his art ('Tea steam' linked to 'ink stains');
but the connection is undercut first by the line break, second by
the nature of the parallel itself. The tea-making may be a private
ritual, but it is a far cry from the more profound ceremoniousness
implied in a poem such as 'Sleep & Death'. 'Snow Water' is, of
course, a poem about transformation – of the self as much as any-
thing else (not least in its 'Eyebrows of Longevity'). But its self-
indulgent playfulness is also the means by which it mocks the self-
importance of the poet (and doubtless of the critic too).

The strategy is not dissimilar in 'Moon Cakes', which, as with
earlier poems such as 'Alibis', adopts a persona who bears some
resemblance to the poet, 'painting almond / and plum blossom'.
The persona is also one who parodies aspects of self, with his 'wee
transcendental...cottage' in which the imaginative power of the small-
scale – a Longley hallmark – is humorously rendered in terms of an
over-refined preciosity. 'I overdose,' the poet concludes, 'on jasmine
tea and / moon cakes (a complicated recipe).'

This is deliberate fodder for those who see Longley only as the
poet of miniaturism, refined tastes and oriental aesthetics, and who
has sated himself on such things. The poem itself is a 'complicated
recipe' of some of Longley's favourite images – plum blossom, snow,
the full moon, the mountain cottage. Yet despite its light-hearted-

ness, there is a more serious issue about the poet's reception at stake in reading 'Moon Cakes'. The 'recipe' may be 'complicated'; the end product should not seem so. The simplicity of the finished work is therefore deceptive: once again, as 'An October Sun' puts it, the poems are 'comfortlessly constructed, / Each sod handled how many times'.

Longley's poems, whose technical complexities have become, through a growing technical assurance, less immediately visible to readers, are too often assumed to be an uncomplicated recipe. That problem may be compounded by a critical climate in which surface difficulty is treated as synonymous with depth, and in which experimentalism is sometimes worn on the sleeve. Longley's poems run counter to this particular critical *zeitgeist*: they play surface lucidity against complicated depth; their formal experimentation is integral to, but never overtly intrudes upon, their effect; and that they are not susceptible to easy explication is a measure of their subtlety.

In *Snow Water* is also detectable an increasing consciousness about Northern Irish poetry as the subject of academic debate. That consciousness is a long way from Muldoon's epic intervention in such debates in *Madoc*, but there is in *Snow Water* a mischievous tendency to send readers on a (false) critical trail. In the early 1990s, Longley's papers, along with those of a number of other Irish poets, became available in the special collections of Emory University Library in Atlanta. Heaney observed, having visited the library, that 'it's odd to see the whole thing turning into "an archive". Before we've been archived ourselves. But Mahon-San is probably right – there's no such thing as privacy no more.'[18]

Longley's own observations in 1983 are not without a certain ironic relevance too: 'I have my doubts,' he wrote, 'about the modern manuscript trade. I do not feel dead enough to take my own work sheets that seriously! It does seem a bit like emptying the sink-tidy over the dinner table, or wrapping the afterbirth in swaddling clothes.'[19] The availability of private material during the lifetime of the poet brings some questions to bear on criticism of contemporary Irish poetry, and its methodology, more generally. One more immediate consequence of the archive, however, has been the urge to tell the "true", or at any rate untold story of Northern Irish poetry – in particular of the Belfast Group – in the 1960s.[20]

The history of the Group under Philip Hobsbaum's auspices (from 1963 to 1966) seems to be one about which an interpretive consensus can never emerge. Perhaps such a consensus would be antipathetic to the Group ethos itself. Perhaps this is also one reason for the

appeal of the subject to critics – that there is always a different
narrative to tell. Heaney's account of the Group, and of Northern
Irish poetry in the 1960s more generally, for instance, interprets
the Group's significance in terms of his own aesthetic preoccupa-
tions. For Longley and Mahon, on the other hand, their concern
has been to shift the emphasis by affirming Trinity College Dublin,
not the Belfast Group, as their apprenticeship; Alec Reid, not Philip
Hobsbaum, as their 'father-figure'. Even the Group's membership
is still contested, the tendency to think of Longley, Mahon and
Heaney as a trio contributing to the assumption that Derek Mahon
(during this period resident mostly in Dublin, the US and Canada)
attended regularly. In Philip Hobsbaum's recent obituary in the
Guardian, Mahon's membership of the Group was once again
affirmed, in spite of his frustrated corrective of many years ago.[21]

Snow Water includes a poem entitled 'The Group', made up of
seven short numbered stanzas, each of which deals with a minor
classical poet – Lamprocles, Telesilla, Charixenna, and others –
about whom very little is known. The title is an obvious tease,
directing its "academic" reader to the Belfast Group, and encouraging
a parallel between the (forgotten) poets of ancient Greece with the
(presently remembered) poets of contemporary Ireland. It is tempting
to think of the poem as the puzzle, the archive the key to solving
it. It is also the case that some identifications prove as irresistible
as they are speculative. Longley notes that 'Hobsbaum once said
to me "The fight is about the fight"'.[22] Philip Hobsbaum's third
collection of poems, published in 1969, is entitled *Coming Out
Fighting*, and the spirit of Hobsbaum does seem to hover behind
section VI of Longley's poem:

> A certain person boozes and gorges
> And says scandalous things about us all,
> Punching the air, 'I've plenty of blows left
> If anyone wants to take me on,' he bawls.
> The Group would be far better off without
> Timocreon of Rhodes (poet, pentathlete).

When 'The Group' was first read in public, at a tribute evening
for Philip Hobsbaum in the Lyric Theatre in Belfast in November
2003, a slight unease greeted this stanza, as if the identification
proved equally irresistible for the audience. The stanza, read this
way, encapsulates Hobsbaum's revitalising energy in relation to
the poetry scene of the 1960s, his combative approach to criticism,
and some of the tension in his relationship with Longley. It is, in
other words, both tribute and rebuke.

But 'The Group' is also a cautionary poem, a warning against ever really understanding the truth about the Belfast Group (and cautionary, too, as regards the partial, fragmented stories which are all that can ever be told from archival material – ancient or modern). To excavate the poem for its contemporary resonance, to find Medbh McGuckian or Joan Newmann behind Telesilla or Myrtis, James Simmons behind Diagoras, Seamus Heaney behind Ion of Chios ('the prize-winning poet'), and so on, is to miss the point. The poem is, Longley writes, 'a red herring which is meant to put researchers of the 1960s Belfast Group off the trail for as long as possible'.[23]

Even that comment, however, is something of a red herring, since it presumes that there is a trail to find and follow. The Belfast Group meetings are hardly a modern day equivalent of the 'Eleusinian Mysteries' evoked in the poem, and the mischievous ironies at work in 'The Group' cut the Belfast Group down to size. In a sense, Longley, unlike Diagoras, isn't 'blowing the whistle (in poem and dance)' on Group mysteries because there is nothing to expose. To take this a step further, if it is read this way, the poem implicitly validates the narrative of the Belfast Group Longley has all along endorsed – that it mattered very little to his own development.

III

As Jody AllenRandolph argues, 'the arch, playful tones in Longley's work…may be seen as part of a broader process of resistance and destabilisation – resistant to accepted ways of being a poet and destabilising to many of Irish poetry's fixed points.'[24] Poems such as 'The Group', or 'Moon Cakes', implicitly challenge accepted ways of reading Longley, even as they show off, sometimes in quite calculated fashion, the qualities which have made him admired. There is also a more serious side to that playfulness, however, through which *Snow Water*, if less wittingly, raises important questions about the poet's reception. Two critical responses to Longley's poetry are significant here. The first is to see him as the apolitical poet of birds and flowers; the second, and related, is to see the Longley poem as a finished, perfected object, a work of art which exists in a glass case.[25]

Throughout *Snow Water*, the relation between reality and the *objet d'art* is exposed in uncomfortable ways. There are no poems in glass cases; but there are poems which throw that view of poetry – and its applicability to Longley's own work – into question. *Snow*

Water is full of decorative, ornamental objects, and works of art:
the 'woodcut by Hokusai' in 'Two Pheasants'; the owls in their
glass cases in 'Owl Cases'; the 'skunk spun out of glass' in 'Two
Skunks'; the 'stuffed pine marten' in 'Pine Marten'; the 'framed /
...oblong flower-head' in 'The Painters' among them. That these
objects are all in some way 'exquisite' (a word used by Longley
for the first time in this book) is part of the reason they are there.
But their exquisiteness in terms of their elegance, beauty, or degree
of perfection carries alongside it the further implication of that word:
a sensitivity to, or intensity of, pain.

So to the owls in glass cases, or the stuffed pine marten, we have
to add, surely, the soldier in 'Pipistrelle':

> They kept him alive for years in warm water,
> The soldier who had lost his skin.
> > At night
> He was visited by the wounded bat
> He had unfrozen after Passchendaele,
>
> Locking its heels under his forefinger
> And whispering into the mousy fur.
>
> Before letting the pipistrelle flicker
> Above his summery pool and tipple there,
>
> He spread the wing-hand, elbow to thumb.
> The membrane felt like a poppy petal.

Preserved before death, not after, in his own glass case of 'warm
water', the image of the soldier without his skin is the traumatic
counterpart to the taxidermic preservation of the exterior else-
where in the book. 'Pipistrelle' is another metamorphosis of Keith
Douglas's mosquito in 'How to Kill', who 'touches / her tiny shadow
on the stone' at the moment of death.

The poem is also obliquely related to the book's title *Snow Water*,
itself akin to the earlier poem 'Frozen Rain', in that it encapsulates
the rigid, entrapped, or immobile and what has been 'unfrozen'.
The frozen bat, the soldier preserved 'alive': these are disturbing
parallels whose counterparts must be the 'unfrozen' bat, his fur
warmed by breath and, presumably, the soldier after death, as fore-
shadowed in the 'poppy petal'. That motif repeats itself throughout
the book, in the 'unfrozen lust' and unravelling otters of 'Dipper'
for instance, or in the 'running water' and 'preservative' of 'Sleep
& Death'.

The artist's role implied here – both to preserve and transgress, to
fix in memory and render fluid – takes us into familiar territory as
regards Longley's work. In *Snow Water*, however, we find poems

in which pain and beauty, life and death, are almost indistinguish-
able, in a way which also puts the book in dialogue with *Man Lying
on a Wall*. *Snow Water*, like the earlier collection, shows us the
world aslant, challenges habitual perception. The soldier 'kept...alive
for years in warm water' is a work of art; so is the poem which
contains him. The parallel unsettles what we understand by 'art',
or by what is 'alive'.

Similarly, the 'skunk spun out of glass', which is 'so small as to be
almost unbreakable' is shadowed by its other: 'a freshly / Flattened
skunk so pongily alive in death' ('Two Skunks'). The 'stuffed pine
marten in the hotel corridor' ends up 'making it across No Man's
Land', escaping the medium by which it has been contained ('Pine
Marten'). And in 'The Painters', the 'framed...oblong flower-head
packed with purple flowers / Shaped like hooks, a survivor from
the battlefield' has its parallel with another survivor:

> When I shouldered my father's coffin his body
> Shifted slyly and farted and joined up again
> With rotting corpses, old pals from the trenches.
> William Orpen said you couldn't paint the smell.

Longley shoulders his father's coffin once again by invoking him
as a representative of the boy-soldiers of the Great War; like the
'oblong flower-head', the coffin is metaphorically packed with the
rotting corpses of those who died. In this poem, his father slips the
net; he shifts 'slyly', refusing to be pinned down. Like the smell
that can't be painted, his is a body that won't be contained even at
the moment it is, in effect, 'framed'. The body in the coffin, the
flower in its frame: awareness of one alters our perception of the
other, contaminating flowers with corpses, complicating the dis-
tinction between life and death, the work of art and a brutal reality.

The seven First World War poems at the heart of *Snow Water*,
which include 'Pipistrelle' and 'The Painters', are in some respects
more disorienting than anything Longley has written on the subject
previously. Conscious that the Great War is ground he has trodden
many times before, Longley writes that 'after each previous collec-
tion I have felt that it was time to leave in peace the ghosts of my
father and the other boy-soldiers of he First World War. But they
won't go away. They haunt my mind just as the problems they
fought in vain to solve still menace the Balkans, the Middle East
and my own little patch, Ulster.' [26] In this he shares the compul-
sion felt by many Great War survivors themselves – the need to,
as Edmund Blunden put it, 'go over the ground again'. [27]

The ground, however, is not merely traversed again; it is also reinvented. As Peter McDonald rightly observes, Longley's war poetry 'can stand comparison with the best of its century; and *Snow Water* adds to the distinguished total, while also doing something radically new'.[28] Some of these poems are notable for their surreality, their strange juxtapositions, as in 'Sycamore':

> The sycamore stumps survived the deadliest gales
> To put out new growth, leaves sticky with honeydew
> And just enough white wood to make a violin.
>
> This was a way of mending the phonograph record
> Broken by the unknown soldier before the Somme...

Longley talks of his admiration for Apollinaire, who 'finds connections in a bombardment of distractions', who 'manages to be all-embracing in a world that is being blown apart'.[29] In 'Sycamore', we see an elliptical compression of seemingly dissociated events and images into a surreal narrative, one that reaches into 'all corners of the battlefield' – past, present, real, metaphorical.

The newness is also related to style. The music of 'Harmonica', for example, which itself irregularly 'breathes in and out', is unlike anything he has produced before in his war poems: 'Our souls are air. They hold us together. Listen. / A music-hall favourite lasts until the end of time. / My dad is playing it. His breath contains the world.' The style both compresses and creates time and space. Longley has described an increasing interest, as he grows older, in 'a lighter utterance that can somehow accommodate everything'.[30] 'Harmonica' shows how effective that 'lighter utterance' can be.

In 'The Front', too, the deceptive simplicities of style contribute to the profoundly unsettling effect of the poem:

> I dreamed I was marching up to the Front to die.
> There were thousands of us who were going to die.
> From the opposite direction, out of step, breathless,
> The dead and wounded came, all younger than my son,
> Among them my father who might have been my son.
> 'What is it like?' I shouted after the family face.
> 'It's cushy, mate! Cushy!' my father-son replied.

This kind of deadly repetitiveness has been seen before, in 'Poppies', where it serves to expose political determinism. There is an inexorability to the rhythm and repetition of the opening lines here as well, one which mirrors the relentless stream of recruits sent to the Western Front, and which contrasts with the (unrhymed) 'out of step, breathless' return. Yet this is also a confusing dream-state, in which the living and the dead are ultimately indistinguishable, corpses eerily brought to life.

The line between conscious and unconscious, real and imagined is not easily drawn in this poem, for all its surface transparency. Past, present and future selves are brought into collision; the 'family face' of the speaker's 'father-son' is also an alter ego. The apparently clear phrase 'my father who might have been my son' is also far from being so, evoking as it does the family resemblance, the generation reversal (his father as someone's son, and, seeing time in reverse, a figure towards whom the poet now feels paternal), and the imagined possibility his own son might have been one of those sent to die. In that sense, the familiarity is disturbing, rather than reassuring, in its implications. Similarly, the 'Cushy' of the final line, as McDonald notes, with its mix of 'irony and archaism', disconcerts rather than consoles.[31]

As the war poems suggest, care and precision are 'exquisite' qualities in Longley's writing; so is an equally exquisite sensitivity to impressions, a susceptibility to, and acute perception of, pain as well as pleasure. That these things are not separable makes *Snow Water* both a darker and stranger collection than the one which precedes it, much of it reminiscent of the sometimes sinister precision of his mid-1970s writing.

In 'Snipe', the poet describes himself as an 'amateur ornithologist[s]'; and precision of observation in relation to the natural world is typical of his writing. But the visual acuity in the poems also opens up their more disturbing depths. In 'Two Pheasants', the traumatised cock pheasant, whose 'bride' has been 'crushed', is held in a split second:

> I got the picture in no time in my wing-mirror
> As in a woodcut by Hokusai who highlighted
> The head for me, the white neck-ring and red wattles,
> The long coppery tail, the elegance and pain.

The pheasant is framed at two removes – by the wing-mirror, and by the comparison to Hokusai – but in being so is brought into devastating focus. To freeze-frame the object in this way – as if it were a work of art – makes of the poem a painting, which captures an instant in time. Yet the picture caught 'in no time' is also held indefinitely outside time – literally in no time – a permanent inscription on memory. The colours observed – white and red – are evocative of emotional extremes, and also, obliquely, of the 'elegance and pain' (purity and blood) of the final line.

That 'elegance and pain' go hand in hand in this 'picture' has broader implications for understanding the work of art, and for understanding why Longley's poems unsettle expectations; the two things are held in tension, each compromising the other. The

woodcut – or the poem – is the inscription of pain and the preser-
vation of beauty. That ambiguity is found also at the close of 'Snipe:
in memory of Sheila Smyth', where the remembered 'exquisiteness'
(again encompassing both elegance and pain) of her 'birdlike…body
and behaviour' is paralleled with the bird that 'froze like an illus-
tration' in the poet's headlights.

IV

The poet's gaze in *Snow Water*, its perception of surface and depth,
complicates the relation between dream and reality, conscious and
unconscious, self and other, interior and exterior. In doing so, it
also complicates the relation between art and life. These are, of
course, familiar themes in Longley, although the trigger behind
their exploration may have changed since the mid-1970s – then a
fear of domesticity, now an apprehension of mortality. The poet is
also subject to the gaze, his agency displaced.

As with the bird caught in the headlights, Longley both freeze-
frames the objects he sees and is himself transfixed by them, thereby
entering into dialogue with his own earlier preoccupations in 'The
Ornithological Section' from *No Continuing City*. In 'Owl Cases',
the poet stares into the 'glass case that contains / Barn-and-steeple
familiars'; but by the close of the poem, the 'snowy owl…whose
yellow gaze / Follows around the museum / Me and you' has turned
the 'owl-lovers' rather than the owls into the specimens under
observation.

In 'The Yellow Bungalow', the poet becomes a character in, as well
as author of, the 'composition'. Gerard Dillon's 'Yellow Bungalow'
painting on the kitchen wall is a 'dream-mirror', a parallel life in
art that is not, in the end, distinguishable from this one. In one
sense, the 'young man' in the painting, with his 'accordion' and
'new tunes' moves out of the painting into 'another room'; at the
same time, in the final stanza it is as if the poet moves into the
frame of the painting:

> As soon as I've switched the fan-assisted oven on
> And opened the bombinating refrigerator
> (I've a meal to prepare) I hear bellows wheeze
> And fingernails clitter over buttons and keys.
> Cooking smells become part of the composition.

Sight, smell, sound, touch: all the senses intermingle by the close of
the poem. It is impossible to tell whether the 'buttons and keys'

and wheezing sounds are those of the accordion, the oven or the refrigerator. The 'composition' is the poem, the tune, the painting, and the cookery – its own kind of 'complicated recipe'. As in the companion poem 'Primary Colours', in which 'The footprints of wild animals' are 'spattered with primary colours', literally painting the landscape, the work of art overspills its boundaries.

That the poems render it impossible to draw lines between things we might usually demarcate without difficulty is part of their subversive effect, their ability to render the familiar extraordinary and to look at the world the other way around. The effect is compounded by a deceptive surface simplicity – in the intimate tone and sometimes colloquial register, in the grammatically contained stanzas which simultaneously cross boundaries, and in the 'new tunes' (that 'lighter utterance') of rhythm and syntax.

The poems directly about art are not the only examples to be found in this collection of the boundaries between things breaking down, of objects merging one into the other. In 'Dipper', an oblique marital love poem, the dipper merges into the golden plovers and then into the otters who 'unravelled out of view', each slipping into and out of view to replace its predecessors, and all entangled with the couple themselves. Altered perception, and the play of interior against exterior are also at the heart of one of the outstanding love poems of Longley's career, 'The Pattern':

> Thirty-six years, to the day, after our wedding
> When a cold figure-revealing wind blew against you
> And lifted your veil, I find in its fat envelope
> The six-shilling *Vogue* pattern for your bride's dress,
> Complicated instructions for stitching bodice
> And skirt, box pleats and hems, tissue-paper outlines,
> Semblances of skin which I nervously unfold
> And hold up in snow light, for snow has been falling
> On this windless day, and I glimpse your wedding dress
> And white shoes outside in the transformed garden
> Where the clothesline and every twig have been covered.

In this poem, the 'Complicated instructions for stitching bodice... box pleats and hems' have their self-reflexive elements. Longley has always been fascinated with assembling fragments to make the whole, as seen in the patchwork quilt poems of *The Weather in Japan*. Here, the 'pattern' might be read as an image of the underlying pattern of his own poems, with their complicated syntax and structure, and yet the surface appearance of seamlessness. Past and present are stitched together to make an imagined future.

'The Pattern' itself is, unravelled, an unusually complicated poem, which seamlessly connects its multiple images to play surface against depth. The 'revealing' wind that lifts the 'veil' anticipates both the marriage ceremony, and its consummation. Opening the 'fat envelope' is its own kind of deflowering, a discovery that recreates an earlier anticipation, as the 'Semblances of skin', 'nervously' fingered, are both disturbing and erotic. The poem begins with a memory of the wedding dress; it unravels through the paper pattern that preceded it to the skin which it covers. It then works backwards (forwards) to recreate imaginatively the dress, whole once again, in the 'transformed garden' of the present day. That the garden is 'covered' with snow suggests innocence and purity, but it is also evocative of the sexual act. Past and present, interior and exterior, are simultaneously refracted through the poem, which sees through the 'tissue-paper outlines' in more ways than one.

The play of interior and exterior in this poem, and Longley's fascination with perception as it shapes the work of art, are also related to a delving into interior consciousness. In 'The Sett', the abuse of the badger serves as a metaphor for a state of mind:

> A friend's betrayal of you brings to mind
> His anecdote about neighbours in Donegal
> Who poured petrol into a badger's sett, that
> Underground intelligence not unlike your own
> Curling up among the root systems.

That petrol is poured into the sett for sport is also an indictment of the emotional damage caused when one human being betrays another. 'The Sett', as with 'The Pattern', shows an interior consciousness, and 'Underground intelligence' at work (and this time under threat), even as its surface observation is characterised by precision and transparency.

The second stanza of the poem is revealing in terms of Longley's own sense of self, and of self-protection: 'why / Can the badger not have more than one address / Like the otter its hovers...?' Implicit here is the need for 'hovers' of the mind, areas which the poet can 'safeguard', moments where the self can be held intact against forces which threaten it. The poem is fiercely protective of its betrayed subject, as earlier in 'The Yellow Teapot', from *The Weather in Japan*; but it reverberates more widely in terms of Longley's own betwixt and between sensibility, the capacity to hold on to individual integrity in sometimes difficult (political) circumstances.

Another version of that 'Underground intelligence' may be seen in 'The Miner', where the network of underground tunnels

and seams which pervade the mining area symbolise the poet's own
memory, and repressed areas of consciousness more generally:

> When they turn the page tomorrow, William Longley
> Will disappear back into darkness and danger
> And crawl on hands and knees in the crypt of the world
> Under houses and outhouses and workshops and fields.

The name recorded in 'the Durham Miners' Book of Remembrance'
brings to the fore issues of memory and selfhood. In part, this is a
poem about the politics of remembrance, where each page turn
symbolises both a forgetting and a remembering. As 'William
Longley...disappear[s] back into darkness', he disappears from
consciousness. But the extent to which he forms and re-forms,
through the coincidence of the name, the poet's own sense of self
and his understanding of his own past ('How many of my relatives
worked down the mine?'), means that 'William Longley' crawls
permanently in that 'underground intelligence' of the poet's own
subconscious. Surface and depth, the seen and unseen, are held
simultaneously at the close of the poem.

The theme of interiority and exteriority, surface and depth,
takes us back to Longley's most disturbing collection, *Man Lying
on a Wall*. *Snow Water* also has its darker side, a probing into the
unconscious, into difficult memories. Significantly, as in 'The
Miner', the darkness is embedded in the collection's return to that
most traditional of forms, the sonnet. Robert Bly once suggested
that 'the sonnet is where old professors go to die'.[32] Yet the form,
reinvigorated in the 20th century, is much more than this, accom-
modating as it does extremes of experience, and some of the cen-
tury's more traumatic events, including the world wars.

For Longley, the sonnet in *Snow Water* is a form whose appeal
lies partly in its traditionalism: it has become the vehicle for a
number of his love poems, and for an elegiac pastoral mode, its
permanence a way in which to shape an apprehension of mortality.
Given the changing rhythms and syntax of *Snow Water*, in which
the longer lines that gave his earlier quatrain poems their formal
depth are far less in evidence, the sonnet-length has also become an
vehicle within which to play 'lighter utterance[s]' and pentameter
lines against each other. But as such poems as 'The Miner', and
more notably the sonnet-sequence 'Woodsmoke' suggest, its appeal
for him is also implicated in the collision of traditional assumptions
about the form (and its subject-matter) with the difficulty – and
darkness – it can contain.

Longley has, of course, been here before, in the exploded sonnet which comprises four holocaust poems in *Gorse Fires*, or in the epic reverberations of 'Ceasefire'. In *Snow Water*, the sonnet is a double-edged form, one which accommodates two different modes at work in the book. In the sonnet 'War & Peace', 'Achilles hunts down Hector like a sparrowhawk / Screeching after a horror-struck collared dove / That flails just in front of her executioner...'. The 'double well-heads' in the poem show two different possibilities: 'in one / Warm water steaming like smoke from a bonfire, / The other running cold as hailstones, snow water', which epitomise the trauma of its opening as against the tranquillity of the 'good old days' at its close.

The predominant imagery of *Snow Water* is that of whiteness, snow, ice, and feathers: the 'covering of snow' in 'Moon Cakes'; the 'snow stains' of the mountain in 'Above Dooghatry'; the 'white nightdress' and 'whitewashed cottage' of 'Arrival; the 'snowy owl' of 'Owl Cases'; the 'snowy weather' of 'Aschy', and so on. The title phrase itself appears half a dozen times, and the various strands of imagery are brought together in the hidden poem at the end of the collection: 'feathers on water / a snowfall of swans / snow water'. But as in 'War & Peace', that imagery is shadowed by its "other", by an alternative imagery of blackness and burning that symbolises a journey into the recesses of memory and into the 'underground intelligence' of consciousness.

'The Miner' disappears into 'darkness'; 'Montale's Dove' 'craves darkness'. Elsewhere we find the 'black soggy land' of 'Up There', the 'blackened...face' of 'Earthshine, and, in 'Woodsmoke', a 'black rainbow, a darkbow', a 'black' feather, a 'dark plantation'. The 'blackness' of imagery in 'The Miner' and 'Woodsmoke', or the 'horror' of 'War & Peace', thus counter-balance the celebratory mode of the love sonnets and nature sonnets earlier in the book. If there's no such place as heaven, there may be such a place as hell, or at least a hell of the mind, the 'darkness and danger' of that 'crypt of the world'. In 'Woodsmoke' the work of art is wrought from pain and trauma, and from a hellfire imagery. As in 'The Miner', the darkness is also about difficult or repressed memories and narratives resurfacing.

A celebration of Helen Denerley's sculpture's, 'Woodsmoke' has an underlying, traumatic narrative glimpsed in fragments, compromising its surface. Denerley's sculptures – often of animals – are, she explains, 'made from scrap metal using relics of the horse drawn days of agriculture alongside discarded modern machinery. Some of the parts have been made by blacksmiths and used to farm the land until they are worn out.' [33] The amateur blacksmiths in

'Woodsmoke' are 'balancing / Buckets of terror as the furnace roared'. The iron bridge – the 'black rainbow' – created from fragments becomes a memorial for the 'neighbour's two boys...burnt alive'. The deaths by fire haunt the whole poem, from the 'Buckets of terror' through 'Smoke and steam' to the 'bonfire, catherine / Wheels ...roman candles', and 'smoke and uneasiness' of its close.

In the final sonnet of 'Woodsmoke', the poet writes: 'We have to imagine one another / Quickly, and then go home...'. 'Home' remains a problematical concept in Longley, never an inviolate space: to 'go home' is also to take home that 'smoke and uneasiness', the darker, and unresolved, tensions at work in the poem. The fear and urgency here that must imagine 'Quickly', that see the moment of recognition and communion under threat, pervade the sequence, and, in other ways, the whole book. This is to live 'from poem to poem, from hand to mouth', to see beginnings in endings and vice versa, each moment held as both the first and the last. The changing rhythms and perspectives of *Snow Water* suggest that this volume is itself unresolved in the best possible way, another stopping-place on a journey whose arrivals are also departures. It ventures into uncharted territory for the poet, not least in terms of form. As such, it is also continuous with preoccupations that have haunted him from the start – from 'no continuing city', to 'no such place as home', to 'no such place as heaven' – where it is not the final destination so much as the journey towards it that matters. As Longley himself puts it, 'Wherever I'm going, I hope I'm still headed there, still travelling to Ithaca.' [34]

Notes

CHAPTER 1: **'In two minds'**: *No Continuing City* (pp.13-50)

1. *Icarus*, 30 (March 1960), p.38.
2. See *Icarus*, 41 (December 1963), pp.30-31.
3. Michael Longley, *Tuppenny Stung: Autobiographical Chapters* (Belfast: Lagan Press, 1994), p.35.
4. Michael Longley, letter to Heather Clark, n.d. [*c.* 2002.], Michael Longley private collection.
5. *Tuppenny Stung*, pp.35-36, 38.
6. Derek Mahon, interview by William Scammell, *Poetry Review*, 81.2 (Summer 1991), p.4.
7. See Boland's letters to Longley in the mid to late 1960s, held in Longley papers, collection 744.
8. 'Q & A with Derek Mahon', interview by James J. Murphy et al, *Irish Literary Supplement*, 10/2 (Fall 1991), p.27.
9. Michael Longley, interview by Siobhan McSweeney, January 1981, box 43 folder 1, Longley papers, collection 744.
10. See below ch. 2 n.46.
11. See *Tuppenny Stung*, pp.38-39.
12. Michael Longley, interview by John Brown, *In the Chair: Interviews with Poets from the North of Ireland* (Cliffs of Moher, Co. Clare: Salmon Publishing, 2002), p.89.
13. Derek Mahon, telegram to Michael Longley, 3 June 1965, Longley papers, collection 744.
14. *Tuppenny Stung*, p.41.
15. Derek Mahon, letter to Michael Longley, *c.* December 1966. Longley papers, collection 744.
16. Michael Longley, *Ten Poems* (Festival Publications, Queen's University of Belfast, 1965), n.p.
17. See Derek Mahon's poem 'Matthew V. 29-30', where the phrase may be read as an ironic comment on his own habitual processes of revision. Derek Mahon, *Poems 1962-1978* (Oxford: OUP, 1979), p.71.
18. Michael Longley, 'The Longley Tapes', interview by Robert Johnstone, *Honest Ulsterman*, 78 (Summer 1985), p.27. Longley here echoes a principle outlined by Keith Douglas earlier. See Keith Douglas, letter to J.C. Hall, 10 August 1943, *The Complete Poems*, ed. Desmond Graham (Oxford: OUP, 1987), p.124.
19. See the different versions of 'Courtyards in Delft' in Mahon's *Courtyards in Delft* (Dublin: Gallery Press, 1981), *The Hunt by Night* (Oxford: OUP, 1982), and *Selected Poems* (London: Viking; Oldcastle; Gallery Press, 1991).
20. Michael Longley, letter to Heather Clark, n.d. [*c.* 2002]. Michael Longley private collection.
21. Sean Lucy, 'Also Often Beautiful', review of *No Continuing City* by Michael Longley, *The Tablet*, 7 February 1970.
22. Eavan Boland, 'A Vision of Risk', review of *No Continuing City* by Michael Longley, *Irish Times*, 20 December 1969.

23. See Seamus Heaney, *The Government of the Tongue* (London: Faber, 1988), p.xii.

24. Quoted in Rachel Buxton, *Robert Frost and Northern Irish Poetry* (Oxford: Clarendon, 2004), p.142.

25. See Michael Longley, 'A Tongue at Play' in Tony Curtis, ed., *How Poets Work* (Bridgend: Seren Books, 1996), pp.113, 118.

26. Longley, interview by Siobhan McSweeney, Longley papers, collection 744.

27. 'The Longley Tapes', p.16.

28. 'The Longley Tapes', p.28.

29. *Tuppenny Stung*, p.25.

30. Michael Longley, 'Strife and the Ulster Poet', *Hibernia*, 33/21 (7 November 1969), p.11.

31. *Tuppenny Stung*, p.24.

32. *Tuppenny Stung*, p.42.

33. Philip Hobsbaum, *A Theory of Communication* (London: Macmillan, 1970), pp.6, 14, 58-59.

34. Jacques Derrida, 'Différance', 1968, repr. in Julie Rivkin and Michael Ryan, eds., *Literary Theory: An Anthology* (Oxford: Blackwell, 1998), pp.388-89.

35. Seamus Heaney, 'Feeling into Words', *Preoccupations: Selected Prose 1968-1978* (London: Faber, 1980), p.41.

36. Derrida, 'Différance', p.389.

37. See Edna Longley, 'Atlantic Premises', *Poetry & Posterity* (Tarset: Bloodaxe Books, 2000), p.336 n.12.

38. James Joyce, *Ulysses*, ed. Hans Walter Gabler (Harmondsworth: Penguin, 1986), p.363.

39. Michael Longley, interview with Peter McDonald, *Thumbscrew*, 12 (Winter 1998/9), p.10.

40. Peter McDonald, 'From Ulster with Love', review of *Poems 1963-1983* by Michael Longley, *Poetry Review* 74/4 (January 1985), p.14.

41. A cancelled stanza from the drafts of 'No Continuing City' makes the point:

> Holiday snaps, littered through my mind,
> Expand to frantic close-ups
> In this last alcove of my youth –
> Since this is the last time they'll be screened
> The zoom lens I remember with
> Throws their legend
> Out of focus...

As is usually the case, the over-obvious or self-conscious approach is excised by the time the poem reaches a final version.

42. Michael Longley, interview by Jody AllenRandolph, *Colby Quarterly*, XXXIX/3 (September 2003), p.294.

43. The typescript held in Emory University is incorrectly dated 2 April 1963 instead of 1964.

44. *Secret Marriages: Nine Short Poems* (Manchester; Phoenix Pamphlets Poets Press, 1968), pp.2-3.

45. Derek Mahon, 'Poetry in Northern Ireland', *Twentieth Century Studies*, 4 (November 1970), p.93.

46. Michael Longley, *In the Chair*, p.88.

47. *Tuppenny Stung*, p.20.

48. Longley, interview by Siobhan McSweeney, Longley papers, collection 744. Edna Longley gives some autobiographical detail in the introduction to *The Living Stream; Literature and Revisionism in Ireland* (Newcastle upon Tyne: Bloodaxe Books, 1994).

49. Michael Longley, miscellaneous handwritten notes, box 43 folder 9, Longley Papers, collection 744.

50. The poem was inspired by a visit to an elderly relative of Edna Longley's, who was a nun in a Dominican convent outside Dublin. Interview with the author, 16 April 2005.

51. See Longley, 'Self-portrait', in *The Echo Gate*, and 'Readings' in *An Exploded View*.

52. Heaney, 'Feeling into Words', *Preoccupations*, pp.41-42.

53. See Seamus Heaney, *Reading the Future: Irish Writers in Conversation with Mike Murphy* (Dublin: Lilliput Press, 2000), pp.84-85.

CHAPTER 2: 'Stereophonic Nightmares': *An Exploded View* (pp.51-101)

1. Michael Longley, 'Yeats's Effect on Young Contemporary Poets', box 37 folder 11, Longley papers, collection 744. The lecture was reported in the *Irish Times* on 13 August 1969.

2. *Irish Times*, 16 August 1969. Prof. A. Norman Jeffares, then Director of the Yeats Summer School, was also quoted as saying: 'An age which demands instant potatoes equally may desire instant poetry.'

3. Michael Longley, 'A Field of Light': address for the opening of the Yeats Summer School, 2003, *Irish Pages* 2/2 (Autumn/Winter 2004), p.68.

4. Edna Longley, *Poetry in the Wars* (Newcastle upon Tyne: Bloodaxe Books, 1986), p.185.

5. Michael Longley, Yeats Summer School lecture, 1970, box 37 folder 11, Longley papers, collection 744.

6. Ezra Pound, 'A Retrospect', *Literary Essays of Ezra Pound*, ed. T.S. Eliot (London: Faber, 1954), p.9.

7. Eavan Boland, 'The Northern writers' crisis of conscience: 3', *Irish Times*, 14 August 1970.

8. Louis MacNeice, *The Poetry of W.B. Yeats*, 2nd ed. (London: Faber, 1967), p.191.

9. Stephen Spender, rev. of *Wintering Out* by Seamus Heaney, *New York Review of Books*, 20 Sept. 1973, quoted in Robert Buttel, *Seamus Heaney* (Lewisburg: Bucknell UP; London: Associated UP, 1975), p.69.

10. Douglas Dunn, letter to Michael Longley, 25 July 1972, Longley papers, collection 744.

11. Michael Longley, 'Strife and the Ulster Poet', *Hibernia*, 33/21 (7 November 1969), p.11. Roy McFadden and James Simmons also wrote pieces for *Hibernia* following the same remit. See *Hibernia*, 33/19 (October 1969), p.16.

12. Eavan Boland, 'The Weasel's Tooth', *Irish Times*, 7 June 1974.

13. Michael Longley, letter to the *Irish Times*, 18 June 1974. The Ulster Workers Council strikes in 1974 delivered the death-blow to the Sunningdale agreement, and received a degree of Protestant support that rendered the position of more liberal Protestants in the North, dismayed by the turn of events, particularly difficult.

14. Edna Longley, *Poetry in the Wars*, p.185.

15. Michael Longley, draft of a letter to *Hibernia*, 10 December 1974, Longley papers, collection 744.

16. Padraic Fiacc, 'Violence and the Ulster Poet', *Hibernia* (6 December 1974), p.19. The article describes the process of putting together *The Wearing of the Black*.

17. Padraic Fiacc, 'Introduction', *The Wearing of the Black: An Anthology of Contemporary Ulster Poetry* (Belfast: Blackstaff Press, 1974), p.vii.

18. Michael Longley, Introduction, *Causeway: the Arts in Ulster* (Belfast: Arts Council of Northern Ireland; Dublin: Gill and Macmillan, 1971), p.8.

19. See *The Poems of Wilfred Owen*, ed. Jon Stallworthy (London: Chatto & Windus, 1990), p.192.

20. Mahon, 'Poetry in Northern Ireland', *Twentieth Century Studies*, 4 (November 1970), p.93.

21. The handwritten draft is untitled and undated. Its reference to Graves's visit dates it as 1975; its style suggests it may have been written for radio broadcast. Box 35 folder 7, Longley papers, collection 744.

22. David Jones, preface to *In Parenthesis* (1937; London; Faber, 1963), p.xv.

23. Michael Longley, letter to Paul Muldoon, 17 July 1972. Box 3, folder 17, Paul Muldoon papers, collection 784, Robert W. Woodruff Library, Emory University, Atlanta.

24. Douglas Dunn, letter to Michael Longley, 15 June 1972, Longley papers, collection 744.

25. The buried village of Skara Brae was discovered in the 19th century. Originally believed to be an Iron-Age settlement, it was carbon-dated in the 1970s as Neolithic. The village houses are connected by covered passages (with insulating midden). Architecturally, it bears a resemblance to the nearby tombs; its design is seen as both functional and symbolically significant. The site is under constant threat of erosion by sea, sand and the weather, and is now situated at the very edge of the shore.

26. Peter McDonald, 'Faiths and Fidelities: Heaney and Longley in Mid-Career', *Last before America: Irish and American Writing*, ed. Fran Brearton and Eamonn Hughes (Belfast: Blackstaff, 2001), p.7.

27. Michael Longley, interview by Jody AllenRandolph, *Colby Quarterly*, XXXIX/3 (Sept. 2003), p.300. A manuscript of 'Caravan' in Michael Allen's possession is dated 29 December 1970.

28. Michael Allen, 'Rhythm and Development in Michael Longley's Earlier Poetry', *Contemporary Irish Poetry*, ed. Elmer Andrews (Basingstoke: Macmillan, 1992), pp.224, 229, 231.

29. Draft index for *An Exploded View*, n.d. but probably early 1972, box 18, folder 25, Longley papers, collection 744.

30. Martin Dillon, review of *An Exploded View* by Michael Longley, *Belfast Telegraph*, 7 August 1973.

31. Peter Porter, 'A Poet from Ulster', review of *An Exploded View* by Michael Longley, *Observer*, 5 August 1973.

32. Douglas Dunn, 'The Poetry of the Troubles', review of *Selected Poems 1963-1980* by Michael Longley, *Times Literary Supplement* (31 July 1981), p.886.

33. See Allen, 'Rhythm and Development', p.224ff.

34. It is interesting to compare these poems by Longley with Heaney's own 'Casualty' and 'Badgers', which appeared side by side in *Field Work* six years later, and have an obvious debt to Longley's poems. All these poems may be read as inspired by the Troubles of the early 1970s, although the response in Longley's work is far more oblique.

35. See Louis MacNeice, *The Poetry of W.B. Yeats*, 2nd edn. pp.197-98.

36. Darwin encountered giant tortoises in what he describes as a 'strange Cyclopean scene', one of whom 'stared at [him] and slowly walked away; the other gave a deep hiss'. *Voyage of a Naturalist* (2nd edn, London: Routledge, 1845), p.272. He is also fascinated with opening up the stomachs of the various animals to inspect the contents; with pulling the tails of lizards in the interests of scientific discovery; and with animal "consciousness", frequently attributing thoughts and ideas, sometimes feelings of his own to the various creatures he encounters.

37. Paul Bew and Gordon Gillespie, *Northern Ireland: A Chronology of the Troubles 1968-1993* (Dublin: Gill and Macmillan, 1993), pp.54, 57.

38. By this time, Edna Longley was running an annual series of readings at Queen's University with Arts Council support. Both Peter Porter and Anthony Thwaite (albeit reluctantly), declined invitations under pressure from family and friends not to expose themselves to the dangers of Belfast. See the early 1970s correspondence held in the Longley papers, collection 744.

39. Nicholas Grene, *The Politics of Irish Drama: Plays in Context from Boucicault to Friel* (Cambridge: CUP, 1999), p.97.

40. Michael Longley, letter to his mother, Constance Longley, 18 July 1973, Longley papers, collection 744.

41. Michael Longley, letter to Marie Heaney. The draft is undated, but is written after Mahon's 1975 collection *The Snow Party*, and before the appearance of *Man Lying on a Wall* in June 1976. Although the letter was unsent at the time, Longley sent a copy of the draft to Marie Heaney in 2002. Longley papers, collection 744.

42. Douglas Dunn, 'Longley's Metric', *The Poetry of Michael Longley*, ed. Alan J. Peacock and Kathleen Devine (Gerrards Cross: Colin Smythe, 2000), p.21.

43. Michael Longley, interview by Dermot Healy, *Southern Review*, 31/3 (July 1995), p.560

44. Allen, 'Rhythm and Development', p.228.

45. Michael Longley, interview by Jody AllenRandolph, *Colby Quarterly*, p.294.

46. The phrase appears in notes on the verse letters made by Longley for a poetry reading, box 38, folder 15, Longley papers, collection 744.

47. The dates of the final drafts are as follows; 'Letter to Derek Mahon', March 1971, 'Letter to Seamus Heaney', September 1971, 'To Three Irish Poets', 5 April 1972, 'Letter to James Simmons', 11 April 1972.

48. Heaney describes the relationship in 1975 as 'a sustenance even in the solitude...a kind of continuum of the imagination' which is strengthened through 'separate enterprises'. Letter to Michael Longley, 17 June 1975. Box 15a, Seamus Heaney correspondence, Longley papers, collection 744.

49. Seamus Heaney, letter to Michael Longley, 17 June 1975, Box 15a, Longley papers, collection 744.

50. Mahon, 'Poetry in Northern Ireland', p.92.

51. 'Q & A with Derek Mahon', interview by James J. Murphy et al, *Irish Literary Supplement*, 10/2 (Fall 1991), p.28.

52. Untitled, undated prose piece by Michael Longley on contemporary

poetry, box 37, folder 21. Longley papers, collection 744. A reference to the burgeoning younger generation of Muldoon and Peskett places it *c.* mid-1970s.

53. See Seamus Heaney, 'Belfast' and 'Feeling into Words', *Preoccupations* (London: Faber, 1980), pp.35, 37, 41.

54. A typescript of Mahon's poem is held along with the manuscript of Longley's 'Letter to Derek Mahon', Longley papers, collection 744.

55. Derek Mahon, interview by Terence Brown, *Poetry Ireland Review*, 14 (Autumn 1985), pp.12-13

56. Notes made by Michael Longley for a poetry reading, some time in the 1970s. He also describes 'Letter to Seamus Heaney' in the same terms. Longley papers, collection 744.

57. See *New Statesman*, 10 December 1971, p.821.

58. Derek Mahon, letter to Michael Longley, n.d. [December 1971], Longley papers, collection 744.

59. 'The Longley Tapes', p.24.

60. Louis MacNeice, 'Epilogue: For W.H. Auden', W.H. Auden and Louis MacNeice, *Letters from Iceland* (London; Faber, 1937), p.253.

61. MacNeice, *The Poetry of W.B. Yeats*, 2nd edn., p.191.

62. Quoted by Derek Mahon, interview by William Scammell, *Poetry Review*, 81/2 (Summer 1991), p.5.

63. See W.B. Yeats, 'Poetry and Tradition', *Essays and Introductions* (Dublin: Gill and Macmillan, 1961), p.260.

64. Derek Mahon, letter to Michael Longley, n.d. (*c.* late 1960s), Longley papers, collection 744.

65. MacNeice, *The Poetry of W.B. Yeats*, 2nd ed., p.197.

66. Michael Allen 'Rhythm and Development', p.233 n.25 and Michael Longley, letter to Heather Clark, n.d. [*c.* 2002], Michael Longley private collection.

67. Quoted in Geoffrey Grigson, ed., *Poems of John Clare's Madness* (London: Routledge, 1949), p.48. This edition of Clare's poems, with a biographical introduction by Grigson, was Longley's first serious introduction to the poet, and provided the inspiration for 'Journey Out of Essex'.

68. Neil Corcoran, 'My Botanical Studies: The Poetry of Natural History in Michael Longley', *The Poetry of Michael Longley*, ed. Peacock and Devine, p.106.

69. 'Q & A with Michael Longley', interview by Dillon Johnston, *Irish Literary Supplement*, 5/2 (Fall 1986), p. 20.

70. Edna Longley notes that 'on 14 August 1969, an RUC tracer bullet killed a Catholic child, Patrick Rooney, in his bedroom', suggesting that this event is also a trigger behind these lines in the poem. See Edna Longley, 'Northern Ireland: commemoration, elegy, forgetting', in *History and Memory in Modern Ireland*, ed. Ian McBride (Cambridge: CUP, 2001), p.247.

71. The death of a five year old girl, in February 1971, who was knocked down by an army vehicle, outraged the community, as did the death of a seven month old boy in an explosion in December of the same year.

72. Jahan Ramazani, *Poetry of Mourning; The Modern Elegy from Hardy to Heaney* (Chicago: Univ. of Chicago Press, 1994), pp.4, 6.

CHAPTER 3: 'There's no such place as home': *Man Lying on a Wall* (pp.102-29)

1. The details of those murders are also evoked in 'Love Poet', from *New Poems*.

2. Michael Longley, interview by Siobhan McSweeney, January 1981, box 43 folder 1, Longley papers, collection 744.

3. Michael Longley, interview by John Brown, *In the Chair: interviews with poets from the North of Ireland* (Cliffs of Moher, Co. Clare: Salmon Publishing, 2002), p.91.

4. See Alex Davis *A Broken Line: Denis Devlin and Irish Poetic Modernism* (Dublin: UCD Press, 2000), pp.160-61 for discussion of the Irish 'well-made poem' as against the Irish 'neo-avante-garde' poem.

5. Longley, interview by Siobhan McSweeney, Longley papers, collection 744.

6. Longley, promotional blurb for *Man Lying on a Wall*.

7. James Simmons, review of *Man Lying on a Wall* by Michael Longley, *Honest Ulsterman*, 52 (May/October 1976), pp.72-73

8. The paradox wherein 'Descriptions of objects in fiction are simultaneously creations of that object', since literary fiction constructs a context and text 'through entirely verbal processes'. Patricia Waugh, *Metafiction* (London: Routledge, 1984), p.88.

9. Peter Porter, 'Away from the Troubles', review of *Man Lying on a Wall* by Michael Longley, *Observer*, 22 August 1976.

10. Douglas Dunn, 'The World and His Wife: new poetry', *Encounter*, XLVII/5 (November 1976), p.81.

11. George Mackay Brown, 'Poetry without Obstacles', review of *Man Lying on a Wall* by Michael Longley, *Scotsman*, 4 September 1976.

12. Eavan Boland, 'Private Violence', review of *Man Lying on a Wall* by Michael Longley, *Irish Times*, 12 June 1976.

13. Longley's handwritten notes on a selection of poems, possibly for a reading, n.d. box 38, folder 15, Longley papers, collection 744.

14. Longley, promotional blurb for *Man Lying on a Wall*.

15. Michael Longley, letter to Kevin Crossley-Holland, 27 June 1975. Longley papers, collection 744. Crossley-Holland was Longley's editor at Victor Gollancz in the 1970s.

16. Michael Allen, 'Rhythm and Development in Michael Longley's Earlier Poetry', in *Contemporary Irish Poetry*, ed. Elmer Andrews (Basingstoke: Macmillan, 1992), p.227.

17. Longley returned to the poem at the end of the 1970s, taking these two stanzas and a rewritten version of the last stanza of 'Mother' and entitling the revised three stanza poem 'Father'. It was not ultimately included in the 'New Poems' section of *Poems 1963-83* in any version.

18. Boland, 'Private Violence'.

19. Quoted in Waugh, *Metafiction*, p. 90.

20. Michael Longley, letter to Kevin Crossley-Holland, 27 June 1975, Longley papers, collection 744.

21. *Macbeth*, Act V. Sc. V.

22. Michael Longley, letter to T.G. Rosenthal, 2 July 1980, Longley papers, collection 744.

23. See *The Diary of Edward Thomas*, ed. Roland Gant and Myfanwy Thomas

(Gloucestershire, Whittington Press, 1977). The particular diary entries Longley draws upon in the poem are those for 14 & 22 February, and 11, 14, 16, 21 & 22 March 1917.

CHAPTER 4: 'The last time in reverse': *The Echo Gate* and *New Poems* (pp.130-60)

1. Anthony Thwaite, 'Weekend Supplement', BBC Radio Ulster, 8 December 1979.

2. See Michael Longley, 'Memory and Acknowledgment', *Irish Review*, 17/18 (Winter 1995), p.158.

3. Peter McDonald, 'Michael Longley's Homes', *The Chosen Ground: Essays on the Contemporary Poetry of Northern Ireland*, ed. Neil Corcoran (Bridgend: Seren Books, 1992), p.81.

4. Paul Muldoon, interview by John Haffenden, *Viewpoints: Poets in Conversation* (London: Faber, 1981), p.130.

5. Robert Graves, 'Ecstasy', *Collected Writings on Poetry*, ed. Paul O'Prey (Manchester: Carcanet Press, 1995), p.497.

6. Neil Corcoran, 'My Botanical Studies: The Poetry of Natural History in Michael Longley', *The Poetry of Michael Longley*, ed. Alan J. Peacock and Kathleen Devine (Gerrards Cross: Colin Smythe, 2000), p.108.

7. Michael Longley, *Tuppenny Stung: Autobiographical Chapters* (Belfast: Lagan Press, 1994), p.76.

8. Corcoran, 'My Botanical Studies', p.110.

9. Corcoran, 'My Botanical Studies', p.111.

10. The poem was written in July 1976, preceded only by 'Oliver Plunkett'.

11. Paul Fussell, *Killing in Verse & Prose* (London: Bellew, 1990), p.188.

12. See Paul Fussell, 'Threes', in *The Great War and Modern Memory* (London: OUP, 1975), pp.125-31.

13. Only Gibson is named in the poem. Edna Longley identifies McBirney as the subject of 'The Civil Servant' in *History and Memory in Modern Ireland*, ed. Ian McBride (Cambridge: CUP, 2001), p.248. The killings are detailed in David McKittrick et al, *Lost Lives* (Edinburgh: Mainstream Publishing, 1999).

14. Michael Longley, interview by Dermot Healy, *Southern Review*, 31/3 (July 1995), p.560.

15. 'Q & A with Michael Longley', interview by Dillon Johnston, *Irish Literary Supplement*, 5/2 (Fall 1986), p.20.

16. Terence Brown, 'Who Dares to Speak? Ireland and the Great War', *English Studies in Transition: Papers from the ESSE Inaugural Conference*, ed. Robert Clark and Piero Boitani (London: Routledge, 1993), p.234.

17. 'The Longley Tapes', inteview by Robert Johnstone, *Honest Ulsterman*, 78 (Summer 1985), p.23.

18. See *Tuppenny Stung*, p.20.

19. Jahan Ramazani, *Poetry of Mourning: The Modern Elegy from Hardy to Heaney* (Chicago: Univ. of Chicago Press, 1994), p.80.

20. Fussell, *The Great War and Modern Memory*, p.69.

21. 'No Man's Land' is not alone in *New Poems* in being a rewriting of earlier work. 'The Rag Trade', from *The Echo Gate*, is cut from *Poems 1963-83* and parts of it reappear in 'Maggie Moore's', although in this instance it becomes an entirely different – and one might argue less effective – poem.

22. Paul Durcan, 'Poetry and Truth', review of *The Echo Gate* by Michael

Longley and *The Strange Museum* by Tom Paulin, *Irish Press*, 20 March 1980, p.6.

23. Derek Mahon, 'An Enormous Yes', review of *Poems 1963-83* by Michael Longley, *Literary Review*, 80 (Feb. 1985), p.55; and Longley, 'Q & A with Michael Longley', interview by Dillon Johnston, p.21.

24. Corcoran, 'My Botanical Studies', pp.116-18.

25. McDonald, 'Michael Longley' Homes', p.75.

26. McDonald, 'Michael Longley' Homes', p.75.

27. Michael Longley, interview by Sarah Broom, *Metre* 4 (Spring/Summer 1998), p.17. See also Michael Longley, 'A Tongue at Play, *How Poet's Work*, ed. Tony Curtis (Bridgend: Seren, 1996), p.113.

28. Interview with the author, 16 April 2005.

29. 'The Longley Tapes', p.27.

30. 'A Tongue at Play', pp.112-13.

31. Repr. in *Tuppenny Stung*, pp.28-29. See also the reference to Grandpa George and Maud on p.23.

32. *Tuppenny Stung*, p.19.

33. *Tuppenny Stung*, p.21.

34. See *Tuppenny Stung*, pp.15, 16, 22.

35. 'The Longley Tapes', p.30.

36. The poem is in typescript with some minor handwritten alterations which have been incorporated into the version quoted above, and is dated 2.iv.75. Longley papers, collection 744.

CHAPTER 5: **Between Hovers:** *Gorse Fires* (pp.161-87)

1. Michael Longley, 'A Tongue at Play', *How Poets Work*, ed. Tony Curtis (Bridgend: Seren, 1996), p.113.

2. 'A Tongue at Play', p.112.

3. Memo from Kenneth Jamison, Director of the Arts Council of Northern Ireland, to Michael Longley, 23 January 1986, Longley papers, collection 744.

4. Memo from Michael Longley to Kenneth Jamison, 15 October 1985, Longley papers, collection 744.

5. Michael Longley, letter to David Cabot, 6 February 1986. David Cabot private collection.

6. 'A Tongue at Play', p.112.

7. Diary entry, 5 March 1986. Michael Longley private collection.

8. Michael Allen, *Michael Longley* (British Council: Contemporary Writers Pamphlet, 1993).

9. 'A Tongue at Play', p.114.

10. For instance, where Matthew Arnold advocated the English hexameter, a line of six metrical units, S.O. Andrew has noted that the Homeric line itself usually carries around five stresses, and therefore adopts a five-stress metre that may be broadly scanned as dactylic. (See S.O. Andrew, trans., *The Odyssey* (London: J.M. Dent, 1953), pp.xiv-xv. Chapman translated *The Odyssey* (though not the *Iliad*), in heroic couplets. Robert Fitzgerald's translation is in blank verse, the constraints imposed by this both its virtue and, at times, its weakness; Robert Fagles has more recently taken a flexible approach, with varying line-lengths throughout, in an inspired version that may yet not be outstanding poetry. Unsurprisingly, some of the more successful translations – by E.V. Rieu most notably – have been into prose.

11. Douglas Dunn, 'Longley's Metric', *The Poetry of Michael Longley* ed.

Alan J. Peacock and Kathleen Devine (Gerrards Cross: Colin Smythe, 2001), pp.28-29.

12. Dunn, 'Longley's Metric', p.18.

13. See translations by those cited in note 10 above. The relevant passage is from book 13 of the *Odyssey*.

14. Typescript for a radio broadcast, Michael Longley private collection.

15. Helen Lewis, *A Time to Speak* (Belfast: Blackstaff Press, 1992), p.27. Helen Lewis now lives in Belfast. The manuscript was read by Longley before publication, and the memoir carries as epigraph a quotation from 'Ghetto'.

16. Michael Longley, interview by Sarah Broom, *Metre*, 4 (Spring/Summer 1998), pp.18-19.

17. 'Walking forwards into the past: an interview with Michael Longley', by Fran Brearton, *Irish Studies Review*, 18 (Spring 1997), p.38.

18. George Steiner, 'The Hollow Miracle', *George Steiner: A Reader* (London: Penguin, 1964), p.211.

19. Michael Longley, 'A Few Thoughts about "Ghetto"', undated typescript, box 38 folder 15, Longley papers, collection 744; 'Walking forwards into the past: An interview with Michael Longley', p.39

20. See Steiner, 'Introduction', *A Reader*, p.14; and 'Privacies of Speech', *A Reader*, pp.386-87.

21. Teaching was forbidden in the camp, but drawing was allowed 'on sufferance'. Over 4000 drawings have survived, most dating from 1944-45. The majority of the children who were sent to Terezín were then transported to and died in the extermination camps in Poland. *Detske kresby z koncentracniho tábora Terezín*, commemorative booklet (Olomouc, Czech Republic, 1991).

22. *A Time to Speak*, pp.23-24.

23. Longley writes: 'If [Helen Lewis] had disapproved of my poem, I would not have published it.' 'A Few Thoughts about "Ghetto"'.

24. Dunn, 'Longley's Metric', p.29

25. 'Walking forwards into the past', p.39.

26. 'A Tongue at Play', pp.114, 115.

27. Paul Fussell, *The Great War and Modern Memory* (London: OUP, 1975), p.235.

CHAPTER 6: **Metamorphoses:** *The Ghost Orchid* (pp.188-213)

1. 'Where is our home key anyway?': an interview with Michael Hofmann, by Fran Brearton, *Thumbscrew*, 13 (Spring/Summer 1999), p.41.

2. Ovid, *Metamorphoses*, trans. Mary M. Innes (Harmondsworth: Penguin, 1955), p.29.

3. John Kerrigan, 'Ulster Ovids', *The Chosen Ground: Essays on the Contemporary Poetry of Northern Ireland*, ed. Neil Corcoran (Bridgend: Seren, 1992), pp.266, 242-43.

4. 'Ulster Ovids', pp.248, 250.

5. Derek Mahon, 'Each Poem for me is a new beginning', interview by Willie Kelly, *Cork Review*, 2/3 (June 1981), p.11.

6. Michael Hofmann and James Lasdun, eds., *After Ovid: New Metamorphoses* (London: Faber, 1994), p.xi.

7. Peter McDonald, 'Lapsed Classics: Homer, Ovid, and Michael Longley's Poetry', *The Poetry of Michael Longley*, ed. Alan J. Peacock and Kathleen Devine (Gerrards Cross: Colin Smythe, 2001), p.47.

8. These are translated by Innes as: 'Whom the gods love are gods them-

selves, and those who have worshipped should be worshipped too', *Metamorphoses*, p.198.

9. Michael Longley, letter to the *Irish Times*, 18 June 1974.

10. Michael Longley, in Clive Wilmer, *Poets Talking* (Manchester: Carcanet, 1994), p.115.

11. Paul Muldoon, quoted in 'Profile: Michael Longley', *The Guardian*, *Saturday Review*, 21 August 2004.

12. The white garden of the poem is inspired by Vita Sackville-West's garden at Sissinghurst, Kent. The quotation (a trivial, everyday message), is taken from an ancient shard which is an artefact in a Greek museum. Interview with the author, 16 April 2005.

13. Michael Longley, postcard to Edna Longley, May 1989, Longley papers, collection 744.

14. See Neil Corcoran, 'My Botanical Studies: The Poetry of Natural History in Michael Longley', *The Poetry of Michael Longley*, pp.102-03.

15. Neil Corcoran, 'Ovid in Ulster': review of *The Ghost Orchid* by Michael Longley, *Times Literary Supplement*, 7 July 1995, p.13.

16. Brian John, 'The Achievement of Michael Longley's *The Ghost Orchid*', *Irish University Review*, 27/1 (Spring/Summer 1997), p.141.

17. Michael Longley, 'Memory and Acknowledgement', *Irish Review*, 17/18 (Winter 1995), p.158.

18. Derek Mahon, 'Poetry in Northern Ireland', *Twentieth Century Studies*, 4 (November 1970), p.93.

19. See Longley, 'Memory and Acknowledgement', *Irish Review*, and Longley, 'Say Not Soft Things', in *Remembrance*, ed. Gordon Lucy and Elaine McClure (Armagh: Ulster Society (Publications) Ltd, 1997).

20. The museum was put together by the East German regime which has now fallen, and for whose "agenda" in relation to the past the museum subsequently offered the "apology".

21. Note to Edna Longley appended to the manuscript of 'The Stone Garden' and dated 8/11/91, Longley papers, collection 744.

22. McDonald, 'Lapsed Classics', p.45.

23. McDonald, 'Lapsed Classics', pp.45-46.

24. McDonald, 'Lapsed Classics', p. 46.

25. Longley, 'Memory and Acknowledgement', p.158.

26. See McDonald, 'Lapsed Classics', p.46.

27. The typescript of the speech is held in box 35, folder 1, Longley papers, collection 744. The poem written in December 1995 is 'All of These People', and appears in *The Weather in Japan*.

CHAPTER 7: **Outwitting Winter:** *The Weather in Japan* (pp.214-36)

1. There is a colour reproduction of the quilt pattern at the front of the pamphlet. See Longley, *Broken Dishes* (Belfast: Abbey Press, 1998).

2. 'The Yellow Teapot' and 'Damiana' were written in late January and early February 1998. Both poems respond implicitly to the betrayal of Edna Longley, then academic director of the John Hewitt Summer School, by other members of its organising committee in 1996. A public protest and petition followed, along with the boycotting thereafter of the School by many leading writers and critics in the field of Irish Studies. Local and national newspapers carried the story in Ireland. The Hewitt Summer School has since offered an apology to Edna Longley. Michael Longley gave a poetry reading at the School in the summer of 2004.

3. Michael Longley, interview by Peter McDonald, *Thumbscrew*, 12 (Winter 1998/99), p.7.

4. See Longley, interview by Peter McDonald, pp.5-14.

5. 'The Fox', written in February 1999, is the only poem added after these dates.

6. Michael Longley, in Clive Wilmer, *Poets Talking* (Manchester: Carcanet, 1994), p.118.

7. Peter McDonald, letter to Michael Longley, 17 December 1997, Longley papers, collection 744.

8. The moment is also captured on the film, *The Corner of the Eye*, made by Michael Viney and David Cabot (Wild Goose Films, 1988).

9. 'Walking forwards into the past: an interview with Michael Longley', by Fran Brearton (11 July 1996), *Irish Studies Review*, 18 (Spring 1997), p.36.

10. Josephine Balmer's translation of Sappho's 'The Evening Star' – almost certainly Longley's source for his own version – runs as follows: 'Hesperus, you bring everything that / the light-tinged dawn has scattered; // you bring the sheep, you bring the goat, you bring / the child back to its mother.' *Classical Women Poets*, ed. and trans. Balmer (Newcastle upon Tyne: Bloodaxe Books, 1996), p.31. The influence of Balmer's translations – many of them fragments from almost forgotten poets – may be seen in others of Longley's poems from the late 1990s and early 2000s.

11. It seems Longley flirted with the idea of some Sappho translations in the late 1970s. His friend Fleur Adcock, who admitted to feeling 'possessive' about Sappho, tried to warn him off the territory: 'get yourself a male Greek poet' she writes to him on 20 February 1979, 'there aren't many female ones for us ladies'. Longley papers, collection 744.

12. Balmer, *Classical Women Poets*, pp.15, 25.

13. Guy Rotella, *Castings: Monuments and Monumentality* (Nashville: Vanderbilt UP, 2004), p.2.

14. Longley, 'Say Not Soft Things', in Gordon Lucy and Elaine McClure, eds, *Remembrance* (Armagh: Ulster Society Publications Ltd, 1997), p.122.

15. See Homer, *The Iliad*, VIII, *l*. 306ff. The image also appears in Virgil's *Aeneid*, IX, *l.* 436 to describe the death of Euryalus.

16. The photograph, which appeared in a local newspaper at the time, was uncovered by the historian Jane Leonard in her explorations of Great War memorials in Ireland, and shown to Longley in the spring of 1995.

CHAPTER 8: **A Complicated Recipe:** *Snow Water* (pp.237-59)

1. Rachel Campbell-Johnston, 'The weight of years', rev. of *Snow Water* by Michael Longley, *The Times*, 27 March 2004.

2. Michael Longley, interview by Jody AllenRandolph, *Colby Quarterly*, XXXIX/3 (September 2003), p.306.

3. Longley, interview by Jody AllenRandolph, p.295.

4. Michael Allen, review of *Snow Water* by Michael Longley, *Fortnight*, 425 (May 2004), p.28

5. Interview with the author, 16 April 2005.

6. Longley, interview by Jody AllenRandolph, p.305

7. Longley uses the phrase to describe his Uncle Lionel's disappearance in the Great War. It reverberates more generally in his sense of those who were

lost, and whose bodies were 'not recovered' in the conflicts of the twentieth century. See Michael Longley, interview by Dermot Healy, *Southern Review*, 31/3 (July 1995), p.558.

8. Peter McDonald, 'Cold Comfort', review of *Snow Water* by Michael Longley, *Guardian*, 22 May 2004.

9. Interview with the author, 16 April 2005.

10. Chris Agee, 'Of peace and nature', review of *Snow Water* by Michael Longley, *Irish Times*, 17 April 2004.

11. McDonald, 'Cold Comfort'.

12. Interview with the author, 16 April 2005.

13. Robert Graves, *Goodbye to All That* (London: Jonathan Cape, 1929), p.446. The passage is from the dedicatory epilogue for Laura Riding, which was cut from the 2nd edition of 1957.

14. Rachel Campbell-Johnston, 'The weight of years'.

15. Chris Agee, 'Of peace and nature'.

16. Michael Kinsella, 'Poetry and Ceremony', review of *Snow Water* by Michael Longley, *PN Review*, 163 (May-June 2005), p.93.

17. Michael Longley, interview by John Brown, *In the Chair: interviews with poets from the North of Ireland* (Cliffs of Moher, Co. Clare: Salmon Publishing, 2002), p.91.

18. Seamus Heaney, letter to Michael Longley, 13 November 1997, box 15a: Heaney correspondence, Longley papers, collection 744. Heaney had recently been in Japan – hence 'Mahon-San'.

19. Michael Longley, letter to Sotheby's, 13 January 1983, Longley papers, collection 744.

20. Heather Clark's forthcoming study of the Belfast Group draws extensively on archive material in its re-evaluation of the period.

21. 'I was not a member of Philip Hobsbaum's fucking group.' Derek Mahon, 'Q & A with Derek Mahon', interview by James J. Murphy et al, *Irish Literary Supplement*, 10/2 (Fall 1991), p.27. See also the *Guardian*, 7 July 2005.

22. Interview with the author, 16 April 2005.

23. *Poetry Book Society Bulletin*, 2004.

24. Jody AllenRandolph, 'The Wandering Voice', review of *Snow Water* by Michael Longley, *PN Review*, 163 (May-June 2005), p.92

25. See for instance Stephen Knight, 'Swaddled in white silence', review of the Weather in Japan by Michael Longley, *Times Literary Supplement* (7 April 2000), p.29, where he describes some of the poems as 'refined', as if 'in glass cases'.

26. *Poetry Book Society Bulletin*, 2004.

27. Edmund Blunden, 'Preliminary', *Undertones of War* (London: Cobden-Sanderson, 1928), p.viii.

28. McDonald, 'Cold Comfort'.

29. *Poetry Book Society Bulletin*, 2004.

30. Longley, interview by Jody AllenRandolph, p.308.

31. McDonald, 'Cold Comfort'.

32. Quoted in X.J.Kennedy, *An Introduction to Poetry* (London: Harper-Collins, 1990), p.173.

33. *Sculpture* by Helen Denerley (Kilmorack Gallery, Invernessshire, 2003), www.kilmorackgallery.co.uk

34. Longley, interview by Jody AllenRandolph, p.308.

Selected Bibliography

1. Works by Michael Longley:

POETRY BOOKS

Ten Poems (Festival Publications, Queen's University of Belfast, 1965).
Secret Marriages: Nine Short Poems (Manchester: Phoenix Pamphlet Poets Press, 1968).
No Continuing City (London: Macmillan, 1969).
Lares (Poet & Printer, 1972).
An Exploded View (London: Gollancz, 1973).
Fishing in the Sky: love poems (Poet & Printer, 1975)
Man Lying on a Wall (London: Gollancz, 1976).
The Echo Gate (London: Secker & Warburg, 1979).
Patchwork, with drawings by Jim Allen (Dublin: Gallery Press, 1981)
Selected Poems 1963-1980 (Winston-Salem, NC: Wake Forest UP, 1981).
Poems 1963-1983 (Edinburgh: Salamander Press; Dublin: Gallery Press, 1985).
Gorse Fires (London: Secker & Warburg, 1991).
The Ghost Orchid (London: Jonathan Cape, 1995).
Selected Poems (London: Jonathan Cape, 1998).
Broken Dishes (Belfast: Abbey Press, 1998).
Out of the Cold: drawings and poems for Christmas, with Sarah Longley (Belfast: Abbey Press, 1999).
The Weather in Japan (London: Jonathan Cape, 2000).
Cenotaph of Snow: sixty poems about war (Enitharmon Press, 2003)
Snow Water (London: Jonathan Cape, 2004).
The Rope-Makers: fifty-eight love poems (Enitharmon Press, 2005)
Collected Poems (London: Jonathan Cape, 2006).

POETRY RECORDINGS

The Ghost Orchid (Random House Audio Books, 1995), cassette.
The Poetry Quartets 4 (British Council/Bloodaxe Books, 1999), double cassette with Paul Durcan, Brendan Kennelly, Medbh McGuckian, half-hour recordings of each poet reading and discussing a selection of work.
Michael Longley reading from his poems (The Poetry Archive, 2005), CD.

AS EDITOR

Causeway: the Arts in Ulster (Belfast: Arts Council of Northern Ireland; Dublin: Gill and Macmillan, 1971).
Under the Moon, Over the Stars: young people's writing from Ulster (Belfast: Arts Council of Northern Ireland, 1971)
Selected Poems by Louis MacNeice (London: Faber & Faber, 1988).
Poems by W.R. Rodgers (Oldcastle: Gallery Press, 1994).
20th Century Irish Poems (London: Faber & Faber, 2002)

INTERVIEWS

'Making Some Kind of Sense', interview by Fintan O'Toole. *Sunday Tribune* (17 March 1985).

'The Longley Tapes', interview by Robert Johnstone. *Honest Ulsterman*, 78 (Summer 1985).

'Q & A with Michael Longley', interview by Dillon Johnston. *Irish Literary Supplement*, 5/2 (Fall 1986).

Interview by Clive Wilmer, *Poets Talking: Poet of the Month Interviews from BBC Radio 3* (Manchester: Carcanet Press, 1994).

'An Interview with Michael Longley', by Dermot Healy. *Southern Review*, 31/3 (July 1995).

'"Walking forwards into the past": an interview with Michael Longley', by Fran Brearton. *Irish Studies Review*, 18 (Spring 1997).

Interview by Sarah Broom, *Metre*, 4 (Spring/Summer 1998).

Interview by Peter McDonald, *Thumbscrew*, 12 (Winter 1998/99).

Interview by Mike Murphy, *Reading the Future: Irish Writers in Conversation with Mike Murphy* (Dublin: Lilliput Press, 2000).

Interview by John Brown, *In the Chair: Interviews with Poets from the North of Ireland* (Cliffs of Moher, Co. Clare: Salmon Publishing, 2002).

Interview by Jody AllenRandolph, *Colby Quarterly*, XXXIX/3 (September 2003).

PROSE WRITINGS

'Louis MacNeice: A Misrepresented Poet', *Dublin Magazine*, 6.1 (Spring 1967).

'Strife and the Ulster Poet', *Hibernia*, 33/21 (7 November 1969).

'The Neolithic Night: A Note on the Irishness of Louis MacNeice', *Two Decades of Irish Writing*, ed. Douglas Dunn (Cheadle Hulme: Carcanet Press, 1975).

Tuppenny Stung: Autobiographical Chapters (Belfast; Lagan Press, 1994).

'Memory and Acknowledgement', *Irish Review*, 17-18 (Winter 1995).

'A Tongue at Play', *How Poets Work*, ed. Tony Curtis (Bridgend: Seren Books, 1996).

'Say Not Soft Things', *Remembrance*, ed. Gordon Lucy and Elaine McClure (Armagh: Ulster Society Publications Ltd, 1997).

'A Field of Light': address for the opening of the Yeats Summer School, 2003, *Irish Pages*, 2/2 (Autumn/Winter 2004).

2. Reviews and critical writings about Michael Longley:

Adair, Tom, 'Of Flock and Fold: A Consideration of the Poetry of Michael Longley', *Linen Hall Review*, 4/1 (Spring 1987).

Agee, Chris, 'Chinese Whispers, Epic Recensions', review of *The Ghost Orchid* and *Tuppenny Stung* by Michael Longley, *Poetry Ireland Review*, 49 (Spring 1996).

Allen, Michael, 'Options; The Poetry of Michael Longley', *Éire-Ireland*, 10/4 (Winter 1975).

———, 'Rhythm and Development in Michael Longley's Earlier Poetry', *Contemporary Irish Poetry*, ed. Elmer Andrews (Basingstoke: Macmillan, 1992)

———, *Michael Longley* (British Council: Contemporary Writers Pamphlet, 1993).

————, 'Louis MacNeice and Michael Longley: Some Examples of Affinity and Influence', *Louis MacNeice and his Influence*, ed. Kathleen Devine and Alan J. Peacock (Gerrards Cross: Colin Smythe, 1998).

AllenRandolph, Jody, and Douglas Archibald, eds. *Colby Quarterly: Michael Longley Special Issue*, xxxix/3 (September 2003).

Boland, Eavan, 'A Vision of Risk', review of *No Continuing City* by Michael Longley, *Irish Times* (20 December 1969).

————, 'Private Violence', review of *Man Lying on a Wall* by Michael Longley, *Irish Times* (12 June 1976).

Brown, George Mackay, 'Poetry without Obstacles', review of *Man Lying on a Wall* by Michael Longley, *Scotsman* (4 September 1976).

Corcoran, Neil, 'Ovid in Ulster': review of *The Ghost Orchid* by Michael Longley, *Times Literary Supplement* (7 July 1995).

Davis, Dick, 'King Image', review of *The Echo Gate* by Michael Longley, *The Listener* (31 January 1980).

Duhig, Ian, review of *The Ghost Orchid*, by Michael Longley, *Fortnight*, 340 (June 1995).

Dunn, Douglas, 'The Poetry of the Troubles', review of *Selected Poems 1963-1980* by Michael Longley, *Times Literary Supplement* (31 July 1981).

John, Brian, 'The Achievement of Michael Longley's *The Ghost Orchid*', *Irish University Review*, 27/1 (Spring/Summer 1997).

Johnstone, Robert, 'Harmonics between Electrified Fences', review of *Gorse Fires* by Michael Longley, *Honest Ulsterman,* 92 (1991).

Kennelly, Brendan, 'Wonder and Awe', review of *Gorse Fires* by Michael Longley, *Fortnight*, 295 (May 1991).

Lyon, John, 'Michael Longley's Lists', *English*, 45/183 (Autumn 1996).

McDonald, Peter, 'From Ulster with Love', review of *Poems 1963-1983* by Michael Longley, *Poetry Review*, 74/4 (January 1985).

————, 'Michael Longley's Homes', *The Chosen Ground: Essays on the Contemporary Poetry of Northern Ireland*, ed. Neil Corcoran (Bridgend: Seren Books, 1992).

————, 'Cold Comfort', review of *Snow Water* by Michael Longley, *Guardian* (22 May 2004).

Mahon, Derek, 'An Enormous Yes', review of *Poems 1963-1983* by Michael Longley, *Literary Review*, 80 (February 1985).

Motion, Andrew, 'Burning Snow', review of *The Echo Gate* by Michael Longley, *New Statesman* (11 January 1980).

Murphy, Hayden, 'Grace Under Pressure', review of *Poems 1963-1983* by Michael Longley, *Scotsman* (27 April 1985).

Peacock, Alan J., 'Michael Longley: Poet Between Worlds', *Poetry in Contemporary Irish Literature*, ed. Michael Kenneally (Gerrards Cross: Colin Smythe, 1995).

Peacock, Alan J. and Kathleen Devine, eds. *The Poetry of Michael Longley: Ulster Editions and Monographs 10* (Gerrards Cross: Colin Smythe, 2000).

Porter, Peter, 'Away from the Troubles', review of *Man Lying on a Wall* by Michael Longley, *Observer* (22 August 1976).

————, 'A Poet from Ulster', review of *An Exploded View* by Michael Longley, *Observer* (5 August 1973).

INDEX